# MISSION ACCOMPLISHED

David Stafford is the author of several books on intelligence history, including *Britain and European Resistance*, *Churchill and Secret Service*, *Roosevelt and Churchill: Men of Secrets*, *Flight from Reality*, *Ten Days to D-Day* and *Endgame 1945*. He was Professor of History at the University of Victoria in British Columbia, Executive Director of the Canadian Institute of International Affairs, Chairman of the Canadian Association for Security and Intelligence Studies, an Associate Member of St. Antony's College, Oxford, and Project Director at the Centre for the Study of the Two World Wars at the University of Edinburgh, where he is currently an Honorary Fellow.

# DAVID STAFFORD

# Mission Accomplished

## SOE and Italy 1943–45

VINTAGE BOOKS
London

Published by Vintage 2012

2 4 6 8 10 9 7 5 3 1

First published in Great Britain in 2011 by
The Bodley Head

Vintage
Random House, 20 Vauxhall Bridge Road,
London SW1V 2SA

www.vintage-books.co.uk

Addresses for companies within The Random House Group Limited
can be found at: www.randomhouse.co.uk/offices.htm

The Random House Group Limited Reg. No. 954009

A CIP catalogue record for this book
is available from the British Library

ISBN 9780099531838

The Random House Group Limited supports The Forest Stewardship
Council (FSC®), the leading international forest certification
organisation. Our books carrying the FSC label are printed on
FSC® certified paper. FSC is the only forest certification scheme
endor

# Contents

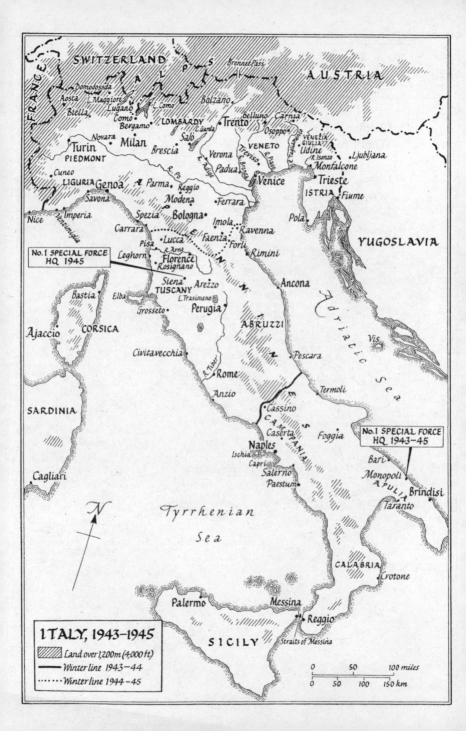

SWITZERLAND
AUSTRIA
*Brenner Pass*
*Domodossola*
Aosta
*L. Maggiore*
Biella
*L. Lugano*
Bolzano
*Como*
*L. Como*
Bergamo
LOMBARDY
Belluno
Carnia
Novara
Milan
*Salò*
Trento
Osoppo
Turin
*L. Garda*
VENEZIA
PIEDMONT
Brescia
Verona
Treviso
GIULIA
*Cuneo*
*R. Po*
*R. Adige*
Udine
*R. Isonzo*
Ljubljana
LIGURIA
Genoa
Padua
*R. Brenta*
*R. Tagliamento*
Monfalcone
Savona
Parma
Reggio
Venice
Trieste
Nice
Imperia
Spezia
Modena
ISTRIA
Fiume
*Ventimiglia*
Carrara
Bologna
Ferrara
Pola
Pisa
*Lucca*
Imola
Faenza
Ravenna
YUGOSLAVIA

NO.1 SPECIAL FORCE
HQ 1945
*R. Arno*
Leghorn
Florence
*Rosignano*
Forlì
Rimini

Siena
*Arezzo*
TUSCANY
Ancona
Bastia
Elba
*L. Trasimeno*
Grosseto
Perugia
ABRUZZI
*Vis*
CORSICA
Ajaccio
Civitavecchia
*R. Tiber*
Pescara
Adriatic Sea

Rome
Anzio
Termoli
SARDINIA
Cassino
CAMPANIA
Caserta
Foggia
NO.1 SPECIAL FORCE
HQ 1943–45
Naples
Ischia
Bari
Cagliari
Capri
Salerno
Monopoli
APULIA
Paestum
Brindisi
Taranto

*Tyrrhenian*
*Sea*

↑
N

CALABRIA
Crotone

Palermo
Messina
Reggio
ITALY, 1943–1945
▨ *Land over 1,200m (4,000 ft)*
—— *Winter line 1943–44*
······ *Winter line 1944–45*
SICILY
*Straits of Messina*

0     50     100 miles
0   50   100   150 km

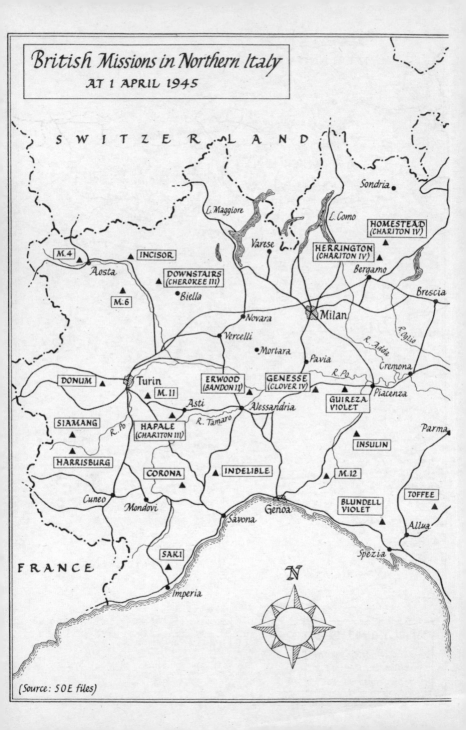

# British Missions in Northern Italy
## AT 1 APRIL 1945

SWITZERLAND

Sondria

L. Maggiore

L. Como

HOMESTEAD
(CHARITON IV)

M.4

INCISOR

HERRINGTON
(CHARITON IV)

Aosta

DOWNSTAIRS
(CHEROKEE III)

Varese

Bergamo

Brescia

M.6

Biella

R. Oglio

Novara

Milan

Vercelli

R. Adda

Cremona

Mortara

Pavia

DONUM

Turin

ERWOOD
(BANDON II)

GENESSE
(CLOVER IV)

R. Po

Piacenza

M.11

Asti

Alessandria

GUIREZA
VIOLET

SIAMANG

HAPALE
(CHARITON III)

R. Tanaro

Parma

HARRISBURG

INSULIN

CORONA

INDELIBLE

M.12

TOFFEE

Cuneo

Mondovi

Genoa

BLUNDELL
VIOLET

Allua

Savona

Spezia

SAKI

FRANCE

N

Imperia

(Source: SOE files)

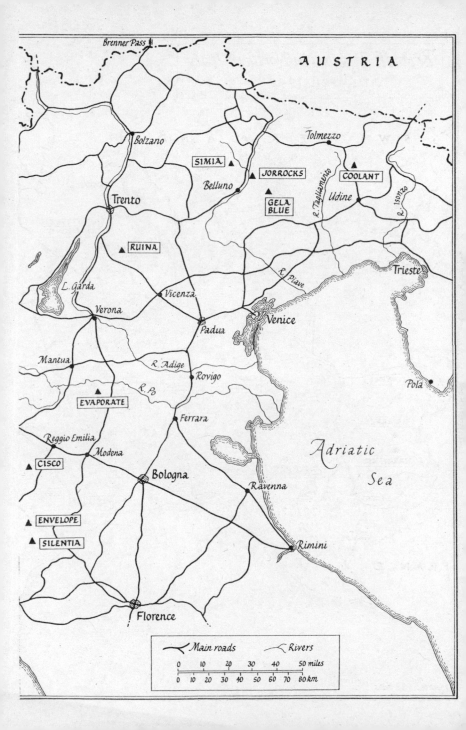

# Glossary

**'A' Force**: The Mediterranean deception unit (using training in escape as its cover).

**AAI**: Allied Armies in Italy.

**ACC**: Allied Control Commission.

**AFHQ**: Allied Forces Headquarters.

**AMG**: Allied Military Government.

**BCRA**: Bureau Central de Renseignements et d'Action. The Free French intelligence and special operations service.

**BLO**: British liaison officer.

**CLN**: Comitato di Liberazione Nazionale – Committee of National Liberation.

**CLNAI**: Comitato di Liberazione Nazionale di Alta Italia – National Committee of Liberation for Upper (Northern) Italy.

**CVL**: Corpo Volontari della Libertà – Corps of Volunteers of Liberty. The armed partisan units of the resistance.

**FSS**: Field Security Section.

**FANY**: First Aid Nursing Yeomanry.

**GAP**: Gruppi di Azione Patriottica. Small city-based resistance hit squads.

**GCI**: Gruppi Combattenti in Italia. Volunteer organisation formed by General Pavone but quickly dissolved by the ACC.

**GL**: Giustizia e Libertà – Justice and Liberty, an Italian anti-Fascist movement.

**ISLD**: Inter-Services Liaison Department. Cover title for SIS in Italy.

**IS9**: Title for MI9 in Italy.

**MAS**: *Motoscafo antisommergibile*. A fast Italian submarine hunter.

**MI5**: The Security Service.

**MI6**: The Secret Intelligence Service, or SIS.

**MI9**: The Escape and Evasion Service.

**MI(R)**: Military Intelligence (Research), a branch of the War Office.

**MS**: *Motosilurante*. An Italian motor torpedo boat.

**ORI**: Organizzazione della Resistenza Italiana. Resistance group formed by Raimondo Craveri.

**OSS**: Office of Strategic Services (USA).

**OVRA**: Organizzazione per la Vigilanza e la Repressione dell'Antifascismo. The Fascist secret police force.

**PdA**: Partito d'Azione – Action Party.

**PWB**: Psychological Warfare Branch.

**PWE**: Political Warfare Executive.

**SD**: Sicherheitsdienst. Intelligence agency of the SS.

**SHAEF**: Supreme Headquarters Allied Expeditionary Force (North-West Europe).

**SIM**: Servizio Informazione Militare – Military Intelligence Service.

**SIMCOL**: Operation launched by Lt Col. A. C. Simonds to rescue escaped prisoners of war in Italy.

**SIS**: Secret Intelligence Service.

**SOE**: Special Operations Executive.

**SOM** (sometimes **SO(M)**): Special Operations (Mediterranean).

**SPOC**: Special Project Operations Centre.

**TAC HQ**: SOE's forward tactical headquarters in Florence.

**USAAF**: United States Army Air Force.

# Introduction

Florence, 7 August 1944. After weeks of gruelling fighting in the Apennines, allied armies finally reach the southern bank of the River Arno. On the other side, in the heart of the old Renaissance city, the Germans are under constant fire from the resistance. The population hovers on the edge of starvation. The only bridge linking the two parts of the city left standing by the Germans is the tenth-century Ponte Vecchio. To prevent the allies from using it, they have demolished the houses standing on its southern end, mined the approaching streets and given their machine-gunners and snipers a clear line of fire.

But high above their heads runs a secret passageway across the bridge known as Vasari's Gallery, designed in 1565 by the painter and architect Giorgio Vasari to allow the Medici family to move between their various residences unobserved and safe from potential assassins. Unknown to the Germans, it shelters a secret telephone wire. Installed just two days before by an Italian resistance fighter after a perilous crawl past enemy guards, it gives his headquarters in the ancient city a continuous and direct twenty-four-hour link with the allies.

This morning, as the sun begins to warm the yellow of the city's walls, a British officer scurries through the rubble and scrambles up a rope to the gallery. Its floor has been largely destroyed, and as he crawls through the shattered beams he wonders if the secret has yet been discovered by the Germans and if he's about to be shot. If he is captured alive, his fate might be worse – he's not carrying a suicide pill with him – and he might well be tortured. Apart from his commando dagger, he's armed only with his automatic pistol. The city of the Medicis is infested with German snipers and booby traps.

His mission is to see whether there is any chance that an allied battalion might exploit the bridge and its secret passage to cross the river undetected. He also wants to check out personally the reliability of the telephone link; has it been discovered by – or been betrayed to – the Germans?

On inspection, everything turns out to be as it should. The wire still lies well concealed, and there is no evidence that the Germans have discovered the passageway. He also rapidly concludes that it will not be practical for even a specialised company to use the bridge to surprise the Germans. It might reach Italy's greatest art gallery, the Uffizi. But it would then be at the mercy of German guns that could easily destroy any building that the battalion occupied.

After completing his reconnaissance, he makes it safely back to the other side. Over the next few days the telephone link offers a running commentary on the state of fighting between the Germans and the resistance and provides invaluable tactical intelligence to the allied forces who stand poised to enter the city. By contrast with Rome, liberated two months before without a struggle, in Florence the resistance is offering serious help to the allies. So important is it considered, indeed, that the officer is flown back to London to report personally to his superiors on what he has witnessed.

The officer, Major Charles Macintosh, was head of the Florence mission of SOE, the Special Operations Executive, the top-secret agency created in July 1940 following the collapse of the French Army. British strategic planners had originally counted on France to provide the principal ground force that would lead the fight against Hitler's Germany and take the offensive back to the Nazi heartland. But with the capitulation of the French a drastic alternative had been required. Out of the crisis, the chiefs of staff and prime minister turned to a new weapon of warfare.

SOE was designed to mobilise and support popular resistance inside occupied Europe in the hope that together with the continued naval blockade of the continent and the strategic bombing of Germany, popular revolt would so weaken the Germans that the eventual landing of British forces in Europe would spark the collapse of the Nazi regime. 'Set Europe ablaze' was Churchill's legendary injunction to the man he placed in charge of SOE, the veteran Labour

politician and minister of economic warfare, Hugh Dalton. After
Pearl Harbor SOE's mandate became global, and by the time the
Second World War ended it could boast a staff around the world of
some thirteen thousand men and women, with at least half of this
total having worked as secret agents in neutral countries or behind
enemy lines.[1]

Its achievements have been extensively celebrated. SOE agents
who were parachuted into Norway famously destroyed the Norsk
Hydro plant that was manufacturing heavy water for the Nazis'
atomic bomb project. Before and after D-Day in June 1944, dozens
of SOE agents, both men and women, were infiltrated into France
to help obstruct and delay German reinforcements intended for the
Normandy beaches, and they often paid for their bravery with their
lives. More controversially, agents trained by SOE assassinated SS
Obergruppenführer Reinhard Heydrich, Hitler's 'Protector' of
Bohemia and Moravia – an undeniably heroic mission but one with
dire consequences for the internal resistance and domestic population of Czechoslovakia. Notoriously, SOE's networks in Holland were
penetrated by the Abwehr at the cost of some fifty agents who fell
directly into German hands, nearly all of whom were shot.[2]

Yet SOE's achievements in Italy have undeservedly long remained
in the shadows. It was, after all, to Italy that Major General Colin
Gubbins, SOE's head and directing genius, deliberately chose to fly
to celebrate victory in Europe in May 1945, and on the day that
German forces in north-west Europe finally surrendered at Rheims,
in France, he was in Siena, at SOE's Italian headquarters, thanking
its staff for all they had done. There was considerable personal
poignancy in this visit, too, for his elder son Michael had been
killed some fifteen months before at Anzio while working with an
SOE mission. Six years later, in his history of the Second World
War, Churchill made his own tribute to the Italian resistance by
noting that it had been 'created in a cruel atmosphere of civil strife,
assassinations, and executions' and that, as elsewhere in occupied
Europe, it had 'convulsed all classes of people'. W. J. M. Mackenzie,
the historian officially commissioned after the war to record the
worldwide achievements of SOE, came closest to giving the resistance it supported in Italy its proper due, although by the nature of
his volume he could offer it only a few lines. 'It flowered very quickly

in what had seemed a barren land,' he wrote in 1948, 'and was in the end one of the greatest Resistance movements in the West.'[5]

But Mackenzie's verdict, along with his volume, remained secret until 2000, and, in Britain at least, recognition of the scale and achievements of the Italian resistance suffered alongside much else connected with the war in Italy. Controversial from the start, and proving far more costly than ever anticipated, the long, gruelling and attritional allied campaign there was then, and has been ever since, frequently dismissed as a sideshow, an irrelevance, or even a mistake. Whereas the Eastern Front has its Stalingrad, and the Western Front its D-Day, the best the Italian front can usually offer historians is the bloodbath of Monte Cassino, which, with its four separate battles, can be considered as much a failure as a success. Inevitably, SOE's achievements, along with those of the resistance it supported, have also suffered from this sidelining and criticism of the Italian campaign. The partisans, claims one history of the campaign dismissively, were 'lavishly armed by the Allies, and capable of little more than murder and noisy fire-fights with their fellow Italians of a different political hue'.[4]

Nor did post-war Italian history help enhance its reputation. For while SOE gave crucial and widely acknowledged support to the partisans in the German-occupied north, its story in Italy is separate from theirs. It also worked with, and greatly benefited from, the co-operation of the royalist government in the south as well as with significant elements of the Italian armed forces who continued the national struggle against the Germans. For this, it was frequently condemned by anti-Fascists who had suffered under the long dictatorship of Mussolini, who had been appointed by the King in the first place. After the abolition of the monarchy in 1946, it became unfashionable, or in some cases even professionally unwise, to acknowledge any positive aspects of the royal government's activities between the September 1943 surrender and the nation's liberation. This, together with what may loosely be termed a 'centre-left' consensus myth that long dominated perspectives on the resistance, rarely gave SOE its proper due. Instead, debates focused almost exclusively on its role in allegedly quashing the revolutionary impulse that animated its most militant groups. Only recently has this changed, which, together with the opening of the archival record, now makes it possible to provide a more balanced account of SOE's operations there.[5]

This is an official history, commissioned by the Cabinet Office, and the sixth about SOE to appear in print: previous histories have been those by Mackenzie, referred to above, the two on France and the Low Countries by Professor M. R. D. Foot, and the volumes on Scandinavia and the Far East written by Charles Cruickshank. It completes the project first started by Christopher Woods, CMG, MC, a veteran of SOE Italy himself, whose volume covering the period 1940 to September 1943 has been substantially completed but is not yet in print.[6] It is, it should be stressed, a history of SOE *and* Italy, not of SOE *in* Italy, which means that it makes no attempt to cover operations to other countries that were launched from Italian soil, such as Yugoslavia, Albania, Poland, Hungary, Austria or Bulgaria. Although SOE bases in southern Italy devoted a considerable amount of energy and personnel to servicing these operations, they are merely tangential to the main story told here of SOE's relations with Italy and the Italians. So, too, are the operations of 'A' Force or IS9, which represented the interest of MI9, the agency charged with organising the escape and evasion of allied personnel from enemy-occupied territory, and of the Secret Intelligence Service (SIS), which operated in Italy under the title of Inter-Services Liaison Department (ISLD). Neither the collection of intelligence nor the evacuation of escaped prisoners of war or evading aircrew was ever a primary concern of SOE in Italy, and nor indeed was black propaganda and political warfare conducted by the Psychological Warfare Branch (PWB), although at times it helped with the work of all the clandestine agencies involved in those operations.

To some critics the term 'official history' suggests at best a dry-as-dust volume of bureaucratic prose, and at worst a 'whitewash' that sacrifices objectivity to produce some bland or diluted version of the past to please officialdom. The reader alone can decide whether what I have written here is readable and interesting. All I can say is that I have done my best to make it so. As for the widespread notion that official history is a contradiction in terms and cannot be honest, this misunderstands both the purpose and track record of official histories, at least in Britain, if not in totalitarian states such as the former Soviet Union where glorification of the Communist Party was always an explicit goal.

The British series of official histories was born in the aftermath of the disasters of the South African War of 1899–1902, when the British Army was roundly humiliated by the Boers, and was expressly designed to identify mistakes, in the hope that future policy-makers and strategists would not repeat them. In other words, far from seeking a whitewash, it was *the truth* that was being sought by the officials who commissioned them. This imperative continued to guide the multiple volumes of the official history of the First World War edited by Sir James Edmonds, although, paradoxically, it was this series that did most to generate the critical view of the official historian as one who is afraid or unwilling to include material unfavourable to, or critical of, high-ranking officials and generals. That charge was led by the well-known journalist-cum-strategist Basil Liddell Hart, an influential figure in his day, who nurtured polemical views of his own about the conduct of the First World War and took issue with some of the official history's conclusions. The word 'official', he suggested, cancelled out 'history', and only those who were 'unfettered' could produce history that was honest.

Yet Liddell Hart's view of Edmonds's efforts was itself a distortion created by his own very passionate opinions, and in reality the volumes were of substantial historical and military value. The same may be said of the numerous official histories of the Second World War, although the many different professional historians involved brought their own individual approaches and skills to their particular topic. All, however, were guided by the precept articulated in 1953 by the Cabinet Secretary Sir Norman Brook to Sir Edward Bridges, head of the Civil Service, that the official historian's duty was 'to give an exact and truthful picture of events', a sentiment that was echoed in the words of the general editor of the military series, Sir James Butler, who insisted that his authors should provide an accurate and objective account of events 'giving honour where honour was due but not disguising failure'. Anyone doubting that an official historian can be highly critical of 'official' policy has only to read General Sir William Jackson's scathing indictment of the decision made by Generals Alexander and Leese to launch Operation 'Olive' in August 1944 as 'one of the most dramatic and perhaps unfortunate decisions taken during the Italian campaign'.[7]

The official historians also enjoyed full access to the records and were free to express their own opinions, their only constraint being, as it has been in this case, to submit their volume for clearance before publication. But this has to do with national security, not the censorship of views, and I can assure the reader that none of the opinions expressed here has been changed by any explicit or implicit official request. Nor have I exercised any sinister self-censorship to head off some anticipated clash of views with the Cabinet Office or anyone else.

It is, however, written from a British and not an Italian perspective, and it is a history neither of the partisans nor of the wider Italian wartime resistance movement, a subject that has been amply covered by dozens of Italian historians since the end of the war some sixty years ago. While the book takes into account their many passionate and often informed opinions, here too I have reached my own 'unfettered' views on the subject at hand.[8]

One significant difference between this and the preceding volumes on SOE should be stressed. This is the first volume to have been written after the vast bulk of SOE files were deposited from the late 1990s onwards in The National Archive (formerly the Public Record Office) in Kew, London, which means that anyone interested in fully exploring the minutiae of any operation or any other aspect of the story can now do so by examining the original documents. There is thus no need here either for an encyclopedic account or an exhaustive chronicle of events. Instead, what I have sought to do for the general reader is to present the 'big picture' of SOE activities in Italy, with as many pointers as possible to the sources I have used, to help those specialists who wish to follow up on particular episodes or themes in greater detail.

Here, a cautionary note is in order. The surviving SOE archive is far from complete, as much of it was weeded out and destroyed immediately after the war, so that the documentary record for Italy — as for its other fields of operation — remains essentially fragmentary. It has to be supplemented, if at all possible, by other archival sources as well as by personal memories and testimony. As one well-informed historian has written, any serious student of the subject 'will find him or herself required to ply a difficult course through a sea of patchy paperwork and a host of personal accounts of uncertain accuracy'.[9] In any case, even if all the documents *had* been preserved, they can mislead, intentionally or not. A false antithesis

is often drawn between oral testimony, regarded as inherently un-
reliable, and the documentary record preserved in some file, which
is assumed to be objective. But files, too, are human products, and
even when compiled in good faith can be partial, biased and
misleading, especially when produced, as many are, for immediately
operational reasons and not for the sake of some future historian.
'When a few people are asked to describe in detail the simplest event
which all have just witnessed,' noted one of those who fought in
the clandestine war in Italy, 'their accounts tend to vary so much as
to make one believe that each of them is talking about a totally
different event.' From such memories were after-action reports
written, sometimes hurriedly, and these now quietly repose as
apparently reliable sources in the documentary record.

Even those official records constructed in less harried circumstances, such as the many internal histories that chronicle the achievement of this or that section of SOE, often possess, for all their
usefulness, an inbuilt flaw, namely the attribution of coherence and
purpose to what was often contingent and unplanned. This was well
expressed by Lieutenant Colonel Cecil Roseberry, the head of SOE's
Italian section, when he was invited shortly after the war to comment
on an internal history written by some anonymous author. 'I consider,'
he wrote, 'that the report . . . [does not] bring to anyone without a
previous knowledge of the subject an adequate idea of the extent
of the frustrations and disappointments which had to be endured
and which were to a great extent never eliminated. To the uninitiated
the report will convey the impression of "planned progress" whereas
those concerned know that this was far from the case . . . If the
history is intended solely as a "look at what we did," it is good; its
omissions of or glossing over of failures, disabilities, and handicaps
reduces its value as a guide for future planners and at the same time
detracts from the excellence of the achievements of SOE.'

In telling the story of SOE and Italy I have certainly sought to
explain aims and outcomes. But history is indeed intrinsically messy,
and it is within its murky crevices that its reality can often best be
understood. Where secret operations are concerned, this might lie
with the airdrop thwarted over and over again by bad weather and
finally aborted; the arrival of the pick-up boat just thirty minutes
late which causes a carefully planned operation to miscarry; the fully

briefed and intensively trained agent who breaks a leg at a critical moment, or whose radio set is damaged during a parachute drop, thus wrecking an ambitious plan worked on for months by staff officers; or a sudden and unexpected change in the larger strategic picture that throws everything into question and puts a sudden end to a particular kind of operation to the benefit of another. Such contingency I have tried to convey, and I have done my best to ensure that what appears here is accurate and truthful. But, like any history, this reconstruction of the past can only present a palimpsest of the reality.[10]

There are many people I wish to thank for helping me bring this book to fruition. My greatest single debt is to Christopher Woods, CMG, MC, from whom I took over the project. He has been unstintingly helpful and gracious with his advice and commentary, especially on my final text, where his critical eye and profound knowledge of the Italian resistance suggested many improvements and saved me from numerous solecisms. Over many years, his assiduous researches created an encyclopedic archive which he placed at my full disposal and which has proved indispensable on so many counts. This material has now been deposited in the Cabinet Office and is referred to throughout this text as 'the Woods Archive'. Mr Wood's personal experience as a British liaison officer in Italy during 1944–1945, and later as SOE Adviser to the Foreign and Commonwealth Office, also provided him with a wealth of knowledge which, again, he shared most generously with me. By the time I came to the project it was too late to interview most veterans. But over many years, he had traced and corresponded with a large number of them and the fruits of this research, too, were available to me. All in all, I owe him an immense debt of gratitude – not to mention the generous hospitality that he and his wife, Patricia, frequently provided at their home in Suffolk.

I wish also to thank those who assisted with the handing-over of the project, namely Tessa Stirling, head of the Histories, Openness and Records Unit in the Cabinet Office, who with Mark Seaman helped guide me through the Whitehall maze and assisted me in gaining access to material essential to the book's completion. Along with Sally Falk, who was my principal point of contact in the unit and who herself facilitated much of the work, as well as Chris

Grindall, they have my most sincere and heartfelt gratitude. Amongst others in Whitehall whom I wish to thank in particular for their support and friendship are Gill Bennett and Duncan Stuart, CMG. The staff at the Imperial War Museum, the depository of a great deal of invaluable written and oral material relating to SOE, also proved most helpful. To Rod Bailey in particular, who was working there at the time and who has since taken over the task of completing the earlier part of the story prior to September 1943, I am especially grateful for pointing me to several useful leads, sharing information and providing an invaluable sounding board on a number of topics.

At the University of Edinburgh, my home for the duration of the project, I wish to thank all those in the school of History, Classics and Archaeology who recognised the importance of the project and gave me facilities to complete it. The late Professor James McMillan, and Professors Douglas Cairns and Tom Devine, as successive heads of the school, gave me their full support, while the School's administrator, Francine Shields, translated all this into practical terms by ensuring me the space and other facilities that I required. At the Centre for the Study of the Two World Wars, Pauline Maclean, Paul Addison, Jeremy Crang and Yvonne McEwan all helped create a friendly and cooperative environment that made it a pleasure to work there.

Over many years of studying and writing about SOE and the Second World War, I have accumulated many debts of gratitude. For this particular project I especially wish to thank the following: Peter Davies and Roger Vincent, sons of No. 1 Special Force officers Jim Davies and Hedley Vincent respectively, who very kindly lent me material, including photographs, from their fathers' private collections. Likewise Julia Korner, the daughter of Andrew Croft, was extremely generous in letting me browse through her father's papers at leisure and letting me use material from them. Sir Tommy Macpherson, the head of SOE's 'Coolant' mission in north-east Italy welcomed me to his home in Scotland and lent me some useful material as well. I also wish to record my thanks to David Ellwood, Guy Puzey, Terry Hodgkinson, John Earle, Tom Wales, Richard Aldrich and Neville Wylie. Clara Muzzarella Formentini, the niece of Max Salvadori, generously permitted me to reproduce the photograph of her uncle.

The project could not have been carried out without the help of the Holdsworth Trust, which provided me with financial support, while the welcome award of an emeritus professorship by the Leverhulme Trust came attached to a grant that enabled me to carry out much of the travel necessary to my research. Thanks to an invitation to deliver the 2010 Joanne Goodman Lectures, I was able to present some of my preliminary ideas and conclusions to a wider public audience than would otherwise have been possible; the series was established by Joanne's family and friends to perpetuate the memory of her blithe spirit, her quest for knowledge and the rewarding years she spent at the University of Western Ontario. My agent, Andrew Lownie, and my editor at The Bodley Head, Will Sulkin, showed gratifying faith in the project at a difficult moment in the publishing world when it seemed as though history of any kind had lost all appeal, and Will's editorial comments have been astute and helpful. I am also grateful to his colleague Kay Peddle for her work on the illustrations and other technical matters, and to Tim Waller for his eagle-eyed copy-editing of the final text. At more than one critical stage of the project my wife Jeanne Cannizzo was ready with necessary advice, and in its final stages she gave me much-needed and greatly appreciated practical help in bringing it to fruition. It is to my great sorrow that her father, Walter Mario Cannizzo, an American Second World War veteran who showed consistent interest in the project, did not live to see it in print.

Finally, I wish to dedicate the book to the memory of Roger Absalom, a fine scholar and friend of Italy and Italians, whose company and friendship during the final stages of my research gave me considerable pleasure and reward. His sudden and unexpected death as I was completing the project dealt a heavy blow. But his knowledge and understanding of the Italian resistance proved incomparable, and although he never read this text and might indeed have dissented from some of its conclusions, his generous spirit provided me with much welcome encouragement and support.

David Stafford
September 2010

# CHAPTER ONE

# 'Of capital and urgent importance'

As darkness fell on Wednesday 8 September 1943, an armada of more than six hundred ships assembled off the beaches at Salerno, some 80 kilometres south of Naples. The sea was calm, and in the moonlight the isle of Capri was clearly visible to the north. The invasion fleet was carrying a landing force of four American and three British divisions under the command of the US Fifth Army's Lieutenant General Mark Clark, some 170,000 troops in all. It was codenamed 'Avalanche'. Together with the landings a few days earlier across the Straits of Messina from Sicily into Calabria by General Bernard Montgomery's British Eighth Army, the Salerno assault marked the start of the allied military campaign on the mainland of Italy.

Shortly after midnight, and 19 kilometres offshore, the men of the three assault divisions that would spearhead the invasion clambered down into their landing craft for the two-hour run in to the beaches. There were over 32 kilometres of them, stretching south of Salerno with no shoals and good underwater gradients that offered perfect landing conditions. Dead on schedule, the ramps came down and the first riflemen scrambled hastily ashore. Then flares went up, the heavy rattle of German machine guns hidden in the dunes shattered the silence, and mortar fire and shells began to rain down on the beaches. Half an hour later, as dawn broke, Luftwaffe planes arrived on the scene, bombing and strafing. Concealed amidst the ruins of medieval watchtowers built centuries before to ward off Saracen raiders, enemy snipers began their deadly work. The battle for Salerno had begun. The allies were not to break out of the bridgehead for another week.[1]

Floating offshore through the first day of battle lay a reserve division, the US 45th. On board one of its dozens of landing craft, packed with tanks, guns and transport vehicles, a small party of eight men waited and watched patiently for their turn to disembark. Two days before, they had heard the news over their ship's radio about the signing of an armistice with the Italians and celebrated with a bottle of brandy, congratulating themselves on the prospect of an unopposed landing. But that same day German planes had appeared overhead and machine-gunned the ship, which was later shaken from stem to stern by a depth charge, a sobering reminder that the war was still on. Now, amidst the deafening noise of heavy artillery, they saw the beach where they were due to land lit up by the vivid orange flashes of exploding shells.

The leader of the group, which had recently been given the official title of 'Special Force', was Major Malcolm Munthe of the Special Operations Executive, a slim, six-foot-tall 33-year-old wearing the kilt of the Gordon Highlanders. Before the war he had worked as an assistant to the High Commissioner of the League of Nations, and in 1940 had been recruited by SOE for operations in Scandinavia, where he'd ended up in Stockholm training Norwegian exiles in sabotage before being expelled after a mistimed bomb blew up a train in neutral Sweden instead of, as intended, enemy-occupied Norway. '[He] had infinite charm, a wonderful sense of humour, and the ability to improvise in an emergency,' wrote one of his companions.[2] 'I liked his frank open friendly manner, plus ruthless efficiency,' wrote another. 'He was one man who didn't seem to know the meaning of the word fear.'[3]

Most recently, Munthe had been in charge of SOE's mission in Sicily, attached to the Eighth Army, and, while contributing little to the success of military operations, had acquired some useful experience in working with allied forces in the field. Now enlarged for its tasks on the mainland, the mission was codenamed 'Vigilant'. Its general objective as described by Munthe was 'to establish contact with elements who could harass the enemy behind his fighting line acting on instructions from the 5th Army H.Q. to be transmitted over our clandestine W.T. sets'. With it, the group was bringing radio equipment for six such possible 'outstations'. It had joined the American division at the port of Termini Imerese in Sicily just four days before.[4]

In addition to Munthe, the SOE group consisted of Lieutenant Adrian Gallegos, Captain Max Sylvester, Second Lieutenant Henri Boutigny and two signallers, Sergeant Donald Macdonnell and Corporal 'Bill' Beggs, both experienced radio operators who had joined up with Munthe in Sicily. The father of the 25-year-old French-speaking Boutigny had been known as 'the uncrowned King of Egypt' because of his control of the Société Orientale de Publicité, which enjoyed a monopoly of advertising in all Egyptian papers. But the family fortunes had taken a tumble during the financial crash of 1929/30 and Henri had ended up living in Greece. When war came he worked as an interpreter in the British Censorship Office in Cairo, before joining SOE, working briefly in its Greek section, and then becoming a demolitions instructor at its training school in Haifa and a conducting officer for several of its Greek recruits. After his own training at Arisaig in the west of Scotland, he had been posted to 'Massingham', SOE's Mediterranean head-quarters outside Algiers, and then on to Sicily. The 35-year-old Adrian Gallegos had spent the first part of the war with the Royal Navy before being sent to Gibraltar to work with the Joint Intelligence Centre on Operation 'Goldeneye', a plan to counter a possible German invasion of neutral Spain, where he produced a regular intelligence summary. Born in Rome, with a Spanish father and an English mother, he had been a City broker and insurance agent, enjoying a high-flying social life in London, and was fluent in several languages.

In the long term, however, the most important member of Munthe's group was the tall, fair-haired and blue-eyed Captain Sylvester. At least, that was his name on the papers that identified him as a commissioned British officer. In reality, he was an Anglo-Italian with British nationality named Massimo ('Max') Salvadori. His principal mission was to liaise with the large number of Italian anti-Fascists who were impatient to help liberate their country from Fascism and the Germans.

For this, he had impeccable credentials. Born in London in 1908, he was the son of an Italian count and had grown up in Florence, where his liberal-minded family made little secret of their opposition to the Fascist regime. Within a year of Mussolini's seizure of power in 1922, both he and his father were beaten up by Fascist blackshirts, and two years later they fled into exile in Switzerland. After taking a degree at the University of Geneva, Salvadori joined the exiled radical group Giustizia e Libertà (Justice and Liberty, or GL) and in 1929 he returned to Italy, ostensibly to attend the University of Rome, but in reality to organise GL clandestine resistance groups. Two years later the Italian secret police, the OVRA, arrested him and he was interned on the island of Ponza, although his ten-year sentence was greatly reduced after pressure from high-ranking English relatives – a first cousin was a senior Foreign Office official. Shortly afterwards he secretly crossed back into Switzerland, and in the years that followed he married, had two children and farmed in Kenya.

Crucially, however, during an interlude in London, his anti-Fascist record had come to notice and in 1938 he was recruited by Section D (the sabotage and subversion unit of the SIS) to take part in a scheme to broadcast anti-Nazi propaganda from a small boat in the North Sea. 'But the scheme went up in smoke, literally,' writes one source, 'when the boat with its transmitter was destroyed by fire in the port of Boulogne.' After this, he had briefly taken a teaching job at St Lawrence University in New York State before returning to Britain on the outbreak of war to work on various intelligence and propaganda campaigns for Section D. But having failed in his principal ambition – to gain a commission in the British Army – on grounds of his age (he was 31) he returned in frustration to the United States. Here, over the next two and a half years, he did valuable work for SOE in recruiting fellow Italian anti-Fascists in Mexico and arranging their passage to London.[5]

Finally, he had been allowed to enlist in the British army as a commissioned officer and he officially joined SOE's Italian section (J Section) as 'JF' in March 1943 before undergoing standard training in various locations in England and the Scottish Highlands. Roseberry, the section's head since September 1941, had spent much of his time toiling hard but mostly unsuccessfully to launch operations into Italy, and was so delighted to have him on board that he handed him a number of files to help evaluate the merits of SOE's contacts in Italy. But Salvadori was sceptical about many of their claims and suspected that some or even most of them were not genuine at all. They were, he feared, 'either with agents of O.V.R.A. or of the Fascist information services (political or military)'. He also worried that 'the "agents" who have gone to Italy have been caught and are speaking and writing under duress'. Despite, or perhaps because of, this scepticism, Roseberry regarded him highly. 'He has done superb work since he joined this section,' he reported in July 1943, 'and is of outstanding ability and energy.'[6]

Salvadori's decision to join SOE required some personal courage and many of his anti-Fascist friends were horrified at his wearing allied uniform. But he saw things quite differently. 'If one is convinced that the war is right and necessary,' he argued, 'one should take part in it as a combatant, not as an arm-chair critic or radio orator.' He also expressed some other firm convictions: that the only reliable people were those who had opposed Fascism from the very start; that the Communists 'always try to sabotage what they cannot lead'; and that Italian nationalists (as opposed to patriots) had sold their country to the Germans. Nationalists everywhere, he believed, 'were stupid'. On the form he completed on joining SOE he described himself as a 'nineteenth-century Liberal'.[7]

With such fierce anti-Fascist views and widespread contacts in exile circles, Salvadori was to prove a valuable asset from then until the liberation of Italy in April 1945. Yet, like most anti-Fascists, he was often severely critical of the inevitable compromises SOE had to make with forces in Italy that shared little or none of their record as opponents of Mussolini. Two of the most important such anti-Fascists earlier brought to SOE's attention by Salvadori were also travelling with Munthe's group, and landed with him at Salerno: Alberto Tarchiani, a former editor of the Milan-based newspaper *Corriere della Sera*, who had fled into exile in 1925 and since 1940 had been living in the United States; and Alberto Cianca, a former editor of the influential journal *Il Mondo*, who had also spent years of exile in France as a 'warrior of the pen' before fleeing across the Atlantic after the fall of Paris. A third anti-Fascist made up the Italian group: Signor Corrado Ferentini, described by Munthe as a 'former sailor, grocer, and anti-Fascist agitator'. It was hoped that in the first fluid stage of the battle it would be possible for the Italians, dressed in civilian clothes, to be infiltrated through the lines, from where they would make their way north to Rome. With this in mind, Munthe had requisitioned two saloon cars, a Lancia and a Fiat.[8]

*    *    *

This SOE party finally landed on mainland Italy shortly after noon on Friday 10 September. It was baking hot, and shimmering on the edge of the beach ahead of them they could see the three great Doric temples of Paestum, the Graeco-Roman city originally known as Poseidon, or city of Neptune, founded in the sixth century BC by Greek colonists from the city of Sybaris. 'Aircraft were screaming and screeching overhead,' recalled Gallegos, 'swooping down and then climbing steeply up again, looking like huge swallows or perhaps hawks.' Bursts from machine guns churned up the sand in little lines. White puffs of smoke from the ships' anti-aircraft shells punctuated the sky. He saw a jeep on the beach suddenly blown up by a landmine. There was a bang, the jeep went up in a mass of sand and the driver was hurled out, apparently unharmed. 'And then he started running at terrific speed,' Gallegos remembered, 'as if the very devil was chasing him. He must have gone temporarily off his head.'[9]

They were amongst the first vehicles to disembark, impatiently revving their engines under a hail of fire from German tanks hidden on the road running behind the beach. But the landing was a confused affair that provided an inauspicious start to their mission. Back in Sicily, the two saloon cars had been waterproofed for the journey, not by the military transport specialists of the division with which they were travelling, who were equipped with the tools needed to make a certain job of it, but by the Special Force's own mechanics, who were not. The result was that they got water into their engines, and at the crucial moment they stalled.

Worse followed. Somehow, no one had noticed how low the Lancia and Fiat were slung on their axles. 'It should be taken into account,' noted Munthe drily in his official report, 'that their body work cannot clear the top of the drawbridge of the L.S.T., let down probably on some very uneven floating pontoon leading to the beach.' The result was that they incurred the rage of the unloading officer as they struggled frantically to get off the craft, blocking the exit of the other vehicles waiting impatiently behind.[10]

Finally, however, they succeeded. Driving rapidly along the improvised pontoon bridge on to the pitted sand, they headed speedily for the cover of the low cork trees fringing the beach. There was still furious fighting going on. White tape marked the path where mines had been cleared, and almost adjoining it Gallegos spotted a group of dead soldiers half covered by the sand, lying just as they'd fallen. Further on, where the sand met the dunes, they passed yet more corpses, a dozen or so bodies covered by a blanket laid out neatly in a row – young Americans, wrote Salvadori, 'who would never again see Main Street, the drugstore, the home town where their friends and relations were not too sure just where to find Italy on the map. I bowed my head.'[11] Eventually they reached the village of Paestum, where they found a farmhouse to shelter for the night.

At almost exactly the same time as Munthe's party hit the beach at Paestum, a corvette of the Royal Italian Navy, the *Baionetta*, was nudging its way cautiously into the harbour at Brindisi, on the Adriatic coast on the heel of southern Italy. On board were the 74-year-old King of Italy, Victor Emmanuel III, with his wife Elena, as well as his son and heir, Prince Humbert. Accompanying the royal party were Marshal Pietro Badoglio, the prime minister, General Vittorio Ambrosio, the commander-in-chief of the Italian armed forces, and Admiral Raffaele de Courten, head of the Italian Navy. Several dozen other government ministers and senior officers of the Italian supreme command made up the rest of the group. Badoglio had led the Italian forces to their victory over the Emperor Haile Selassie in Abyssinia in 1936 and had briefly headed the supreme general staff before falling out with Mussolini over the 1940 invasion of Greece.

It was two days since the party had hurriedly quit Rome, leaving behind chaos and confusion in the Italian capital. Since the King's dismissal of the Fascist dictator Benito Mussolini on 25 July, he and Badoglio had embarked on secret, lengthy and complex discussions with the allies on the subject of surrender. A week before, these had culminated in the signing of an armistice at Cassibile outside Syracuse on Sicily, where General Harold Alexander, commander of allied forces in Italy, had pitched his headquarters in an almond grove – the site, appropriately enough, where the Athenians had surrendered to the Syracusans in 413 BC. It had been agreed, however, to delay any public announcement of the surrender in order to avoid provoking the Germans into retaliating violently against their Italian allies for abandoning them, and thus to help safeguard the imminent British and American landings on the mainland.[12]

But when, exactly, should the armistice be announced and implemented? On this, the allies and the Italians had reached an impasse, and it was this that lay behind the scenes of confusion in Rome. On their side, the allies had wanted the Italians to surrender *before* their main invasion force landed at Salerno but, for obvious reasons of security, they could not reveal the date to the Italians much in advance. The Italians, however, preferred to surrender *after* the landings, when allied forces would be at hand to help protect them from the Germans. Since Mussolini's fall, Hitler had moved eight of his divisions over the Brenner Pass and drawn up a detailed plan to occupy Italy and replace Badoglio with a Fascist government. His forces were positioned threateningly on the outskirts of Rome, and on the eve of the allied landings it was far from clear that Badoglio and his ministers would keep to the terms of their agreement with the allies. In order to encourage them, at the very last minute General Dwight D. Eisenhower, the supreme allied commander in the Mediterranean, had promised to land an airborne division outside the capital to bolster the Italian defence. But fear of the Germans appeared to paralyse Badoglio, the King and his ministers, and no significant preparations had been made to assist it.

Meanwhile, Badoglio continued to drag his feet on the timing of the armistice announcement, hoping to put it off as long as he could. Finally, just hours before allied forces were due to land, an exasperated Eisenhower cancelled the airdrop and broadcast news of the armistice to the world. 'Today is X Day,' he curtly informed the Italians by telegram, 'and I expect you to do your part.' This ultimatum finally forced the Italians' hand. Whatever they did now, argued the King, they could expect little mercy from the Germans, so they should at least honour their deal with the allies. Thus, on the evening of Wednesday 8 September, at 7.45, Badoglio went on Rome radio to broadcast news of the surrender to the Italian people.[13]

Now he and his government were scrambling for safety. Behind, they left a nation in chaos. At first, most Italians greeted the armistice with relief, a sign that the war was over. 'Crowds poured into the streets singing,' recalled one witness of a scene in San Remo that was typical of towns across the nation. 'Soldiers were shouting: "Now we can go home again," and bars and cafes were packed with people drinking to the peace.'[14] But the euphoria rapidly passed as it became clear that Italy was now a theatre of fighting and that Germany's occupation in the north could be harsh and vengeful.

This quickly became apparent in its treatment of the Italian Army. In his broadcast about the armistice Badoglio had directed the Italian armed forces to cease hostilities against the Anglo-American forces and to retaliate 'against any attack from any direction whatsoever'. Its failure explicitly to mention the Germans, however, combined with the purely passive nature of its injunction, as well as the vacuum in Rome caused by the hasty flight to Brindisi, had led to utter confusion. Telephone calls to the War Office from local commanders all over Italy asking whether they should fight the Germans were answered by junior officers, who could only reply that they could not advise them because 'no-one was there'.[15]

Some units immediately surrendered to the Germans. In others, senior officers simply slipped surreptitiously away while their men were confined to barracks, subsequently to be taken prisoner by the Germans. A few units pledged their continuing loyalty to their erstwhile Axis ally, while many in Yugoslavia and Albania actively joined the partisans. Several put up a vigorous fight against the Germans, and when they were defeated often suffered terrible reprisals. Such, notoriously, was the case on the Greek island of Cephalonia, where the occupying Italians, unable simply 'to go home', chose actively to fight, only to have some 5,000 of the 12,000 garrison massacred in cold blood after they surrendered.[16]

Everywhere, Italian soldiers captured by the Germans were deported to Germany, where eventually some 700,000 of them were held in dozens of labour camps. It was scarcely surprising that many Italians believed that they had been betrayed by their own supreme command and experienced the events of 8 September as a national tragedy. This was all too vividly and painfully brought home as the trains loaded with prisoners began to head slowly north over the Brenner Pass to Hitler's Reich, observed by silent and weeping civilians along the track.[17]

In Rome, the Italian Motorised Corps resisted strongly and took heavy casualties before finally capitulating to the threat of a Luftwaffe carpet-bombing of the city. They formally surrendered to the Germans on the afternoon of Friday 10 September, at almost exactly the same time as the royal party was sailing into Brindisi.

The Adriatic port appeared to offer an obvious safe haven, but how safe remained uncertain until the very last moment. As the King and his ministers sailed down the coast from Ortona, a German plane circled overhead for several minutes before flying off without firing on them, deterred no doubt by the presence of their heavily armed escort, the cruiser *Scipione Africano*, but with no guarantee that it would not return later with a fleet of bombers.

Any lingering worries, however, must have been rapidly dispelled on disembarking. Just that morning, an advance party of one of the more unorthodox units of the British Eighth Army, Popski's Private Army, a small special-forces sabotage unit consisting of fewer than a hundred men, had entered the town, and its commander, Lieutenant Colonel Vladimir Peniakoff (the legendary 'Popski' himself), had discussed armistice arrangements with the local Italian admiral. Now the town was bedecked with Union flags, hanging from windows and balconies, alongside a blizzard of green, red and white Italian flags. Relieved to be safe from the Germans, the royal party thankfully made its way to the scattered accommodation that had been hastily improvised for it. Troops of the British First Airborne Division arrived the next day and firmly secured the town and its surrounding region.[18]

Amongst those disembarking from the *Baionetta* was a blond young man in his early twenties. Despite his fluent Italian, he was a member of neither the government nor the supreme command. In fact, he was not even an Italian. He was an Englishman, and his name was Cecil Richard Mallaby.

Known as 'Dick' to his friends, he had spent his formative years on the Tuscan estate of his father, a former tea planter from Ceylon who had married an Italian, and had fought in the North African desert with the commandos. But for the previous year and a half he had been working for SOE, largely in training recruits, had himself received the full range of its specialised skills from sabotage to parachuting, and had just been awarded his commission as a lieutenant. More important, however, was that in addition to being bilingual in Italian and English, he was a trained and experienced wireless operator. Unexpectedly and unpredictably, this had cast him as a central figure in the recent armistice negotiations.

Just a month before, he had been dropped by parachute with an inflatable dinghy into Lake Como. The plan was for him to paddle ashore and to reach a safe house where a radio set would be waiting for him, along with various contact addresses, so that he could act as a link between SOE and Italian resistance groups. Unfortunately, on the previous night Milan had been subjected to a heavy air raid by the Royal Air Force. Refugees had poured north out of the city to Como, and to help them find their way after dusk the shores of the lake were still brilliantly lit up. So instead of descending in darkness, Mallaby's parachute had been easily spotted and he'd fallen into the hands of the Servizio Informazione Militare, or SIM, Italian military intelligence, without even having had time to inflate his dinghy.

By sheer good chance, however, this mishap had coincided with the start of the secret negotiations about the armistice. Unexpectedly, Mallaby and his radio set had provided the crucial top-secret communications network for discussions between the British and the Italians. From the top floor of the headquarters of the Italian supreme command in Rome with a senior Italian wireless operator at his side, Mallaby had been responsible for coding and decoding the scores of messages that culminated in the agreement of 8 September, using a signal plan codenamed 'Monkey'. The Italians had assumed, and SOE had been careful not to disabuse them, that Mallaby's drop into Lake Como had been a legendary act of foresight by the all-powerful 'British intelligence'.[19]

He was bringing to Brindisi his wireless transmitting set, along with its Monkey signal plan and ciphers, with which he could keep in direct touch with SOE and provide a direct and immediate link between the allied high command and the Italian government. Events were moving fast, and the picture was confused. Even en route he had received an urgent message from Massingham. 'You must make immediate arrangements for connections with all parts of Italy,' it told him. 'This is of capital and urgent importance.' Within hours of landing, Mallaby and his radio set were installed safely in one of the towers of the castle in Brindisi where Popski had met the Italian admiral just hours before.

Two days later, four men dressed in tropical uniform arrived from Taranto, the Italian naval base, and moved into the Hotel

Internazionale. They, too, were attached to SOE, and they brought
with them a radio set as well as signals plans and ciphers which
had travelled on top of a bundle of straw – with matches to hand
in case they were intercepted by unfriendly forces.

The leader of this group was Captain Edward ('Teddy') De Haan,
who had worked under Roseberry in the Italian section in Baker
Street before being transferred that June to North Africa to take
charge of Italian affairs. Aged 24, he had passed a decade of his
childhood in Milan, was fluently bilingual and had spent the last
two years of peace as a trainee manager at the Savoy Hotel in
London. Most recently, he had served in Sicily as official military
interpreter during the armistice talks and his arrival in Brindisi was
the result of an order from Allied Forces Headquarters (AFHQ) in
Algeria to locate the whereabouts of the Italian government. With
him were Captain Freddy White, a cipher expert, and two signallers,
Sergeant Royle and Sergeant Case, the latter a Jamaican who had
worked as a telephonist in Kingston before the war.

This party, like Munthe's, had been despatched by Massingham.
Based at the Club des Pins, a former French beach club situated
in a secluded copse of pine trees at Guyotville, 24 kilometres west
of Algiers, Massingham had been established after the allied landings in North Africa to provide an advanced command, communications, supply and training base for subversive operations into
southern France, Corsica, Sardinia, Sicily and mainland Italy, and
it had country sections like the Baker Street headquarters in London.
Quite separate from, but working closely with the American Office
of Strategic Services (OSS), it was under the command of Lieutenant
Colonel Douglas Dodds-Parker, a former member of the Colonial
Service in Sudan, who'd joined SOE in 1940 and cut his teeth on
irregular operations helping Orde Wingate, 'the unorthodox king
of irregular warfare', wage guerrilla war against the Italians in East
Africa.

The Guyotville site, explained Dodds-Parker, was ideal. 'It was
a playboy's paradise,' he recalled. 'The airfield at Blida was about a
quarter of an hour away and people could get on a DC3 and do
their operational training drops in the sand dunes enclosed within
the barbed wire fence. There was a good beach for practising going
ashore at night from a submarine, and with American help we built

some store rooms there . . . There were basically Americans, British, French and all sorts of other people who turned up after having got out of Europe through Gibraltar who came to us . . .' The base was also close to AFHQ, the command centre for allied operations in the Mediterranean under General Eisenhower, located in the city's Hotel St Georges. The links SOE established here with the regular military and other specialised allied agencies were to prove invaluable for its operations into Italy.[20]

De Haan's small group was part of a 'two prong' strategy towards Italy being pursued by SOE – Munthe's group with the Fifth Army on the west coast being one of the prongs and his own group forming part of another on the east coast. Whereas the former had a fairly limited tactical role, the latter was designed to be built up as quickly as possible into a full-scale unit equipped to exploit the opportunities of a secure base in southern Italy for mounting operations by land, sea and air. As yet it was unclear whether it would be an independent unit, or merely the preliminary stage of a transfer of Massingham onto Italian soil. Since Brindisi was also an excellent base for launching operations into the Balkans, SOE had in mind that it might act as a base for these too.[21]

The origins of De Haan's mission lay in the final armistice talks at Cassibile. From the very start of the delicate and highly secret talks with the Italians in Lisbon, Roseberry, as head of J Section, had played a vital role, and he had flown out from London for their culmination. In his early fifties, and described by one insider as 'small, dark and earnest', he brought experience and skill to the task. By profession an East India merchant specialising in commodities such as jute and cotton, he had more than twenty years of international commercial dealing behind him. De Haan had been with him in discussions with the Italians. More importantly, however, Roseberry was no stranger to secret service work. During the First World War he had worked in postal censorship and served as British vice-consul at Narvik, to which he returned as consul in April 1940 before moving to Stockholm and then on to Helsinki as vice-consul. He was therefore used to handling often delicate and tricky diplomatic problems.

On the Italian side the principal negotiator was General Giuseppe Castellano, a senior officer on the staff of General Vittorio Ambrosio, the chief of the Italian general staff. With him, he brought for the final session his military intelligence staff officer, Major Marchesi.

Immediately after the signing of the armistice, Alexander informed Churchill that Castellano was remaining close by his headquarters and that they intended that very evening to start detailed military talks as to the most effective assistance the Italian forces could provide to allied operations. 'I have given them [the Italians] specific instructions,' Alexander reported to the chiefs of staff in London, 'to carry on [measures] which will help us in the sabotage line, sit down strikes, forming guerrilla bands, etc.'[22] The next day Roseberry himself met Castellano and they agreed in principle both to prepare a large-scale sabotage campaign against German communications in northern Italy and to inaugurate close liaison between the British and SIM – at least that part of it which remained loyal to the King.

Results followed promptly. Italian officers were brought down from Rome with up-to-date information and couriers were despatched instructing SIM officers in the field to direct all their future efforts against the Germans. Shortly afterwards, De Haan had also received his orders to proceed to Brindisi with the twofold mission of placing SOE services at the disposal of the Allied Control Commission (ACC) and of establishing contacts with the Italians. Here it would be his task to build up firm links with SIM and to make sure that their efforts tallied with allied needs. Given that Italian military intelligence had been, in the words of one distinguished British historian of the Second World War, allied intelligence's 'most brilliant professional opponent operating in any European country', this was a bold and extraordinary proposal and was to prove one of the most beneficial fruits, along with the delivery of its navy, of the Italian surrender.[23] A few weeks later Marshal Giovanni Messe, Ambrosio's replacement as chief of the Italian general staff, issued a general directive to all regional commands to start organising guerrilla warfare. 'It is our duty,' he declared, 'to develop with all our energy such form of warfare in all occupied territory.'[24]

De Haan acted rapidly to enlarge his team. Within days, he and Mallaby had joined forces, moved into the less conspicuous Hotel Imperio, and made contact with Marchesi and SIM. 'Two or three days after the arrival in Brindisi,' recorded Marchesi in his memoirs, 'Major Maurice Page and Captain De Haan, whom I had met at Cassibile, came to see me. They quickly convinced me that the programme of collaboration [with SIM] they had agreed had become even more important than ever [and that] I should be head of the Italians who collaborated with [them]. My "special group" would be distinct from SIM with the title of 810th Italian Service Squadron directly dependent on [British] control. I also had to agree to accept the difficult condition of their control over all my incoming and outgoing cipher messages.' In control of SIM's relations with SOE was the 42-year-old Lieutenant Colonel Giuseppe Massaioli, formerly an intelligence battalion commander who had served on both the Greek/Albanian and Russian fronts, and who was selected by allied authorities for the task.

One immediate objective was to establish communications with Rome, where Mallaby had left behind a radio set. After an Italian volunteer courageously travelled from Brindisi on horseback, carrying the necessary codes, contact was established with Colonel Giuseppe Montezemolo, a royalist sympathiser who was acting as an agent of Badoglio, organising resistance in the capital. Codenamed 'Rudder', the signal plan, all of whose traffic at first was encoded and decoded personally by Mallaby, provided a vital clandestine link with the Italian capital. In mid-December, Montezemolo began to ask for arms supplies and early in the New Year two attempted drops were made, but without success. Although Montezemolo fell into the hands of the *Sicherheitsdienst* (SD), the security service of the SS, in late January 1944, the radio link was never compromised and continued to operate until the liberation of the city.

The SOE group in Brindisi also began training additional Italian radio operators recruited by SIM from the Italian Navy – a bonus from the surrender of the Italian fleet. Taking a B2 W/T set with him to the nearby Italian naval barracks, Sergeant Royle showed the recruits how to work it, taught them basic operating procedures and took them out into the surrounding Apulian countryside to practise transmitting. In all this he was helped by several Italian wireless operators, one of whom spoke excellent English and acted as interpreter. Meanwhile, Captain White successfully established radio contact back to Massingham using a signal plan, codenamed 'Drizzle', devised by Massingham's signals expert, Lieutenant Dorothy Temple.[25]

*   *   *

The presence of this trained and experienced SOE nucleus in Brindisi was one of the few rays of light in an otherwise gloomy Italian scene. Not surprisingly, given the hasty evacuation from Rome and the confusion surrounding the armistice, there was little sign of Badoglio's government having any clear sense of direction or showing firm leadership. Indeed, for the first few days, Badoglio was even without a typewriter and had to write out all his communications in longhand. Harold Macmillan, Churchill's personal representative in the Mediterranean who arrived in Brindisi a few days later, concluded that the royal party could hardly be dignified with the title of a government at all, as it consisted merely of the King and his family, the aged (72-year-old) Badoglio, a sprinkling of generals and courtiers, and only one civilian minister, the rest having opted to remain in Rome. The characters of the men he had seen so far, concluded Macmillan, 'inspire sympathy rather than confidence' and an atmosphere of 'well-bred defeatism' surrounded the group.

It did, however, possess one great advantage: an unchallenged claim to legality. This was to prove important for SOE in the weeks and months ahead. And while the Italian Army had more or less disintegrated, and only a fraction of the Italian Air Force's three thousand planes had fallen into allied hands, a significant section of SIM was cooperating, the Italian fleet was under allied control, and locally the Italian Navy was showing every sign of cooperating. Eventually, on 13 October, the Badoglio government formally declared war on the Germans and was accepted by London and Washington as a 'co-belligerent'.

In this generally barren soil, only special operations appeared to offer much immediate prospect of flourishing. 'There is tremendous scope and a fruitful field for [sabotage and propaganda],' reported the head of the allied military mission in the town, Lieutenant General Sir Noel Mason-Macfarlane, the former Governor of Gibraltar, four days after Mallaby's arrival. 'We must go flat out on SOE and PWE [Political Warfare Executive, or propaganda].'[26]

By the end of the month strategists at AFHQ had reached agreement. In a directive issued under the name of General Eisenhower's chief of staff, Major General Walter Bedell Smith, they gave the green light to both SOE and OSS for 'the instigation of the Italian population to carry out acts of resistance to German forces . . . Direct attack on communications and transport in that area of Italy now held by the enemy . . . Destruction of enemy aircraft on the ground [and] Destruction of enemy supply dumps.' It also approved the establishment of SOE bases in southern Italy and the establishment of a forward OSS base near Bastia in Corsica. 'OSS/SOE will proceed at once,' the directive concluded, 'to infiltrate the necessary agents, supplies, and communications equipment.'[27]

Meanwhile, on the other side of the peninsula, Munthe and Salvadori had decided to drive as quickly as they could to Salerno to reach reliable contacts who could help their Italian anti-Fascist passengers reach Naples while the fighting lines remained fluid and permeable. As the main highway heading north was still held by the Germans, late in the afternoon on the following day they set off in a jeep. Driving behind hedges and skirting the swampy fields and coastal marshes full of water buffalo, they reached the mouth of the River Sele, the boundary between the British and American landing sectors. 'Here,' reported Munthe, 'while Tarchiani and Cianca hunted for signs of the enemy approaching through our field glasses, standing on top of the vehicle, Salvatore [Salvadori] and I pulled up sufficient fallen trees to form a bridge for our car.'

Once across, they drove rapidly along the sand and eventually reached Salerno. 'It was dusk,' remembered Munthe,

> the town seemed deserted: broken houses, doors unhinged, nothing moved. Suddenly shots rang out. We sheltered in a doorway; plaster and stones from the road were spattering around. We understood what we should do in what was obviously a German-occupied city. We could hear the trundle of tanks and armoured cars coming along the road. We stood in the shadow of a wall on a stone staircase. Our wretched jeep was outside, in full view. The cars were rattling nearer every minute. Then we saw them in the dark passing rapidly. We strained to hear the voices — German or Italian? It was difficult to make out. Then, with more than usual pleasure, we heard the familiar swear words of the British Army.[28]

The town had been heavily bombed by allied planes and only a tenth of the population remained. Hundreds of civilians had been killed and the rest had fled to the nearby hills. The port was in ruins, flour and food had run out and looting was rampant. 'There wasn't a soul to be seen,' remembered Salvadori, 'on either side were ruined buildings and fire-blackened walls. We had no idea whether Salerno was still in our hands, whether it had been occupied by the Germans, or whether it was No Man's Land. We broke open a door. On the second floor there was a dentist's brass plate. We went in. Nobody there, nobody in that building or any others nearby.' The next day, he and the two Italians went over to the town hall, where Cianca immediately recognised the octogenarian mayor as an old friend from pre-Fascist days. As a Member of Parliament he had withdrawn from public life during the Mussolini years and had recently been appointed by the Badoglio government. 'His age would have entitled him to stay away from trouble,' commented Salvadori. 'Yet there he was, doing everything possible to keep things in some sort of order.' With his help, they quickly despatched their first volunteer emissary over the hills to stir up trouble behind the lines.

Maintaining any sort of order proved difficult in the circumstances. Quite apart from the battered state of Salerno itself, fighting continued all around as allied forces struggled to consolidate the beachhead in the face of determined German resistance. At one point an enemy counter-attack even forced Mark Clark to consider abandoning the landings altogether. Every morning, recalled Salvadori, who described the following two weeks as pure 'hell', the Germans started firing on the town and the surrounding plains. 'A salvo of about forty shells whistled past every eight or ten minutes to land a little below us,' he wrote. 'After three hours they stopped, and started up again in the evening. At night, the dry thud of shells exploding three or four hundred yards away got on one's nerves . . . I recommend bombardments,' he added drily, 'to all who suffer from constipation.'[29]

Munthe's group kept the dentist's office as their base for a couple of nights until it was hit by shellfire, when they moved to a sturdier villa next door. By this time they had been joined by Gallegos and the rest of the party from Paestum, as well as by the mission's main signals detachment, which landed five days after Munthe's initial party. This was headed by Captain Derrick Scott-Job and included another signaller, Corporal Harry Hargreaves, as well as

several reserve W/T sets, signals plans and ciphers for use by the
missions they planned to send behind the lines. It also included an
Italian, Sergeant Leo Donati, a former prisoner of war who'd been
trained as a wireless operator at Massingham, as well as a finance
officer, Basil Evans. Hargreaves, like the majority of personnel in
Italy, had spent months at Massingham and was a graduate of the
SOE radio training school at Fawley Court near Henley-on-Thames.

Shortly after this, the sniping at night got really bad. The final
straw came when a bullet hit the wall just a foot from the head of
Munthe's batman, who had taken to cooking their meals in a foun-
tain, sheltered from sniper fire only by the brim of its marble bowl.
At this, Scott-Job insisted his section move out of Salerno in order
to avoid the shelling and protect its equipment — without radio
communications the mission would be both helpless and useless.
German patrols had also been reported operating close to the Salerno
villa and Scott-Job decided that the risk of ciphers falling into enemy
hands was simply too great to take. He and his team had already
established contact with the Massingham base, and radio communications were flowing well. They were made even easier a few days
later when a 15 cwt truck fitted with signals equipment, jocularly
christened the 'Gin Palace', landed at Salerno with the third SOE
group to step ashore. The truck had seen sterling service in North
Africa and was in the charge of Captain 'Dumbo' Newman.[30]

Despite all these hazards, by the end of September Munthe and his
men could mark up some useful progress and there was a steady
build-up of the mission. Two days after the third group landed, yet
another party disembarked at Paestum that included four more anti-
Fascist Italians returning from exile: Leo Valiani, Renato Pierleoni,
Aldo Garosci and Dino Gentili.

Valiani, aged 34, was an exiled journalist from Fiume, where he
was born in 1909 as Leo Weiczen into a Jewish family of Hungarian
origin. He spent a number of years in Mussolini's prisons, five of
which were endured in the fortress at Civitavecchia, before fleeing to
Paris in 1936, covering the Spanish Civil War as a war correspondent,
quitting the Communist Party in disgust at the signing of the
Hitler–Stalin pact, and then joining the Justice and Liberty group.
After a brief stay in Mexico, thanks to a strong recommendation from

Salvadori he was brought back across the Atlantic to work alongside SOE. MI5, asked to vet him, noted that he had 'a long record of socialist and anti-fascist activities. We have no reason,' they added, 'to doubt his integrity from a security point of view.' Pierleoni and Garosci were also former activists of Justice and Liberty who had fled to exile in Mexico, while Gentili had recently been living in the United States. Pierleoni and Valiani had both been flown from Britain to the Massingham base, where the latter had received instruction in coding before travelling on to Sicily and embarkation for Salerno. Pierleoni was a 41-year-old precision-tool mechanic running a lucrative business with his brother in Mexico City at the time of his recruitment. Like many of the Italian anti-Fascists, he had fought in Spain with the Republican forces. 'During the whole of his service with us,' it was noted in his SOE file at the end of the war, 'he has proved himself loyal, honest, exceptionally keen and courageous.' He also received an average daily allowance of 200 lire for his services.[31]

Accompanying the Italians was one of the more remarkable members of Munthe's mission, Adolphus Richard Cooper. A natural roustabout with a chequered career, Cooper had been born forty-four years before in Baghdad where his father served as British consul. Abandoned by his mother at birth, he had trailed round various Middle Eastern cities with his father, picked up numerous languages, including French, Italian, Greek, Turkish, Spanish and Arabic, and at the age of 15 joined the French Foreign Legion. He won the Croix de Guerre while fighting with French forces in the Dardanelles, briefly became a merchant seaman, worked as an interpreter with the British Army and then rejoined the Foreign Legion to fight in the Rif campaign in Morocco. Altogether, he spent eleven years with the Legion which, in his colourful published memoir, he referred to as 'my parent, torturer, friend and home'. It is possible, too, that he had once briefly worked for British Army intelligence.[32]

He lived for most of the 1930s in England, doing odd jobs such as school teaching, acting as a Thomas Cooks' guide and interpreter, and working as a linguist in an international telephone exchange. He knew how to look after himself and get things done, and in 1941 SOE recruited him for work in North Africa, where he was arrested by the Vichy French authorities and sent to prison in mainland France, from where he promptly escaped. In Sicily, he spent most of his energies training the Italian exiles for work behind the lines. Salvadori, for one, was duly grateful. 'If it were not for Cooper,' he noted in Salerno, 'I would still be on my way here. He threw his weight about and got people to take us from one place to another until we found our unit . . .' One of those who recruited him described him as 'a very good type of *débrouillard* [resourceful] tough'. Only after his recruitment did SOE find out that he also possessed a minor criminal record.[33]

He brought with him to Salerno ten million lire, packed in sandbags, to finance their operations. Shortly after landing, the ancient Aprilia car he was driving broke down irreparably on the road south of Salerno. After unloading the bags, he stood by the roadside and hitched the first of several lifts that finally allowed him to hand over the money, with great relief to all concerned, to Basil Evans.

In the meantime, Munthe's mission had started to work. Capri was liberated on Sunday 12 September and two days later Gallegos and Munthe embarked for the island from a battered Salerno harbour in a commando landing craft accompanied by Tarchiani and Cianca.

The island had long been a sybarite's delight and a magnet for tourists. As the men stepped ashore, civilians were casually strolling down to the beach wearing multi-coloured shirts, shorts, beach hats and sunglasses, as though they had never heard that a war was going on. Mingling with them were several Fascist militiamen and other people in uniform. 'Elegant ladies in sun suits and big hats strolled about followed by their little dogs and gigolos,' remarked one angry anti-Fascist veteran who arrived on the scene shortly afterwards. 'If I had seen an anarchist slip a time bomb or two under the tables I certainly would have done nothing to stop him.' The cafés on the island's small central square were crowded with people sipping their aperitifs and exchanging gossip. Such were the bizarre incongruities of war.[34]

The scene was all too familiar to Munthe. His father Axel, a wealthy Swedish doctor, had been physician to the Swedish royal family, spending much of his adult life on Capri in attendance on the delicate Crown Princess Victoria, who always wintered there. Just over a decade before, his account of life as a doctor on the island, *The Story of San Michele*, had become an international bestseller.

Malcolm, the younger of his two sons by his second wife, an Englishwoman, had himself spent much time on the island, and the Villa San Michele was almost a second home. 'I was touched to see how much loved Munthe was by the Capri people,' noted Cooper. 'As the son of their beloved Dr. Axel they regarded him as one of themselves. They approached him with smiles, almost ready to kiss his hand. It was touching to see, too, how Munthe knew them all. It was "Buon giorno, Giuseppe" here and "Buon giorno Maria" there all the way.'[35]

The island also attracted other celebrities. On the night he arrived, Munthe was standing on the pier in his kilt helping unload the commando vessel that had brought them over from Salerno. In the moonlight, an American destroyer glided into the harbour and a voice from the bridge called out, 'Say, Scottie, I'm landing thirty-two of Mussolini's political prisoners. Look after them – they haven't been free for seventeen years!' Munthe looked up and saw a lieutenant commander dressed in a crumpled shirt, trousers and battered cap. Round his waist he wore straps and chains and belts from which dangled an assortment of deadly weapons. 'By the time I had grasped the full significance of thirty-two prisoners,' Munthe recalled, 'the lieutenant commander had re-embarked and was sailing away, like the romantic prisoner of Zenda liberator he was – for he was Douglas Fairbanks, Junior.' On board the USS *Knight* with Fairbanks was the novelist John Steinbeck, now working as a war journalist.[36]

After they were installed comfortably in the Hotel La Palma, with their wireless operator established in an attic of the nearby Hotel Quisisana, Gallegos made contact with the allied admiral-designate in Naples, Admiral Morse, who had set up a temporary base in the villa belonging to Mussolini's daughter Edda Ciano, and who responded positively to Gallegos's request for help to find small boats. The island was ideally suited for the operations he planned, strategically placed as it was, opposite the Sorrento peninsula and close to Naples, which was still in enemy hands. 'From Capri night after night,' recalled Boutigny, who was now the main escort for Tarchiani and Cianca, 'we could watch our bombers delivering their loads of death on the port area. The heavy German ack-ack fire, the fires started by our bombs, the tracer bullets, all combined to create phantasmagorical fireworks.'[37]

In addition to providing a base for allied small craft, Capri also had a flotilla of Italian MAS boats (motoscafo *antisommergibile* – submarine chaser) which, thanks to the cooperation of the Italian Navy, were placed promptly at the allies' disposal. Over the nights that followed, several fishing boats were able to escape from Naples, unseen by the Germans, bringing Italians eager to help and with valuable contacts behind enemy lines.

From now on, the military campaign was to play an increasingly determining role in the deployment of SOE forces and the direction of their efforts in Italy. Its strategic goal from start to finish was *not* to chase the German armies out of Italy as quickly as possible. Instead, it was to contain the maximum number of enemy divisions there in order to prevent them from being used to reinforce either the eastern front against the Russians or the western front in France, where the D-Day landings had the highest allied priority and were due to take place in May, later postponed until June, 1944. It followed for the western allies that while the Italian campaign was important, it was essentially a secondary front and could, if necessary, be 'raided' for reinforcements for the main front in France (as it was to be, frequently).

While this strategic goal was known to the principal allied commanders, it did not necessarily filter down to lower commands, nor indeed to most senior SOE officers in Italy, and certainly remained unknown to the Italians. This was to prove significant, not only for its influence on the role and scale of SOE activity in Italy, but also for the misapprehensions and errors of judgement to which it led, especially for most Italian resistance leaders and partisan commanders. The liberation of Italy from the Germans was certainly an objective shared by the allied armies with the Italian resistance. But in their broader strategic view it was subordinate to the overall military aim of winning the Second World War by the defeat of *all* the enemy forces, wherever they were. For the Italian resistance, however, naturally enough, the liberation of Italy itself was the ultimate war aim. Inevitably, these different priorities were to give rise to misunderstandings and disputes about the scale and tempo of operations in Italy – in which SOE frequently found itself at the epicentre.

So far as the political background was concerned, the broad aim of British policy towards Italy so long as the fighting lasted was to keep control by supporting the government that had signed the surrender. Macmillan, despite his initial unfavourable reactions on encountering the King's party at Brindisi, quickly came to accept that in the circumstances support for the House of Savoy was imperative, offering as it did the only unifying force in the country and the only effective counterweight against the threat of a Communist takeover. 'What else was there?' he asked.[38]

The snag here was that this policy involved supporting the King, who was widely discredited for his twenty-year collaboration with Mussolini (even though he had also eventually dismissed him), as well as Badoglio and his government, which was blamed for the catastrophe that had engulfed the country during the surrender. Distaste for the King and his entourage was especially strong amongst anti-Fascist activists such as Max Salvadori, whom SOE had originally seen as leaders of the resistance.

Roseberry was acutely aware of the contradiction. So it was only after Salvadori landed at Salerno that he told him about his own role in the surrender talks, his negotiations with the Italians, and their agreement to collaborate. 'I am afraid that it was necessary to keep you in a state of doubt and uncertainty for longer than was good for your morale,' he told Salvadori by letter, 'but events were such that this was inevitable ... I am fully alive to the fact that such collaboration has its drawbacks and leaves out of account entirely the spiritual side of resistance,' he went on. 'I am therefore of the opinion that our old friends [Giustizia e Libertà] should be kept in tow and fostered. Against this the General Staff consider there is no room in Italy just now for anything but military action and action of our sort carried out by trusted military personnel (not of course operating as military). They are suspicious of all political or revolutionary movements and in fact one of their first decrees was the abolition of all parties.' He continued:

What I am most afraid of in Northern Italy is what we have seen happen in so many other countries which have been occupied by the Germans, namely, a spirit of apathy and a consideration only of how one can work and live. To overcome this tendency to apathy the work of G and L can be valuable, and the presence in Italy of our friends such as the two Alberti, Dino, Aldo and Leo [Cianca, Tarchiani, Gentili, Garosci and Valiani] can have great value. I am therefore sending the last three-named on to you and I want you to give them every assistance possible. It is most important that we, as an official organisation, should not appear to be encouraging what the military delight in calling 'political agitators,' so that from the time of their arrival they must look after themselves and have no contact with [De Haan].

As you can imagine it has not been easy to get them down to concrete planning, but the following is the outline agreed upon:-

(a) They will seek out and establish safe houses and addresses at the bridgehead. When they leave for the interior they will rely on their own resources and the friends of G and L to establish a series of addresses so that these are available for messages and further bodies. If we can possibly arrange it in time, we shall give them a set and an operator for whose safety and utilisation they will be responsible. Failing this, other means of contacting us will have to be worked out.

(b) Their principal business will be to stimulate the spirit of resistance and to encourage those who are physically capable of carrying out definite operations.

(c) They will not encourage any party revolutionary tactics.

A good deal of tact and discretion must be exercised. I consider that such elements can do a lot of good but I must see that our organisation is not compromised vis-a-vis [the] Italian General Staff.

You have had a weary time waiting about and may often have wondered what you were expected to do. This period was unfortunately prolonged as you could not be brought into the picture until the negotiations I was conducting had been concluded. There is only one enemy now; Fascism is dead and we and the Italians must unite to get rid of the Hun. There can be no peace in Italy until there is peace in Europe.[39]

This was the clearest statement ever made of SOE's dual strategy in Italy, and for veteran anti-Fascists such as Salvadori it proved a bitter pill to swallow. In addition, even after the royal government declared war on Germany, Italy was never recognised as a full and equal ally but merely as a 'co-belligerent' which, when the war ended, would have to suffer some punitive peace terms. If this were not bad enough, Italian *amour propre* was not helped further by a widespread tendency on the part of the British in particular, especially those who had fought with the Eighth Army against the Italians in East and North Africa, to treat them not just as a defeated enemy, but also as one for whom they had little military regard. All this was to complicate SOE's task of fostering and supporting resistance behind the enemy lines.[40]

# CHAPTER TWO

# Maryland: 'All in all, it did us well'

As the allies gained their foothold in southern Italy, and as more and more members of the Italian armed forces came forward to help them, so German propaganda railed vociferously at the treachery of Italians and demanded the punishment of those who had resisted or undermined the Fascist regime. The campaign grew more strident after the dramatic rescue of Mussolini by the renowned German commando leader, Otto Skorzeny.

After the July coup the Italian ex-dictator had been briefly imprisoned by the Badoglio government on the island of Ponza before being transferred to La Maddalena, a small island and naval base off the north coast of Sardinia. But word of his whereabouts soon leaked out and the government, fearing a Nazi attempt to abduct him, flew him to a resort hotel high up in the Apennines on the Gran Sasso mountain, 120 kilometres from Rome. Within a matter of days this news too reached the ears of German agents, and just four days after the Salerno landings German parachutists led by the flamboyant Skorzeny carried out a daring and spectacular raid. Landing by glider in the grounds of the hotel, they seized Mussolini and flew him to safety. In Munich he was reunited with his family before being flown to see Hitler at his 'Wolf's Lair' military headquarters at Rastenburg in East Prussia. Here the Nazi dictator made him an offer he could not refuse, to become the head of a new Fascist government in German-occupied Italy. Despite the outward trappings of autonomy, in all essentials this was to be a puppet state of the Nazis or, in Churchill's words, the 'pitiful shadow' of a government. As if to make this clear, Hitler refused all Mussolini's pleas to allow it to take its seat in Rome.'

Instead, early in October, the Italian Social Republic (RSI) set up office on Lake Garda and quickly became known as the Salò Republic, after the small town from which it issued its communiqués. Mussolini himself took up residence in the Villa Feltrinelli at nearby Gargnano, where he served both as head of state and of the government, albeit closely supervised by a senior German 'liaison officer' housed with a small professional staff in the villa next door and with a junior member of its team in the Villa Feltrinelli itself. This did not deter Mussolini from claiming to be the only true leader of Italy. 'Only blood,' he proclaimed in a broadcast to the Italian people over Radio Munich, could cancel the humiliation of the King's betrayal of Fascism and of the Duce himself, as well as of their German allies. The war would continue, he promised, and traitors of all kinds would be eliminated. As a counterweight to Marshal Badoglio, now serving the King, he appointed Marshal Rodolfo Graziani, the former commander of Italian forces in Libya, as his Minister of War.[2]

Who supported Mussolini and the new Fascist regime, and who was against him, thus once again became a vital political issue in Italy. So far as Rome Radio, now controlled by the Germans, was concerned, at least one villain in the drama of what they regarded as Italy's betrayal was obvious. 'Amongst the treacherous Italians most responsible for the breakdown of Fascism and for the under-mining of the Rome–Berlin Axis,' it declared in a broadcast in mid-September, 'must ever stand the name of Benedetto Croce, and he too will soon be brought to justice.'[3]

Croce was Italy's most famous living philosopher. He was also a senator and leading Liberal (which, in Italian terms, meant Conservative), and, despite having flirted with Mussolini's move-ment in its early days, since 1925 he had emerged as a leading symbol of anti-Fascist resistance. Now aged 77, he was living quietly and unobtrusively with his wife and daughters in their villa in Sorrento, on the mainland just across the water from Capri. Here it would be all too easy for the Germans to seize him and rumours rapidly spread that a group had been despatched for this purpose.[4]

Munthe decided that this should be prevented at all costs. So on Wednesday 15 September he sent Adrian Gallegos from Capri on a rescue mission. Late in the afternoon, Gallegos set off in a fast Italian MAS boat placed at SOE's disposal by Captain Alessandro

Michelagnoli, commander of the Italian II MAS Flotilla. The SOE officer was wearing full naval uniform and was accompanied by Signor Brindisi, a Neapolitan lawyer and friend of the Croce family who was also the police commissioner on the island. He knew Sorrento intimately and could guide Gallegos quickly to the philosopher's home in the Villa Tritone.

No one knew whether the Germans had arrived in Sorrento or not, and as he headed for the mainland Gallegos worried about the sort of reception he would receive when he landed. Were there Fascists still active in the town who would turn him in, or even violently resist his small party? Halfway there, they encountered a naval launch heading in the opposite direction. 'Are the Germans in Sorrento?' asked Gallegos. 'They were there yesterday,' came the reply, 'and most probably still are – so watch out.'

As they approached the town, Gallegos keenly scanned the shore-line through his field glasses. Dusk was falling. He could see no sign of any uniforms so decided to make straight for the harbour. As the boat drew alongside the jetty, some bystanders approached. Again he asked if the Germans were still there. 'I believe they left this morning,' answered one of them, doubtfully.

Quickly, Gallegos and Brindisi made their way up the hill. As they passed people in the street they asked them about the Germans. Each time they seemed to get a different answer. Gallegos felt increasingly anxious. Just in case, he'd brought with him his Colt pistol and a tommy gun.

Finally they entered the garden of Croce's villa, thankful to be enveloped in the darkness under the trees. It was about 7.30 p.m. Inside, Brindisi was recognised immediately by Signora Croce, who greeted him warmly. With her were a number of Croce's young followers, all now wondering about their best course of action. Brindisi explained why they were there. 'Yes, I too think that my husband should get away from here,' answered the philosopher's wife, 'but you will find it difficult to convince him.'

She was right. Inside Croce's study Gallegos found the elderly white-haired Liberal reading a book by the light of a candle. He listened carefully as the SOE officer explained why he was there and then, slowly but firmly, responded that he was an old man who did not like the Germans, but that he was not afraid of them. 'I shall remain here,' he declared. 'I would not want the people of Sorrento to think that I am afraid, that I am running away.' Gallegos replied that he did not think they would because he would be clearly helping the cause of freedom, and once inside free Italy his presence would provide a stimulus to anti-Fascist forces. But if he stayed, he pointed out, the Germans would declare a Fascist victory and even claim he had elected to stay there.

But Croce proved obstinate, and it took much precious time and all of Gallegos's patience and skill eventually to persuade the philosopher of the merits of leaving. Brindisi added his own exhortations and persuasions. Finally convinced, Croce asked when he should go. 'Now – as soon as you can pack some things,' replied Gallegos. 'All right,' responded Croce reluctantly. 'I shall tell my wife. I shall try to be quick . . . She will come too of course?'

It was pitch-dark when the small party hurriedly left the villa, the philosopher leaning heavily on the arm of his eldest daughter, Elena. His wife opted to remain behind to pack up their things and promised to follow as soon as she could. Walking furtively and talking in whispers, the group made their way undisturbed to the harbour, where the boat and its crew were patiently waiting. They cast off, and as they reached Capri the moon rose up over the horizon.

Munthe had been anxiously waiting for them for over an hour. 'At last the sound of engines in the mist was clearly heard,' he remembered. 'Round the mole the [boat] was coming; standing on the deck, his white cap visible, Gallegos appeared alongside his precious charge . . . The greatest anti-Fascist in Italy was free at last to lead back to sanity his distraught countrymen.'[5]

Late on the evening of the next day Munthe, accompanied by Brindisi and Tarchiani, set off to bring back Signora Croce along with her younger daughter and a suitcase of secret papers left behind by her husband. Their mission was almost aborted before it began. The MAS boat broke down twice as they struggled to get it ready, then the Italian captain lost his nerve and refused to set off on the grounds that he would be shot by the Germans if he was caught. Munthe promptly placed his sub lieutenant in charge and finally, just before midnight, they set off. As they left, Brindisi fired Munthe's Sten gun into the water for practice.

By now it was widely rumoured that the Germans had at last

entered Sorrento, so Munthe avoided the harbour and headed instead for a small creek known to Brindisi. 'The moon was well behind cloud when we turned off the engine and glided into the creek, which turned out to be the wrong one but was nevertheless quite close to the place where Mrs Croce was,' recorded Munthe. At the villa, she and her party were prepared and waiting, and in five minutes they were all heading back to the boat. They walked along the bed of a little rivulet to the creek in single file, with Brindisi in front and Munthe bringing up the rear. No one appeared to notice them until they were actually embarking, when shots rang out from the hills above. There was a brief delay when Croce's wife snagged her coat on a rock and struggled to free it. A shot hit the back of the boat but it struck above the water line and no one was hurt. A short while later, at 2 a.m., the group stepped ashore on Capri and the Croce family was reunited.[6]

For the allies, the rescue of Croce was a great propaganda coup, a welcome riposte to Skorzeny's rescue of Mussolini, and a feather in SOE's cap. 'The English wireless has today announced that I was taken to safety by English officers,' Croce recorded in his diary on 20 September.[7] For SOE, however, his rescue was by no means the end of the Croce affair. On the contrary, it quickly brought to the surface some troublesome policy issues.

Munthe had first been warned of the risk to the philosopher by Croce's son-in-law Raimondo Craveri of the Banca Commerciale, who had reached Sorrento after escaping from Rome where he was working with the Committee of National Liberation (CNL) as a leader of the newly formed Partito d'Azione (PdA), or Action Party, a leftist wartime offspring of Justice and Liberty. Through Craveri, Munthe met one of Italy's most celebrated First World War military heroes, General Giuseppe Pavone.

The former commander of the famous regiment the 'Arditi', who had assisted the nationalist poet Gabriele D'Annunzio in his daring and controversial seizure of the city of Fiume for Italy, Pavone lived in a tower at Torchiara close to Paestum, and had greeted the allied landings with unalloyed delight. After Munthe was established in Salerno, he took to dropping in to see him regularly and, as he put it, 'at last getting into the smell of battle'. Munthe was deeply impressed by the portly and now elderly Pavone, describing him as 'in more senses than one a tower of strength ... [with] the figure of Henry VIII and a tremendous grey beard'. The idea soon emerged of placing him at the head of a thousand Italian volunteers who would be trained by SOE but fight under his personal command in the name of Italy. This would prevent any damaging idea that they were simply acting as 'agents' for the British and would provide, so Munthe thought, 'excellent cover' for SOE's work. Such a plan also had the advantage of not requiring the volunteers to swear an oath of loyalty to the King.[8]

But Pavone had another suitor, the OSS. Relations between SOE and its American counterpart were governed by an agreement of June 1942 designed to avoid the confusion of two separate agencies operating in the same field. Distinct British and American areas were identified, with either power entitled to set up a special operations mission in the territory of the other, provided it came under the latter's direction and control. Globally, SOE had been given initial pre-eminence in India, East and West Africa, Gibraltar, the Balkans, the Middle East, Western Europe, Poland, Czechoslovakia and Scandinavia, while the Americans were granted China, Australia and the south-west Pacific, North Africa, Finland, and the Atlantic islands (the Azores, Madeira, the Canaries and Cape Verdes). Burma, Siam, Indochina, Malaya, Sumatra, Germany, Sweden and Switzerland were considered joint areas – as was Italy.

While this agreement formed the basis of SOE–OSS relations until the end of the war, it came under constant pressure from the latter's director, General William Donovan, to give OSS greater independence in field operations whilst still preserving access to British training and field support. As a result, occasional pragmatic adjustments were made to it. At Massingham, the two agencies had worked closely together and launched dozens of joint operations, and it was thanks to the US Fifth Army that Munthe's mission had been able to establish itself at Salerno, Capri and Ischia to begin with. But the opening-up of Italy for special operations presented Donovan with an opportunity at last to establish a more independent policy, and after the landings at Salerno the two agencies pursued separate although not necessarily conflicting agendas. Colonel Ellery C. Huntington, Munthe's American opposite number, was friendly and cooperative. But he had his own firm directives from Donovan.[9]

The forceful OSS director, who as ever was keen to set his personal mark on events, lost little time in descending on the scene to see for himself what was happening. Within days of the Salerno landings he turned up at the OSS headquarters attached to the Fifth Army in the Hotel Luna in Amalfi, a former monastery founded by St Francis of Assisi, where the American contingent was being comfortably looked after by uniformed chambermaids and dinner-jacketed waiters. The officer in charge was Donald Downes, who'd worked with Sir William Stephenson's British Security Coordination office in New York during the United States' period of neutrality before Pearl Harbor. 'He arrived in a sort of Churchillian baby's jumper suit with his general's insignia and a musette bag − no luggage,' wrote Downes about his boss, a First World War hero who'd won his nation's highest award, the Medal of Honor, for bravery on the Western Front. 'He wanted to see the beach-head . . . to smell powder, to sleep in a fox hole and eat K-rations.'[10]

Shortly afterwards, Donovan sailed to Capri where he met up with another of his officers, Peter Tompkins, a youthful pre-war correspondent in Rome for the *New York Herald Tribune*. After Tompkins told him that Croce was the one person who, over the previous twenty years, had truly represented the spirit of Italian anti-Fascism, Donovan went to visit him. Croce noted the meeting in his diary. '[He] asked me how the spirit of the Italians was,' he recorded, 'and I said that what all the best Italians wanted, and what would most encourage them, would be permission to form a combatant legion under the Italian flag to co-operate with the Anglo-American armies in liberating Italian soil from the Germans.' Did he have anyone in mind who could command such a legion? asked Donovan. Croce immediately gave him the name of Pavone. The Italian general, he explained to the OSS director, was 'of an old southern family, a patriot, and a liberal'.[11]

Donovan immediately decided to enrol Pavone for the OSS cause and quickly convinced Craveri to help him persuade his father-in-law to go along with the Americans. Just two days after meeting with Croce, he called a joint meeting between OSS, Munthe's mission and the Italians at his own personal headquarters in an olive grove just south of the temples at Paestum. That same day, Croce, Craveri, Pavone and Tarchiani decided to constitute themselves as a provisional committee with the title 'National Liberation Front' and the philosopher agreed to write its manifesto for broadcast to the Italian people. Munthe, when he read the text a few days later, was both 'convinced and moved by it', while Donovan was so enthused that he succeeded in 'selling' the plan to Mark Clark. It was especially valuable, he argued, because the Badoglio government had still not declared war on Germany. Considerable public enthusiasm greeted the news of the Gruppi Combattenti in Italia (GCI) which Pavone launched with a public appeal in Naples on 10 October.[12]

So far, it appeared that SOE and OSS were keeping closely in step and that the Pavone scheme would develop as a joint operation. But this soon changed. For one thing, the Americans were able to promise the Italians supplies on a scale impossible for SOE to match. 'In all matters of instructors, uniforms, food, tents and weapons where we had promised ten, OSS promised a hundred,' acknowledged Munthe, 'and it very quickly became evident that we were hopelessly outbid.'[13] This in itself posed no intrinsic problem as SOE had long before willingly embraced its reliance on superior American resources.

Far more serious was that the Pavone scheme soon ran into opposition from the Badoglio government, which quickly rang alarm bells in the higher reaches of SOE. Already, even before Donovan's meeting with the elderly general, Massingham had warned Munthe of the risk that the Italian high command would complain about the role being given to political exiles. Now De Haan, who was working closely alongside the Italians in Brindisi, again sounded an alarm. 'Obviously we are getting into "big stuff",' he recorded, before adding by way of warning that SOE was entering 'very dangerous ground indeed'. His concern increased when he heard of a proposal by Munthe to provide Craveri and Pavone with transport to Brindisi so that they could explain the project to Badoglio in person. That, he objected, would have 'ghastly results at present'.[14]

Despite his protests, however, the delegation did make the journey to Brindisi to consult the marshal. Accompanied by Salvadori, they took two days to get there. As they were still in a military zone their car could not use its headlights and they were forced to spend the first night at a farm near Eboli. On the second day, their journey was severely delayed because the Germans had blown up most of the bridges, forcing them to make long detours before finally reaching Bari, where they had to spend their second night. When they finally drove into Brindisi, all Salvadori's passionately held anti-Fascist feelings rose instantly to the surface. 'The castle . . . which houses what remains of the Italian government,' he confided to his diary, 'is a fine symbol of fascism – an impressive façade which would collapse at the first shots fired. What particularly struck me were the round paunches and gleaming riding-boots of the officers around Badoglio – an army strictly for parade. They found our uniforms very inelegant (they certainly are!). They cannot understand why we have no batmen, and they disapprove of our lack of sharp distinction between officers and other ranks.'[15]

To the Italian exiles who met him in his office on the afternoon of 4 October Badoglio was polite but reticent, giving them a mere forty-five minutes of his time and explaining that he himself was working hard to raise an effective force to fight alongside the allies. But the Germans, he stressed, while 'barbarians', were good soldiers and the task would be hard. He therefore had his doubts, not about the enthusiasm but about the fortitude of the likely Pavone volunteers, and it was necessary 'to be very careful not to cut a sorry figure'. With this, he effectively dissociated himself from the project, although he was careful not to say so explicitly and even promised that he would willingly express a favourable opinion on the initiative.[16]

In the meantime, Roseberry had arrived in Brindisi to deal with the by now politically awkward project. So far as Churchill and the War Cabinet were concerned, Badoglio and the monarchy had to be supported as the government of Italy for the time being, both to ensure the active participation of the Italian armed forces on the allied side and to ensure the maintenance of order and good administration behind the lines. This did not preclude either making changes to broaden the government's political base or, as insisted on by many anti-Fascists, accepting the abdication of the widely discredited King. But until an acceptable alternative emerged – one that would clearly protect the needs of the allied armies – the status quo, however unsatisfactory, was the preferred option. Churchill in particular believed strongly that Marshal Badoglio was the 'only solid peg' on which to hang policy in Italy, and had instructed Macmillan accordingly.

Baker Street was fully briefed on the policy through its regular monthly meetings with top Foreign Office officials. The permanent under-secretary, Sir Alexander Cadogan, emphasised that the inevitable corollary of the policy was that 'groups in opposition to the King and Government should not be given too much encouragement at present', while Sir Stewart Menzies, the SIS chief, said that his latest and best information showed that 'any change of regime in Italy at this moment would have unfortunate consequences for us'. All his evidence indicated that the Officer Corps in Italy was strongly loyal to the King.[17]

So when, on 22 October, Roseberry met Salvadori at the Albergo Nazionale he explained that there was no choice but to work for a broad-based government under the King and that the resistance should collaborate with it. In making the point, he was taking special aim at the refusal of the Rome Committee of National Liberation and the Action Party, one of its constituent members, to agree to any collaboration with the royal government at all. This, he emphasised, went against the will of the allies and showed a lack of gratitude for all that SOE had done to help them. Hanging over Roseberry's visit were fears that if the Germans evacuated Rome before the allies arrived a revolutionary movement akin to the Paris Commune of 1871 might come into being. Also present at the meeting as an interlocutor was Prince Filippo Caracciolo, the Italian consul in Lugano, Switzerland, and a prominent member of the Action Party. Married to an American, he was willing to help the allies and keen to broker an arrangement with Count Carlo Sforza, one of the most respected anti-Fascist exiles, who enjoyed considerable American support but had alienated Churchill by refusing to back the King.[18]

For Salvadori, as for other anti-Fascists, the official line as expounded by Roseberry was difficult to swallow. Whilst he accepted that some of the returning exiles and resistance militants had unrealistic ideas about holding immediate elections and appointing a new government, he thought that the Allied Control Commission was worrying unnecessarily about a possible threat from revolutionary forces and was not giving the anti-Fascists their due. 'Now that some measure of liberty has returned to Italy,' he told Harold Caccia of the Commission, 'it seems absurd to expect the survival of a government of fascist fellow-travellers and ex-frondeurs, such as Badoglio.' Increasingly, he felt he was being sidelined by events. 'All I can do,' he noted resignedly in his diary, 'is write reports which probably go straight into the waste-paper basket.'[19] Three weeks later, he recorded a lengthier analysis of SOE's direction.

Alp [Roseberry] and his collaborators have decided that the Resistance in German-occupied territory must be contacted and organised through *badogliani*. There is a practical reason for this decision: since the end of October, members of the Italian military Intelligence have crossed the lines and kept in constant touch with Brindisi by radio. I have tried to explain that Intelligence is not the same thing as Resistance; that the two must be dealt with separately – as the British Army has recognised since the beginning of the war; that the organisers of the Resistance are people very different from those useful as Intelligence agents. As far as one can tell, the Resistance groups are being organised mainly by anti-fascists, who may be willing – to some extent – to work with Badoglio and all that he stands for, but who would certainly never consider themselves *badogliani*. Sending followers of Badoglio as Allied representatives and as liaison officers can only be detrimental to the good relations between the Allies and the Resistance. The Liberation Committees represent the break with the past, and should be approached by people who have no connection with the Brindisi government. Otherwise, instead of encouraging the Resistance, the Allies will run the risk of paralysing it.[20]

It was a criticism of SOE policy that was to gain widespread currency both then and later in resistance circles. In fact, however, as Salvadori himself immediately acknowledged, Vigilant under Munthe's direction was continuing in its efforts to contact the anti-Fascist underground in Rome.

Early in November, the Allied Control Commission published orders for Pavone's corps to be disbanded. It had, in any case, received far fewer suitable volunteers than hoped for and by the end of October only ten officers and thirty-five other ranks had been selected. Within the ranks of the OSS, enthusiasts of the scheme blamed SOE for sabotaging the project, but by November even they were losing interest.[21] As it slowly disintegrated, Munthe himself had begun to dissociate himself from it. 'I was asked to attend the joint meetings,' he recorded, 'but now pleaded excessive work and sent an observer only, pointing out to Huntington that he was not authorised to engage in political movements.' Nonetheless, he felt that the episode had ended badly for SOE. 'All this made a confusing and unfortunate impression on those Italians who might have been valuable to us,' he recorded, 'and Pavone, bewildered and disappointed, retired once more to his tower at Torchiera . . . He was not well handled.'[22]

Naples was liberated by Fifth Army troops on 1 October. On the following day, Munthe moved his headquarters from Salerno to a large old house with a walled garden high up above the sprawling city. The villa had just been evacuated by the German Field Security Service and portraits of Hitler still hung in the main rooms. This was to be Vigilant's headquarters until the Anzio landings in January.

The city was in chaos. For days, Fifth Army forces streamed through its crowded streets. 'Veteran jeeps with fancy names, battle-scarred and dusty, were decorated with flowers, and mascots, ranging from a fragment of an antique bronze to a modern German helmet, were wired to the bonnets as they paraded the Via Roma,' wrote an entranced Munthe. 'At the doors of the churches priests stood holding up thin fingers in benediction. One aged prelate in tattered, white lace cassock, stood on the steps of the cathedral where lies the miraculous shrine of San Gennaro. He was leaning forward, pinning a medal, dangling from a piece of ribbon, on the tunics of the men who passed by . . . [they] were made of yellow, shiny metal, displaying the saint surrounded with an inscription asking his blessing on the liberators. The old man had the face of an El Greco portrait.' Munthe himself had one of the medals pinned on his uniform as he passed by.

During the last few days of fighting, Naples' supplies of water, gas and electricity had all been cut off by bombing. 'The port and area behind the royal palace was a scrapheap of tangled ironwork and ruined masonry,' wrote Munthe. 'Yellow-faced queues of dying men, women and children stood along the pavements, begging for bread.' The author Norman Lewis, who was serving in the city with Field Security, compared life to what he imagined it was like in the Dark Ages. 'People camp out like Bedouins in deserts of brick,' he wrote. 'There is little food, little water, no salt, no soap.' Everywhere, noted a shocked Italian woman returning from years of exile, 'ragged, darting children [emerged] from the ruins and fetid alleys to beg cigarettes and sweets'.[23]

Yet amidst the shambles Munthe's mission managed to establish some form of regular existence. 'I took a reveille parade every morning at 0700 hours and a roll call was also held at 1900 hrs to act as a check on the system of leave passes we issued to the men,' he reported. Close liaison was also established with British 10th Corps headquarters, which was responsible for selecting the targets for the behind-the-lines groups being trained by SOE. During the following months, up to January 1944, recorded Munthe, 'some seventy missions across the lines were successfully carried out from our Naples HQ'. Of these, twelve became casualties.[24]

In addition to military targets, Munthe's group, despite Salvadori's strictures against Roseberry's 'line' in Brindisi, was eager to establish contacts with the civilian resistance in Rome. Here, the way was unexpectedly opened up by a woman named Joyce Lussu.

Married to Emilio Lussu, a fellow anti-Fascist exile and resistance leader, she and her husband had been strongly courted by Roseberry and SOE in 1942 to lead a guerrilla movement in Sardinia. 'I learned the Morse code and how to work radio transmitters and receivers,' she recalled. 'I took a special course in codes and ciphers of the most complicated nature. I explored the mysteries of invisible inks and their reagents. I practised with all the weapons of the saboteur and fire-arms in accordance with the most up-to-date guerrilla techniques.' But after the scheme fell through, when Lussu failed to win promises about the post-war treatment of Italy, they'd broken with SOE and, by a circuitous underground route, succeeded in reaching Rome shortly after the armistice. Both were radical activists in the Action Party. Eager to establish links with the allies as well as to make contact with the Badoglio government, the Committee of National Liberation had made three unsuccessful efforts to send messengers through the German lines. One was shot, one disappeared and the third turned back after deciding the mission was impossible. Finally, Lussu had proposed that she herself should try, on the grounds that it might be an easier task for a woman than a man.[25]

In late September she set off. Travelling first by train, she then hiked her way south on foot, dodging German patrols, mingling with pitiful groups of refugees, fleeing from bombing and artillery strikes, scrabbling up mountainsides through unforgiving scrub and once even trekking through a dark and abandoned railway tunnel – until, several gruelling days later, she reached the American lines on the edge of the Salerno plain, where she turned herself in to some friendly GIs. But at the local divisional headquarters she was taken for a spy and sent to Fifth Army headquarters at Paestum, where she was roughly interrogated for several days. Finally, after going on a two-day hunger strike, she was handed over to the Allied Military Government (AMG) headquarters at Agropoli and was given more comfortable accommodation and good food in a villa occupied by British officers. She gave her word not to try to escape for two days. But, by now exasperated at her treatment, she insisted that she would certainly try to get away thereafter.

On the morning of the third day she had just got up when a major knocked on her door and told her that a captain wanted to talk to her. Is he English or American? she asked. 'English,' came the reply. Ah, she thought to herself with irritation, another intelligence officer come to grill me. But, as she later wrote, 'when the captain entered in his dusty battledress, a khaki beret on his fair hair, I threw my arms around his neck and greeted him noisily in Italian so shrill that the footsteps of several sentries could be heard rushing up the stairs. The English major lowered his eyes in embarrassment,' she continued, 'blushed and turned towards the door. He was shocked. He could never have guessed that the captain was my brother.'

He was also Max Salvadori. The two siblings had not seen each other since a brief encounter in France a few days before the fall of Paris, where she and her husband were living in exile, and she had heard nothing at all of him since – and certainly not that he was now wearing British uniform. The first thing they did was head for Torchiara to see General Pavone and hear his plans. Then Salvadori drove her to Salerno to meet members of the Naples Liberation Committee as well as his own SOE companions.[26]

Munthe, for one, was profoundly impressed by her. 'I have never met,' he wrote, 'any one who could better combine cool courage with a lady's gentle qualities.' She held fiercely hostile views on the King and Badoglio, whose previous complicity with Fascism and their sudden abandonment of Rome she was not prepared to forgive. She made no secret of her opinions either to Croce, a long-standing intellectual father figure, to whom she also paid a visit. 'She urges war not just against the Germans but against the King and Badoglio,' noted the philosopher. Though broadly sympathetic, her brother Max thought her views extreme. 'My sister uses harsh words: I don't believe that all the Ministers, senior officials and generals were fascists and traitors,' he wrote.[27]

Not surprisingly, she rejected an offer by Munthe to join SOE. Nonetheless, he immediately realised her value as a source of intelligence about the resistance in Rome and as a conduit to its leaders. With her help, he was able to arrange the first drop of supplies to partisans near Lake Bracciano. Then, although she was pregnant, she insisted on returning to the capital. 'My sister,' recorded Salvadori in his diary, 'has agreed with Munthe on plans to drop arms and explosives near Rome for the use of the Resistance. They need wireless equipment so as to keep in touch with the Allies, arms for the Partisans, and explosives for the underground in the city. They also need money.'[28]

Dressed in the uniform of an American officer so as not to attract attention, Munthe personally drove Lussu and a trusted guide northwards for a day and a half until they reached a town evacuated by the Germans only three hours beforehand. American troops were just moving in and were attracting heavy mortar fire. They left the vehicle in a field and an American colonel pointed out on a map a route over the mountains he thought would be safe. He also insisted that Lussu take a trusted Italian officer as a guide. Then, recorded Munthe, 'in the confusion of the German retreat down the hill she and her guide ran into the shrubs of the hillside above the enemy and got into the valley ... walking in broad daylight like a bewildered evacuee [*sic*].' Lussu's journey to Rome proved as perilous as her earlier trek in the opposite direction, and one night, sheltering with some impoverished and frightened peasant women in a farmhouse, she had an unpleasantly close encounter with a drunken German platoon. Finally, however, four days after saying farewell to Munthe, she reached the occupied capital, her husband and her comrades in the Partito d'Azione.

\*   \*   \*

Joyce Lussu's arrival in Salerno, along with her enthusiastic reports on the resistance in Rome, had prompted Leo Valiani and Renato Pierleoni to leave at once for the capital. Having worked out a cipher and arranged with Munthe to have a radio dropped to them in the next suitable moon period near Lake Martignano, they set off as soon as they could. They chose as the key to the cipher the final sentence from Plato's *Apology of Socrates*: *I go to die, you to live, but who goes to a better end, only God knows*. It was arranged that the BBC would announce the timing of the drop with the message 'Tevere uno, Tevere duo' (Tiber one, Tiber two).[29]

Both men were wearing civilian clothes and Valiani was carrying a suitcase. In 1939 he had been imprisoned along with other foreign Communists in the notorious French internment camp at Le Vernet in the foothills of the Pyrenees, where he befriended the Hungarian-Jewish journalist and novelist, Arthur Koestler. Passing through London on his way to Italy, he paid his former comrade-in-arms a visit, for Koestler was now living comfortably in England on the proceeds of his bestselling novel about the Stalinist purges, *Darkness at Noon*. Koestler did his old friend a favour by getting him an advance to write a book about the Italian campaign, and the proceeds were now secreted in the double-bottomed case that Valiani had had specially made for him in Palermo. Despite being warned by Munthe of the security risks, he was determined to take his own funds. For, as he later explained, his life as an émigré had taught him what he should already have known from Dante's *Divine Comedy*, 'that other people's bread tastes of too much salt, and it is better to run risks to live according to your own means'.

He and Pierleoni were escorted to the front line by soldiers of the US Third Division, and, at the fourth attempt, the two Italians made it across. After reaching Cassino on foot, they hitch-hiked a lift and finally arrived in Rome at midnight on 9 October. The airdrop was made soon afterwards as planned, but the radio was not recovered. A second drop was made a month later. Yet again the radio was lost.[30]

Later that same month, another Italian was infiltrated through the lines, helped by Dick Cooper. Whereas it had once been relatively easy to find large gaps with no enemy troops in sight, the German line had now hardened and the task was becoming more dangerous. It was left to Cooper to find the right spot. The agent's mission was to prepare dropping zones for the reception of SOE supplies in November at a place east of Rome.

They set out in a jeep, crossed the River Volturno north of Caserta, headed further east into the mountains and then abandoned their vehicle and went forward on foot. The fighting was heavy and American mortars were firing amongst the pines. None of the GIs they met appeared to know exactly how close the Germans were. So they went on climbing cautiously, seeking shelter behind boulders and trees with the agent's six-foot-two body doubled up. Eventually, they could look down on the valley. Nearly 300 metres ahead was a small olive grove and they had to duck suddenly as a group of Germans emerged and began scanning the hillside with field glasses. When the Germans had gone Cooper decided it was time for him to disappear, too:

'Well, Giuseppe,' I said, 'this is it. We'd better shake hands now.'

He nodded. I handed him a small Italian map of the district and he pocketed it. We shook hands and he turned and began to make his way down into the valley, crouching and taking advantage of every spot of cover. For a long time I followed him, marking his every movement as he descended. When he reached level ground he kept the Boiano road on his left and disappeared into a small pine forest.

I could do no more. Carefully I retraced my steps.

Later, Cooper heard that the operation was a success and that the Italian had got through the lines.[31]

As the autumn passed, several agents failed to get through. Such was the case with an Italian group that attempted to cross the German lines on the night of 30 November with the purpose of reaching Rome and arranging supply drops to partisans in the Lazio region. One of the five-man party was named Giaime Pintor, a 24-year-old anti-Fascist who had recently reached Raimondo Craveri's group from Rome with the hope of organising Italian armed units.

Most of the group had received explosives training at SOE's school on Ischia and they were conducted by Cooper and Salvadori. By this time it had become clear that the River Garigliano, once a promising crossing place for agents, had come to form part of the heavily patrolled German right flank and was too dangerous to use, so the two SOE officers tried elsewhere. 'Below Castelnuovo in the direction of the Meta mountains,' recorded Salvadori, 'Cooper and I explored the valley between the American and German lines until two in the morning. It looked as if one could get through, but of the five young men ... who tried to get over the mountain that night, four were forced back by German gunfire and the fifth, Pintor, failed to return.'

The next afternoon, Salvadori went to look for him. Eventually, he spotted the agent's body lying in a field, face down. Determined to recover it for burial, Salvadori approached the corpse only to be knocked out by a landmine. When he recovered consciousness he realised that the agent's body lay in the middle of a minefield and he was forced to abandon his efforts. He himself was lucky to escape with little more than slight shock, a superficial face wound and a blood-spattered uniform. He did, however, succeed in retrieving some documents from the body that could have proved compromising, and he was also able to warn off the Americans who had planned to send out a patrol that night in the same location. For the bravery displayed he was awarded the Military Cross.

Thwarted in such terrestrial efforts, SOE turned to airdrops, and two weeks later, in mid-December, two of the same party were dropped blind behind German lines near Tivoli. Others were briefed for drops scheduled to take place later the same month or early in the New Year. But after several postponements, the project was abandoned at the end of January.[32]

In the meantime, Munthe's mission suffered the serious loss of Adrian Gallegos. Since rescuing Croce, he had busied himself arranging seaborne infiltrations by Italian agents behind the German lines, and on the night of 24 September he set off in a MAS boat with an Italian crew. He was accompanied by an agent codenamed 'Farina' he had recruited a few days before in Capri. The mission was to land him on a secluded beach between Gaeta and Terracina, where he would reconnoitre the terrain and carry out some specified sabotage tasks before being picked up at the same spot four days later. 'On the bridge of the MAS boat the evening air swished refreshingly across my face,' remembered Gallegos. 'This was the life!' A couple of hours later, carrying his tommy gun, he stepped ashore from a dinghy accompanied by the agent. After watching him safely across the beach and whispering his farewells, Gallegos clambered back aboard for the journey home. Hardly had they got under way, however, than the boat hit a floating acoustic mine and was badly holed in the stern and began to sink. Taking to the dinghies, Gallegos and the crew endured the next thirty-six hours afloat with no sleep and hardly any food before eventually making it ashore, where they were picked up by the Germans, taken to Rome and declared prisoners. To protect the Italian crew in their agreed pretence of wishing to join the Fascists, Gallegos destroyed any evidence identifying him as a British officer and assumed the identity of an Italian. This he successfully maintained over the next twelve months spent in various camps in Germany before escaping and making his way back to Italy, where he was initially treated as a suspected Fascist spy.[33]

Exploiting the Brindisi foothold for special operations meant establishing a forward base for Massingham in Italy as soon as possible. Within days of the armistice, yet another SOE group was on its way from North Africa to southern Italy, with a mandate to launch operations by land, sea and air, both into German-occupied Italy and across the Adriatic into the Balkans. Greece, Yugoslavia and Albania had long been SOE targets. But distant Cairo had provided the main base for these operations. Southern Italy was far closer and held out much greater promise of producing rapid and effective results.

Late on the afternoon of Tuesday 28 September, a small 60-ton yawl sailed into the harbour at Brindisi flying the White Ensign, only the second British ship to enter the port since the Italian surrender. She was named the *Mutin*, and with her sails and broad-beamed hull she resembled a kind of French fishing boat typically to be found sailing the Bay of Biscay in search of tuna, although in fact she had been built as a training ship for the French Navy. 'She'd sail very close to the wind,' one crew member recalled many years later, 'and you could nearly talk to her. She was the most wonderful sea-going ship I've ever been on.'

On board was the latest SOE mission to Italy. A few days before, they had set sail from Massingham's naval base at Malta, where they saw the Italian fleet surrendering as they left. It was a tense voyage. According to Royal Navy reports, the sea lanes were still plastered with mines, and as they rounded Capo Santa Maria di Leuca at the tip of the Italian heel, the captain hugged the shore as closely as he dared. But eventually they reached Brindisi and made fast in the centre of the port. They were later given a permanent mooring on the north side of the port, under its gigantic monument dedicated to the Virgin Mary.[34]

The leader of the group was Commander Gerald ('Gerry') Holdsworth, RNVR, one of the legendary figures of SOE. A quiet character with an occasionally explosive temper, he was an expert small-boat sailor and former rubber planter in Borneo. One of those who worked closely with him said he was 'brave, brave as they came', while the Italian resistance leader Edgardo Sogno, who came to know him well, described him romantically as 'more southern than northern, generous and warm, half hero and half pirate, the ideal companion for a big game hunt or an adventure in Shanghai'. Major General William Stawell, who headed special operations throughout the Mediterranean during the final phase of the war, penned the following note on Holdsworth in one of his periodic reports on offi- cers serving under his command: 'A most forceful personality. An expert in clandestine warfare in all its aspects. Never spares himself − somewhat mercurial in temperament but with careful handling will give most loyal and conscientious service.' Holdsworth's heroes were Nelson and Wellington, and, as one obituarist later recorded, he was 'a traditionalist as well as a rebel; and a pirate as well as a patriot'.[35]

He was born in Stourbridge near Birmingham in 1904 and his mother, Gertrude Attlee, was related to the Labour Party leader and deputy prime minister, Clement Attlee. After returning from Borneo, Holdsworth had spent the thirties in London making films for the J. Walter Thompson advertising agency before receiving the proverb- ial 'tap on the shoulder' from SOE's predecessor, Section D of the Secret Intelligence Service. In the long-established tradition of the English gentleman spy, such as the hero of Erskine Childers's novel of pre-First World War days, *The Riddle of the Sands*, in 1938 he was recruited along with other members of the Royal Cruising Club to help secretly survey parts of the coastline of continental Europe. After the outbreak of war he was one of the team sent to sabotage iron-ore exports from Sweden to Germany. But the mission was rumbled and he was lucky to make it back to England via Finland after being arrested by the Swedish police.[36]

In the late summer of 1940 he organised and was placed in command of the so-called 'Helford Flotilla', a fleet of small boats that over the next two years carried out a series of daring and dangerous clandestine operations to transport dozens of agents for both SOE and SIS, as well as some high-level refugees, across the English Channel in a two-way traffic with occupied France. Its base was a house named 'Ridifarne' on the secluded Helford River near Falmouth in Cornwall, close to the setting for Daphne du Maurier's swashbuckling historical novel about a French pirate's secret hide-away from which he terrorised the Cornish coast, *Frenchman's Creek*. It was run by Holdsworth's wife, Mary, a graduate of the Royal College of Art, who had turned her skills to forging documents for Section D and had also been trained in demolitions. In addition, she had accompanied her husband on a pre-war clandestine survey of the Scandinavian coastline during a walking tour from Stavanger to Bergen. 'Her porcelain-like complexion and almost fragile appearance did not at first sight suggest an intimate knowledge of explosives,' writes one source. 'In fact she was so intimately acquainted with them that as a skilled commercial artist she had made detailed draw-ings on such subjects as "How to construct a home made mine" for a handbook for saboteurs.' One of the Helford Flotilla crew members described her as 'a very kind-hearted lady . . . [but] not to be bossed about by a bunch of idiots'.[37]

The *Mutin* had been sailed to Britain by her skipper after the collapse of France and she was the first of the small boats Holdsworth requisitioned for the task. He not only fell in love with her, but spent a lot of money having her refitted with a powerful new German Deutz diesel engine originally intended for the private yacht of Ettore Bugatti, the racing car designer and builder. So attached did he become to the vessel, indeed, that when he was assigned to North Africa in November 1942 to carry out similar small-boat oper-ations in the Mediterranean, he sailed her across the Bay of Biscay to Gibraltar and then on to Algiers. A Bay of Biscay tunny boat was obviously unsuitable for clandestine operations in the Mediterranean, where she would have instantly come under suspicion. But she provided useful accommodation for crews, transport for stores and a mobile base facility. She had even briefly sheltered one of the Frenchmen implicated in the assassination on Christmas Eve 1942 of Admiral Jean Darlan, the Vichyite High Commissioner for North Africa, from the unwelcome attentions of the French police.

The skipper was Lieutenant Richard ('Dick') Julian Laming, a tall blond-headed 29-year-old. Born in Amsterdam, where his father had been the British consul, he had spent his time ferrying agents in and out of the Netherlands. Tom Long, the coxswain, who was regarded by Laming as a 'solid gem', had been with Holdsworth since Helford River days, as had another crew member, Jim Pervis, a salmon fisherman from Berwick-upon-Tweed. On board, along with Holdsworth himself, the crew and a load of stores, were men from Massingham who had worked alongside him on various operations. One was Lieutenant Commander Hilary Scott, a Bradford-born solicitor who had been recruited, like many of SOE's top officials, from the City of London law firm Slaughter and May, and who, prior to joining the naval section, had headed SOE's Iberian and North African section in Baker Street. Another was Captain Charles Macintosh, who'd first met Holdsworth when they were co-guests at a dinner held in Gibraltar by the governor, General Mason-Macfarlane, when Macintosh was training Spanish Republicans for sabotage operations in case the Germans invaded Spain. Born in Montevideo of New Zealand parents, the 27-year-old Macintosh had been working for Shell in the oilfields of Venezuela when war broke out and had joined SOE early in 1941. Most recently, he had been rounding up abandoned Italian equipment in Sicily, where he worked closely with Munthe and Gallegos. 'Tall and broad-shouldered and full of good humour,' recalled one veteran, 'the opposite sex went crazy about him.'[38] Also on board were Captain Edward Renton, a peacetime operatic conductor who before the war had been a *répétiteur* at the newly opened Glyndebourne Opera, as well as a wireless operator.[39]

Their mission, as briefly explained in a telegram to Allied Forces Headquarters, was to 'continue work now being carried on from NAF [French North Africa] and establish base for supply to Balkans asap . . .'[40] It also had a codename that had been agreed with Holdsworth before leaving Algiers: 'Maryland', in honour of his wife. Later, Dodds-Parker recalled how, when he told Holdsworth that he was placing him in charge of SOE in Italy, he had demurred, saying that he was a simple sailor. 'I pointed out,' wrote Dodds-Parker, 'that he had just been awarded his second DSO, which was an important asset. He finally agreed when told that he could name his special command with the codename Maryland.'[41] And that, as well as No. 1 Special Force, was how his mission would generally be known for the rest of the war. 'It was conceived,' writes the first official historian of SOE operations in Europe, 'only as an operational "out-station", not a directing HQ, and was designed primarily to take prompt advantage of a new jumping-off ground, which would be useful for many destinations besides Italy.' But in practice, as time was to prove, it became the directing force for practically all Italian operations.[42]

Once ashore, Holdsworth's party wasted little time. By that evening Laming had called on Admiral De Foscari, the Italian Navy's Chief of Staff–Intelligence, to find out whether and how the Italian Navy could help SOE in running clandestine operations up the coast. He was 'an absolutely splendid fellow,' reported Laming, 'and had on hand a flotilla which could do the job under SOE guidance.'[43]

The next day, Wednesday 29 September, a second boat arrived in Brindisi harbour. The *Gilfredo* was a two-masted schooner requisitioned not long before by Gallegos in Sicily to collect abandoned enemy arms and ammunition from Tunisia and, to the dismay of those on board, it turned out to be infested with rats. She was skippered by Lieutenant Robin Richards, the 21-year-old younger brother of Francis Brooks Richards who was about to take over the French section at Massingham, and had worked for the Helford Flotilla ferrying agents to and from Brittany. Amongst those on board were Richard Hewitt, Peter Lee, Francis Donaldson (a Field Security Section NCO, commissioned on arrival in Italy, the only Italian-speaker in this advance party) and Captain Michael Gubbins, along with several ratings. All came with experience of running operations at Massingham. Gubbins had organised the 'small boat landings' exercises for SOE and OSS trainees; Hewitt was responsible for arranging Mallaby's drop to Lake Como in August; and Lee had headed its security section.

It was a memorable journey for all concerned. 'I had all my Italian and North African security records on board with me in a tin trunk,' recalled Lee. 'We slung our hammocks wherever we could on deck. And I remember going to sleep my first night as this thing went clonk-clunk-clonk-clunk-clung across the Mediterranean. It only did about five knots.' Richards recalled that the drinking water came out of some old abandoned fifty-gallon oil drums and that they managed to keep reasonably clean by stopping the boat in the middle of each day and bathing in the ocean. Sanitary arrangements consisted of a bucket that was regularly emptied overboard.[44]

Waiting to welcome the *Gilfredo* into Brindisi was Douglas Dodds-Parker, who had flown to Italy two days before with units of the British Sixth Airborne Division bound for Foggia and completed the journey on his motorcycle. 'There,' Dodds-Parker recalled, 'I found Holdsworth and his well-trained crew. For the first time, we were in ex-enemy territory and felt justified in "liberating" any government property which might be used to advantage.'[45] Donaldson noted likewise: 'We set about house hunting stage immediately,' he recorded, 'our finds ranging from kitchen stores and cars to razors and silk stockings.' Holdsworth had already requisitioned a house which was to serve as his headquarters for the next few weeks.

But competition for accommodation in Brindisi proved fierce, so Donaldson and Major Maurice Bruce, a training officer who had also flown in from Massingham, headed 72 kilometres up the coast to the small town of Monopoli. Here they managed to requisition several houses, and by mid-October had established their training headquarters in the town. Shortly after that, in early November, Holdsworth followed suit by shifting his Maryland HQ there as well.[46]

When asked later why he had selected Monopoli as his base, he replied that the choice had been quite fortuitous. 'It was a small place not already committed to one of the armed forces, and, therefore, requisitionable. A harbour for a couple of boats from Africa, it also provided the opportunity of keeping ourselves to ourselves without being too hopelessly remote.' With a population of about fourteen thousand, the town's income largely depended on fishing and farming. The past glories of the surrounding region, Apulia, which had been much sought after and colonised by both the Greeks and the Romans, had long since faded and like most of southern Italy it had missed out on the prosperity enjoyed in the industrial north and was suffering from considerable poverty and even starvation. To the SOE staff who arrived there from the former holiday camp now housing the Massingham mission in North Africa, conditions in and around Monopoli came as a shock. 'All in all,' said Holdsworth, reflecting his seafarer's perspective, 'it did us well.'[47]

# CHAPTER THREE

# No. 1 Special Force

Barely had Holdsworth and his party arrived when they got their first taste of action.

Some 80,000 allied prisoners of war were held in POW camps throughout Italy. In the chaos of the surrender, and with no clear orders from Rome, hundreds of their guards simply disappeared overnight, leaving the gates open behind them and the inmates to an uncertain fate. On the mistaken, and in retrospect extraordinary, assumption that the allied campaign would last only a few weeks, orders had been given that prisoners were to stay in the camps until they were overrun by the advancing armies.

The result was a disaster. More than half the prisoners were immediately rounded up and shipped off to camps in Germany and Poland, while many of those who initially escaped were soon recaptured and also bundled on to trains heading north for the Reich. The lucky remainder dispersed into the Italian countryside. Some took shelter with Italian families, expecting to be liberated by Christmas. Others went north, hoping to cross the frontier into neutral Switzerland. Several thousand more trekked south in the hope of reaching allied lines or the coast, from where, somehow, they might make good their escape.

One of hundreds of such men was Eric Newby of the Special Boat Service, who'd been captured in August 1942 during an operation off the coast of Sicily and who was later to become one of Britain's most distinguished travel writers. At the time of the armistice he was in a prison hospital near Parma, nursing a broken ankle. As the Italian guards disappeared, he hopped through the deserted corridors of the building and was spirited through the perimeter barbed wire by two of his comrades before being carried on a donkey to a farmhouse nearby where a small army of women, girls and young boys soon arrived heavily laden with wine, bread, cheese, eggs and cigarettes for him and other prisoners being sheltered there. It was the beginning of a lengthy odyssey in the Apennines, where the generous hospitality of the impoverished population, given at considerable risks to their own lives, was to provide him with months of welcome shelter. Similar help was to provide SOE and the Italian resistance with valuable support in the months ahead.[1]

A special secret service to help escapers and evaders, MI9, had been established at the beginning of the war, and as the scale of the problem in Italy became apparent Lieutenant Colonel A. C. (Tony) Simonds, the head of its Cairo office, was ordered to launch an operation to rescue as many prisoners as he could. Later, he recalled being told that the instructions to this effect had come from Churchill himself, a plausible enough claim as the prime minister retained vivid memories of his own life on the run behind enemy lines after escaping from the Boers during the South African War.[2]

Simonds possessed energy, a flair for intelligence work and hard-won experience in mounting irregular operations. He had worked in Palestine and Ethiopia with Orde Wingate and served briefly with SOE as head of its Greek country section before turning to rescue work. In no time at all he concocted a plan that envisaged a small role for Holdsworth's force. It was completed by 1 October, and on that same day Laming received orders to set sail for the port of Termoli.[3]

Simonds's plan was to drop uniformed parties by parachute up the Italian coast where they would contact allied prisoners of war and escort or direct them to four preselected rendezvous points on the coast. Here, they would be met at prearranged times by parties coming by sea who would embark them to safe territory. The troops forming the operational parties were drawn from the First Airborne Division, the Special Air Service and the OSS, which had recruited a goodly number of second-generation Italian-Americans for work in Italy. The sea transport consisted of eight Italian fishing vessels hastily commandeered by Simonds. It was SOE's job to supply three officers and six 'marine soldiers' to help run the sea operations.

Codenamed SIMCOL (after Simonds), the operation soon encountered a multitude of problems. Escaped prisoners could not always be found quickly, and even when they were located they often proved frustratingly slow in getting to the collecting points on the coast. As one British officer who was mobilised to help keep escapers on the move lamented, they had 'an exasperating tendency to linger, wherever they found a beautiful valley or a beautiful girl'.[4] Sometimes, indeed often, the fishing vessels broke down or encountered unfavourable weather and failed to reach the beaches in time, and they were certainly not helped by an initial lack of radio communications. Moreover, operations could only safely take place during the so-called 'dark period', when the moon was low, which limited them to about two weeks in the month. Even when all went according to plan, at the very last minute things could go unpredictably and dismayingly wrong. On one occasion, just twenty minutes before a group of three hundred ex-prisoners were due to be taken off a beach, they heard a burst of gunfire in the darkness. In panic, someone shouted out 'It's a trap!', and all but fifty or so vanished back into the farms and hills from which they'd been painstakingly collected over several perilous days.[5]

Laming, along with Hilary Scott and Michael Gubbins, as well as the intrepid Tom Long, was given a requisitioned trawler named the *San Vito* and set sail according to orders for Termoli. British forces had only just reached the town and a fierce battle was still raging onshore. Ships at anchor were coming under regular bombardment from deadly German 88 mm fire and attacks by Heinkel fighter-bombers were an almost daily event. Soon, one of these proved deadly for the *San Vito*. After two frustrating operations in which the rendezvous beach had been successfully reached on time but no one turned up, another Heinkel attack put paid to her efforts. '2 small bombs fell on either side of her,' recalled Laming, 'while I stood at the end of the gangway; they opened up all her underwater seams and she settled quietly on the bottom.'[6]

Their boat was not the only one to be knocked out of action. In all, German dive-bombers sank four of the eight vessels commandeered by Simonds and damaged two others. By this time it had become clear anyway that they were not of much use for the task, and a handful of landing craft were hastily brought in as substitutes.

But by then the first favourable moon period had ended and not a single prisoner had yet been brought back by sea, although some did succeed in infiltrating across by land. In the end, it was the Italian Navy that saved the day.

By the time that operations resumed ten days later the Italians had put three MAS boats with a speed of up to 45 knots at Simonds's disposal and, thanks to their help, by the end of October approximately five hundred allied prisoners of war had been rescued. Laming's team helped with these operations, and Michael Gubbins, at least, appears to have gone on shore more than once to help.

Despite the minor part played by the Maryland party, and tangential though the recovery operation was to its main mission, the experience proved useful. From the moment Holdsworth's group arrived in Brindisi they had found themselves involved in naval activities in support of the military campaign that were strictly outside their SOE brief. But Dodds-Parker, as head of Massingham, thought it important that Holdsworth should help wherever he could as a quid pro quo for getting the support he needed from other parties for his primary tasks. Baker Street agreed, provided that SOE needs did not suffer. Holdsworth himself calculated that his co-operation put some badly needed credit in the bank when he in turn came to request help from the regular allied armed forces, who were still somewhat suspicious or ignorant of SOE. More tangible and immediate, though, was that the whole affair had cemented the burgeoning cooperation with the Italian Navy, which Laming described as 'marvellous to work with'. The commander of the MAS flotilla, Captain Giorgio Manuti, was 'a fine fellow. He had sunk our cruiser *Manchester* off Cape Bon 6 months earlier, in MAS 73 and had the silhouette painted in black on the bridge!'[7]

But helpful though this all was, SIMCOL was called off at the end of October when Simonds had to return to Cairo to take care of his many other similar responsibilities in the Balkans and Middle East. On his own reckoning, about nine hundred prisoners had come through southern Italy by the end of the year. More were to follow in the coming months, with 'A' Force officers sailing with SOE missions to landing places along the coast. But overall, SIMCOL had not been a great success.

A major source of irritation in these early days was the shortage of sea craft. Holdsworth's natural instinct was to purchase or charter boats, but London vetoed this and told him to obtain them through regular naval channels. This seemed all very well, but in practice it was unhelpful because of the tight competition for transport from SIS, which also had agents to land and pick up. However, matters improved in late October after the Commander-in-Chief Mediterranean, Admiral Sir Andrew Cunningham, agreed to provide as many fast craft as possible for mounting clandestine seaborne operations in the Adriatic and Western Mediterranean. These included the MAS boats made available after he signed an agreement on naval cooperation with the head of the Italian Navy, Admiral De Courten, at Taranto in mid-September.[8]

The foundation laid by these joint efforts led to a whole series of combined operations up the Adriatic coast that lasted until the early summer of 1944: mainly hit-and-run sabotage attacks, the infiltration of agents and stores, and the exfiltration of agents and prisoners of war. It was a considerable advantage in these early days to be able to infiltrate the mainland by sea because, quite apart from the stores that could be sent (arms, ammunition etc.), it provided a way of sending in agents when air operations were still difficult, given not just the shortage of aircraft but also the lack of information about dropping zones. It was also useful to have first-hand knowledge about conditions on the ground from people arriving from behind the enemy lines. All the arrangements, intelligence and laying-on of the operations were done in close cooperation with the Royal Navy. Here, it helped that Holdsworth was himself a naval officer.[9]

The first clandestine sea operation in the Adriatic, using Italian naval craft based at Brindisi, illustrates the close collaboration forged between SOE, SIM, and ISLD at the time of the armistice. On 4 October two Italian agents, briefed jointly by the three intelligence agencies and under the control of the SIM liaison officer with both British services, embarked on an Italian MAS boat. Their mission was to operate in the Bologna area, and they were to be landed as far north up the coast as possible, with an intermediate refuelling stop in the Tremiti Islands where fuel had been secretly landed in advance. Although the first effort had to be abandoned because of heavy seas or engine failure, perhaps a combination of both, it was successfully completed when the agents were landed south of San

Benedetto del Tronto two nights later. Eventually, the two agents moved on from Bologna to the Veneto, their native area, where they continued to operate right up to the end of the war. The MAS boat, however, was less fortunate. On its way back to Brindisi it ran into a storm and was forced to run aground. As a result, SIM success-fully pleaded with the Italian Navy for the use of submarines for future operations.[10]

Four more sea operations took place before the end of November. The next was able to use a submarine to drop off three parties, one for SOE and two for SIS, who were landed at the end of October at different points up the Adriatic coast as well as the Lussino Islands off the Dalmatian coast. At about the same time five Italian agents bound for an SOE mission in the Marche (a region wedged between the Apennines and the Adriatic) were landed near Cupra Marittima using a landing craft, and on its return it picked up some prisoners of war as part of the SIMCOL rescue effort. A second submarine operation was then followed on the night of 27/28 November with the landing of two Italian missions for SOE from an Italian fast boat near Porto Civitanova at the mouth of the River Chienti.[11]

This last operation involved Dick Laming, Robin Richards and Tom Long. The next day, Holdsworth sent an exuberant letter to Brooks Richards back at Massingham. 'We reckon we have had quite a lot of fun getting ourselves all set up' he wrote, 'and we have pretty well reached the point when our efforts look as though they are beginning to bear fruit.'[12]

SOE sea operations, like its airborne ones, were always subject to the vagaries of the weather, human error and the dozens of other factors that can derail even the best-laid plans in war. No better illustration of this can be found than a frustrated note made by Max Salvadori in his diary as the winter of 1943/44 came to an end. After his bruising encounter with the landmine a few weeks before he had been given convalescent leave, but once he recovered he was summoned to Monopoli by Holdsworth to help with operations. 'We are in fairly regular contact with the Resistance in the Abruzzi, the Marche and Romagna . . .' he noted on 31 March 1944. '[They] are asking for more supplies. They are exasperated by our slowness. I wish they had been with me during the last ten days, to get an idea of the difficulties we are up against when we try to send supplies by sea. One night we started out in a converted trawler, but the engines gave out. Another night we were forced back by heavy seas. A third time we encountered a German or repubblichino [Fascist] torpedo boat, and again had to turn back. One night we actually reached shore, but it turned out to be the wrong beach – or at any rate there was no one there to receive the cargo we had brought. In the course of another little undertaking, instead of destroying the track to be used by a train bringing German supplies, we mistakenly blew up a disused railway line.'[13]

By November 1943 Maryland had become a viable operational base and was beginning to resemble a mini-Massingham on the heel of Italy. There was now a parachute training school for agents at San Vito dei Normanni, 13 kilometres west of Brindisi, a paramilitary battle school on the coast at nearby Castello di Santo Stefano, a series of 'holding houses' for agents, and in the centre of Monopoli itself a complex of requisitioned buildings that housed the country and operational offices, stores, motor transport, workshops, messes and accommodation for officers and other ranks. One of the two NCO instructors at the training school was Sergeant Major George de Relwyskow, whose speciality was unarmed combat. A small, dark man, and in peacetime a professional wrestler, he came from a White Russian background and his father and mother (a former Gaiety Girl) had featured in the First World War Army Physical Education manual. Recruited to SOE by Maurice Buckmaster of the French Section, he had been a member of the original SOE team that set up STS 103, the SOE training school in Canada. Here, he had impressed new recruits with his sometimes chilling instruction on how to incapacitate an opponent by pushing in his eyes with the fingers.[14]

Sixteen kilometres south of Monopoli, amidst hills covered with olive groves, was La Selva (also known as 'Hillside'), a unit for training wireless operators. The signals unit itself moved to Monopoli from Brindisi at the end of November. Wireless communications were the *sine qua non* of SOE operations. The radio sets and ciphers that arrived with Mallaby and De Haan in September worked via Massingham, even when communications were destined for agents within Italy, and it was soon decided that Maryland had to have its own independent communications. This also required more staff. In mid-November, seven members of the FANY (First Aid Nursing Yeomanry) were despatched by sea from Massingham to augment Holdsworth's team.

The FANY was founded in 1907, and as the first of the female services amply demonstrated its worth during the First World War by providing dozens of ambulance drivers on the Western Front. Of the three thousand women who worked for SOE during the Second World War, the large majority were FANYs, an army of women who proved indispensable as administrative, teaching and domestic staff and generally keeping the wheels functioning smoothly. While the majority were secretaries, some had important staff jobs, a few were agents and a significant number worked as cipher staff and wireless operators – the lifeline for agents in the field, whose safety and lives very much depended on messages being received and transmitted correctly. A skilled and experienced wireless operator could even learn to distinguish the 'fist' of an individual agent and detect if he or she was operating under enemy control. Leo Valiani, who received radio training at Massingham, was not alone in finding these young and capable women also a welcome distraction from the grim business of war. They were, he wrote, as 'enchanting as though they had stepped out of the pages of a novel by Walter Scott'.[15]

Two of the seven FANYs who arrived in November, Ensign Gundred Grogan and Ruth Hermon-Smith, were to work as personal assistants to Gerry Holdsworth and Peter Lee respectively, while another, Dee Evans, took charge of the coding office. Lieutenant Prudence Macfie, who had served as a conducting officer in Britain for female agents for the French Section, was assigned to help agents with their training, and herself took a parachute course. The remaining four were coders, one of whom, Chris Marks, was later to marry Dick Mallaby. In the New Year, six FANY wireless operators arrived from Massingham, followed by two more coders in April. The operators worked alongside British Army signallers as well as Italian operators provided by SIM.[16]

The FANYs have left far fewer and generally less detailed accounts of their part in the secret war. Many appreciated that compared to

British agents and Italian resisters their contributions were rarely dangerous. In their letters home outlining their hopes, fears, expectations and experiences they were acutely aware of security concerns and often self-consciously played down or remained silent about 'the job' while writing much more expressively about social events and good-looking men. Diaries were forbidden, which they knew, and those who did keep journals were discreet about personalities and operations.

Some of them had learned their coding and decoding at Thame Park, near Oxford, and a few spent time at Grendon Underwood, in Buckinghamshire, dealing mostly with French traffic. The women at Fawley Court at Henley often trained for four months learning their Morse code. A few were sent to Chicheley Hall in Buckinghamshire, where they drilled and became skilled at map reading. On the successful completion of their training, they were issued with uniforms and kit which included, among other items, so one recalled, two corsets, a greatcoat and a respirator. Having volunteered for duty in Italy, they were flown to Cairo or Algiers, where some received further training at the Morse code school at Massingham. From Algiers or Cairo they were taken to Bari and then onward to their posts.

From Monopoli some of them wrote home about the poverty of the local population, many of whom seemed to be of mixed Arab and European blood, and of the strangeness of the traditional Apulian 'beehive' houses which could still be found dotting the landscape. There were the usual cross-cultural mix-ups as they settled in: on one FANY's first morning at the mess the Italian cooks mixed the porridge and bacon together at breakfast. Many took to eating bread and melons when available, and some grew tired of spaghetti, while others found the food wonderful. Red wine often replaced the problematic drinking water and they sometimes went days without a bath. Some found the atmosphere rather 'Bohemian'. There were a few excursions to the Officers' Club up the coast in Bari, and on Christmas Day 1944 in the town square of Monopoli they played a netball match against the men of No. 1 Special Force. Later in the war the magnificent Villa Cimbrone in the hilltop town of Ravello on the Amalfi coast became the site of a week's leave for a few of the lucky FANYs after Gerry Holdsworth started a leave rota which paired two women and two male officers. The villa had been built by Lord Grimthorpe and was made available to SOE thanks to Manfred Czernin, one of No. 1 Special Force's officers whose mother was Grimthorpe's daughter. No doubt adding to the pleasures of luxuriating in its huge, comfortable rooms with private baths, and walking the magnificent gardens and the grand terrace overlooking the Bay of Sorrento, was the frisson of knowing that the villa had been a haunt of the Bloomsbury Group and the secret trysting site for Greta Garbo and Leopold Stokowski during their grand love affair before the war.

But mostly it was work. Twelve-hour shifts were initially the norm as there were few operators and much traffic – priority being given to messages concerning supply drops. Gerry Holdsworth once described the young women as looking 'wilted' – 'no wonder', one remembered, as they were also encouraged to go dancing with visitors before and after their shifts. Eventually working alongside them as W/T operators were uniformed Italian soldiers – one described them as the 'cream of the Italian Army Signals'. Certainly the FANYs found them very competent, although some recalled having trouble telling the difference between the continental *1* and crossed 7 used by the men. Radio operators did not know the identity of the agents at the other end or even whether they were British or Italian. 'Mainline' traffic was handled as well as that from the 'field'. Often the signals were quite faint. One or two recalled seeing messages carefully labelled 'NOT to be decoded by a woman'. With overlapping shifts, there were often six to eight coders in the room at one time, but most remembered a cheerful, efficient crew not given to any 'back-biting' and grateful to be completely trusted, as there were no overseers or 'checkers' as there were in Cairo. A series of contraptions consisting mostly of tin cans or little boxes and string webs, rigged up by Holdsworth's second-in-command Dick Hewitt to carry W/T messages, never failed to amuse the FANYs, although if any had slipped, all the precious messages would have gone awry. The women found Hewitt exceptionally hard-working, sometimes not sleeping at all, and very serious-minded – but of course an agent's life or death could rest on his decisions. As one of his staff remarked, 'We didn't work Mediterranean hours, and occasionally would continue to 2 or 3 a.m. but it was still 8 a.m. prompt in the office the same morning.' And Hewitt was always already waiting for them.

In early August 1944, when the first batch of British liaison officers (BLOs)was being sent behind the lines, there was bandied about the idea of giving a few FANYs field training and then parachuting them into occupied territory. In a note from Gerry Holdsworth to the FANY captain in Monopoli, he suggested that 'The conditions under which the personnel selected might be required to work should be assumed to be rigorous. It is, therefore, essential that only the toughest and most illness-free FANYs be considered.' But the idea never materialised after Major General Stawell made it clear that no British women were to be despatched behind enemy lines. One FANY who got as far as the parachute course was then told that her red hair would attract attention and always be hard to disguise.

Eventually, in early 1945, the No. 1 Special Force headquarters moved to Siena and for the FANYs this proved a great improvement. Their mess was in a small hotel where they enjoyed the comfort of real beds, although the cold often necessitated the frequent taking of brandy. They were thrilled to find oranges and cherries, which they hadn't seen since 1940, and a unique attraction was the fencing master, whom Dick Mallaby had known in pre-war Siena. Among their improvised work sites were an old morgue and part of a hospital for incurables where they worked in whitewashed cells, each overlooked by a large crucifix over the door. As in Monopoli, all were given the rank of 'Cadet Ensign'; there were no NCOs, and senior officers could be identified only by their superior accommodation. When on duty everyone was addressed by her surname and again, as at Monopoli, a kind of 'family' feeling was generated. Some of their colleagues stood out as well. One was a catering expert, 'a real old trooper' from South Africa, who came to Siena early in January 1945 to help prepare for the influx from Monopoli and would cheerfully proclaim that 'You can do anything if you've been brought up in the bush.' Few FANYs had been raised in the veldt, but all tried their best to uphold their unofficial motto – 'I cope' – in a 'flap'. There was also a USAAF HQ in town, which provided one FANY with a real taste of the shadow war when she accompanied – strictly unofficially – an Italian-speaking American officer on his trips to find possible landing sites for British and OSS agents.

In a town north of Pisa, which had just fallen into American hands, their jeep was shelled and huge boulders were rolled down the hillside in a crude attempt to kill them.

Some of the FANYs left Monopoli not for Siena, but for Rome, where Holdsworth moved after the city's liberation in June 1944. Those who went with him found it exhilarating and enjoyed their exposure to a much wider world, including operational agents and escapees from behind the lines, as well as some of the leaders of Italian resistance groups who were called to top-security meetings with Holdsworth before returning to the partisans in the occupied north.

Slightly further up the coast from Monopoli, Major Peter Lee established his security and interrogation centre in Bari, operating under the cover title of Field Security Section No. 300, or 300 FSS, a title dreamed up by Lee, so he claimed later, 'while swinging in my hammock on the deck of the good but rat-infested schooner *Gilfredo*'. The number 200 was the highest one he could recall having been assigned to any existing Field Security Section. The section's staff all shared a flat in the town. 'We'd taken it off a German who'd had to leave in rather a hurry,' explained Lee, 'and the place was absolutely stuffed full of scent. There was one ottoman there [which] was literally full of [the] most expensive perfumes. So all our girl friends had a wonderful time. They thought we were marvellous because we used to dish these things out.'[17]

Security was vital to SOE. But the work of its security section, which operated in close liaison with MI5, was not always popular in the country sections, which were psychologically geared to recruiting agents and launching operations as quickly as possible and were therefore frequently impatient of the cautionary and restraining hands of the security experts. A case in point was that of the resourceful ex-Foreign Legionnaire Lieutenant Dick Cooper, who so successfully took care of Max Salvadori and other anti-Fascist exiles in Sicily as they prepared for their missions.

After his unpleasant brush with the Vichy authorities in North Africa he spent a leave in England seeing his family and taking a refresher course. Over lunch one day in the Grand Hotel in Northampton he boasted to an officer sharing the same table that he was an escaped prisoner of war, had interrogated a famous captured Italian general, and was connected with MI5. News of his claims soon reached Baker Street. 'It is clearly undesirable to have in this organisation a man who is prepared to make to a perfect stranger such glib and fantastic statements . . .' recorded one alarmed officer in SOE's security section. 'I do not think his employment with us should be continued.' But this evoked a robust response from those preparing Cooper for his forthcoming mission. Noting that as the agent's claims were totally fictional they could hardly be considered a breach of security, an operations officer made the point that Cooper was 'a man who has had to get out of a number of tight corners in his time and it probably comes naturally to him to spin a bit of a yarn. Indeed,' he went on, 'a certain amount of glibness is surely an essential quality for an agent who must always be ready to give a quick answer to an awkward question . . . [and] you cannot perhaps expect the sort of person who is going to be a good agent in the field to have the same characteristics and reactions as the ordinary peaceful citizen.' All that he was prepared to do was give Cooper a cautionary talk about over-embroidering his tales to the point where he drew too much attention to himself. And there the matter was left.[18]

By the time SOE got to work in Italy, security fears about German efforts to penetrate the organisation had heightened following troubling experiences in Belgium, and they were to come to a climax in December with the revelation that most of the Dutch network had been thoroughly penetrated by the Abwehr and some fifty agents had been dropped directly into enemy hands.[19]

In Bari, Lee's principal task was to interrogate agents and would-be agents crossing over from behind enemy lines who had been, or might have been, in enemy hands, or who were thought to possess intelligence that could be useful in any security case he had to deal with. As Italy had been enemy territory until only shortly before, it also meant that he had the task of interrogating all potential Italian recruits for SOE work. Transferred in April from Baker Street to Massingham as chief of security, he had been shocked on arrival at the Club des Pins to be told that his first task was to train about a hundred Spanish Communists as security guards.

To the vigilant Lee, these anti-Fascist left-wingers were all politically suspect, although so far as Dodds-Parker was concerned there was 'no problem' with security and 'they couldn't have been better' — another example of the conflict between the professional suspicion of the security man and the action-orientated officer working with the best material he could find at any given moment and keen to get results. All in all, Lee considered that until far too late in the day Massingham's security had mostly been 'a shambles', and so he was gratified at being in at the very start of Maryland operations in Italy. For this reason, too, he deliberately decided to keep his physical distance from what he termed 'the operational boys' in Monopoli, who were, he believed, far too prone to run risks in their impatience to take action.

But his initial optimism soon gave way to bitter complaints about the shortage of personnel to help him, and by the end of November he was deploring that 'security work in general is being skimped willy-nilly' and insisting that he couldn't guarantee that all the recruits taken in by Maryland were 'O.K.'. One of the main reasons for his discontent was that Italian-speaking members of his section were being constantly diverted to other miscellaneous tasks in creating the Maryland base, a complaint wearily registered by his assistant Donaldson early in the New Year. 'I have been asked, and even ordered on many occasions to do jobs which were absolutely no part of my duties,' he told Lee. 'I have bought countless pairs of stockings and packages of cosmetics for officers to send home; I have bought table lamps, typewriters, and office equipment; I have spent a lot of time finding and employing domestic staff, carpenters, electricians, mechanics and the like . . . If someone wishes a request for something to be made to the mayor or the police, I am sent. If civilians are to be turned out of requisitioned property elsewhere, I am sent.'[20]

None of this helped Lee's relations with the action-orientated Holdsworth, who also took the view that Lee's first responsibility was to him as head of Maryland rather than to the security section in London and any directives or guidance he might receive from Baker Street. Not surprisingly, friction marked relations between the two from the very start. 'He [Holdsworth] had to get on with his job which was dropping agents into northern Italy,' Lee explained later, 'and I had to get on with mine. And I wanted to try and make sure that if anybody got caught in northern Italy we knew and could warn the operational section concerned of exactly who knew who and who was liable to talk about what after the statutory forty-eight hours of silence had been gone through, because these agents were told "If you get caught for God's sake try and put up with anything that happens in the first forty-eight hours to give your comrades a chance of getting away and going to ground." I also thought it was better that when I was interrogating prospective agents and recruits that it should be done in Bari rather than down in Monopoli. So Bari was a sort of safe house . . .' Six months later, after SOE's deputy head of security in London had made an inspection visit to Italy, he reported, with masterly bureaucratic understatement, that 'there had not been complete understanding as between [Holdsworth] and Major Lee'.[21]

Tensions between Maryland's operational and security requirements were to continue until the end of the campaign in Italy. The Dutch disaster had appeared at one point to threaten the very existence of SOE by handing a lethal weapon to its bureaucratic enemies in Whitehall; and Baker Street continued to press Maryland to adopt operational procedures analogous to those developed in London, especially with a view to safeguarding against penetration by the Germans. To this end, in the spring of 1944 it sent out a senior officer, Lieutenant Colonel Hoyer Millar, to coordinate all security measures in Italy, including those of Advance Force 133, SOE's forward Balkan section, which was working in the same building as Lee's section in Bari, yet entirely separate from it. Shortly afterwards, a Security Intelligence Panel was set up to serve both Maryland and the rest of SOE in Italy. But this too ran into the persistent turf war between Holdsworth and Lee, with the former insisting that the panel's work under Lee had little or no relevance to the increasingly paramilitary nature of SOE's work.

In this he was backed by Lieutenant Colonel J. G. Beevor, the former head of SOE's mission in Lisbon, who by now was in charge of plans and operations for Italy at the recently established SOE Mediterranean headquarters. 'The speed at which events in Italy are moving and the development of open Partisan guerrilla activities,' noted Beevor in July 1944, when optimism was running high about a swift end to the campaign that year, 'have gone far to remove Italy from our category of a purely clandestine country where a more highly developed security organisation is a first necessity.' In the circumstances, he believed, the immediate priority of SOE was to meet its 'urgent operational commitments in the next three months which may well be the climax of the war'.[22]

The Baker Street security section remained vigilant, however, and never ceased insisting on the stringent application of security measures – not least for their importance in counter-intelligence tasks for which SOE would have responsibility in the immediate aftermath of the fighting. As a result, problems between Lee and the operations side of Maryland persisted, and even led Hoyer Millar in January 1945 to call in exasperation for Lee's replacement – but with no effect.[23]

The creation of the Maryland base urgently raised the question of who was in charge of operations into Italy. There were three possibilities: Roseberry and his J Section based in Baker Street; Dodds-Parker and Massingham in Algiers, which had provided the forward base for special operations in the Western Mediterranean since the North African landings; and Holdsworth and his group, which had arrived as an advance mission of Massingham but was rapidly taking on·a life of its own. Behind the question of control lay that of the nature of SOE strategy in Italy now that allied forces were waging active warfare there. What, in short, should SOE be trying to do? Up till now, its efforts under Roseberry and J Section had largely been focused on keeping SOE activities broadly in step with policy towards Italy as articulated by the Foreign Office, and on building up contacts through the SOE mission in Berne with anti-Fascist resistance groups, mostly in northern Italy. But was this now enough and what, if any, was the military pay-off from such contacts? With Italy now both a co-belligerent and major theatre of war, should the emphasis not shift to more military-orientated goals? And, if so, what did this mean for issues of control and command?

By chance, the Salerno landings coincided with the appointment of a new head of SOE, the third since 1940, and the first to be a professional soldier, Major General Colin Gubbins. His predecessor, the merchant banker Sir Charles Hambro, whose multifarious business contacts had served SOE extremely well but cut severely into his available time, had fallen out with the SOE minister, Lord

Selborne, over the issue of the control of SOE operations in the Middle East.

Trained at the Royal Military Academy at Woolwich, Gubbins had served as a battery officer on the Western Front and been awarded the Military Cross. Service against the Bolsheviks in northern Russia during the allied war of intervention, followed by several months' fighting the IRA in Ireland, sparked his interest in irregular warfare, and in 1939 he joined MI(R) — Military Intelligence (Research), a branch of the War Office — where he helped prepare training manuals specifically on guerrilla war. Later, as chief of staff to the British military mission to Warsaw at the time of the German invasion of Poland, and subsequently as head of a mission to the Czech and Polish forces under French command, he began thinking seriously about the potential of resistance movements behind enemy lines. This took on an immediate urgency after Dunkirk, when he was placed in charge of creating the Auxiliary Units, a civilian force hastily improvised to operate behind German lines if Britain were invaded. In November 1940, and by now a 44-year-old brigadier, he became SOE's head of training and operations ('M').

Gubbins possessed energy, imagination and will. Above all, he implicitly understood the need to coordinate special operations with the operational needs of the regular military forces and theatre commands. In this he was firmly backed by the prime minister. On 30 September 1943 Churchill presided over a special conference of ministers to consider the future of SOE. 'At last,' commented Gubbins, 'we had moved into smoother waters . . . I was called more frequently to the chiefs of staff . . . [and] was personally allowed to see the agenda of all [their] future meetings.' The ministerial review also ruled that the execution of SOE policy in operational theatres would be under the control and direction of local commanders-in-chief.[24]

From the very start of his involvement with SOE, therefore, Gubbins argued that its irregular activities would prove their worth only when properly integrated with the military operations of the regular armed forces. The allied landings in southern Italy had transformed the strategic scene both in Italy and throughout the Balkans, where the Italian surrender of arms had given a significant boost to the partisans in Greece, Albania and Yugoslavia and thereby promised a rich yield for SOE. To help ensure that his doctrine was applied in the Mediterranean, in mid-October Gubbins flew out from London for high-level talks with the military commands and SOE missions concerned. The biggest problem that faced him lay in Cairo, where relations between SOE and GHQ Middle East had long been a major source of conflict and controversy. After dealing with that he flew to Brindisi to sort out the 'muddle' in Italy. He arrived amidst an acrimonious row between Roseberry and Dodds-Parker.

After his important supporting role in the surrender arrangements, Roseberry, now a lieutenant colonel, spent most of October in Brindisi working closely with the Allied Control Commission, joining in discussions between Marshal Badoglio and a succession of Italian politicians, and consolidating the important relationship he had established with SIM. He also worked closely with 'C's' man in Brindisi who, amongst other favours, allowed SOE infiltrees to be briefed by SIS before they left for the field. So far as Roseberry was concerned, he himself was still obviously the man in charge of SOE Italy. 'You know more about the work than we can tell you,' he claimed that Gubbins told him, 'and all we need to say is that wherever J [Roseberry] is, the policy of J can be decided, whether he is in Algeria, Brindisi, or Rome. Just keep us informed and ask us for any help you want.'[25]

But on arriving at Brindisi, Roseberry discovered that this was far from being the case and that Dodds-Parker considered that all the SOE missions in Italy — Munthe's in Naples as well as those of De Haan and Holdsworth — came under *his* control for both policy and administration. On one of his frequent visits to Brindisi, learned Roseberry, Dodds-Parker had even 'read the riot act' to De Haan, insisting that no 'separatism' would be countenanced. He had also flexed his muscle by withdrawing two of SOE's signallers and retaining a third, Captain White (who had arrived with De Haan in September), in Algiers after he'd travelled there to train some Italian recruits. So far as Dodds-Parker was concerned, Roseberry was both 'wasting his time [in Brindisi] with politics' and getting too closely involved with SIS.

To sort things out, Gubbins met with both men on 13 November for what was a heated meeting. Roseberry argued strongly that as SOE depended for political guidance on the Foreign Office, Baker Street should retain overall direction, and he threatened that if it did not, he might as well resign. Furthermore, he alleged, Dodds-Parker was solely intent on furthering 'his own scheme of personal advancement'. For his part, Dodds-Parker, who had established good relations with AFHQ in Algiers, insisted that military, not political, factors should now be paramount and that Baker Street's influence was, rightly, becoming remote. Gubbins, in an effort to calm things down, declared that Holdsworth, with whom Roseberry got on reasonably well, was really now the commander of the Italian mission, although ultimately responsible to AFHQ through Massingham. In the circumstances, therefore, he suggested that it would be helpful if both Roseberry and De Haan were to move from Brindisi to Monopoli to be closer to Holdsworth.

Given the personalities and strength of feeling involved, this was a solution doomed to fail. Although he began to visit Monopoli more frequently, Roseberry remained firmly entrenched close to SIM and SIS in Brindisi, while for their part Dodds-Parker and others at Massingham complained bitterly about his 'disruptive' influence and the lack of any coherent plan for Italy. Soon, Gubbins himself began to refer to Roseberry's 'cagey and uncooperative attitude' towards Holdsworth and also became increasingly concerned about the lack of direction being given by SOE through Berne to the resistance in northern Italy. Finally, after a triangular blizzard of telegrams between London, Algiers and Cairo, in early December he decided to send Roseberry back to London as 'the advance post for Maryland' with the principal task of focusing on the vital work of the Berne mission in mobilising anti-Fascist resistance groups inside Italy. As a sop, J Section in Baker Street was transferred from the Western European Directorate to the newly formed Mediterranean Directorate and was raised to the status of a 'Region', with Roseberry at its head. Despite his dislike of the arrangement, he had to live with it and for the rest of the war friction continued to colour his relations with No. 1 Special Force and Holdsworth, who referred to him dismissively as 'Rosebud'. 'What a nuisance that old man is,' he confessed to De Haan as the campaign in Italy ended.[26]

*      *      *

One of the consequences of Gubbins's decision to make Holdsworth's mission – now renamed No. 1 Special Force, or 1SF – the effective nucleus of SOE operations in Italy was the closing-down in January 1944 of Munthe's Vigilant mission in Naples. This included five 'holding pens' for locally recruited agents, the training school on Ischia, a liaison section with the [British] 10th Corps of Mark Clark's US Fifth Army, and the base on Ischia used for sea operations run by Adrian Gallegos. After his capture in late September, he had been replaced by Lieutenant Peter Simpson-Jones.

A 29-year-old naval reserve officer fluent in French, and yet another Helford Flotilla veteran now on service in Italy, Simpson-Jones had been sentenced to five years in a Vichy prison on Madagascar after being captured during an SOE operation on Réunion Island but was fortunate to serve only six months before the island was liberated in September 1942. Setting up base in a villa he shared with the naval officer-in-command Ischia, during the last three months of 1943 he carried out several special operations using a couple of Italian MS (*motosiluranti* or motor torpedo) boats. These were ideal for SOE operations, as Simpson-Jones recalled. 'They were about 80 feet long,' he wrote, 'their speed was 38 knots, they had two Isotto Frascini wing engines of 300hp each, and an Alpha Romeo straight-8 centre engine, with underwater exhaust for close, silent inshore work.' To help him as crew he had two British able seamen, ten Italian naval officers and two hundred Italian ratings. He also acquired as a base ship the *Eduardo*, built originally in Viareggio for the Atlantic fishing trade but converted by the Italian Navy into a minesweeper. Eventually, he was able to arm this with Bofors and Oerlikon guns fore and aft, two machine guns on the bridge and a bazooka and, a nice final touch, to surround the wardroom with the armoured plate-glass windows from Mussolini's personal train.[27]

Operating only during the dark (non-moon) periods of the month, which lasted for fourteen days, he carried out one operation for SOE in early November, and another four weeks later. The former, code-named 'Tideway', took place on the night of 5/6 November and successfully landed an Italian agent named Gino Mangiavacchi (alias Giorgio Mancinelli) equipped with two cases holding 80 lb of explosives for a sabotage mission in Rome. An electrical engineer by trade,

Mangiavacchi had been released from imprisonment in Rome for anti-Fascist activities just prior to the armistice and immediately made his way south through the German lines, where he was recruited by Munthe in Naples in mid-October.

The landing took place near Sabaudia, south of Anzio, at about 3 a.m. The agent clambered from the torpedo boat into a small dinghy, accompanied by a British and an Italian sailor, the latter acting as pilot. They had reached land and begun to unload the boxes when a light appeared a mere 90 metres away. Ordering the others to re-embark, Mangiavacchi managed to shift the boxes further inland before hiding behind a bush as two German patrols passed. He waited for some time before digging a hole to hide the two cases. But his troubles had only just begun. His report continues:

I chose a point on a rise, and here buried one, while the other I hid a short distance away. Having safely disposed of the material, I began to take a look around. While I was thus employed the two patrols with others re-passed and stopped a few feet away from me, that is, in the thicket behind which I was hiding. I think they were parachute infantry; they waited there for a good hour and then walked away towards the north. As the dawn was approaching I made haste to get away from the landing point. I climbed a small rise and saw before me Lake Caprolace to the north, which flowed into a canal, and which served as a sea base garrisoned by Germans. To the south was an explosives factory surrounded by a wire fence which from the lake stretched to the road, and beyond the road towards the sea was a fort manned by Germans on coastal defence services. I remained there throughout the day. The only way of escaping . . . was to cross the wire enclosure of the factory. I waited for night to fall and observed towards evening that a sentinel was posted at the fence but . . . decided to try. I crossed the fence towards midnight, the ground was boggy, I sunk in up to my knees and it took me a long time to get across. The dawn was breaking when I got to the other side.

Having continued on for 200m I came to a broad canal which, having no outlet, was full. The bridges were all blown. I undressed and forded across. The area was completely deserted, the houses abandoned, the bridges were no more. After walking for some hours I finally encoun-

tered an inhabited house and asked for food . . . That evening I reached
Littoria, the following day Genzano, and on the 11th November I arrived
in Rome.

Once again, however, things did not go according to plan. In the
capital he contacted the military committee of the Communist Party
and began planning to recover the explosives. As there was no transport available and the cases were too heavy for women to carry, he
set off back to Lake Caprolace with his brother Massimo. When
they arrived, however, the moon was full and there was no chance
of crossing the factory enclosure without being spotted. So they
returned to Rome and tried again a few days later. This time they
contacted a carter who was employed by the Germans and offered
him money to let them take his place with his cart and permit. He
at first agreed, but when the time came reneged on the deal. At this
point Mangiavacchi decided to abandon the effort. Instead, he
persuaded the Communist Party to supply him with explosives.

By late November he had managed to accumulate a significant
cache, along with fuse wire and adhesive tape, in his flat on the via
Giulia. He also set about recruiting a sabotage group, including his
brother, which went on to carry out some successful operations. Once
these were under way he left Rome to organise another sabotage
group in Viterbo. This was fortunate, because on 2 January 1944,
thanks to an informer, several members of his Rome group were
arrested by the SS. Four were shot, one hanged himself in prison
after severe torture, a couple were imprisoned, one was released after
five days, and he himself was sentenced to death *in absentia*.
Eventually, after things quietened down, he returned to Rome shortly
before the allies arrived in June and was subsequently taken on by
the OSS, although soon after that he was discharged from service
after breaking a leg during a parachute exercise.[28]

The second operation, codenamed Gerrard III, consisted of a four-
man Italian team led by Domenico di Gennaro, a tank officer who
had joined up with Munthe's group after the armistice. It was a
short-term sabotage mission aimed at German road transport behind
the lines on the Garigliano front, but in the event it was to remain
behind the lines for about six months before being overrun by the
advancing allied forces in late May; all its members survived. Eight

further operations, however, scheduled either for SOE or OSS in December, had to be cancelled or aborted because of bad weather.

The Italian agents were trained at the Castello Mezzatorre on Ischia, held incommunicado for at least three days before their operations and kept unaware of their landing date. Simpson-Jones and his crews encountered them only as they embarked from a small cove reached by a steep winding path to the villa. 'For obvious security reasons,' recalled Simpson-Jones, 'we and the crew of the transport were kept as far as possible from the agents so that in the event of capture neither knew anything about the other.' Besides serving as a training area, the villa also acted as a security holding area, from which one or two recruits were let go after it became clear they were simply interested in getting back to their families living on the other side of the German lines.[29]

Not all Simpson-Jones's operations were at the service of SOE. In mid-November he was summoned to 15th Army Group headquarters in the old Bourbon Palace at Caserta, outside Naples, where top-secret planning had begun for the Anzio landings – an attempt to 'leapfrog' German defences on the now largely static front line north of Naples that was blocking the advance towards Rome. His own contribution was to undertake seaborne reconnaissance of the target area, and over the next few weeks he led three night-time missions, taking samples of sand and noting the texture and gradient of the beaches involved. He also carried out for the Royal Navy an operation in bright moonlight with an American radio team on board, making as much noise as possible in order to test enemy defences. He made a final reconnaissance just forty-eight hours before the landings, and served as a lead marker for the invasion fleet itself. Some of these missions were run jointly with the Special Boat Service or the Royal Marines and typified the joint nature of many SOE operations both on the west and east coasts of Italy at the time – all of which helped enhance its credibility with the regular armed forces.

Having distinguished himself at Anzio, in mid-February 1944 Simpson-Jones and the *Eduardo*, along with one of the two *moto-siluranti*, were sent to Bastia on the north-east coast of Corsica. A mere 40 kilometres from Elba, the French island was ideally suited for launching seaborne operations to penetrate the northern Italian mainland. Almost immediately, Simpson-Jones helped land an eight-man Italian commando group at Moneglia, 48 kilometres down the Ligurian coast from Genoa, with the mission of blowing up a railway bridge. He was efficient, noted one observer of Simpson-Jones's operations, 'but a tough nut'.[30]

Even before the Germans had evacuated the island the previous October Massingham had set its eyes on Bastia as a base for its naval operations. Once the enemy left, it immediately established an SOE mission there. Codenamed 'Balaclava', it came under the command of Major Andrew Croft, who had since successfully launched dozens of operations, using fast small boats to the Italian mainland as well as to the coasts of Spain and Provence. Similar operations from Bastia were also run for SIS, the Deuxième Bureau and other French services, such as de Gaulle's Bureau Central de Renseignements et d'Action (BCRA), Britain's 'A' Force, dealing with escapers and evaders, and the OSS. Croft's opposite number in SIS, Lieutenant Commander Patrick Whinney, who had worked on naval irregular operations in the Mediterranean since early 1942, later described the Bastia headquarters as 'a minestrone of nations'. The cooperative and friendly atmosphere was enhanced by the fact that the head-quarters of Fighter Wing, Coastal Forces, ISLD, OSS and SOE were all situated within 90 metres of each other. Attached to Balaclava was also an 'A' Force representative and its highly qualified intelligence officer helped create a first-class intelligence 'pool' shared by all the services involved.[31]

Such close inter-allied and inter-service cooperation was a rare commodity and was not acquired without considerable skill, diplomacy and effort. On occasion, it required the intervention of higher authority. Early in the New Year, for example, when Francis Brooks-Richards, the head of the Massingham French section, paid Croft a visit from Algiers, the two men invited Captain Norman Dickinson, the senior naval officer commanding the fleet of craft being used for these clandestine services, to dinner for a 'council of war'. Something, Croft insisted, 'had to be done to keep SIS in general – and [Whinney] in particular – from swallowing us [SOE] up whole and removing all our freedom of action'. Dickinson agreed that while Croft's operation could certainly help SIS when asked, it should remain an independent unit. Thereafter matters proceeded more smoothly, so that in later life, as author of the official history of clandestine operations in the Mediterranean, Brooks Richards was able to note the 'uniquely friendly atmosphere' that prevailed in Bastia.

At the operational level, friendly cooperation applied especially to relations with the Americans. Whinney recorded that they were always ready to lend him boats and that they 'proved themselves to be kind, hospitable, efficient, and good company to work with'. Croft's initial second-in-command was an OSS American naval lieutenant named Fisher Howe, 'an enthusiastic charmer with a wide grin,' recorded Croft, 'who added greatly to our spirit of adventure'.[32]

Croft himself was an almost stereotypical Boys' Own hero for whom SOE frequently appeared to provide a natural home and for whom it might even have been invented. '[He] was a splendid man,' recalled Cooper, who, during his years in the Foreign Legion, had already encountered an impressive cast of buccaneers. 'He is tall, with finely chiselled features, but physical description does him less than justice. He is determined and strong, a man of action, indefatigable, his body so finely tuned and disciplined that he could never understand a man complaining of tiredness. "Tired?" he would say, frowning in perplexity, "surely that is not a condition? It is a weakness."'

Already aged 38, the perfectionist Croft had quickly abandoned an intended career in the cotton trade to become a hardened veteran of gruelling pre-war expeditions to the Arctic, during one of which, as principal dog-handler on the 1934 British Trans-Greenland Expedition, he completed the longest self-supporting dog-sledge journey on record, at 1,738 kilometres. Having also witnessed the Reichstag fire during a year in Germany learning the language, he was an early recruit for Section D missions alongside Malcolm Munthe in Scandinavia. He also worked as chief intelligence officer to Gubbins in Norway, helped organise Auxiliary Units in Suffolk and Essex, and served with the commandos before flying out to Algiers in April 1943 to join SOE's naval section at Massingham.

'If I could relive any chapter of my life during the war,' he nostalgically recorded later, 'it would undoubtedly be Corsica [where] I had the fun of running my own show to a large extent unsupervised.'[33] This was not strictly true, as he operated within AFHQ guidelines, followed methods and procedures in close liaison with the French, the Americans and the other British services involved, and was in daily contact through his own signals unit with both Massingham and Maryland. It was certainly the case, however, that inspection visits from higher authority were rare and that he was left broadly to his own devices. Between December 1943, when the first operation was launched, and late July 1944, when it was closed down following the allied landings in southern France, Balaclava carried out fifty-two sorties. Croft personally took part in about half of them.

Of this total, however, slightly fewer than half, some twenty-four, were successful. The others failed because of bad weather (seven), hostile craft such as German E-boats (seven), faulty navigation (six), the non-arrival of an onshore reception party (four), and other complications such as engine failure or the sudden unwelcome arrival of a German patrol on the scene (four). This was par for the course for seaborne clandestine operations, for in addition to the elements the situation in occupied territory for the resister was, in Whinney's words, 'highly fluid, making lightning changes [to plans] the order of the day – or night'. During the fourteen or so nights per month when moon conditions prevented operations, boats had to be repaired, experiments and improvements carried out, and operational personnel thoroughly trained and briefed for impending missions. A staff of six Royal Corps signallers kept in contact with Massingham, Maryland and agents in the field.[34]

Operations to Italy, however, dominated the scene in Bastia. In all, seventy-five agents and an unknown quantity of radio sets and light arms were safely landed there, while some twenty-one men were brought back to Corsica. Not all of the agents that were safely put ashore were working for SOE, however, and the majority of operations were for 'A' Force, SIS [ISLD], OSS or the Italian commandos. This was all achieved with no more than twelve trained operational personnel. The small boats deployed to land agents ashore from the fast craft involved were either rubber – for rocky shores – or Royal Engineers assault boats. Various types of rubber boats were used, including German and American makes. Equipped with sails, emergency repair outfits and iron rations, and both camouflaged and adapted for rowing, they proved reliable and surprisingly fast.[35]

The first of Croft's total of five successful sorties carried out for SOE took place in early December 1943 with the object of landing a 27-year-old Massingham-trained Sicilian radio operator named Silvio de Fiori a few kilometres north of La Spezia to establish communications with a resistance organisation in Genoa known as 'Otto'. Established by Professor Ottorino Balduzzi, a distinguished neurologist and an anti-Fascist with Communist Party contacts, Otto was linked with a group of partisans up in the mountains behind Genoa who were protecting some escaped British prisoners of war whom they hoped to use for sabotaging a number of railway targets. In November, a small group of Otto's men, along with a couple of the Britons, including a senior British officer named Colonel Gore, had succeeded in making the hazardous crossing by sea to Corsica, whereupon Gore had been flown to Algiers to report on the Otto group. By this time, an airdrop by three British aircraft had already provided it with a million lire, and a later drop supplied it with armaments and equipment. One of the Italians who had come out with Gore was named Paolo Risso. It had been decided that he should accompany De Fiori back to the group in Genoa. The operation was codenamed 'Valentine/Cunningham'.

The first two attempts to get them ashore, on the nights of 29 November and 1 December, were foiled by bad weather. But the sea was comparatively calm on the following night when an Italian MAS boat, No. 541, under the command of naval Lieutenant Cosulich and with an Italian crew, slipped out of Bastia harbour bound for the Ligurian coast. The wiry, red-headed Cosulich, who inevitably became known to his new British colleagues as 'Ginger', was a member of a well-known Triestine ship-owning family and was regarded as the most experienced and reliable of the young MAS boat captains. In charge of the operation was Pat Whinney, with Croft also on board. Accompanying them was Sergeant Geoffrey Arnold, formerly of the Long Range Desert Group, who was an experienced navigator.

After safely skirting an enemy minefield near the harbour entrance, the boat's engines shifted easily into their cruising speed of 30 knots. What, wondered Whinney, was the state of mind of the crew? This was the first of their operations to Italy for their ex-enemy, the British, and he wondered where their loyalties now lay.

Not long before, while inspecting the MAS crews just recently turned over to the allies, he had been present when one of those lined up on the deck had suddenly stepped forward, given the Nazi salute and said firmly 'Heil Hitler!' Further down the line, one or two others joined him. The Italians in charge had promised there would be no repeat of such incidents. The loyalty of Cosulich seemed certain. But his crew? Only time would tell. Perhaps the assurance that the crews would not be involved in offensive actions against their compatriots fighting on the other side, nor indeed against their erstwhile allies the Germans, would do the trick.

After an hour or so, one of the lookouts reported pinpricks of red light on the starboard bow. Some of the crew were becoming visibly nervous and asked the captain to stop the boat because they didn't know what the lights were. 'We can't stop the ship for that!' replied Whinney. 'The longer we go on the easier it'll be to find out. Please tell them – no stopping.' Cosulich conveyed the decision while the crew peered anxiously ahead. Suddenly, Whinney realised it wasn't the lights they were afraid of.

> They were very anxious, however, about what this foreigner – me – might be up to. A series of extra bright flashes in and around the lights provoked a further wave of unease and nattering, obliging Ginger [Cosulich] to ask once more if we might ease down. In explanation he said that once the crew knew what the lights were there would be no further worry. Reluctantly I agreed and speed was reduced; almost immediately it became plain that the whole display was the result of an air raid on la Spezia. Various among the more religious members of the crew crossed themselves as we resumed our 30 knots.[36]

An hour later, they stopped the main engines and switched over to the auxiliaries for the two-hour run in to the shore. Still, even at 6 knots, they emitted a high-pitched whine and it had to be hoped that they wouldn't be heard or identified by sentries on shore. As they went, they watched the air raid and saw many fires in and around the city. What was the crew feeling about that?

Gradually, the silhouette of the coastline became visible and the cliffs and the mountains beyond began to tower over them. Their priority now was to get close inshore so they'd be screened from enemy detection by the sheer height of the cliffs and inside the normal run of inshore patrols. Passing a village, they saw the occasional flicker of light from a door being opened. Whinney and Croft checked their position. Within 180 metres of the beach, Croft reported that,

> the rubber dinghy was put over the side with Geoffrey in the bows acting as armed look-out. I put the two agents in the stern with their radio and equipment then rowed for the shore. But it all looked far more precipitous than the aerial photographs had indicated, and in almost total darkness the outlying rocks showed up only when the breakers washed over them. Suddenly Geoffrey spotted phosphorescence-making surf away to port, and with a few quick strokes I grounded the dinghy on the tiny beach. Geoffrey was first ashore and made a thorough reconnaissance before we lifted the men clear of the surf to give them a dry start.[37]

Once the agents' safety was assured Arnold signalled seawards by torch to the ship, which, owing to her small silhouette, could hardly be seen. By 0100 Arnold and Croft were safely on board and arrived back at Bastia at 0800.[38]

Risso returned to Corsica in mid-February 1944 with another boatload of allied prisoners of war and downed airmen, and was subsequently taken on by OSS for one of their missions into Italy. De Fiori's fate, so far as it is known, was less happy. He eventually came on air with his radio set in January, but at the end of March fell into enemy hands when almost the entire Otto organisation was rounded up by the Germans. Many were shot, and it seems likely that De Fiori was one of the victims.

Few operations were as straightforward as this, however. On 30 December a party of four SOE agents bound for Italy arrived in Bastia under the control of the irrepressible ex-Legionnaire, Captain Dick Cooper. It consisted of two men and two women. Of the men, one was an Italian and the other a Canadian radio operator. The two women were known only as Fiammetta and Anna. Both, along with a third woman who had subsequently dropped out, had been successfully infiltrated by Cooper through Eighth Army lines just before Christmas but then immediately overtaken by allied troops before they had gone very far. As a result, it had been decided to send them in by boat instead. 'All sparkled with vivacity. Their irrepressible high spirits had included such japes as throwing hand grenades at the Germans as they pulled out of Naples,' wrote Cooper.[39] 'Two excellent men and two women – one frightful,' noted Croft in his log the day they arrived, adding that the women had later been found trying on the clothes of Paddy Davies, the officer in whose room they were billeted, and making them (as Cooper delicately recorded) 'bulge in all the wrong places'.[40]

New Year's Eve and Day were too stormy at sea for any operations at all, and on the night of 2 January a first attempt to land the group was thwarted by an alert ashore and the appearance of two E-boats. On the following night another effort was made with Croft in charge, assisted by an indispensable member of his team, Sergeant Harry Coltman, another French Foreign Legion veteran, whose experience and knowledge of small arms was of paramount importance in training and operations. Croft's log tells the story of what happened:

> We were again late on schedule on arrival in the target area. The Radar in the P.T. boat said we were 300 yds. from the Monseglia peninsula, but in actual practice we were at least 1200 to 1400 yards. We had a tiring row inshore in almost pitch darkness and a most exhausting one along a precipitous coast. Absolutely no loop hole in these 'rocky defenses' could be found – certainly not for women and we had once more to give up the operation. In a post-mortem afterwards it was found that we had been embarked in the rubber boat (heavily loaded with six persons) too far north and that in our wanderings southwards we had eventually turned round only about six hundred yards from the pin-point. It was a maddening final to this dark period, but we have learned a lot and shall be more fully prepared than ever next time, i.e. in a fortnight's time. We must have better oars since [we] broke three on their last operation and only just managed to struggle back to the ship.[41]

When they got to Bastia Cooper took the agents to Calvi for a much-needed rest during the non-operational moon period. They proved a difficult quartet to handle as the two men fell in love with

Fiammetta and jealousy reared its head. On 19 January, the first night suitable for operations to resume, yet another attempt to land them failed because, despite a calm sea, the boat started late, failed to find the right pinpoint and ran out of time for further reconnaissance. Two nights later they made another attempt. 'Early meal for ops party who were on board with [Cooper's] party by 1730 and away by 1800,' recorded Croft:

> All our hopes went with them as this is the fourth attempt! Alas – they were back at 2330 with the sad news that the MAS boat had had to turn back owing to a broken petrol pipe. Such bad luck – so much thought and preparation had been given to this attempt that otherwise might have been successful.

A fifth and final attempt was made the following night but had to be aborted when three enemy vessels appeared in the target area. At this point, with the agents' morale at rock bottom, Anna sick and the wireless operator showing some serious health problems, it was decided to abandon the mission altogether and the two women were flown back to Naples escorted by Henri Boutigny. 'Dick Cooper jubilant at getting women off his hands,' recorded Croft in his log. As they left, one of the male agents, Ranieri, flew off the handle, protesting that the whole operation had been carried out inefficiently, that it was criminal having been assigned a wireless operator with a weak heart and that he refused to proceed with the operation.[42]

This was not quite the end of the story, however. Cooper's job was now to take care of Ranieri, so he took him to Ajaccio and a safe house belonging to French intelligence. Here, from an Italian source, he learned that Ranieri was not to be trusted, so he was escorted to Maryland, which was instructed to place him under house arrest. Instead, Field Security put him under surveillance and soon discovered that he was paying regular visits to Fiammetta, who along with Anna had been sent on from Naples to a safe house in Brindisi to await a suitable dark period before being parachuted in behind the lines. At this, Ranieri was taken to Naples and ordered not to return to Brindisi. Then, in February, Cooper spotted him back in town and immediately reported it to the police. The same day,

Fiammetta passed on information she had discovered from the Italian. 'He had protested his love for her,' recalled Cooper, 'and she, shrewd woman, had humoured him, pretending to be in love with him until she could find his true allegiance. Ranieri was, in fact, a Fascist who had never changed his views and if we had managed to land him in German-held territory he would have betrayed every member of the organisation he could lay his hands on.'[43] All in all, therefore, the frustrating failure to land the group had proved to be a blessing in disguise. Of one thing at the time, however, Croft was sure. If women were ever sent again, he told Holdsworth, 'they should preferably not be accompanied by men'.[44]

Later that month Croft embarked on yet another operation to help the Otto group. This was Operation 'Tail Lamp 2', to land a three-man Italian mission, codenamed 'Charterhouse', close to Genoa, where Otto had agreed to provide a reception party by the pier at Voltri on the western edges of the city. On the night of 28 January 1944 the party set off in an Italian MAS boat. Unfortunately, its crew was inexperienced in clandestine operations. Outside Genoa harbour they spotted some ships just over a kilometre away and panicked. 'Within two minutes,' recorded Croft ruefully, '[they] had the boat retreating at top speed, the rear gunner optimistically firing at flares sent up by ships in the area and at various points along the coast.' The excitement also proved too much for the captain, who passed out, leaving the SIS navigator on board to take over and get them all safely back to Bastia.[45]

Three nights later, and this time using two American PT (Patrol Torpedo) boats equipped with radar, Croft's team tried again. Now there were seven agents on board. On the way, one of the boats broke down and there was an anxious delay while some of the agents and equipment were hurriedly transferred to the other craft. At 2 a.m., in pitch-darkness, they reached the point offshore where they were to wait for the signal from the reception committee that all was safe. No signal came, but three of the agents volunteered to go ahead anyway. Seaman Donald Miles, a member of Croft's team, clambered into one rubber dinghy with the three Italians. Escorted by Croft and Harry Coltman in another, they paddled along the shore until the Voltri pier loomed up above them out of the darkness. They could hear German sentries talking and see the glow of their cigarettes. One or two cars passed on the coastal road. 'Suddenly,' recorded Croft,

a group of men flashed a light in our direction: they looked like an enemy patrol. Donald knew exactly what to do: he sheltered his dinghy under the seaward end of the pier. Harry and I waited watchfully. When the coast was clear we crept ashore to see if any other dangers lurked in the darkness. The beach was empty but there was a shipyard alongside. We spent precious minutes, eyes and ears on the alert. Nothing stirred. We flashed our signal to Donald and he brought the three agents ashore. Then suddenly a cottage door opened not twenty yards from where I was standing; an old woman came out carrying a lamp. We all froze as she placed the lamp carefully on the ground not taking her eyes off it. Was she part of the reception committee? The seconds passed. She picked up the lamp and in that instant I flashed the pre-arranged signal towards her, but she was probably blinded by her own light and went back into the cottage. The door was firmly closed.

The agents were our first thought, we mustn't risk their lives, so we took them to what looked like a secure hiding place, spotted by Harry and me during our recce, and went back to the cottage. I shouted the password 'Panzer.' I could hear a door being opened, then a man's gruff voice from inside asking apparently what the hell was going on . . . I repeated the password. Dead silence.

So the reception committee just hadn't materialised; how absolutely infuriating! We went back to the agents and saw them safely on their way.

Despite the lack of a reception committee, the three men quickly made contact with the Otto organisation through an address that the leader of the group, Italo Cavallino, who was a native of Genoa, had been given before his departure. Their mission was to establish communications with, and provide support for, partisan groups in Liguria and south Piedmont, and both Cavallino and the wireless operator, Secondino Balestri, codenamed 'Biagio', were duly passed on to some bands in Piedmont led by a Captain Piero Cosa. Here they arranged supply drops and gave instruction on the use of British arms and supplies until Cavallino was caught by the Germans in March. A month later, Biagio was also captured, but he later escaped and was able to return to base. Here, however, he was received not with praise but with suspicion as an enemy infiltrator. Paradoxically, this was because he'd managed to insert a warning in one of his messages that was so ingenious that the security section could not credit the explanation from someone so young – he was only 18 years old – and so held him for some considerable time before clearing and releasing him. The third member of the mission, Nino Bellegrande ('Annibale'), was retained by the Otto organisation in the Genoa area. Although he was lucky enough to survive the round-up of March 1944, he was eventually caught and was shot just a month before his country's liberation.[46]

Croft was back again at Voltri pier on the night of 17 March, in a spectacular operation to land ten agents and six W/T sets. This was a 'composite' operation, meaning that agents from more than one organisation were being handled. In this case, eight were for SOE and two for SIS. All were successfully put ashore before midnight without any serious problem. The SOE agents were in two teams and guided by Giuseppe Conforti, a native of Voltri who'd arrived in Corsica shortly before with Paolo Risso and the boatload of prisoners of war. One of the missions, codenamed 'Winchester', reached its destination in Val di Susa but had difficulty in establishing wireless communications, and two of its members eventually crossed over into France, later to be despatched back on further missions in Italy. Their radio man operated for a time in Turin and then joined an SOE mission in the Langhe. The second group failed to make radio contact at all and its leader was apparently captured and shot.[47]

Six nights after this Voltri operation, disaster struck when Ginger Cosulich's MAS 541 was lost with all hands when it struck a mine during an operation to land two agents in the Savona area. Early in April, Croft lost another of the MAS boats when its crew mutinied, shot their captain and two other Italian officers, threw the bodies overboard and took their boat to the mainland, where they surrendered to the Germans. When the news reached Bastia, all Italian-manned boats were withdrawn from special operations. This did not prevent Croft continuing to land agents in Italy (as well as France) over the next four months, using American PT and British MTBs, but the rapidly changing strategic scene meant that Italian operations were finally closed down on 25 July 1944. Ten days later

Croft and his best hand-picked men were flown to the Massingham base at Algiers and soon after that were parachuted into southern France for operations there. 'So ends Balaclava!' records Croft's log on Sunday 6 August 1944. '[Not] the close of the book but only the finish of a chapter.'[48]

# CHAPTER FOUR

# The Swiss connection

The previous October, nine days after Leo Valiani and Renato Pierleoni arrived in Rome, the wireless transmitting set promised to them by SOE had been dropped by the Royal Air Force near Lake Martignano. To their dismay, however, the reception party that travelled out from Rome was unable to locate it in the dark. 'Damn it!' recalled Valiani. 'We'd lost any means of communication with the allies.'[1]

By now, underground anti-Fascist groups in the occupied capital had formed a Committee of National Liberation (CLN) under the chairmanship of a former prime minister from pre-Mussolini days, Ivanoe Bonomi, head of the small right-wing Labour Democratic Party. Overtly hostile to Badoglio and the King, the CLN consisted of the six main anti-Fascist parties: the Communists, the Socialists, the Christian Democrats, the Labour Democrats, the Liberals and the Action Party. In a model followed across German-occupied Italy, where local CLNs also sprang into existence, decisions were made wherever possible on the basis of unanimity. In Milan, the Committee of National Liberation grew into the Committee of National Liberation for Upper Italy (CLNAI) and became, in effect, the controlling body for resistance in the occupied north of the country. Its chairman from January 1944 was a prominent banker, Alfredo Pizzoni, who did his best to remain impartial amidst the clamour of always passionate and frequently contradictory voices.[2]

The Rome committee's secretary was drawn from the Action Party, which, as its name implied, was one of the most dynamic of the resistance organisations. Without the long-anticipated radio set, the CLN quickly decided that someone from the Action Party would have to go to Switzerland in person to contact the allies and brief them on its aims and activities. The most obvious candidate was Ferruccio Parri, who was based in Milan and was in charge of building relations with partisan groups, springing up all over the German-occupied north. It was agreed that Valiani should escort him on his journey and report back to Rome.

In late October, accompanied by his wife, Valiani set off for Milan, where he found that Action Party activists were keeping a close guard on Parri, who was leading a precarious clandestine existence in the city while outwardly living under the respectable cover of research director for the Società Edison, the company supplying northern Italy with its electricity. Their meeting lasted only a few minutes – 'just enough,' recorded Valiani, 'to be struck by his marvellous white hair, dignity and deep scrutinizing gaze'. Already in his fifties, Parri was a venerated figure within the Italian resistance. Wounded in action during the First World War, he had also helped plan the great Italian victory at Vittorio Veneto as a staff officer, and since the 1920s had been imprisoned more than once for anti-Fascist activities. The two men agreed to meet up three days later on a train heading to the Swiss border. Finally, on 3 November, they reached Lugano.[3]

SOE had been represented in Switzerland since February 1941 by John ('Jock') McCaffery, an old Section D hand who was based at the legation in Berne under the cover of assistant press attaché. Perched at the crossroads of Europe, the landlocked neutral state was surrounded by Hitler's Reich, Vichy France and Italy, and had long been a fertile ground for espionage. The writer Somerset Maugham, who worked for British intelligence there in the First World War and based his famous *Ashenden* spy stories on the experience, wrote how 'agents of the secret services, spies, revolutionaries and agitators infested the hotels of the principal towns'. The British minister in Berne at the time, Horace Rumbold, recalled sitting in his room 'like a spider . . . attracting every day news and information.'[4] By the same token, however, life for an intelligence officer could be lonely and stressful. The Swiss were vigilant in guarding their neutrality, the legation's work on all its fronts was far too important to be jeopardised by wild cloak-and-dagger operations, and communications were limited and difficult, with couriers having to travel by the lengthy and hazardous land route through southern France and Spain to Lisbon.

On the plus side, however, McCaffery received sympathetic if guarded support from the legation's minister, established close working relations with the military and air attachés, and received considerable assistance from SIS. Historians have frequently remarked on the conflicts and rivalries between SOE and the long-established Secret Intelligence Service. The latter's mission of acquiring intelligence required quiet and undetectable methods – not for nothing was it sometimes referred to as 'the silent service' – whereas SOE's task of encouraging sabotage and subversion inevitably drew hostile attention. 'SOE was a raw and untrained organisation,' acknowledges its official historian, 'and . . . it necessarily worked in an atmosphere fatal to the quiet methods of an intelligence service. In the nature of things, an SOE organisation must eventually expose itself to open violence, and even in its beginnings it must indulge in some political activity and move in circles where recklessness of consequences is one of the qualifications for leadership.'[5] In the course of the war this meant that at the highest level SOE and SIS frequently fought a battle for influence that on more than one occasion appeared to threaten SOE's very survival as an independent organisation.[6]

Yet this did not preclude frequent close cooperation and liaison at the operational level, especially during SOE's early life, when it had to lean heavily on the experience of SIS for practical help. Under cover as British vice-consul in Basle, Sir Frank Nelson, SOE's first director, had worked in the 1930s for the secret intelligence network known as the 'Z' Organisation set up by Sir Claude Dansey, himself a former head of station in Berne and now assistant chief of SIS under Sir Stewart Menzies. In September 1940, Nelson signed an agreement with SIS about projects, transport, communications, spheres of interest and the recruitment of agents. He also visited Menzies at frequent intervals, and even gave Dansey a room of his own at Baker Street to help further good relations between the two services. It was hardly surprising, therefore, that he sent McCaffery to see Dansey for a briefing before the Scotsman left for Berne. Over lunch, the assistant SIS chief told him that his men in Switzerland would be delighted to provide all the cooperation they could, and even gave him a list of their names. 'They did,' recorded McCaffery, 'far beyond anything he [Dansey] had ever dreamed of.'⁷

McCaffery found Frederick ('Fanny') Vanden Heuvel, the Geneva-based head of the Swiss SIS station, especially cooperative and helpful. 'We had the same common objective of penetrating enemy territory,' wrote McCaffery, 'and eventually we were able to swap people or groups which either of us thought would be more useful in the other people's field.' A tall, handsome man – 'the perfect figure of a European aristocrat,' thought McCaffery – Vanden Heuvel was not only a Papal count but also had long experience of Europe, working with the Beecham pharmaceutical company; a 'smooth operator,' remarked the SIS officer-turned-Soviet spy Kim Philby, who once dined with him at the Garrick Club. The deputy SIS officer in Geneva eventually handled most of McCaffery's French traffic – although this, so the latter claimed, was 'not only without the knowledge of his London HQ but without that of his local superior officer'. Geneva also had the only SIS transmitter in Switzerland. As in all SOE stations abroad, McCaffery had relied entirely on SIS channels for his radio communications to London until Baker Street established its own separate cipher traffic in March 1942. SOE officers often chafed at the restrictions placed on its operations by SIS and on occasion suspected that the senior secret service was at best deliberately less than cooperative and at worst actively obstructionist. So far as Dansey was concerned, the important thing was that SOE should keep out of his own agents' way.⁸

For the first few months of his posting McCaffery had run a virtually one-man show helped by Elizabeth Hodgson, who handled most of the German and Austrian work out of the Zurich consulate-general, and with some part-time assistance from locally employed British female staff from the legation. These were later reinforced by an experienced secretary from Baker Street, Mary Bailey, who had worked with Gubbins and brought both valuable knowledge about the personalities and inner workings of the rapidly expanding SOE headquarters and a keen sense of security, and by Robert Jellinek, an Englishman in his late twenties. With a Swiss-German wife, and always known as Peter, he had worked for a number of years for the Bally shoe company before being taken on first by the military attaché and then by McCaffery. He was to become the

Scotsman's indispensable right-hand man until the end of the war, taking charge of the station whenever McCaffery was away from Berne; a man, recorded his grateful boss, 'for all seasons and all tasks'. His fluent knowledge of Swiss-German proved a particular asset.[9]

McCaffery was born in 1905 of Irish parents in Glasgow, where his father was a policeman. In later life he hinted mysteriously at 'a mis-spent youth in Canada' where he acquired a familiarity with poker, and claimed that as a football enthusiast he was once offered a trial by a First Division team.[10] At some point he also trained for the priesthood at the Gregorian University in Rome, and Jellinek described him as 'very Catholic and anti-communist'. But in the end he stayed in Italy as a teacher, married and became head of the British Council in Genoa. In addition to his initial primary task of encouraging subtle sabotage against German trains transiting Switzerland laden with coal supplies for Italy across the Brenner Pass, he also had the mission of assisting SOE efforts in France, Germany and Austria. So far as Italy was concerned, before the armistice Roseberry and Baker Street's J Section had seen Switzerland as the principal gateway into the country. This was McCaffery's own keenest interest, and he had given it high priority by establishing contacts with the Swiss Italian press, providing financial support to anti-Fascist groups in the north and recruiting agents there. Again according to Jellinek, he was 'an obsessive worker – and party-goer'.[11]

He was also in touch with Allen Dulles, who headed the OSS mission in Berne. The future post-war Director of Central Intelligence had arrived in the Swiss capital the year before, openly going about his business, noted one observer, 'as head of the American Secret Service; a tall, heavily built man, with rimless spectacles . . .'[12] At first this very openness had, in his own words, 'terrified' McCaffery, who, like many of his 'sharp-end' professional colleagues, considered the Americans to be dangerously naive and ingenuous in the affairs of intelligence. He had therefore avoided Dulles for weeks. Eventually when they met, McCaffery explained that having 'sweated considerably in learning and operating a business not in facts and figures but in the lives of men' he could not agree to the actual running of it by someone who knew nothing about it. British–American collaboration, he explained, would have to be 'on the understanding that whilst all important figures who showed up would be seen by us both, the actual mechanics of the operation would have to be run, at least for some time, by myself and the organisation I had created.'¹³

As Dulles's principal interest anyway was in gathering intelligence from inside Hitler's Third Reich, he had not taken umbrage at this and had been largely content to leave operational work in Italy to McCaffery. For one thing, there was no US consulate in Lugano to provide cover for operations across the border, and for another he lacked sufficient personnel who spoke Italian. In his telegrams to Washington and London he codenamed the British 'Zulu', and within weeks of the armistice he was assuring his superiors that his work in Italy was 'well-synchronised with Zulu SOE'. This did not preclude friction, especially when the Italians tried to play off the two allies for their own advantage; and McCaffery was never entirely at ease with Dulles's security, nor Dulles with McCaffery's jealous guarding of his assets. But strategically, the two men enjoyed a generally amicable relationship.¹⁴

Most importantly, through his principal Swiss-Italian socialist contact in Lugano, a man whom he referred to simply as 'Paul' but who in reality was Piero Pellegrino, the Swiss editor of *Libera Stampa*, McCaffery had established a line to what he told London was an active and effective subversive anti-Fascist movement in northern Italy known as the 'Tigrotti' ('Tigers'), a body that he described as formed in large part of army officers but also included professional men. He provided it with significant supplies of explosives and it reported excellent results, including the destruction of oil tanks in Genoa and the wrecking of the engine room of a corvette under construction. He was also lending similar support to another such group known as the 'Wolves' that was operating in and around Milan.¹⁵

Not long after establishing the first operational line into Italy for the delivery of sabotage material to the Tigers, in April 1942, he had also recruited a highly promising Italian contact whom he described enthusiastically to London as '1st class and worth backing all out . . . I do not think we have any abler man on our books.' This was a Signor Almerigotti, who was introduced to him by Group Captain Freddie West, the air attaché in the legation, who had met him through an American assistant naval attaché in Rome where West had previously served. Presenting himself as a former army officer, Almerigotti claimed to be playing a leading role in an anti-Fascist organisation of some 1,500 people covering most of northern Italy. Impressed, McCaffery had given him the symbol 'JQ900' and provided him with 30,000 lire as a start to produce results, an amount that London immediately upped to 100,000 lire. To supply Almerigotti's network, McCaffery used a Swiss-Italian contact in Lugano, whom he codenamed 'JQ701', who held a regular frontier permit for his business journeys by road to Milan. Another anti-Fascist contact, an Italian businessman who frequently travelled to Germany, was also recruited as 'JQ800' and put in touch with Almerigotti so that he could use the latter's lines of communication. Almerigotti had also proved useful in the infiltration into northern Italy of a 22-year-old agent recruited and trained as a radio operator by SOE in Britain named Giacomo Sarfatti, an Italian-Jewish anti-Fascist from Florence who went by the war name of 'Galea'. Radio contact had been established and a few messages exchanged.[16]

McCaffery had also been in touch with the Action Party through Filippo Caracciolo, who'd been one of Roseberry's contacts during the post-armistice discussions in Brindisi, as well as with one of its leading Rome-based members, Ugo la Malfa, whom he met with Allen Dulles after the Italian briefly took shelter across the border to escape arrest. He had also, again in cooperation with Dulles, made contact with the Italian industrialist Adriano Olivetti, who had been actively working to get rid of Mussolini in the months before his overthrow. In addition he had held several promising talks with Ignazio Silone about organising joint operations with the Italian Socialist Party. A founder of the Italian Communist Party and former head of its underground network, Silone was the author of two powerful anti-Fascist novels, *Fontamara* and *Bread and Wine*, who, since falling out with the Communists in 1930, had been living in Switzerland to concentrate on his writing. 'But the old fascination for clandestine work against the Fascist regime was still there,' noted McCaffery, 'and after agreeing to be an adviser and consultant, gradually he had come round to wanting to participate.' He put Silone in touch with Paul and discussions took place about providing him with radio equipment. Despite a setback in late 1942 when he was briefly detained by the Swiss police, Silone proved useful in establishing links with socialist groups.[17]

All these contacts had been made before Mussolini's downfall. The weeks between then and the armistice had been confusing and frustrating. But they at least had the advantage of bringing out into the open the leading anti-Fascists and allowing them to start organising on a nationwide scale, so that by the time the Germans finally occupied the north, SOE was no longer, as McCaffery put it, 'working confusedly and in the dark'.[18] On the day following the announcement of the armistice, London sent him the signal that the time had now come for all the groups he was in contact with to intensify their action against enemy communications across northern Italy. Amongst other things, use could now be made of five tons of stores that had been laid towards the end of October in underwater containers off the Ligurian coast. This too, suggested London, could be the moment for Sarfatti to play 'a most important role as a centre of communication'. There followed a month of intensive and frantic action and McCaffery received a number of highly positive reports from and about Almerigotti.[19]

In the meantime, dozens of anti-Fascists fled into Switzerland. Most of them settled in Ticino, the Italian-speaking region where Lugano, its largest city and lakeside resort with its dozens of hotels and palm-fringed promenades, became a virtual Italian enclave — full, wrote McCaffery, 'of Italian refugees, few of them with anything to do, and all of them anxious to have some connection with the patriots across the border. It was a hotbed of gossip, rumour and whispered information, wide open for infiltration.' It was not long before the exiles formed a Liberation Committee that echoed the party political make-up of the CLN in Milan. Alberto Damiani, of the Action Party, was responsible for its military affairs and liaison with the allies. McCaffery described him as 'a dynamo'.[20]

Helped by half a million lire provided by McCaffery, the Italians quickly got to work on establishing lines of communication and escape routes across the border, setting up reception committees, storing explosives and producing propaganda leaflets, to be printed and dropped by the allies to encourage resistance groups. In late October Damiani reported that they were busy organising partisan bands in the mountains, recruiting action squads in all the major

centres of population, working on building liaison between the
resistance in Piedmont, Lombardy, the Veneto and Liguria, and
raising financial support. What they sought as immediate goals were
cross-border links with the allies, agreement on targets for sabotage
and anti-sabotage, and supplies of food, clothing and arms. He helpfully supplied a map showing possible drop sites, provided a couple
of contact addresses in Bergamo and Milan, and stated firmly that
the CLN wished to avoid any contact with openly monarchical and
'Badogliani' elements. For this reason he was highly critical of allied
propaganda that was, he claimed, 'not contributing' to the anti-
German and anti-Fascist struggle. 'Either,' he stressed, 'give news
that responds to reality . . . or, rather than lying, be quiet.' This
political plea was the opening shot in what would be a continuing
tension between the stridently anti-monarchist sentiments of the
anti-Fascist resistance and the more pragmatic and action-orientated
goals of SOE, with its commitment to working with the government
of the King and Badoglio.[21]

McCaffery had been fully briefed by London on the agreement
with SIM about working together on behind-the-lines sabotage.
But he had also been informed, along the lines of Roseberry's
guidance to Max Salvadori, that SOE could not rely entirely on
such collaboration and would continue to work with independent
channels: thus the 'spiritual' [i.e. anti-Fascist] side of resistance was
paramount in mobilising sentiment in German-occupied Italy. So
he should do all he could to support the anti-Fascists from Switzerland
while making it clear to them that, for the time being at least, it
was essential for military reasons to work with Badoglio. Eisenhower,
he was told, had placed sabotage on a high level and had called on
SOE for an 'all-out' effort. Confidentially, however, Roseberry also
told him that the real power within the royalist government lay
with Generals Castellano and Ambrosio, who would willingly
'discard' Badoglio when he was no longer needed.[22]

The massively increased volume and urgency of his tasks in Italy
inevitably forced McCaffery to spend a great deal of his time travelling to and from Ticino, and within weeks he was urgently asking
London for more staff, especially an Italian-speaker who could help
with the Italian work. 'Travel, travel, travel; tiredness and utter
weariness,' he noted later about this period. The stress was all made

worse by the absence of his wife and son. It quickly took its toll. In early October, two days after his plea for more staff, he suffered a complete nervous collapse, 'going out like a light,' he recalled, 'in a ... hotel and waking up in a Lugano clinic with leeches draped around my neck'. Exhaustion was diagnosed, and he was to spend the next four weeks resting in the clinic. The collapse did not come entirely out of the blue. Shortly before, returning on the night train via Zurich after yet another long day of discussions in Lugano, he'd been so furious at being woken by the ticket inspector that he'd taken the man by the throat and banged his head against the seat before realising his identity.

While he recovered, Peter Jellinek took over the running of the Berne office, where eventually most of the Italian workload was taken over by Captain Julian Hall, with Major John Birkbeck installed to take care of Italian affairs in the Lugano consulate. Hall, the heir to a baronetcy, and, in McCaffery's words, 'quintessential Eton and Oxford of those days', was one of the thousands of British prisoners of war who'd made the long trek north into Switzerland after the armistice. So was Birkbeck, who in peacetime had been the manager of two large country estates in Britain. The former took over the handling of reports, evaluations, correspondence and telegrams relating to Italy, acted as both 'shield and filter' dealing with the growing stream of prospective recruits who found their way to Berne, and in the end had more continuous contact with Dulles and the OSS than did McCaffery himself. In Lugano, Birkbeck took over the task of dealing with Damiani and the Italians; together, the two young officers proved 'the finest supply team one could have had'. All this allowed McCaffery, when he recovered, to concentrate on policy and planning. London also agreed to provide him with a house of his own, a car and separate accommodation for interviewing and housing agents. They also authorised the employment of additional cipher clerks, who were found from amongst British Army ex-POWs.[23]

The reason McCaffery required a car was not just for his personal convenience but also to keep up with the Americans. In the wake of the Salerno landings he was becoming acutely aware that there was also a competitive edge to Britain's relationship with its powerful ally. That September, he told London that whereas SOE in Switzerland had been run from the start 'with little noise and low expectations', the recent turn of events and the arrival of the Americans who 'splashed money' and had large houses and fleets of cars meant that SOE must evolve and not appear 'poor second fiddles'. Indeed, he complained, he had almost 'lost' Caracciolo and La Malfa because he had not been able to put them up and had no car, so they had stayed with Dulles instead.[24]

McCaffery met Valiani and Parri in Lugano the day after he left the clinic. Parri had also gone out of his way to stress the anti-Fascist and political, as well as purely anti-German, goals of the CLN in Milan, so McCaffery was prepared for a lengthy and difficult discussion. He spent four hours alone with the Italians before being joined in the evening by Allen Dulles for further talks. For the first part of their encounter Damiani kept the notes, then Dulles took over. 'Surrounded by a motley group of advisers,' recalled McCaffery, 'we spent nine hours in conference studying the present situation and planning the future. The North Italian Committee was in the process of formation and so also was the scheme of linking up the entire centre and north of Italy under its supreme guidance.'

What he did not record for posterity, however, was that after listening to the Italians' complaints about the pro-Badoglio tone of allied propaganda he went 'off the deep end' and told them bluntly that if the Italian opposition to Mussolini had managed to do anything concrete, *it* would have been running things instead of Badoglio. The prime British interest, he emphasised, was military, and if the Italians insisted on pushing their own propaganda line they would simply be playing the German/Fascist game of splitting their opponents. To this, Damiani and Parri suggested that at the very least the British could keep quiet about the King – a comment that McCaffery passed on to Roseberry.

The J Section head, who was still in Brindisi keeping close to the royalists and SIM, predictably deplored 'the extremism' of the Italians' views but described their action programme as 'splendid'. Nonetheless, he took a cautious view of extending SOE's relations with them. He warned McCaffery about passing on any information about allied military plans in case their networks were penetrated by the Germans, and he was sceptical about the long-term value of a number of the groups being reported on by Damiani. Berne should continue to pass on all the information it received, he instructed

McCaffery, but he should make no promises to the Italians and bear in mind that ultimately any support by way of arms to resistance groups would be decided by AFHQ 'broadly on the basis of their location, strength and composition'. He also thought it important to supply groups with organisers and W/T sets *before* any serious action was attempted. In late November, he was still largely unmoved by the expansive and enthusiastic prospects being floated by Damiani and Parri. The greatest contribution the Italians could make, he told McCaffery, continued to be the 'constant and large-scale interruption of traffic from the Brenner' – the target given to SOE in Switzerland back in 1941, long before the armistice and the emergence of a resistance movement in the north of the country.[25]

Still, small steps continued to be made in developing relations with the Italians. Despite the heated words at McCaffery's meeting with Parri and Valiani, one immediately practical result was that the latter took the opportunity to report the failure of his Rome comrades two weeks before to find the radio set dropped by the RAF. 'I asked [McCaffery] for a repeat, letting us know via the BBC,' he wrote. 'He did this, sending a telegram in code to Roseberry ... The second drop was more fruitful. The radio was not found, but the explosives were and were used by the Roman resistance.' From now on, the Italians remained in twice-weekly contact with SOE Switzerland through messengers crossing the border.[26]

The encounter also raised questions about McCaffery's relations with Dulles, who was now beginning to question whether SOE should be left alone to handle the Italians. 'Giving Zulu entire control over our support for the maquis groups in Italy would have an unfortunate outcome,' he told his superiors in Washington. McCaffery was quite prepared to keep Dulles in the picture. But he was unwilling to work on the technical side with the Americans, whose methods he dismissed as 'so divergent', and he continued to run his agents on his own lines in absolute secrecy from the OSS – as Dulles was still complaining to Washington in March 1944. In practical terms, however, these disagreements made little immediate difference. Both men agreed on the need to support the CLNAI, and policy in any case was becoming an inter-allied affair with most major issues being discussed and resolved at AFHQ.[27]

\* \* \*

Two days after McCaffery's meeting with Parri and Valiani in early November Jellinek received an urgent telegram from Roseberry in Brindisi, where he had just bid goodbye to Gubbins at the end of the SOE director's visit to sort out control of Italian affairs. It delivered a brutal shock.

SIM, it transpired, during a 'let's be frank with each other' session between the J Section head and the two SIM senior officers principally concerned, had revealed that Almerigotti, McCaffery's much-lauded 'catch' in northern Italy, was in reality a man named Dr Eligio Klein, from Trieste. Moreover, he had been operating under *their* control in a deception campaign ultimately directed to West, the air attaché and holder of both the Victoria and the Military Cross for his exploits as a Royal Flying Corps pilot, who had strong personal links with Italy.[28] In addition, they told Roseberry, 'JQ701' (Elio Andreoli) was also in their pay, and they knew about 'JQ800', as well as a couple of Yugoslavs additionally recruited by McCaffery, who had promised to run operations from across the Yugoslav border. Others cultivated by McCaffery also appeared on the list. The 'Wolves', not surprisingly, also turned out to be a creation of SIM. The only agents of McCaffery *not* to have been controlled by SIM were Caracciolo and La Malfa.

'I am investigating further', reported Roseberry by telegram, 'to ascertain whether A) SIM revealed their knowledge to Police or kept it to themselves for their own ends and B) whether line [is] still likely to be controlled by Its [Italians] hostile to us.'[29] The J Section head was well aware of McCaffery's fragile state and that he had gone off to the mountains for further rest and quiet after meeting Parri and Valiani. So he suggested that Jellinek should hold off for a while before passing on what he delicately termed the 'intimate details' furnished by SIM. McCaffery's deputy duly waited a week before breaking the news. When he was finally told that the man he believed was one of his best contacts in Italy had in fact been working under SIM control, McCaffery understandably clutched at straws by asking whether Klein had been a willing agent or merely an unwitting dupe. And what, he asked anxiously, about the 'Tigers', as well as the young Italian, Sarfatti? He felt especially deeply about the latter because it was he who had recruited him from a Pioneer Corps camp at St Ives in Cornwall back in 1940, and he had closely tracked his mission to Italy. Only a few weeks earlier he had bid him a moving farewell in Berne before Sarfatti left for his journey by train to Lugano and across the border to Milan.

More revelations followed over the next few days. Some were reassuring, others embarrassing and worrying. SIM had not, they assured Roseberry, informed either OVRA – the Fascist political police, or the Questura – the regular police, or the Germans, about any of these operations, and no records of their operations had been left behind in Rome. But they *had* deliberately planted Klein, and all the money and stores provided by SOE had been passed on to SIM. Likewise, all the safe houses named to McCaffery by Klein in Naples, Genoa, Bari, Taranto and Trieste were under SIM control. So far as Sarfatti was concerned, he had been known to SIM from the start and they had provided his reception and safe housing. But the SOE agent had been entirely unaware of the fact and SIM's motive had been to 'protect' him in the hope he would inadvertently lead them to others. Reassuringly, SIM had given Roseberry no indication that they had any knowledge of the Tigers, who proved ultimately to have been a product of the OVRA.[30]

What remained disturbingly unclear, however, was whether the communications link via Lugano was now under the control of SIM officers who remained loyal to the King, or to others who had gone over to Mussolini's new Fascist Republic and the Germans. If it was the former, then SIM and SOE together could send them new instructions; if the latter, the consequences could be dire. By 23 November Roseberry felt confident enough to reassure McCaffery that the cross-border link was secure, although he recommended that for the time being he should not commit any supplies to it. If it turned out not to be safe, it could be used for deception. As for Sarfatti, Roseberry had no doubt at all that his loyalty to SOE was 'unshaken'. But he considered him now 'useless' as an agent and suggested that he should be extricated from Italy as soon as possible. To help him unravel the tangle, McCaffery was assured by Baker Street that he had the full cooperation of SIS. In January, however, McCaffery was still trying to piece together the picture of the debacle and was deliberately stalling on Almerigotti's demand for several million more lire until he knew that Sarfatti was safe; he had no desire to make the SOE agent a hostage.[31] Fortunately, the SOE wireless

operator remained safely in the occupied north for the next twelve
months until returning to Switzerland in October 1944.

As for Klein, in May 1945 he turned himself over to the allies in
Rome, was thoroughly interrogated by SOE and OSS, and released.

In the weeks following his crucial meeting with Parri and Valiani,
McCaffery came under constant pressure from Damiani to deliver
results by way of supply drops to the burgeoning resistance in the
north, a demand so insistent that by the end of November he was
even threatening to break off relations altogether with the allies
unless something was done. McCaffery himself was losing patience
with his superiors. At the very least, he stressed, a symbolic drop
would help – 'start a snowball rolling,' he said – with the partisans.[32]

But this was an issue completely outside his control. Although he
could and did pass on Damiani's pleas for help, SOE controlled no
aircraft of its own and was entirely dependent on the few planes
provided for such purposes which, until January 1944, were all based
in North Africa. These consisted of one Royal Air Force squadron
(No. 624) of Halifax bombers and a Polish flight (No. 1586) of two
Liberators and four Halifaxes, and were mostly reserved for missions
to France and Poland respectively. So new demands for Italy had to
compete with well-established requirements elsewhere. Even if
planes were available, the weather did not always oblige. Only a few
nights in any month were suitable anyway, even if the weather *was*
good. In the event, poor conditions prevented any drops in November,
and it was only on 23 December 1943 that the first successful one
took place.[33]

The Italian anti-Fascists suspected, then and later, that the delays
were political in nature, caused by their hostility to the King and
Badoglio. But this was emphatically not the case. Whatever stance
Parri and company took on the monarchy, in early December
Roseberry, McCaffery and Gubbins all agreed that this should *not*
affect their decisions about providing support, and they put their
money where their mouth was by giving Damiani three million lire.
Nonetheless, the tenor of meetings with the Italians in Lugano
remained constant, with the CLN representatives invariably asking
for more – and more *now* – and McCaffery explaining the limits of
what the allies could provide. 'We strongly supported [the Italians]

behind their backs,' explained McCaffery later, 'and scolded them vigorously to their faces. In one somewhat heated meeting with Party representatives in Lugano I told them that Allen [Dulles] and I were the only two Italians in the room, because we were the only ones who were not motivated by sectional interests and who saw Italy as one sole piece on the international checker-board.' Such plain speaking inevitably left the Italians feeling bruised, and nourished the grievances of those who wished to think ill of the allies.[34]

Despite all this, however, the information provided by the Italians via McCaffery helped build up a picture of the growing popular resistance to the Germans in northern Italy. Max Salvadori, who by now was recovering from the injury he'd incurred the month before, found himself in Algiers in mid-December, talking to Italian volunteers recruited by Gentili and Garosci who were waiting to be parachuted behind the lines. 'With the news that reaches us here from France and Switzerland,' he recorded in his diary, 'one gets a more complete picture of the C.L.N. and Partisan activities. Evidently the C.L.N. are consolidating, and there are the beginnings of some cohesion between what previously were innumerable separate initiatives ... there are more Partisan groups than we had thought.'[35] Nonetheless, there remained significant gaps in SOE's understanding of the CLN structure and the relationship between various regions and groups, and hence an understandable reluctance to commit themselves to any large-scale assistance.

The final channel of communication with Italy established by McCaffery was through General Bianchi, the Italian military attaché in Berne. On Mussolini's downfall, the general had made a public declaration that his oaths of loyalty were to his king and country and that this was the way he intended it to remain. Shortly afterwards, Brigadier Henry Cartwright, the British military attaché and a legendary First World War escapee, who had known Bianchi before the war, brought him to the legation. 'We were extremely chary of him but all our checks gave the same satisfactory answer and eventually we began to use him as a whole-time collaborator,' recalled McCaffery. Bianchi's transmitter did 'yeoman work' for contacts with Italian officials in Bari and Rome, the Italian supreme command, and contacts in the field. Bianchi and his assistant, Major Davveri, organised lines of communication to the 'Green Flames', bands with

no obvious political affiliation and formed mostly of army men –
predominantly Alpini, the elite mountain warfare soldiers of the
Italian Army, whose collar patch gave the movement its name. From
the ranks of Italian officers interned in Switzerland after the
armistice, Bianchi and Davveri selected several to cross back into
Italy and join the partisans.[36]

It was not until March 1944 that McCaffery found suitable accommodation for his agents. This was a house in Berne that inevitably
became known to those who used it as the Casa Rossi, after the cover
name he used for his dealings with the Italians. 'I needed the right
kind of place,' he recalled, 'to be able to put people up and ... found
it in a commodious chalet-type house standing in its own grounds
on the edge of town ... Its position prevented any overlooking or
unobtrusive watching; it had a rear entrance which came up through
a wood, bringing a road at a considerable distance from the normal
approach road.' Ex-POWs also provided him with a staff that was
both British and hand-picked. The traffic that passed through it, he
later recalled, was 'unremitting and intense, and most of it came
from Italy. [To it] came our numerous couriers; delegates from Milan,
from Turin, from Lugano; [and] our own agents and British Liaison
Officers ...'[37]

One of the first Italians to arrive was the 28-year-old army officer
Lieutenant Edgardo Sogno, who left a compelling account of his
introductory cloak-and-dagger encounter with McCaffery in the
middle of April. After a seven-hour train journey via the St Gotthard
Pass from Lugano, he arrived in the Swiss capital shortly before nine
o'clock in the evening. In the main subway of the station, at the
foot of the exit stairs, he saw a large brightly illuminated adver-
tisement for Caran d'Ache pencils. In Lugano his contact had told
him to look out here for a man wearing black, holding an umbrella
and reading the *Gazette de Lausanne*. When the swarm of passengers thinned out, Sogno saw the man bent at an angle leaning on
his umbrella. It was Julian Hall.

The British officer led him out into the medieval centre of the
Swiss capital and the cobbled Neuengasse with its arcaded shops.
They walked for a while in silence down various side streets and on
to the riverside embankment beside the fast-flowing River Aare.

Here they paused for a while. It was pitch-dark and there was an icy wind. A tall slim woman appeared from nowhere. Without stopping she simply said: 'All clear.'

When they reached 32 Alexanderweg, a manservant in a white jacket opened the door. 'In the small hall,' recalled Sogno,

I was startled by the many Alpine hunting trophies. There were the heads and horns of deer, chamois and mountain goats everywhere. A door opened and a square, supple man of moderate height came out. He had a wide, sanguine face, a frank expression and penetrating eyes. It was McCaffery. He shook my hand and slapped me on the shoulder with his other hand, exclaiming 'Well done. You are just as I imagined you to be' . . . Although he talked through his clenched jaw, his Italian was perfect, nearly without accent.

We went into the living room. There was a lighted fire, a few book cases full of books, walls covered in dark wood and some leather armchairs.

'Would you like a Martini?' asked McCaffery.

'Yes, thank you.' I stretched myself out with my glass in my hand. I had the feeling of being at home with friends. On top of a small, low table, I saw an open book on the works of Shakespeare.

He picked it up. 'It's Julian who recites,' McCaffery said. 'You should hear him. Hall smiled but said nothing. McCaffery then stood up, abruptly put his glass down and stood in front of me, forefinger pointing. 'How is your mother?' he enquired.

I looked at him uncomprehendingly. He continued to stare at me with a half smile but still did not lower his hand. Then suddenly I remembered. It was a coded message.

'Wait a minute,' I replied. 'I will say it now. Wait. At least I think I remember that Manolo came into it . . . I detest Manolo.'

'Well done. Now I'm sure you are who you say you are.'

Having cleared the security test, as well as some far more extensive interrogation by McCaffery, a few days later Sogno passed back across the frontier along an 'official' route that was recognised by Swiss intelligence, and where Captain Guido Bustelli facilitated many of the crossings. Here, Sogno was destined to become SOE's 'star turn' in northern Italy.[38]

Born in Turin, Sogno was a dyed-in-the-wool loyalist to the Savoy dynasty, had fought in Spain alongside the nationalist forces of General Franco, and had been stationed in Nice with Italian occupation troops. Immediately following the armistice, however, he left Turin to join Badoglio's army staff in Brindisi, and he was soon picked up through SIM as a volunteer to go back into northern Italy under allied auspices. He was teamed up with another Italian Army officer and an Italian radio operator, sent to Massingham in Algiers for parachute training and despatch, and dropped blind into Piedmont in early December.

But having lost their radio set during the drop, they decided to go their own separate ways and Sogno devoted himself to 'activist' work rather than intelligence gathering. Politically a Liberal, he became the party representative on the military committee of the Committee of National Liberation in Turin. He also worked closely with the Otto group in Genoa and was visiting the Ligurian city when its members were rounded up by the Gestapo on Friday 31 March 1944. Arrested along with them, and found with several incriminating documents in his possession, before being interrogated he managed to break out from the Gestapo HQ by prising apart the bars of a lavatory window, escaping, and subsequently making his way to Milan. On the same day, the Turin military committee was also arrested, and four of its members were shot. In the aftermath of these disasters, Sogno resolved to rebuild the Otto group and was also asked by the CLNAI in Milan to pursue funding and other subjects with McCaffery in Switzerland.

Sogno's personality and skills being most obviously attuned to the interests of SOE, McCaffery agreed that he should pass to the control of No. 1 Special Force. This visit to McCaffery was crucial, for he was able to give SOE its first direct insight into the state of the resistance and German counter-measures in north-west Italy, especially the repercussions of the Otto arrests in Genoa. He stayed three weeks, during which he also recruited several supporters for his networks from an Italian officers' internment camp at Mürren in Switzerland.

Then, on 8 May 1944, bearing a letter from McCaffery to Alfredo Pizzoni, the chairman of the CLNAI, he recrossed the border back into Italy. He carried with him his directives from SOE. These were to thoroughly train all reception committees and prepare for wide-spread action when the time came. In the meantime, however, he was to exercise 'maximum restraint' except for small raids to secure arms and materiel. When the moment for action came, the resist-ance was to cause continuous and widespread disruption of railways and the cutting of telephone lines. The main railway and road targets were Genoa–Nice, Genoa–Turin, Turin–Ventimiglia, Turin–Modena, Turin–Aosta, and Turin–Savona – i.e. in north-west Italy, where disruption would prevent or delay the Germans from sending rein-forcements to France in response to the allied landings in Normandy.[39]

# CHAPTER FIVE

# Behind the lines

By now, the allied armies were finally closing in on Rome, months after first landing on the Italian mainland, when they had hoped to take the capital within weeks. The gruelling winter campaign had mocked the notion of Italy as the 'soft underbelly' of Europe, and little had gone right since the fall of Naples in early October. Under orders from Hitler, Field Marshal Albert Kesselring, commander-in-chief of Army Group C, who was defending Italy with more than twenty divisions, conducted an obstinate fighting retreat, and by early January his forces were securely dug in along a line of defences north of Naples known as the Gustav Line. Its key defensive position was the Cassino Massif dominated by the old Benedictine monastery of Monte Cassino, and was constructed up to fortress strength.

In January 1944 Hitler declared that with the battle for Rome about to begin all officers and men of the Wehrmacht should demonstrate a 'fanatical will' to end it victoriously, and promised that a merciless battle would be waged against all those who failed in 'the decisive hour'. Between 12 January and 18 May 1944 four great battles were fought at Cassino before the allies finally overwhelmed the heights of the monastery and an officer of Lieutenant General Anders's Polish II Corps triumphantly raised a pennant of the 12th Podolski Reconnaissance Regiment above the ruins. With a quarter of a million men killed or wounded, the struggle grimly recalled the bloodbaths of the First World War and the Western Front.[1]

The slowness of the allies' progress had its effects on SOE. Apart from its boat operations up the Adriatic coast and those of Andrew

Croft's flotilla out of Corsica, in the weeks following Salerno one of its principal early goals had been to contact the Committee of National Liberation in Rome, on the assumption both that it formed the 'central brain' of Italian resistance and that it could play a valuable local role in the liberation of the city by the allied armies. Accordingly, throughout the autumn of 1943, Malcolm Munthe and his Vigilant mission had spent considerable time and effort trying to infiltrate Italians through the lines. But early December found Max Salvadori lamenting the lack of success that was 'preying' on their minds, while the increasingly costly nature of their efforts was made deadly clear by the fate of his own mission a few days later, which ended in the death of one of the Italian agents and almost fatally wounded him.[2]

By the end of the year it was obvious that the usefulness of Vigilant was limited, and it was decided to close it down and transfer its personnel to No. 1 Special Force headquarters (Maryland) at Monopoli. Quite apart from the problems of infiltrating agents into Rome, the mission also now seemed superfluous given that Holdsworth's unit had become what even Munthe himself had to concede was a 'fine base HQ with all accessories such as Parachute, Packing Station, etc.' On Christmas Eve, he returned to Naples from a visit to Monopoli and sadly told his group 'We are obliterated.' Effective 10 January 1944, Vigilant ceased to exist.[3]

Yet this did not mean that SOE efforts to make contact with Rome were entirely abandoned or passed by default to the Americans, as suspected by Salvadori. On the contrary, while he was still digesting the news, Holdsworth threw him a crumb. Along with Munthe, Michael Gubbins and another Vigilant officer, Captain Pickering, he would form a small advance party to proceed to Rome with the US Fifth Army. Included in the group were two Italians, one of whom was Alberto Tarchiani.

Holdsworth made it clear to Salvadori that he would now be responsible to him, and that he would be expected to spend sufficient time at the Maryland base to keep him fully informed about his work. He would, however, be free to travel whenever and wherever his work required in order to recruit new personnel for active SOE work behind the lines, and to acquire, develop and maintain contacts useful to Maryland's immediate aims in Italy. He could also assist by – the words were Holdsworth's own – 'enhancing British prestige and . . . building up pro-British feeling with those elements who are likely to be powerful in post-war Italy'. This was the first explicit evidence that SOE's thoughts were already turning towards peace and the future political shape of Italy. Along with the rest of his remit, it gave Salvadori an exceptionally wide-ranging brief that he would use to the full.

One aspect of his new task was clear. 'I was asked, among other things, to engage in recruiting of a type different from the one in which AM61 [De Haan] was engaged,' he commented later. 'The Country Section of Maryland had been recruiting only one type of agent, the one provided by SIM . . . I was under the impression that it had been a mistake to ask SIM agents to contact the Committees of the National Front of Liberation in German-occupied Italy. A SIM agent represented the Government of Marshal Badoglio, a Government which was despised . . .' As a result, Salvadori promptly met Action Party leaders in Naples to help him find agents willing to contact party groups in German-occupied territory. He soon became frustrated, however, with Maryland's response to his initiatives. Having found four possible groups of agents, he was told by De Haan that there were already so many agents from SIM that there was no room for anyone else. After visiting them, Salvadori also concluded that the SOE schools being established in the Brindisi area were organised exclusively for training of what he termed 'a military type', thus excluding those 'devoid of a military mentality'. All in all, he concluded, the Italian section at Maryland had effectively become a captive of SIM and thus he was wasting his time having anything to do with it. 'The longer I stayed away from [it], the better it was,' he concluded bitterly.[4]

The renewed hope in the New Year of getting Italian agents into Rome was sparked by the decision of the top allied commanders in Italy at a meeting chaired by Churchill in Carthage on Christmas Day to bypass the Gustav Line and pave the way for a rapid advance to the Italian capital with a daring amphibious landing at Anzio, 32 kilometres south of the Eternal City.

Munthe was making his own plans for reaching Rome when he was briefed about the Anzio landing by Admiral Morse. Immediately he decided to jettison his scheme and sail instead with the invasion

force. On 18 January 1944 he was summoned to Fifth Army headquarters at Caserta, where he received instructions to warn 'all and
any organisations you have in Rome to do their damnedest'. Four
days later, as the first allied troops were landing unopposed on the
Anzio beaches, Maryland sent a signal to resistance contacts in the
city to cut all communications and hinder the Germans' mobility
on all roads outside of the capital 'to the utmost capacity of the
patriot forces'. Munthe's group landed just north of Anzio equipped
with a couple of jeeps and a radio set, whose operator, Corporal
William Pickering (no relation to Captain Pickering), left a vivid
account of their landing in heavy seas under fierce Luftwaffe attack.
They expected to be in Rome within a week.[5]

But Anzio did not go according to plan and the allies were to
remain trapped within its perimeter until late May, beached, in
Churchill's caustic words, like a stranded whale. A setback for allied
strategy, the results for SOE also proved tragic.

The effort to harass the Germans during the landings inflicted a
heavy price on the resistance in the capital, with mass arrests and
the loss of radio contact with Maryland. As a result, Munthe's top
priority became the reopening of contact with the capital. Salvadori
by this time had fallen seriously ill with jaundice and was sent back
to hospital in Naples. Pickering, the only German-speaker in the
group, was fully occupied interrogating German prisoners of war
and compiling intelligence reports. This left Munthe and Michael
Gubbins, aged 22, to get on with the task.

One day, they found an Italian who claimed to know a route
through to Rome by which he had travelled only two days before.
After checking out his credentials, Munthe decided to despatch him
back through the lines on a test run which, if it failed, would do
no damage to the mission. Having spent considerable time reconnoitring the front, he decided to try and get the man across on a
section of the line being held by the Sixth Gordon Highlanders
with whom, by happy coincidence, he had served at the beginning
of the war and who were all too willing to help him. The first
attempt failed, and they made a second effort on Sunday 6 February,
when a lull set in after several days of bitter fighting. Munthe's
official report tells what happened next:

We tried to get our man over again, going to fetch him in a cave where the Irish Guards were holding him for us. This necessitated going right forward in a fairly exposed position as our line must have come back a bit though I did [not] realise this at the time. Michael was with me and asked to accompany me as he had drawn the map showing the exact route by which to avoid enemy positions, he thought he could explain it to our man better than I could. He hated to be kept back at any time. It was Sunday afternoon about four o' clock and quite peaceful, and so sunny, I remember, that we sat on the grass to eat our rations, and read a letter he had just got from home. For the first time, I believe, I agreed that second-in-command should come forward at the same time as myself and we walked past the Guards H.Q. and got into a ditch by the side of the road behind the 'factory' [in fact, a ruined church and belfry]. Being thus out of view of the enemy we crept forward. Suddenly, the 'moaning minnies' [*nebelwerfer*, German multi-barrelled rocket artillery launchers that emitted a high-pitched scream] started; mortar shells fell around pretty thickly so we got into a disused slit-trench, Michael as usual in a hot spot, humming the old rhyme 'Abdul the Bull-Bull' as calmly as ever. We crouched in that trench for about ten minutes [and] earth seemed to be flying everywhere. Then something fell right into our trench and Michael was killed instantly. His helmet had come off and his eyes were open, but he was not suffering any more when I called him and shook his shoulders. I went to find a Red Cross van at the crossroads. When they came to Michael they said they could not take him with us and as I could not see much then I asked them to lift me to him so as to make sure they were right. He was undoubtedly beyond help. The mortaring then started again and I have no further recollection of what happened until four days later Pickering found me in the American Casualty Clearing Station.

With shrapnel wounds in his skull and chest, temporarily blind in one eye and nursing several broken fingers, the badly wounded Munthe was stranded for several days in the field hospital at Anzio before eventually being sent back to Naples and hospital, where he stayed for several weeks. From there he was shipped to Algiers and eventually back to England. For Munthe, his war was largely over, and it was left to Pickering to wind up the ill-fated mission.[6]

News about his son's death was cabled back to Major General

Gubbins in London, where he had just returned from yet another tour of inspection of SOE's Mediterranean stations. The officer on weekend duty placed the telegram with its 'killed in action' message about his son in Gubbins's in-tray on top of a pile of operational files, and marked it 'deepest sympathy'. Normally, the SOE director's private secretary or military assistant would have been there first thing the next morning, and thus able to soften the blow. But Gubbins came in early to work quietly on the files before a chiefs of staff meeting that afternoon where SOE's organisation in the Mediterranean was on the agenda. 'Overwhelmed by grief and remorse,' write his biographers, 'he steeled himself to attend the . . . meeting . . . His contribution to the discussion . . . could only have been perfunctory.' His son's death, he remarked later, was 'totally useless'.[7]

Back at Maryland, Holdsworth and No. 1 Special Force continued their operations within guidelines set by Baker Street. Here, Roseberry had now returned from his lengthy autumn stay in Italy and was focusing his efforts on strengthening the links established by McCaffery with the rapidly growing resistance movement in northern Italy on the one hand, and with AFHQ and Holdsworth's Maryland group in the south on the other.

As the New Year opened, SOE's aims in Italy were spelled out firmly to McCaffery by Roseberry's immediate superior, Brigadier Eric Mockler-Ferryman, the director of western European operations and a personal friend of Gubbins who had previously headed the intelligence branch of Eisenhower's Anglo-American forces in North Africa. By now, eight W/T operators were reporting back to Maryland from behind-the-lines groups previously known to the Italian High Command or the Naples resistance committee, and a dozen more operators were about to complete their training. In addition, a hundred Italians who had been previously recruited to work *against* the British had volunteered to work *with* SOE against the Germans and were in their final stage of training, after which they could be delivered as instructors to resistance groups or as the nuclei of small sabotage groups. Within the next moon period, many would be infiltrated into German-occupied Italy south of Florence against targets selected by the military. After accomplishing their missions, they would be sent on to activist groups that could make use of them.[8]

Mockler-Ferryman, in tune with Gubbins's views, was anxious to integrate SOE's activities with the needs of the theatre command. This, of course, depended on McCaffery being able to provide details of the groups passed on to him by the CLNAI and other sources, along with addresses, passwords and details of their financial needs. This in itself would not be enough, however, because everything rested on being able to supply the resistance with weapons and sabotage material. Apart from the small-boat operations under way, this meant relying on airdrops. But so far, SOE had suffered from a severe shortage of aircraft as well as appalling winter weather that severely affected the handful of efforts that had been made. In the three months following September, only nine sorties had been flown by the Royal Air Force for SOE (and OSS) operations in Italy. By contrast, it was estimated that it would take forty sorties a month to provide all the sabotage parties they envisaged with the materiel required.

Thus, stressed Mockler-Ferryman, who was anxious to damp down any expectations by McCaffery's Italian contacts about the creation of some nationwide secret resistance army, 'Our operations will always be limited by the transport available and there are small prospects of being able to drop arms and supplies to support armies.' He defined the main objectives of SOE attention as the French border region, the Ligurian coast, the Brenner Pass and the area bounded by Leghorn, Bologna, Rimini, Rome and Ancona, 'with special attention to coastal and transverse railroads'. Like much of SOE's planning for Italy in the first half of 1944, this reflected the long-term aim of contributing to 'Overlord' – the Normandy invasion – by hampering and diverting the Germans in Italy at the time of the 'Anvil' landings in southern France.[9]

One point Mockler-Ferryman went out of his way to make clear, however, was that while 'the political and guerrilla groups' in northern Italy would become important if the Italian front stabilised again after the fall of Rome – or indeed if the Germans opted for a sudden pull-out from Italy altogether, where the resistance could perform valuable harassing operations – it was the requirements of 'the immediate future' that would have the first call on SOE's available resources. In other words, the unremitting pressure by the

CLNAI through McCaffery in Switzerland for the arming of the resistance in northern Italy would have to take second place to the more immediate needs of SOE and the allies elsewhere. At this stage of the campaign, sabotage and harassing operations were considered more important than partisan warfare. Overall, Baker Street's assessment in early 1944 was that the strategic value of Italian resistance groups was low, and that any assistance provided by SOE would be used mainly to keep them in existence rather than to bring them to action. Support for them should, therefore, 'be given a low priority'.[10]

One of the greatest problems for SOE over the next few months lay in piecing together an accurate picture of the resistance in Italy and deciding on priorities. In dozens of telegrams, McCaffery reported to Baker Street what both Parri and Damiani were telling him about various groups and their activities, and in turn he passed on to them requests from No. 1 Special Force and Allied Forces Headquarters for more detailed information about such matters as likely dropping zones and the links between the myriad groups. The Italians continued to vent their frustration about the shortage of, or delays in, drops, and McCaffery tried to mollify them while simultaneously venting his own frustration to his superiors. The north Italians, he pointed out to Baker Street, had courageously helped escaping prisoners of war, were eager to join the anti-Fascist fight and needed support and encouragement to maintain morale. 'Hope we don't miss another bus for lack of imagination and foresight or for preconceived ideas,' he wrote after receiving one lengthy telegram from London explaining delays.

Not surprisingly, it proved difficult to shift Parri from his determined view that allied behaviour had some sinister explanation – either a conscious decision to withhold support and/or a deliberate rejection of the 'central bodies' – i.e. the CLNs – being set up by the Italians. Based in Milan, he also complained that the resistance in neighbouring Piedmont was 'anti-Milanese' and had received 'excessive' drops, that Turin was offering passive resistance to his plans and that 'vital' sectors like the Lombardy Alps had received no airdrops at all. Not surprisingly, activists in Piedmont had their own grievances to air against Parri and his particular regional perspective.[11]

But the frustration was not all one-sided. London had to point out the 'low strategic value' of many of the groups concerned, which meant that their demands for supplies and weapons could simply not be met, as well as the fact that Italy was 'a newcomer' in the game of requesting special-duties flights that were being heavily stretched by demands from across the Mediterranean. It was also obvious that the CLN movement was scarred by much factional in-fighting, which hardly gave the allies reason to risk life and limb in supporting them.[12]

Nor were the Italians always quick to give the allies information that they urgently requested. In late March, for example, following several requests, London was complaining bitterly about Damiani. 'His inability to furnish safe houses and contacts in Italy throws doubts [on] his standing with the CLNs,' Roseberry remarked acidly to McCaffery. 'By now we should have been provided with such in all principal towns and districts; we have to press on with internal organisations so that all [is] tied up ready for The Day and in particular we need organisation of special reception committees at all key points; for this, our pioneer infiltrees must have safe contacts.'[13]

Italy, as Baker Street constantly had to insist, was not the only country in early 1944 served by its Mediterranean-based support services that required attention. Resistance in Greece, Yugoslavia and Albania was growing apace; the Maquis in southern France was assuming greater and greater importance as D-Day approached; and from bases across southern Italy an increasing number of special-duties flights were being sent to central European countries such as Czechoslovakia, Hungary and, above all, Poland. Holdsworth and No. 1 Special Force in Monopoli were all too aware of this. SOE's Advance Force 133 in charge of Balkan operations was based at nearby Bari, and in add-ition to its Italian tasks Maryland itself was responsible for providing administrative and equipment facilities for the Polish and Czech units stationed nearby, as well as for supplies required by the 'Clowder' party, a mission under London's direct control aimed at penetrating the southern fringes of Hitler's Reich across the Austrian–Slovenian border.[14]

To help bring focus to these disparate SOE efforts in the Mediterranean, Gubbins flew out to Italy in late January 1944 to discuss how they could best be integrated with the plans of the theatre command. The result was the creation of Special Operations Mediterranean (SOM), under Major General William Stawell, located at Mola di Bari between Brindisi and Bari and directly responsible to the supreme commander in the Mediterranean, General Maitland Wilson. However, in the words of W. J. M. Mackenzie, 'its military position remained obscure. On the one hand, there was a staff branch (G3 Special Operations Section) in AFHQ, under an American Brigadier-General, who was interposed between SOM and [the Supreme Allied Commander] as co-ordinator of SOM's requirements with those of other "special" formations – secret intelligence, psychological warfare, strategic deceptions and so forth. On the other hand, SOM had only limited control over its own lower formations, which looked for operational directives to various other commanders and were on the administrative side very well-accustomed to look after themselves . . . HQ SOM remained a good idea in theory which came too late in a period of rapid movement to have much chance of finding its feet.' In short, the creation of this bureaucratic behemoth made little practical difference to the work of No. 1 Special Force. Lieutenant Colonel J. G. Beevor, who had previously represented SOE in Portugal, was sent out by Baker Street to help planning at SOM and later wrote its internal history. 'It is to be hoped in the interest of posterity,' he declared crisply, 'that no similar set-up will ever again recur since it may be said with confidence that the set-up . . . involved problems of remote control which in any future war should be guarded against with every care.'[5]

This organisational upheaval also coincided with the transfer of all aircraft in North Africa specifically earmarked for special duties to Brindisi, where they were combined with a squadron from the Middle East to form 334 Wing. Even then, however, the gains for Italy were limited. Within a month, one of its component squadrons was returned to North Africa to fly exclusively to southern France and was replaced by a smaller squadron whose principal destination at first was the Balkans.[6]

By early May, as the allies readied themselves for a renewed spring offensive, both McCaffery and Holdsworth began to receive directives for mobilising their behind-the-lines contacts when, but only when, the campaign began. Targets were given, along with the messages that would be broadcast over the BBC to mobilise action. *'Avete visto la primula rosa?'* ('Have you seen the scarlet pimpernel?') meant 'Make sure your plans well advanced,' and *'Avete comprato il vestito rosso?'* ('Have you bought the red dress?') instructed them to 'continue your special work until fresh instructions given.' Maryland was also told to submit plans to support the Allied Armies in Italy on and after the start of the offensive. They should concentrate in particular on north-west Italy and the Apennines, and should include the establishment of W/T links with all fighting groups across the north and centre of the country, as well as the provision (stressed once again) of safe houses and passwords for agents and W/T operators.[17]

With the arrival of better spring weather and air crews now benefiting from hard-won experience, airdrops to Italy were also beginning to prove more successful. In April, some 45 tons of arms, explosives, food and clothing were delivered to behind-the-lines groups, and during the first week of May Maryland could count on fifty dropping zones. Contact with resistance groups was also maintained through Radio Bari. This was a station under allied control from which, every night at 2030 GMT, a special resistance programme, produced jointly by No. 1 Special Force and the Political Warfare Board Executive, was broadcast throughout Italy. It was through this link that general directives were sent to resistance groups, and that reception committees were alerted to impending supply drops. It would also be the means by which the resistance in general would be ordered to act when the signal was given.[18]

Throughout the winter, with allied forces bogged down along the Gustav Line, the fragmentary nature of SOE's knowledge of Italian resistance groups had not been of major significance. But now things had changed and the resistance was poised to make an important contribution to the allied effort. SOE's action in Italy was guided by allied strategy, the goal of which remained, as it always had been, to force Kesselring to commit the maximum number of divisions there when Overlord took place in early June. This meant destroying as many enemy formations in Italy as possible to force the Germans to replace them from elsewhere. For maximum effect, this should begin some three weeks before the launching of Overlord.

Codenamed 'Diadem', Alexander's offensive in Italy opened on 11 May. One of its subsidiary components was a sabotage operation to cut all road and rail communications in a belt across Italy, from La Spezia on the west coast to Rimini on the Adriatic.

By 4 June, when Rome fell to Mark Clark's Fifth Army, Alexander's forces in Italy had scored a considerable victory and met the goal of holding a large number of divisions away from Overlord. 'Morale is irresistibly high as a result of recent successes,' reported Alexander on the day that Eisenhower's allied forces landed on the beaches in Normandy. 'Neither the Apennines nor even the Alps should prove a serious obstacle to [the allied armies'] enthusiasm and skill.' He estimated that he could reach Florence in the second half of July, and that by mid-August he would be able to attack the Gothic Line, another of Kesselring's formidable defensive lines, this one stretching from north of Pisa to just south of Rimini.[19]

Typical of the many operations carried out by SOE to support the allies' offensive was the Eighth Army's thrust in the direction of Arezzo and the dropping of twelve detachments, each of four SOE-trained saboteurs, to attack enemy communications. Each detachment carried eight prepared charges. The report of one of the saboteurs tells how the charges were used:

The four of us were dropped blind near Arezzo with orders to blow up the railway line in the district at two points. As soon as we landed safely we took the explosive from the package and divided it evenly between us. We then set out in pairs for our objectives, which were in the opposite direction. It was early morning by now and my companion and I hid in a near-by wood during the day. We placed our charges on the line towards 23.00 hours in readiness for the 23.30 train. We then moved off across country as quickly as possible, and soon heard a terrible explosion. Later we learned that a goods train had been completely wrecked at this point. My companion and I decided to return through the lines to our Command and offer ourselves for a further mission. On the way south we were stopped and taken to the Police Station of a small town by the Brigadiere who, in the presence of a German official, loudly accused us of train-wrecking and ordered us to present ourselves at the prison of a neighbouring town. He then proceeded to divert the German's attention with a bottle of wine and told us in whispers a safe way through the line. We eventually succeeded in crossing and presented ourselves with pride to the first British sentry.[20]

With the liberation of the whole of northern Italy suddenly in prospect, it was obvious that SOE's effort in Italy was poised for a significant new phase. The day before Diadem was launched Max Salvadori, now in Naples, observed that, thanks to the reports flooding in from Switzerland, SOE was beginning to get a clearer idea of the situation in the occupied north of the country. 'There are Partisan bands in nearly all the valleys of the Apennines and Alps,' he noted with satisfaction. 'I should not be surprised if there comes a time when the Resistance will keep more Germans and Social Republic troops engaged than Allied troops do.'[21] On the day Rome was liberated Gubbins urged Holdsworth to seize the initiative. 'At this time it is desperately important to encourage resistance in North Italy by every means possible,' he told him, 'as great things can undoubtedly come from it.' Maryland now suggested that the best way to find out what was really happening behind the lines, and in turn to interpret allied goals clearly to resistance groups, was to send in allied liaison officers. In fact, Holdsworth told London, No. 1 Special Force had already lined up eight to ten such parties for June and July and agreed on a provisional division of labour with an 'enthusiastic' OSS. The Americans would focus on Siena and Florence, and SOE on Ancona, La Spezia and Piedmont. Both organisations could work Lombardy and Venice.[22]

Holdsworth's proposal reflected long-standing pressure from the special operations branch at AFHQ. Since at least March it had been expressing concern at the extent to which Maryland's plans depended on the use of Italian personnel in the field, and had been pressing for British officers to be recruited for its operations. Gubbins, not surprisingly, was enthusiastic, possibly spurred on by another visit to Italy in May when he met up with Dodds-Parker and senior military figures to discuss, yet again, SOE operations in the Mediterranean and the Balkans. 'I am quite convinced,' he declared, 'that the time has come when we ought to send in British officers as BLOs [British Liaison Officers] to activate all guerrilla activities and try to effect some co-ordination and also facilitate the matter of supply.' The next day, Baker Street sent a signal to Holdsworth. 'Now is the time to despatch BLOs,' it told him. 'Do all you can ... keep us posted with progress.' Back in October, McCaffery's deputy, Peter Jellinek, had floated this idea during the initial discussions on liaising with the Italian resistance, with the model in mind of the small army of F Section agents already operating in France. Now this, at least a modified version of it, was about to become reality in Italy. The one thing that London insisted on was that the BLOs concerned should be individuals 'with personality and a knowledge of SOE work and aims and [be] capable of assuming leadership'. Anything but first-class officers, it warned Holdsworth, 'would do harm'.

Support for the idea was also stimulated by a report from two senior British officers who had escaped from a POW camp at the time of the armistice but only recently crossed the lines. Brigadiers J. B. Combe and E. Todhunter had spent months in northern Italy in contact with the partisans and believed they could be exploited 'with excellent results' but only if they were under allied control. 'Any suggestion that they should work under the control of Badoglio or the King will produce no results at all,' they insisted. Senior British officers should be sent to them with wireless sets, arms and explosives.[23]

According to Todhunter, they were both flown to London and taken directly to see the prime minister to be interviewed about the strength of the resistance in Northern Italy. Churchill 'was sitting up in bed in a silk dressing gown with Chinese dragons all over it — a glass of brandy and a cigar in his hand,' Todhunter told his son later. 'He had read the report and completely mastered it, cutting them short if they repeated what was in it and asking about endless details.' If the prime minister harboured any worries about Communist influence over the resistance he can only have been reassured by what he read. 'It is our considered opinion,' stated the two senior officers, 'that no danger need be apprehended of a Communist rising or civil war after the war as a result of arming these so-called Communist bands.' In the meantime, they concluded, the partisans could provide 'an excellent dividend' to the allies both before and after the occupation of Italy — provided they were under allied and not Italian (i.e. Badogliani) control.[24]

*    *    *

If the winter had turned into a slogging match for the allied armies, it severely tested the mettle of the nascent Italian resistance. In late December the Germans launched the first of a series of *rastrellamenti* (literally, 'rakings') against partisan groups throughout the north, especially in Piedmont and Venetia, that threatened their very survival. Then, in late March, they smashed both the Genoa-based Otto group as well as the Turin-based regional military command for Piedmont, and followed this in April by a further devastating series of punitive *rastrellamenti* throughout Piedmont and Venetia, this time assisted by Marshal Graziani's Fascist Italian forces. In these campaigns, writes one historian of the resistance, 'the Germans introduced new raking techniques, often with stunning results. In south-western Piedmont, for instance, they employed an entire division for the combings and blocked off whole valleys with the goal of either destroying or dispersing the troublesome partisans.'[25]

In the towns and cities as well, the tempo of resistance grew. On 1 March, thanks to weeks of planning by the CLNAI, several hundred thousand workers downed tools in all the major Italian cities in the north such as Turin, Milan, Genoa, Bologna, Florence and Venice. For a week, virtually all production came to a halt, although the strike failed to win much support from employees in public services such as the railways, telephones, electricity and gas plants, as well as newspapers. Nonetheless, it was an impressive demonstration of dissent and the Germans reacted accordingly: some two thousand labour leaders were seized and hauled off to Mauthausen, Buchenwald, Dachau and Auschwitz.

By the late winter, the Germans were so worried by spreading Italian resistance that they began to resort to more extreme measures, provoked by a campaign of assassinations directed against leading Fascist and German targets by militant groups of the mostly Communist GAP (Gruppi di Azione Patriottica), small groups of youthful activists, both male and female, operating in the country's major cities. The most widely publicised killing was that of Giovanni Gentile, the neo-Hegelian and self-proclaimed 'philosopher of Fascism', ghostwriter of Mussolini's *The Doctrine of Fascism*, and one-time member of the Fascist Grand Council, who was gunned down while walking along a street in Florence. But there were many others, especially in the capital. On 18 March, Max Salvadori sombrely noted in his diary that Nazi and Fascist repression had seriously worsened in Rome. 'The front is near and the Germans mean business,' he recorded. 'The firing squads are constantly at work.'[26]

Five days later, a GAP squad in Rome killed thirty-three members of a German security police detachment with a bomb concealed in a street cleaner's cart as it marched along the Via Rasella in the heart of the city. An infuriated Hitler ordered severe retribution and it was decided that ten Italians should be shot for every German soldier killed, meaning a total of 330 in all. The victims were selected from amongst dissidents already held in prison as well as others specifically rounded up to fulfil the target, including a large number of Jews. The following day, a convoy of lorries drove them out in batches to the Ardeatine caves on the southern outskirts of the city.

In post-war testimony at his trial, Herbert Kappler, the 35-year-old head of the Rome Gestapo, described what happened next:

At about 1400 hours the first transports began to move and I, and a number of my men, went to the cave. As each truck arrived at the cave the persons concerned, always five at a time and each accompanied by an SS man, were led to the end of the cave. All persons had their hands tied behind their backs. At the end of the cave the five were made to kneel down together, and at the given order they were shot in the back of the head by the accompanying SS men at short range. The next five were shot by officers, and I was one of these officers. After the execution of each five, the five SS men went to the exit and brought in the next five victims.

The executions went on until about eight-thirty in the evening. Amongst the victims was Colonel Montezemolo of the 'Rudder' group, who had been captured in January and severely and continuously tortured by the SD at the Gestapo interrogation centre on the Via Tasso. Heroically, he never talked.[27]

Despite – or perhaps because of – this and other severe reprisals, as well as the many savage *rastrellamenti* launched by Kesselring's forces, the number of armed resistance members in German-occupied Italy grew, so that by May there were some 70,000 guerrillas at work throughout the north, 'holding check,' claimed General

Alexander, on some six German divisions. Recruitment to the resistance was also helped when Mussolini's government responded to mounting pressure from the Germans for more Italian manpower by passing mobilisation decrees in February that impelled thousands of young Italian men to go underground.[28]

In March 1944, five days after the Ardeatine cave massacre, the chairman of the CLNAI in Milan, Alfredo Pizzoni (alias 'Pietro Longhi'), crossed the border into Switzerland with Giambattista Stucchi (alias 'Federici'), a lawyer and socialist from Monza who served on its military committee. Their mission had been agreed on by the committee at a meeting in Milan shortly beforehand.

Their passage was typical of many such clandestine crossings. Led by the most senior of the CLNAI's couriers, an architect by profession, they were driven in the car of another supporter, a doctor, to a point just beyond the town of Malnate, where they were passed on to another contact who handed them bicycles on which they rode along small tracks to a farmstead close to the frontier. Here they rested until dusk before proceeding cautiously on foot to the border fence. 'We exchanged signals with the Swiss customs officials,' recalled the 50-year-old Pizzoni, 'and after a quick dash in which I was the last to arrive – partly because I was inappropriately dressed – we arrived at the fence which had already been cut. We crawled underneath and were met by a customs official and farmer and with them arrived at a nearby house.' At this stage, they were greeted by the Swiss Army Captain Guido Bustelli. Indeed, the Swiss authorities not only turned a blind eye to much of this clandestine activity, but were actively complicit in it. After completing the necessary formalities at the closest customs post, the Italians were driven by car to a nearby village, where a meal and beds were waiting for them.

The next morning, they met up in a small square in the centre of Lugano with Luigi Casagrande, a former treasurer of the Milan CLN and a Liberal well known to Pizzoni, who was unhappy at Damiani's handling of communications and had asked Milan to intervene. Without further ado, he led them to the private residence of the SIS man in the city. Here, waiting for them, was McCaffery. On the agenda were several increasingly urgent issues affecting relations between SOE and the Italian resistance.[29]

Gradually, over the winter, tighter internal discipline and closer coordination of the armed resistance groups had developed, along with a vibrant clandestine press. A major step forward had come with the formation of the CLNAI at the end of January as the principal focal point for northern resistance activity as well as, at least in the eyes of its more militant members, a potential government-in-waiting representing all the major anti-Fascist political groups.

But military coordination was another matter, and no overall headquarters for the fighting forces of the CLN parties and the many autonomous groups had emerged. This was largely because of internal rivalries combined with the hope on the part of the Communists that their numerical superiority in the field would eventually lead, by default, to one of their own leading militants being chosen as the supreme military coordinator. So far as the link with the allies was concerned, since Feruccio Parri and Leo Valiani's meeting with McCaffery in September, this had remained largely a monopoly of Parri and his allies in the Action Party, with Damiani acting as their representative in Lugano. With the growing resistance clearly being of increasing value to the allies as they poised for the breakthrough to Rome, several key issues needed urgent clarification.

McCaffery, who had requested the meeting, came straight to the point with comments that took Pizzoni aback. The Italians in Lugano, and in particular Damiani, had frequently attempted to play SOE off against the OSS in their quest for support, and McCaffery now insisted bluntly that this would have to stop. Ultimately, he explained, the allies coordinated their policy in London and Washington, but at the operational level they had different methods and acted independently. So did the Italians wish to work with him, or with Dulles? They had to make up their minds, he said. Stucchi at least had been partially prepared for this ultimatum. Before leaving Milan he was briefed by Parri, who told him that if he was forced to choose, he should opt to work with SOE on the grounds that the British effectively controlled the Mediterranean and would be better placed to support them than the OSS.

The issue was also troubling Dulles, who was not present at the meeting. Indeed, McCaffery had explicitly declined the Italians' request for a joint meeting with him. Only the week before, the

American had complained to OSS headquarters in Algiers that no satisfactory division of labour had been decided between him and SOE. 'The latter,' he explained, 'is inclined to work on their own lines in absolute secrecy and [I] can appreciate the fact that, from the point of view of security, it would be bad policy to put all our eggs in one basket.' Had the field, he demanded to know, referring to Italy, 'been divided in any way between Zulu [SOE] and OSS?' If not, then he asked for instructions, because from the viewpoint of both safety and efficiency he felt that the number of services (couriers, etc.) operating from the Lugano area were far too numerous. McCaffery, he added by way of footnote, was 'very competent but he is not especially co-operative except following regular crackdowns by me, which are wasteful of time and energy'.[30]

McCaffery also seriously grilled Pizzoni and Stucchi about whether the CLNAI really had the authority over the resistance that it claimed. Many individuals who made contact with him in Switzerland, he told them, were either ignorant of the existence of local CLNs, or sometimes even hostile to them. He also expressed his frustration at the endless obsession of the Italians with politics, which intruded on every discussion. What mattered, he stressed, was military activity. In this respect, he was finding it increasingly difficult to work with Damiani, who tended to argue too much and 'in every matter introduced a political note'. As a result, misunderstandings had begun to occur that were good for neither SOE nor the CLNAI. What he omitted to tell the Italians, but secretly explained to Roseberry in London, was that he hoped to cut Damiani out altogether from his links with them.[31]

To this litany of complaints, the CLNAI representatives delivered a robust response. After twenty years of Fascism, they pointed out, political fervour and intense discussion were inevitable and besides, anti-Fascism was a common denominator which united a huge variety of groups that would otherwise be unlikely to work together. As for the authority of the CLNAI and its associated CLNs, this was demonstrably real, as proven by the huge numbers of former men and officers of the Italian Army who were happy to work with them.

This was a topic to which they returned more than once over the next few days. In the end, McCaffery was largely persuaded. But he made it clear that the allies did not expect a partisan army to fight a war with its own objectives, but instead to provide action-orientated mobile groups to work in conformity with directives based on European theatre strategic plans. In particular, according to Stucchi, he stressed the importance of intelligence on German activity, the sabotage of transport, communications and industrial plants working for the Germans, as well as some limited guerrilla operations to 'disorientate the enemy and disrupt vital points of his organisation'. He was also impressed by a map they brought from Parri showing the positions of partisan units in the north, as well as more extensive and detailed information carried by Stucchi.

By the time they had finished, a better understanding of each other's position and objectives had been established. Stucchi, who was initially sceptical of the British, was impressed by the Catholic and fluently Italian-speaking McCaffery. It had all been 'better than expected', he recorded, subsequently referring to SOE as being 'more engaged, efficient and secure' than the OSS. One further useful outcome was that McCaffery took time to explain and clarify the differing functions of SOE and SIS, and they agreed on procedures that would separate 'operational' (i.e. SOE) and intelligence (SIS) channels – the latter took part in all these discussions. McCaffery was particularly keen to ensure that, by contrast with the purely intelligence channel, all resistance-related material and its courier service should be unknown to the Swiss.[32]

In a lengthy message to London, which took him virtually all night to encipher, McCaffery reported the details of the new arrangements and concluded hopefully that, provided the separate but parallel liaison with the Italian military attaché General Bianchi ('Bernit') worked out, 'we shall have [the] entire resistance of all tendencies in our hands [at] this end.' In a second message, he passed on a full list of all potential dropping zones handed to him by Pizzoni and Stucchi along with a personal plea to provide 'the most and quickest drops possible'.[33]

Having strongly argued the CLNAI case, Pizzoni was nevertheless well aware that some of McCaffery's complaints were justified and that the Italians would have to meet him at least halfway. His own position was delicate. As chairman of the CLNAI, he had to balance the differing views of its various political parties and take a line broadly acceptable to them all, while simultaneously negotiating with McCaffery. Fortunately, he was exceptionally well qualified for the task.

With his experience in banking, Pizzoni had a good working knowledge of English and had briefly studied jurisprudence in Oxford and London. In 1944, he was 50 years old. His family background was military. His father had been a brigadier general during the First World War, and he himself was awarded the Medaglia d'Oro for services with the Bersaglieri (rifle regiment). Captured by the Austrians, he had made two efforts to escape before being repatriated in a prisoner exchange. He served again with the Bersaglieri in 1941, before being demobilised after the ship carrying him and his battalion from Taranto to North Africa was sunk by two British aircraft in January 1942. He had returned to the Credito Italiano and moved from its Genoa branch to its head office in Milan.

Liberal and a patriot of the old school, he slowly and reluctantly abandoned his faith in the monarchy. During the 'forty-five days' between Mussolini's fall and the armistice he emerged as one of the leading spirits of Milan's anti-Fascist Committee, became the chairman of its successor, the CLN, and then, in January 1944, was appointed chairman of the CLNAI. His military background meant that his protestations about the support enjoyed by local CLNs from former military officers and men carried some weight with McCaffery.

As a moderate, he was also acceptable to all factions of the CLNAI, especially the Liberals and Christian Democrats, as well as the Communists, who saw in him a useful ally in opposing Parri's tendency to monopolise relations with the allies. Another crucial factor was that he was fully familiar with the industrial and financial worlds of Italy, where he possessed genuine and influential friends who trusted and were willing to help him. This made him, writes one Italian historian, 'a kind of *fra Galdino* [Lady Bountiful] who knew very well on which doors to knock to fill his wallet with offers'.[34]

But Pizzoni did more than just help fill the coffers of the resistance. In effect he was its leader and organisational linchpin and, in Max Salvadori's words, 'the motor who ensured the proper functioning of the complex machine of the CLNAI.'[35] Crucially, he also established trust with the allies through his relationship with SOE's man in Berne. 'John McCaffery,' he recorded later, 'was always to us a very warm friend.' The feeling was reciprocated throughout SOE. 'A strong pro-British protagonist,' recorded an official post-war summary of his contribution, 'thoroughly sound and reliable.'[36]

It took another couple of months for the results of this crucial meeting to make themselves felt. The new arrangements sparked some furious protests from Parri and the Action Party, but Pizzoni, bolstered by McCaffery, pushed them through. By the middle of June, the 'awkward' Damiani had been replaced, the lines of communication between McCaffery and the CLNAI leadership sorted out, and the security of trans-border communications – where some of Damiani's methods had also sparked McCaffery's concern – tightened. By August a financial agreement was put in place that saw the allies providing ten million lire a month subsidy to the CLNAI, split fifty–fifty between SOE and OSS.[37]

Along with allied victories and the liberation of Rome, this all produced a noticeable shift of tone in relations between the CLNAI and SOE. Whereas before the Italians had loudly complained about what they saw as allied failings in providing support, now the CLNAI seemed almost apologetic in not being able to do more for the allies. 'If sometimes it seems to you that you are receiving from us less than you would expect,' wrote Pizzoni to McCaffery a week after the liberation of Rome, 'I ask you please to realise the difficult situation in which we live and work. We do not doubt,' he went on, 'that within the next few weeks your help to us will not be lacking . . . we recognise what you have been doing for us.'[38]

Another influential factor in this new climate was that some important rifts within the resistance had been overcome, or at least considerably lessened, and that the major issue that had clouded relations with the allies, namely the monarchy, had been largely resolved. On 1 April, the leader of the Italian Communist Party, Palmiro Togliatti ('Ercoli'), who had just returned from an almost two-decade-long exile in Moscow, during which he'd also served as Secretary of the Communist International (Comintern), dropped a political bombshell. The Communists, he announced from Naples, should collaborate with the Badoglio government in a united anti-Fascist front, because the primary goal now was the war against the Nazis and the Fascists; by contrast, the fight against the monarchy was subsidiary. After this, the Communists began to show greater flexibility and willingness to collaborate with the other resistance forces.

On that same day, perhaps by coincidence, Holdsworth and Salvadori met at the Special Force headquarters in Monopoli. The latter's unhappiness at SOE's reliance on SIM for recruiting its agents, followed by his subsequent illness with jaundice, had seen him somewhat sidelined since Anzio, and he was keen to be given a new directive, one more suited to his political skills. He cannot have been displeased. His new mission, Holdsworth told him, was 'to keep informed about the nature, aims and activities of the forces which are at work in both allied-occupied Italian territory and German-occupied territory'. Since then, under cover as an official of the Allied Control Commission, Salvadori had travelled widely throughout the south making contacts with Italians of every ideological persuasion and producing regular reports on the fractious and rapidly changing political scene.

But he did more than report. He also used his influence to support individuals and groups who were friendly to Britain and to block those who were not. Not surprisingly, given both his own liberal political views and Holdsworth's previous insistence on thinking about the end of the war, he was especially alert to the growing power of the Communists, above all in the German-occupied north of the country, and to the need to build up countervailing forces to frustrate them. 'Proceeded to Salerno, which was reached on 9 May,' he reported on one occasion:

> Interviewed there another old friend, MS20 [he gave all his contacts such numbers], editor of the local Christian Democrat paper. Explained to him the necessity for Catholics to establish contact with the organised Catholic groups in German-occupied territory; stressed also necessity of strengthening Catholics in order to check the growing Communist influence among resistance groups. Mentioned fact that it appears that there are already a few bands of Christian Democrats in Aemilia [Emilia] and Venetia. MS20 agreed on necessity of establishing contact and said that he would try to find two energetic and reliable members of clergy to go to the other side.[39]

Salvadori entered Rome within hours of its liberation. The Germans had made no effort to defend the city and had destroyed none of the bridges across the Tiber. Instead, they withdrew their troops to the north, along with some of their prisoners, who were then shot, including an SOE officer (known as Captain John Armstrong – in reality of Hungarian origin) who had been captured before the armistice on a mission to Sardinia. There was no insurrection. Fear had gripped the capital since the Ardeatine massacre in March and the majority of the CLN leaders were either in hiding and inactive, or else under arrest. The resistance was also divided, with its conservative wing, fearful of an Italian version of the Paris Commune, firmly opposed to any violence at the moment of liberation. To this view, which was gratefully echoed by the bulk of the population, the Vatican added its highly influential voice. As for the allied high command, it ordered all armed squads to wait for explicit orders before acting. But as it, too, preferred calm and predictability for its entry into the city, it actually issued no such orders.

Driving down the Appian Way in a jeep with an advanced column of Mark Clark's troops, Salvadori entered the city's deserted streets shortly after midnight on 5 June. At dawn the next morning he set off in search of his sister and her husband, Emilio Lussu, and over the next few days met many other resistance contacts, including Riccardo Bauer of the Action Party, chairman of the military committee of the city's Committee of National Liberation, and his old friend Renato Pierleoni, who back in October had accompanied Leo Valiani on his perilous journey through German lines to Rome, since when he had been helping organise GAP squads in the city. 'The arrival of the Allies has caught the CLN unprepared,' noted Salvadori. 'They have not had time to occupy the Capitol, the Quirinal, or Palazzo Venezia. The situation has not been improved by differences of opinion among the leaders of at least three [resistance] groups.'

He also reported that the city's resistance leaders were 'not well disposed' towards SOE because of the repeated failure to supply the Rome resistance with W/T sets and stores, and were far more friendly to the OSS. Promptly, therefore, he set about counteracting this mood and was able to find a reliable source, the Naples leader of the ORI (Organizzazione della Resistenza Italiana), who was able to testify to the efficiency of both allied special forces. As a result, he claimed, relations immediately improved and 'a contract was signed between No. 1 Special Force and [Bauer].' This governed the formation of a new branch of the ORI to work with the British, which was run by Bauer's military assistant, Captain Antonio Conti. The agreement with Bauer proved important in helping No. 1 Special Force loosen its reliance on SIM, on whom they had become rather over-dependent during the first few months of the year.[40]

On reaching Rome, the allies prevented King Victor Emmanuel from returning to the city and forced him, finally, to hand over power to his son, Prince Humbert of Savoy, with an understanding that after the war a vote would be held on the future of the monarchy. Badoglio also resigned and was replaced as prime minister by Ivanoe Bonomi, heading a government representing all the CLN parties, which included Cianca, as well as Admiral De Courten as head of the navy. Within days, the CLNAI approved a plan for the creation of a Supreme Military Command of the Corps of Freedom Volunteers, in which all military formations were to be represented – in effect, a supreme command for the resistance. Later, in August, Bonomi recognised the CLNAI as the delegation of the Italian government 'for the purpose of the national struggle' in the north, as well as the coordinating authority of all political and military activities of the resistance in occupied Italy. He ended with an appeal to all Italians in the north to collaborate with it.[41]

After crossing back into Italy in early May, Edgardo Sogno had thrown his energies into building a new organisation on the foundations of Otto, known as 'La Franchi' – named after one of his many personal cover names. He spent much of his time organising safe houses for the reception of agents, recruiting groups of saboteurs, reorganising the dropping service and extending it from the valleys of northern Piedmont to cover the whole of the province as well as Liguria and Lombardy. He also managed to locate Otto's principal collaborator and secretary, Conforti, who was in hiding, and get him into Switzerland, and he had several discussions with Ferruccio Parri about the military organisation of the resistance. To this end, he made three further visits to Switzerland over the next two months.

Once the La Franchi group was functioning regularly, Sogno left the north in July by boat for Bastia and from there was flown to Monopoli for his first meeting with No. 1 Special Force officers. Since his escape from the Gestapo in Genoa in March he had been a marked man, and there was considerable doubt both in Baker Street and Monopoli about his return to Italy from Switzerland in the first place, on the grounds that he could be a danger to himself and all his contacts. Not surprisingly, he was interrogated thoroughly on his arrival in the south by No. 1 Special Force security officers. But nothing was discovered to suggest that SOE should not continue to use his services.[42]

On 6 June, at 1600 hours GMT, General Alexander sent an order to Maryland to unleash its maximum effort against the enemy in Italy. In reporting this shortly before midnight, No. 1 Special Force informed Baker Street that by way of a 'crack' (urgent) signal it had ordered all its radio operators to stand by to receive detailed instructions that very night. It also asked that McCaffery be requested to give their 'marching orders' to the groups that he controlled from Switzerland.

A new and significant phase in SOE's efforts in Italy had begun.[43]

# CHAPTER SIX

# 'Squeezing the juice'

The first British liaison officer to parachute to the Italian partisans following the liberation of Rome was Major Hedley Vincent, who, on the night of 9/10 June 1944, was dropped from a converted Halifax bomber into the Friuli region of north-east Italy with two radio operators, Sergeants Donald Macdonnell and Harry Hargreaves. Both signallers had worked with Munthe's Vigilant group during the Salerno landings.

The reception ground lay in mountains flanking the Chiapovano Valley, Italian territory that was populated almost exclusively by Slovenes and dominated, so far as partisan activity was concerned, by the Slovene Nine Corps headquarters, which owed its loyalty to Marshal Tito, leader of the Yugoslav Partisans, who had territorial ambitions in the area. The Clowder mission, which was based with the Slovenes, arranged the reception for Vincent's party after receiving Tito's personal consent.[1] The closest large town was Gorizia. 'It was a beautiful moonlight night,' recalled Hargreaves, 'and I expected the drop would be from 200 to 300 metres. I was surprised when the parachute canopy opened, and below me [bathed] in the moonlight was a panorama of mountains and valleys. We must have dropped from 2,000 metres. Below me appeared a silver ribbon and this turned out to be the rivers Isonzo and Idra whose coldness I would experience on numerous occasions in the near future.'[2]

In fact, he had to test their frigid waters almost immediately. Vincent's stay with the Yugoslavs was designed to be temporary, and after twelve days impatiently waiting for the Slovenes to give them permission and provide guides, the group finally headed out westwards on foot in search of Italian partisans. They were burdened with rucksacks full of their personal possessions as well as their two radio-transmitting sets, six-volt batteries and hand generator. It rained almost continuously, and it took them twelve days walking, including three attempts to wade across the swollen waters of the Isonzo, before they made their first contact, a mere 20 kilometres as the crow flies from their point of departure. 'Each side was wary of the other,' noted Hargreaves. 'As we three came down the mountain track three Italians were coming up, and we noticed that they only seemed to be carrying side arms such as Berettas . . . [Vincent] and the Italian [leader] sat on the grass and spoke together for a period of time, then we all set off together . . .' With his own wry humour, Vincent noted that the journey had served as 'a timely introduction to partisan life [with] sore feet, aching muscles and deep regret that no previous training had been possible at base'.

The Alps of northern Italy were a far cry from Vincent's previous SOE posting in Africa, where he was first based in Lagos, Nigeria, followed by Luanda, Angola. But he had fluent Italian, learned while working briefly before the war in Milan for a British chemical company, and, at 30, he was fit, wiry and healthy. His mission was codenamed 'Coolant', and he adopted the personal cover name of 'Major Tucker'. Later, in mid-August, after he had requested it, a sabotage and explosives team was parachuted to him, consisting of Lieutenants Ronald Taylor and David Godwin, along with Corporal 'Micky' Trent. Taylor and Godwin were explosives experts. Godwin was a chemical engineer who had spent most of his life in Argentina, while Trent in reality was Issack Michael Gyori, a Czech-born Hungarian attached for unspecified 'general duties', including interpreting.[3]

Vincent's real work began at Gradina, a small and desperately poor village that served as the local partisan headquarters for a unit known as the Garibaldi Natisone Brigade – Natisone being the name of a local river. This was a formation of about five hundred reasonably armed men, at least for defensive purposes, who were adequately dressed and in high spirits; its origins lay in a battalion, known as the Mazzini Battalion, which had been founded at the time of the Italian surrender by workers at the nearby Monfalcone shipyards.

Only a small core, however, were reliable fighters, as yet; the majority were young new arrivals from across north-east Italy, both men and women, who had never handled arms or explosives. They greeted him with enthusiasm, seeing his arrival as the head of an allied mission with W/T communications as a sure-fire guarantee of a steady stream of supplies. But Vincent quickly made it clear that there would be a price to pay for this: all supplies were to be used in the most effective way possible against the common enemy, and the allied high command expected that wherever possible their action should be consistent with the general plan of campaign and carried out according to directives that he, Vincent, would communicate. 'They agreed entirely with this proposition,' he recorded, 'and lost no time in convincing me that their partisan movement was an aggressive one and not an instrument for the protection of men who for one reason or another found life in the plains unacceptable.' A reception ground for the dropping of supplies was quickly prepared, and Vincent set about learning as much as he could about partisan life in order to be accepted by those whom, he wrote, 'I had to guide, advise, and direct' – the very stuff, in fact, of a British liaison officer's task.

He spelled his role out more fully in his after-action report:

I was unwilling to assume office or take an open part in the conduct of affairs. We therefore remained a force apart and worked to promote good feeling among all, at the same time directing activities by suggestion and advice which was freely accepted. My policy of living on equal status with the partisans, sharing their fortunes good and bad, participating in all their interests, military, economic, and political, was designed to increase their respect and bring spontaneous expression on matters which often required my mediation. It was not always enough to suggest certain lines of action. Initiative on the part of the mission was demanded in order to ensure the fulfilment of certain projects. This initiative was never resented, never questioned and generally welcomed so long as we trod carefully but firmly using tact and argument. I do not want to imply that the measure of success against the enemy obtained in our zone was due entirely to the work of the mission. I would rather feel that we squeezed as much juice as possible from a fruit which we had not planted, but which we had watered and cared for from an early age.[4]

Not all BLOs in Italy were to encounter such success, although all were to adopt a similar strategy and had to work with existing formations of partisans. Vincent's task was undoubtedly made easier by the fact that he was operating during summer good weather and was able to maintain W/T contact with allied headquarters and thus keep his group regularly supplied with airdrops. 'The B2 set never let us down,' noted the appreciative Macdonnell, writing of his portable thirty-pound short-wave transmitter and receiver, 'and regular communication was maintained with base at Monopoli.' He made it sound easy. But the mission was frequently on the move, often sheltering in lofts, cowsheds and cottages, and its radio would only work if the batteries functioned or if the mains supply could be tapped, a dangerous practice because it could alert the enemy to the radio's presence. In often difficult and dangerous circumstances, Vincent found Macdonnell dependable and cheerful.[5]

As with other BLO missions, all messages were encoded using the double pad system, as described succinctly by Hargreaves, who'd originally qualified as a Merchant Navy radio operator before receiving SOE's specialist training at its radio school at Fawley Court:

> We had a pad with five blocks of five letters printed on this pad in random fashion. There were only two pads. The one that you had and the one that headquarters had. You had a row of letters across the top and you wrote your messages underneath. If the first letter along the top was an A and you were writing ['T'] underneath, you took the A and the T . . . to what we called a silk, a piece of silk in which the alphabet was going horizontally and vertically in random fashion. You would look for A along the top and look for T along the bottom and where the two lines intersected was the letter of your message. If something happened and you lost all this, the pads and the silk, you also had a poem, which you'd use like the pad and send off a message that way. Included in all this we had to use security checks because it was quite possible for the Germans to pick somebody up and send false messages. So you incorporated into your messages your own security check and the girl at the other end, the cipher clerks there . . . would be looking in particular for the security check to make sure they'd got a genuine message.

Poems were individualised, and often chosen by the person concerned for special reasons that helped him or her remember them. In Hargreaves's case, the reason went back to his schooldays in Accrington, Lancashire:

The poem that I always remember for this purpose was 'There was an Ancient Mariner, he stoppeth one in three. By his long grey beard and glittering eyes . . . stoppeth thee/me [sic].' How I remember that was because when I was at school, that was what I used for the hundred lines when I was a naughty boy.[6]

Vincent made airdrops of arms, ammunition, explosives, food and clothing one of his top priorities. After moving to another more permanent base overlooking the plains lying north-east of the city of Udine and carefully reconnoitring the surrounding terrain, he chose a single dropping site high up on the slopes of Monte Joanez, some 1,000 metres above sea level and 300 metres above the small village of Canebola. It offered security from surprise attack, the easy post-drop distribution of stores, and was acceptable to the Royal Air Force crews who would have to pinpoint the spot and make the perilous run-in to make their drop. Careful only to order stores that could be used well, Vincent ensured that the partisans kept accurate records of everything they received in order, he insisted, that they would take care of how they used them, and he made the Garibaldi Natisone Brigade's quartermaster's department responsible to him and the brigade commander for their reception, distribution and checking. Vincent personally supervised the first few drops. Then, satisfied that the partisans knew how to do the job, he let them handle the work themselves – although he made sure that there was one member at least of his mission in attendance at each and every drop, 'more as a duty towards the RAF,' he added, 'than a reflection on the Partisan abilities'.

Typically, a delivery would take place around midnight, after a detachment of partisans based in Canebola heard the BBC 'crack', the coded announcement of an imminent drop that consisted of the message 'The shoes are red.' Then, when they heard the drone of the approaching aircraft, they would light the fires to help guide it in, using the stock of wood, dry hay, petrol and matches they kept permanently to hand. The villagers were organised to turn out every night when a sortie was expected and would take up their positions around the fires and pounce on the packages the minute they touched the ground. Clothes and boots came down without parachutes, which could be a hazard for those busy signalling, but arms, ammunition, explosives and other sensitive equipment floated down in containers. These were then detached from their parachutes and carried down to the village square. Men, women and girls could easily carry a hundredweight on their backs. On arrival they would be met by a representative of the quartermaster, and his team would sort out and check the supplies against load lists. Afterwards, they would be taken to nearby waiting vehicles, and by midday the distribution would be completed. One of Godwin's most vivid memories was of a long line of partisans and villagers carrying enormous loads on their backs and, amongst them, a small boy barely four years old carrying two pairs of heavy army binoculars up and down steep paths all the way to Canebola.[7]

Vincent's task now was to see that such a generous supply of arms and equipment was put to good use. Partisans, he remarked, 'will never be satisfied with the variety or quantity of supplies dropped. This is not just greed but an expression of fear. They gain courage by the possession of equipment but seldom pause to consider its best use or maintenance.' Consequently, his mission spent considerable time in demonstrating, lecturing and handling all stores that were unfamiliar to the partisans. After the arrival of Taylor and Godwin in August, they even set up a small factory under the supervision of an escaped prisoner of war that reconstituted the plastic explosive dropped by the RAF into ready-made charges suitable for every type of target. Before long it was turning out a steady production line of charges tailor-made for the damage or destruction of railway cuttings, rail lines, high-tension pylons, locomotives and factory machinery. It also produced road mines that incorporated tyre-bursters, delayed-action mines of all sizes and delays, hand grenades made out of old cigarette tins filled with plastic explosive, and, an especially popular item with the partisans, anti-pursuit bombs. Equipped with five-second-delay fuses, these could be carried by any partisan transport and rapidly offloaded in case of pursuit to explode underneath the following vehicle. 'Everyone used to smell of almonds

and have terrible headaches after the instructions using Nobel 808,'
complained Hargreaves, referring to the green, plasticine-like
explosive used widely by SOE.

He also recalled the infectious enthusiasm of the mission's two
explosives experts. 'Taylor and Godwin, they were dead keen on
explosives,' he said. 'They did things with [them] that you read about
in [the comics] *Rover* and *Wizard*. I can remember one time they
got a damned big cheese, they were scooping out the middle of the
cheese, and I said "What the hell are you doing there?" They said
"We're going to put plastic in here. We'll put a time pencil in and
get an Italian to take it down into the German mess in Udine."'[8]

In the two months following his arrival, Vincent and his men saw
the partisan brigade evolve into a full-blown division of some two
thousand men. Besides enthusiastic recruiting, the main reason for
this was that they soon encountered another partisan group known
as the Osoppo Brigade, named after the nearby fortress town that
had played a heroic role in the defence of Venice against the Austrians
during the Risorgimento. Whereas the Garibaldini were under left-
wing and largely Communist leadership, the Osoppos were fiercely
anti-Communist and tended to be supporters either of the Action
Party or the Christian Democrats. At first, Vincent noted a complete
lack of collaboration between them and the Garibaldini, with their
respective commanders distrusting and often deprecating each other.
Eventually, however, he managed to persuade the two groups to form
a unified military command, and the joint and significantly
augmented force took the title of Divisione Garibaldi Osoppo. Only
by threatening to withdraw the mission altogether, and thus deprive
them of the supplies they all craved, as well as by one hard-hitting
session reassuring the Osoppos about Britain's, and in particular the
prime minister, Winston Churchill's, attitude towards Communism,
did Vincent get his way. Each formation retained its own identity
and distinctive uniform. But from then on all supplies and other
services were rationed out by a single controlling officer under
Vincent's directives.[9]

With this unified force at his disposal, Vincent set out to create
as much disruption as possible to German lines of communication.
The Udine area lay close to the Austrian border – Villach was barely
97 kilometres away to the north – and roads and railways were

carrying significant military traffic. The area's importance was enhanced in SOE's eyes by the optimism running high in June and July about the advance in Italy. On 3 July Mark Clark's Fifth Army took Siena, followed by Leghorn and Pisa two weeks later, giving the allies a foothold on the lower River Arno. On the Adriatic coast, the Poles of General Oliver Leese's Eighth Army entered Ancona on 18 July, a considerable prize for the allies as it was second in size as a port only to Bari and gave them a significant base for the further advance north. Florence now beckoned and, beyond, the great German defensive barrier across north-central Italy, known as the Gothic Line, that blocked their advance to the Po Valley. But confidence was running high that this could be broken. On 26 July, General Alexander, the allied commander-in-chief, issued a directive that spoke optimistically of securing a bridgehead over the River Po.

The stage was now set for the allied assault on German positions in the northern Apennines. Fuelled by Churchill's enthusiasm for an allied thrust into Austria through the Ljubljana Gap, active talk also began about an amphibious landing on the Istrian peninsula. This reached as far as Vincent near Udine, who later recorded that 'a landing in Istria or at some point ahead of the line was a hope and a possibility. We wished to make a positive contribution with the potential material at our command.' The possibility of a landing in Istria, even though remote, was to remain alive until the allied advance in Italy ground to a halt in October.[10]

Vincent's first step was to establish control of an area sufficiently large to give the partisans several different jumping-off points for attacks on enemy positions and troops as well as sabotage. The longer they could hold the territory, the more damage they could do, and it was hoped, as Vincent later explained, that 'the allied advance would accelerate and coincide with our maximum efforts'. This was not to happen, and eventually the Germans retaliated in force, as Vincent and the partisan commanders always expected. In the meantime, however, they notched up some notable successes. Numerous attacks on enemy forces netted them significant acquisitions of arms, ammunition, vehicles and documents — valuable for intelligence — while a carefully planned campaign of sabotage wreaked considerable damage. Their principal target was the partially electrified railway system. The main line to Austria ran through Udine, which was also a significant junction for regional traffic. As soon as Taylor and Godwin arrived, they set to work, as the latter recorded:

> Immediately on our arrival . . . small groups of hand-picked partisans were made available to us for special training. Within days, these men had begun to assimilate the practical use of every type of fuse and every kind of mechanism for setting off explosives charges; within another few days they could set up a number of linked charges without a single error; within another few days they had shown their newly acquired expertise by successfully interrupting electric power supplies after blowing up a number of pylons and had gone on to derail their first train; after that, they were ready for anything.

Morale and man-management was not overlooked either, as he also noted:

> In a flash of inspiration, Ronald Taylor had at the outset devised a . . . badge that our bunch of dedicated students could wear once they were proficient in what we were teaching them to do, and wear them they did very proudly, returning us the droll compliment of calling us 'Tenente [Lieutenant] Plastico' and 'Tenente 808'.

Over the next two months, small groups of these saboteurs, assisted by armed partisans, derailed, halted or ambushed over forty supply trains and frequently followed up their attacks by laying further explosive charges to delay the enemy's efforts to repair the tracks. The railway yards in Udine became the target for one spectacularly daring effort at sabotage on a grand scale. They were assisted by an effective intelligence service run by local civilians, as recorded by Godwin: 'Much indeed of the credit for knowing when and where to attack the supply trains must go to the civilian station master at Udine, who regularly and at considerable risk to himself copied out the secret military train time-tables given to him at short notice by the enemy authorities, and to the brave young girl who carried this information to us . . .'[11] In addition to the railways, the sabotage teams also blew up several high-tension electricity pylons, damaged a cement factory, destroyed underground international telephone lines into Austria and blocked or mined several roads. It helped that the director of the Electrical Company of Udine was personally willing to enlighten Godwin about the regional electrical supply network.[12]

While the partisans received crucial supplies from the allies, they also depended heavily on support from local civilians. The villagers in the hills and mountains where they operated helped them in countless ways. 'The Friulian peasants gave us what they could in the form of shelter and food (polenta, pasta, etc.),' wrote Hargreaves, 'meat was non-existent, sometimes we managed a little cheese. We slept in the outbuildings in the hay and leaves (the leaves were mulberry leaves for feeding the silkworms which they cultivated).' For the partisan who was captured, death was almost certain. Civilians caught helping them also suffered. Their homes would almost definitely be burned down and they could be transported to Germany. If especially unlucky, they would be shot or hanged. Remarkably, betrayal was rare. After several months' experience, a British Army medical officer reported similarly from another part of Italy. 'We should not forget the *contadini*,' he stressed. 'This community supplies not only the food and shelter for the partisans but also the hostages and the material for German reprisals. My experience of [their] hospitality, generosity and courage is very vivid . . .'[13]

The partisans also relied on significant support from civilian organisations on the plains. 'There was a non-stop campaign,' recorded Vincent. 'Periodically representatives of the town groups would report to the mission for directives, training, and material.' One such organisation was the Communist-run GAP, which had a counter-espionage service that helped eliminate traitors and provided additional provisions from the agriculturally rich plains along with transport to carry it to the partisans. Basics such as flour, salt, potatoes, beans, sugar and vegetables all reached them in this way. Most of this food was acquired through agreement with farmers, who were only too happy to pretend they had been 'forced' to part with it rather than have it requisitioned by the Fascist authorities for use by the Germans.

By the late summer Vincent could legitimately feel that his mission had been a success. The partisans had fought off at least one significant assault by the Germans and now enjoyed a unified command, while Vincent's team had successfully received two new British missions; one, codenamed 'Bakersfield', for SOE (led by Major George

Fielding) and the other for SIS. 'The six bodies [agents] with stores landed accurately in the course of one hectic evening when three aircraft were competing with each other for priority over the target,' reported Vincent. 'The Bakersfield party was safely conducted by our patrol to their zone of operations. The [SIS] party were accommodated at the mission while we arranged for the preparation of forged documents to allow them to proceed on their way into the plains . . .'[14]

By contrast, the next British liaison officer to parachute to the Italian partisans, and the first to the Apennines, got off to a shaky start and never quite recovered. Major Vivian Johnston was dropped near Monte Albano in the central Apennines of Tuscany on the night of 15/16 June along with his radio operator, Quartermaster Sergeant Edward Everitt, to join up with an Italian mission codenamed 'Rutland', headed by Domenico Azzari, an Italian Navy W/T operator who'd been recruited by Malcolm Munthe in Salerno after the surrender and parachuted 'blind' and solo into the La Spezia area in October 1943.[15]

Unfortunately, owing to navigational errors and the presence of fires that were misleadingly read as belonging to their reception party, they landed 25 kilometres from the dropping zone. Shepherds and woodsmen helped them recover their equipment, although they never found one of their two B2 radio sets or part of their money and personal kit. They had also come equipped with a 'Eureka' set, a newly developed portable RAF device designed to act as a beacon to dropping zones for aircraft that were fitted with the corresponding receiving equipment, known as a 'Rebecca'. But without the hands to help carry it, they decided to destroy it instead. Their general brief was to set up a channel of communication with local partisans, supply them with arms and try to coordinate their guerrilla activities as far as possible with the advancing allied armies.

Three days later, close to Monte Tondo, Johnston and Everitt finally reached the local partisan headquarters. Here they also found another Italian mission which had arrived two weeks earlier headed by Giacinto Lazzari ('Alfonso'), a SIM officer, to link up with Rutland and help it receive and distribute supply drops, a task that was seriously hampered before it even began when his wireless operator managed to leave his W/T operating plan behind, either in the plane or back at base. That same night, a team of six Italian saboteurs was also dropped to join Rutland. It was to prove valuable in weapons and explosives training as well as in carrying out various sabotage tasks.[16]

Johnston was a dark and sturdy 23-year-old born in Cairo, where his father was a bank manager. His mother was Maltese and he spoke fluent Italian. He was severely taken aback by what he found. 'I had been given the impression that the partisans ... were commanded by some responsible officer and that I was only to advise and supply them,' he complained bitterly. Instead, he found the partisans in 'the most complete state of disorganisation', consisting of 150 poorly armed, clothed and fed men with little ammunition. One of his early messages from the field conveys his dismay. 'Have met Rutland. Situation most obscure. Band being slowly organised. Mostly composed of young boys evading military service. Organisation in this area has been beyond Rutland's capacity for a long time ... There is a lack of leaders.'[17] Neither was the situation helped when Azzari ('Candiani') was wounded in a needless clash with the Germans, lost his signals plan and was partly out of action for most of the next three months.

After two frustrating weeks, Johnston decided to move across the Apennine watershed into the adjacent province of Reggio Emilia/Modena. Here, in the higher reaches and mountains of the Secchia river valley south of Modena and north-east of La Spezia, partisans had been waging war against the Germans and Republican Italians for months, provoking counter-attacks and often savage reprisals against civilians. The most prominent partisan leader was Mario Ricci, otherwise known as 'Armando', a veteran anti-Fascist and Communist who'd fought in the Spanish Civil War with the Garibaldi Battalion. On 18 June, two days after Johnston parachuted into Italy, the partisans captured the town of Montefiorino, the most important local Fascist garrison, set up a unified partisan command, the Comando Centro Emilia, and in the surrounding area created a liberated zone known as the Republic of Montefiorino, where they held elections and organised relief and sanitation services. It was one of fifteen similar 'oases of freedom' declared by partisans across northern Italy that summer, inspired by what they mistakenly assumed was the prospect of imminent liberation by the allies. Forms of democratic self-government were set up, elections took place – usually by show of hand – food distributed and taxes collected. In a few cases, the property of Fascist sympathisers was confiscated and a local currency established.[18]

Mario Nardi, the chief staff officer of Armando's partisans, which were known as the Modena Division, consisting of some 3,000 men, later recalled the significant impact that Johnston's arrival had on the partisans:

> First of all it boosted our morale as it demonstrated that the long and difficult months of activity had not been useless as they had finally earned us the attention and appreciation of the allies. But furthermore, the material benefits that this link up brought us were invaluable. From that moment on we were regularly supplied with equipment that corresponded exactly to our particular needs, almost as we asked for it. This may need some explanation. Our armaments were for the most part Italian, and we thus had urgent need of Italian ammunition . . . Another matter which was particularly important to us was medical care. Our camp hospital, which could cater for several dozen men with wounds that were serious and even critical, lacked medical supplies. From that moment on, every single request for specific items was attended to in detail . . . Major Johnston's personality helped him to make himself at home with us, to the point that he soon became something more than a co-ordinating officer and could also have been considered a member of the Division Command. He was very young, of pleasant appearance, extrovert, spoke Italian perfectly, was full of enthusiasm and eager to contribute to the operations under hand.[19]

Johnston now prepared three new dropping zones, and by the second half of July supplies for the partisans were beginning to arrive almost daily. Hopes were running high that the partisans could lend significant support to the advancing allied forces, and in mid-July Johnston was suddenly informed of an audacious plan to assist the Fifth Army. After specialist training at SOE's parachute school outside Brindisi, a parachute battalion of the Nembo Division of the Corpo Italiano di Liberazione (the re-formed Royal Italian Army) would be airlifted behind the German lines to join forces with the partisans and mount a diversionary attack to coincide with a push by the US Fifth Army to strengthen the front along the River Arno. Johnston's task was to prepare for this by arranging dropping grounds and alerting the partisans.

Three days after receiving notice of the plan from Holdsworth's headquarters at Monopoli, Johnston gave it the go-ahead. 'Project excellent provided a) made by night b) max supplies,' he messaged. The last-minute planning was frantic, not least because two weeks before the scheduled drop, a staff meeting at AFHQ unexpectedly discussed sending the Nembo parachutists instead to north-west Italy to assist with the allied landings on the French Riviera (initially codenamed 'Anvil' but now known as 'Dragoon'), which were due to take place in mid-August, as well as concentrating supply drops to the resistance west of a line through Lake Maggiore–Milan–Genoa.

Alexander was horrified when he heard the news, and pleaded personally with Maitland Wilson, the supreme allied commander in the Mediterranean responsible for the Riviera landings, to ensure that they stuck with the original plan. In a 'Top Secret. Bigot Anvil. Personal for General Wilson. Eyes Only' message – the highest level of security possible – he stressed the dangers of concentrating all supplies in one comparatively small area and seized the chance to stress how highly he valued the resistance and what he believed was its use to the allies. 'To get the best results and the maximum overall assistance to all your operations from Italian resistance groups,' he insisted, 'I am convinced that we should continue my policy of spreading resistance activities over northern Italy generally with the object of causing the greatest interference with the enemy's general system of communication and forcing him to disperse troops on internal security. The more dropping capacity you can provide for me,' he added with palpable frustration, 'the greater the effect will be and I very much hope you will by some means or another be able to obtain an increase on my present allotment.' Finally, he insisted that his plans for the Nembo Battalion should go ahead because that was where they would pay 'the biggest dividend'.

He won this battle, and three days later No. 1 Special Force was directed to concentrate the bulk of its efforts in Johnston's region of the Apennines. Simultaneously, airdrops were intensified, and

between 10 and 25 July, during the ten nights when weather conditions permitted drops, thirty-eight out of the forty-eight operations
to partisans were to the La Spezia/Modena area. Amongst them
were weapons for the entire Nembo battalion, including a dozen
mortars, four 47 mm anti-tank guns and 250 light or heavy machine
guns. Some dissident voices within SOE queried this tactical diversion of resources from the larger strategic goal of building up the
partisans in the north, but they were overruled.[20]

To help Johnston prepare for this expedition, three SOE officers
were dropped near Frassinoro, south of Montefiorino, during the
last few days of July: Captains Jim Davies, Ernest Wilcockson and
Charles Holland, all of whom had been hastily assembled and mini-
mally briefed in Monopoli the week beforehand. Accompanying them
were Captain G. C. Lloyd-Roberts, of the Royal Army Medical Corps,
two British wireless operators, Corporals Frank Hayhurst and Charles
(Charlie) Barratt, an Italian lieutenant and six Italian radio operators. Their task was to plan and prepare logistical, organisational
and military aspects of the operation. Wilcockson later recalled that
he was briefed by Dick Hewitt, Holdsworth's deputy at No. 1 Special
Force headquarters, with barely a day's notice and struggled to find
time to get the necessary inoculations.[21]

Davies, a 30-year-old sapper and demolitions expert, had grown
up in Switzerland and was an accomplished skier. After studying
forestry at Oxford he'd joined the Bombay Burmah Trading Company
to work in the isolated teak forests of north-west Burma, where one
of his more taxing exploits had been to coax a herd of thirty elephants
on to a raft in order to cross a river, an exhausting task that took
him a full three days. He had also worked with the legendary
Lieutenant Colonel J. H. Williams, whose later wartime exploits
commanding a company which used elephants as light cranes and
winches on the India–Burma frontier against the Japanese became
the subject of a post-war bestseller: *Elephant Bill*. After bouts of
malaria and dysentery, Davies returned to Britain and served as a
sapper platoon commander with the 52nd (Lowland) Division before
a chance conversation with a fellow officer on a train to Scotland
led to his being recruited by SOE. In October 1943 he'd been parachuted into Greece to work with ELAS, the Communist-led resistance,
and had only recently been exfiltrated when the mission was

withdrawn. Wilcockson, an artillery officer who had served as a conducting officer for agents bound for Crete before serving in Monopoli as a small-arms and explosives instructor at SOE's training school, arrived to continue his munitions instruction and to help prepare dropping zones. Holland, a highly trained senior signaller, had worked alongside Davies in Greece after completing two missions to Spain for SOE to plan W/T networks in the event of a German occupation of the country.[22]

This advance party was dropped in three stages over two successive nights – 26/27 and 27/28 July. Unfortunately, as he landed, the medical officer Lloyd-Roberts severely injured a leg as he hit a building and was out of action for the next few weeks. Nonetheless, he was subsequently able to provide valuable insights into partisan casualties as well as medical care, and to investigate what turned out to be a false scare about the Germans using bacteriological warfare by spreading typhoid. 'One will see in rapid succession examples of courage and cowardice, generosity and cruelty, dishonesty and integrity,' he wrote of the partisans he encountered. There emerged, he added, 'the feeling that the Italian partisan is competing under conditions of stress . . . in a creditable manner.'[23]

Fate smiled more kindly on Wilcockson. Because of the height from which he jumped – the Polish air crew dropped him at 550 rather than 250 metres – he became separated from his group and made his way to a trattoria in Frassinoro. Speaking no Italian, he did his best to explain who he was and shortly thereafter, as if by some miracle, there arrived on the scene an Italian called Alfredo Giacomo Venturi speaking fluent English. He was also known as 'Jock', because he'd been born in Scotland where his parents ran a fish and chip shop in Glasgow. He happily agreed to serve as interpreter to Wilcockson and was to remain in the service of No. 1 Special Force until the end of the war.

Barely had the three British officers arrived, however, than at dawn on 30 July the Germans launched a massive *rastrellamento* spearheaded by units of the Hermann Göring Division assisted by Fascist forces. The exceptional number of supply drops as well as leakages from garrulous partisans had undoubtedly prompted them to take pre-emptive action. Some 20,000 enemy forces, using artillery, mortars, flame throwers and armoured cars, quickly overwhelmed the partisans. The battle for Montefiorino has been described as the biggest single battle of the Italian resistance. After some fierce and bitter clashes, Mario Ricci – 'Armando' – gave the order to disband and disperse. Davies, for one, scathingly blamed this decision on 'inexperience, poor leadership, lack of intelligence and discipline'. Instead of the bands dispersing by units under their commanders, he observed, 'individual partisans threw away their arms and bolted, leaving the whole area completely open to enemy patrols and making a bad name for themselves.' Heavy German reprisals followed. Several villages were razed by fire, men under sixty were rounded up and deported to Germany, and both rape and looting were widespread. Captured partisans were routinely tortured before being killed.[24]

With the benefit of hindsight, many of those involved implicitly or indirectly placed the blame for the fiasco on Johnston, whose only previous experience of SOE operations had come after parachuting into the Dodecanese island of Kos in September 1943. Armando's chief of staff, Mario Nardi, for example, felt that Johnston lacked a concrete knowledge of the principles of guerrilla warfare, while Charles Macintosh, SOE's forward operations officer following the capture of Rome, described him as 'clever but [lacking] experience'.[25] Likewise, Jim Davies declared that Johnston was no fool but 'lacked military experience and judgement. On any showing,' he added, 'the Reggio/Modena partisans were not led or trained to resist any German attack or to hold ground. His idea that they were in fact a force to be reckoned with who could defend that territory as an operations base, led to the Nembo plan [which] . . . was too hastily and scrappily mounted, too meagre to cause a worthwhile diversion, even if disposable, unrehearsed and uncoordinated. This was not Johnston's fault and he behaved well. In the crisis the partisans took no notice of him, and when he pulled out in the early autumn I think he had had more than enough.'[26]

These criticisms seem too harsh. From the moment he arrived in the Apennines Johnston had a very clear idea of the partisans' limitations, and he was well aware of Armando's faults. 'He took an interest in everything,' he reported, 'thus achieving very little.' He noted too that 'Armando' was completely under the thumb of his political commissar, Osvaldo Poppi ('Davide'), a hard-line Communist and peacetime lawyer from Reggio, who consistently placed politics above every other consideration, to the point that Wilcockson, who later 'inherited' him from Johnston, eventually manoeuvred his dismissal. It is probably true, however, that the relatively youthful Johnston lacked the experience to make much impact on the partisans' passionate enthusiasm for action. Unlike Davies, he had not worked with Communist partisans before.

Fierce political commitment was certainly not lacking among the Garibaldini, but this was part of their problem. 'The partisan formations on my arrival were strongly Communist which was the natural reaction to twenty years of Fascism,' reported Johnston. 'Most of the leaders . . . had a genuine hate for the Fascists and suspected all the officers of the ex-Italian Army of collaboration. This necessarily entailed the organisation and leadership of partisans to [sic] totally inexperienced men, whose only asset was their political colour and, in some cases, their courage.' The Communists spent a great deal of their time on party propaganda, he went on, sometimes even threatening to eliminate anti-Communists, and they used political commissars to ensure these views held sway amongst the lower ranks of the partisans. Like Vincent in Friuli, Johnston soon encountered equally passionate anti-Communist partisans. After the Montefiorino collapse, he reported, they began to make some significant headway. As in Friuli, the Green Flames operated alongside the Garibaldini under a unified command but kept their own distinct organisation. Each faction, noted Johnston, 'worked feverishly' to enlist as much support as they could.[27]

As soon as the scale and ferocity of the German attack became obvious the Nembo drop was cancelled and the advance British party hastily decided to quit the area and scatter. But as the mules they had been promised had not yet arrived, they had to destroy much of their equipment and all their surplus codes. They also chose to bury their W/T sets before splitting up into four parties. Accompanied by a number of allied escapers and evaders who'd also congregated in the area, and on instructions from No. 1 Special Force, they made their separate ways towards a British mission based to the west in southern Liguria. This was headed by Major Gordon Lett, a 33-year-old professional soldier who'd been captured at Tobruk and after the Italian surrender had walked out of his POW camp to link up with some partisans in the Rossano Valley. After making contact via a message sent through Switzerland, he'd been taken on formally by SOE as a liaison officer.[28]

Five days after dispersing, however, Davies encountered some partisans who told him that Lett's mission, too, was under pressure from the Germans. So the plan of joining him was abandoned and at considerable personal risk Holland, along with Corporal Barratt, returned to the dropping zone and recovered four out of the six buried W/T sets, which the local villagers had carefully and scrupulously reburied more securely within hours of their original forced departure. Eventually, on 20 August, helped by the efficient 20-year-old Hayhurst, Holland was able to make radio contact with No. 1 Special Force and establish his own mission, codenamed 'Toffee'. Shortly after that he moved north across the Apennines towards Parma, and linked up with a Justice and Liberty partisan group near Tizzano.[29]

Meanwhile, Davies set up his own mission near Parma, while Wilcockson and Haycock eventually established a base for another new mission, codenamed 'Silentia', near Modena. Johnston returned to Monte Tondo and briefly linked up with yet another British mission which, like Lett's, was led by an escaped British POW who'd been captured at Tobruk. This was Captain Tony Oldham, who had also joined up with the partisans.[30]

All these missions now had the task of re-establishing contact with the resistance leaders who had survived the German assault and help them re-form their scattered units. Over the rest of the summer they also collected a lot of useful information about German troop movements and gave assistance to downed allied airmen and POWs sheltering in the mountains.[31]

Johnston was not the only pioneer liaison officer dropped behind German lines who anticipated being reinforced by paratroops. On the night of 12/13 June, Major John Henderson, accompanied by two Italians, Lieutenant Angelo Caracciolo and a radio operator, Angelo Fuzio, was dropped near Appignano in the Marche. The region's capital was the crucial port city of Ancona, which the allies now had in their sights and expected to capture about three weeks later. An Italian liaison mission, codenamed 'Marcasite', had already been working in the area for some eight months and partisan forces were well equipped and organised. Twelve members of the partisan

Fifth Brigade, commanded by its leader, codenamed 'Primo', formed the reception committee for Henderson's group, which was bringing stores as well as two million lire. Its mission was to marshal the partisans in preparation for a coordinated attack with the Eighth Army's offensive on Ancona.[32]

A week after Henderson arrived, optimism was still running high about a rapid capture of the port. His initial estimates of the number and quality of the partisans were so encouraging that No. 1 Special Force concluded that the town could be taken by five hundred armed partisans seizing and holding a dropping zone to permit the landing of a British parachute battalion. 'Get on air soonest will have important orders to pass soon,' read a message it sent to Henderson. 'Attack greatest importance preservation port/town Ancona; consult with Primo and other leaders how this can be done as military operation. Give it all you've got.'[33]

But events intervened. The allied advance, spearheaded by the Polish Corps under General Anders, ran into obstinate German opposition and Anders was forced to postpone the anticipated liberation of the city, first to 4 July, then to the 13th, and finally to the 17th (his troops finally entered it on the 18th). It also transpired that no British parachute battalion was available, and in any case, shortly afterwards, Henderson's mission was overrun by allied forces. So, after abruptly telling his radio operator that their mission was over, Henderson returned to base to report on his experiences. He then went back to the Marche with Dick Mallaby on a mission based in the liberated town of Macerata to regain contact with the partisans and assess the value of their work, document their activities in the region, draw lessons that might be useful for northern Italy, recover weapons and stores that might be used for 'brigandage', ensure that partisan leaders now overrun by the allies were well treated, and advise Allied Military Government on the problems they could expect in the future from disbanded partisan forces. As the allies advanced north and more of Italy was liberated, this last issue was emerging as one of the most significant and troublesome.[34]

A self-described 'hotelier and company secretary', the Edinburgh-born Henderson spoke fluent Italian and had worked for two years before the war in Turin. He had joined up in 1939 as a driver for the Royal Army Service Corps and become a sergeant in the Intelligence Corps, working for Field Security in various Persian Gulf ports, before joining SOE in Cairo in October 1943. There he had been trained and briefed for two missions to Yugoslavia, both of which were cancelled. He had arrived in Italy shortly before making his drop into the Marche. Hilary Scott, who met him in Macerata, told Holdsworth privately in a brief handwritten letter that in his opinion Henderson was 'not ideal type for LO [Liaison Officer]; too abrupt and off-hand and not particularly thorough.' Already close to 40, perhaps the Scot found his patience quickly wore thin when confronted with the sometimes anarchic and impetuous enthusiasm of young and eager partisans. After his mission to the Marche, he was to do invaluable work helping the army and AMG handle partisan affairs in liberated Florence.[35]

Scott's letter to Holdsworth was delivered personally by Max Salvadori. After locating his sister in Rome and learning that the Poles were advancing on Ancona, Salvadori had decided to visit his parents whose home a few kilometres south of the city, near Porto San Giorgio, was now in liberated territory. Three weeks later he made a return visit to the Marche with a brief to review the success of No. 1 Special Force in the region. While he claimed – perhaps not surprisingly given his general antipathy to the Badoglio forces – that only one of the SIM agents sent in by the Italian supreme command had had much effect, his assessment of the partisans was scarcely more enthusiastic. In some places, such as the town of Ascoli, he acknowledged, they had, 'within the limits of their possibilities', fulfilled a useful function.

Like Henderson, however, he was more interested in identifying the friction that rapidly emerged between the partisans and AMG officials in newly liberated territory as a serious problem, especially when the latter, in his opinion, continued to 'show leniency to Fascists'. He also warned that this would lessen the chances of the partisans giving up their weapons. Word of 'high-handed' treatment of partisans by allied forces had already leaked out to partisans behind the lines in northern Italy, he claimed, and this would undoubtedly affect their willingness to accept allied instruction. In short, urged Salvadori, if SOE wished to retain the goodwill of the northern partisans and block the Communists, they would have to send in officers able to influence them and not 'straight military types' who were either absorbed by the partisans or else found themselves completely isolated. SOE should also urge AMG to take stronger measures against Fascists in areas close to the front line.[36]

It was the experience of Salvadori's own homecoming, however, as much as anything else, which gave these conclusions their edge. Driving up the Adriatic coast from Bari, and newly promoted to major, Salvadori was in a heady and optimistic mood as the lorry transporting him drove down the avenue of pines that led to his parents' house. As he lingered in the dusk outside for a few moments in his British uniform, powerful memories and images rushed through his mind: the long years in Switzerland, England, Africa and America; all his experiences before and during the war; efforts both successful and unsuccessful; fallen friends. Then he heard a noise and opened the door and went upstairs. 'Someone was walking along the verandah,' he wrote:

> I heard muttered words – they did not seem to be directed particularly towards me, but they were – it was my father's voice.
>
> '*Agente straniero!*' – 'Foreign agent.'
>
> Wrapped in a familiar black cloak, he passed me on the stairs and vanished into the gathering darkness. So that was my welcome after eleven years! I felt a terribly bitter taste in my mouth. Others might not be so outspoken, but might well have the same thought on seeing me in foreign uniform. Eleven years are long. One becomes a *straniero* [foreigner and stranger] after eleven years. And to think that for all these years I had dreamed of that moment, of seeing my home again.[37]

Over the next few days, Salvadori met several people who, back in the 1920s after his arrest, had taken it upon themselves to inform the police of everything he and his family were doing. 'I kept my anger under control,' he recorded, 'out of my respect for my uniform.' But fearful that his strong desire for vengeance would get the better of him, he quickly left. 'I have decided to go away,' he recorded, 'so as not to see these people with their smooth words: "I really wanted to help you" – "I was forced to do it" – "I didn't actually tell the police anything."' He felt better after visiting some surviving anti-Fascist friends, meeting a retired army officer who'd been the heart and soul of the local resistance, encountering a man whose house near the coast had sheltered hundreds of British prisoners of war on their way south by sea, and talking with a priest who had assisted the resistance.

But then, at police headquarters in Ascoli, he got hold of the files concerning him and his family. The names of informers were all there: uncles, cousins, servants, the gardener, the ex-accountant, the schoolmistress. 'This was the kind of servility fostered by fascism,' he wrote, 'which caused so many people to lose their lives . . .' It was little wonder that he thought that the Fascists and their allies should be brought to rapid justice.[38]

SOE's support for the allied advance was not confined to aid for the partisans. On 17/18 July, as the Poles prepared to enter Ancona, a raiding party, including Robin Richards and Dick Laming, landed north of the city to impede the passage of German military vehicles along the coast road. Richards headed the fourteen-man landing party, which included an Italian anti-tank crew led by a Captain Otto armed with a Breda 47 mm anti-tank gun as well as a strange assortment of explosives, road signs and lanterns. The men stepped ashore just after midnight and cautiously crept up to the road and waited patiently for a lull in the traffic. Towards one o'clock they erected their road signs near a fork in the road, complete with German lettering. One proclaimed 'Road Closed' and two others, lettered 'Diversion', directed traffic down a precipitous and ill-surfaced by road sprinkled with mines and tyre-bursters. The party then withdrew, leaving a red light burning on the beach as a target indicator for the 47 mm anti-tank gun and 20 mm machine gun mounted on the fast Italian torpedo boats that had brought them from Ortona. The trap was set and baited.

At about two o'clock a number of German trucks drove straight into it. The waiting party heard two sharp explosions and sounds of confused shouting. Mortar flares from the ships lit up the scene and the guns opened fire from offshore. 'Lines of large trees skirted both sides of the road so that the road was in the shadow of the foliage all the time the parachute flares were burning,' reported Laming and Richards. 'This made observation, notwithstanding the good luminosity of the mortar flares, very difficult. It is however certain that 3 motor vehicles, one of them very large, were put out of action.' Later on, though, Richards recalled its value rather differently. 'The *coup de main* north of Ancona with Captain Otto was rather a schoolboy affair,' he wrote. 'We put spikes on the coast road and then shot up vehicles from the MS when they had run into our road block; not worth the petrol!'[39]

This operation, codenamed 'Leyton', was authorised by Hilary Scott, who was now temporarily headquartered at Salvadori's house where the latter's father, presumably, was now feeling more benign about the allied presence. The day before Richards and Laming's operation, he told Holdsworth that he doubted whether the hopes placed by the latter in the partisans would ever live up to his expectations. 'I hope I am wrong,' he said, 'or at least too pessimistic, but I do not think so.' It was in this letter, too, that he delivered his brief evaluation of Henderson. But if Holdsworth was dismayed either by this or by Scott's estimate of partisan abilities, he would have been cheered by his evaluation of Salvadori. 'Thoroughly good type,' wrote the lawyer and Yorkshireman (Scott). 'Genuine, sincere and anxious to do everything he can. Could be very useful politically as a leader of the moderate groups who are not Communists or Fascists. He could start up in this area where he is well known and universally respected. Any prospect of it?'[40] Time was to reveal that Salvadori had a yet more important role to play in Italy.

At the beginning of July, Roseberry produced a report on assistance to the Italian resistance showing that SOE now had sixteen W/T stations working back to Maryland and eleven operators who had not yet made contact. Some fifty-eight 'organisers and trainers' had been sent to various action groups and thirty-nine *coup de main* sabotage teams had been infiltrated to attack specified targets and then join up with known groups and serve as instructors. So far, three British liaison officers had been infiltrated behind the lines and another had not yet been heard from. So far as supplies were concerned, a total of 355 tons of arms, ammunition, sabotage material, food and clothing had been delivered in the first six months of the year. 'Throughout the whole area of unliberated Italy,' concluded the J Section head, 'active and open hostility to the Germans and neo-fascists is revealing itself. There is no important sector which has not been penetrated by S.O.E. and which help and assistance has not reached . . . Given favourable weather and sufficient lift, the strategic areas should be in a satisfactory state as regards arms and organisation by the end of July.'[41]

# CHAPTER SEVEN

# 'On the right lines'

August 1944 was a key month for SOE and resistance forces across Europe. The Normandy landings had opened the gateway to Western Europe and on Saturday 19 August, five days ahead of the 2nd French Armoured Division's triumphant entry into the French capital, the Gaullist resistance launched an uprising in Paris. Four days before, allied troops had landed on the French Riviera and were heading rapidly north, liberating Grenoble before the end of the month. In the east, with Stalin's Red Army approaching Warsaw, the Polish Home Army launched an uprising on the first of the month. Lasting sixty-three days, it was to be brutally crushed by the Germans. Throughout the month, allied efforts to support both the Maquis in southern France and the patriots in Warsaw were to impose heavy demands on special-duties flights from the Mediterranean.

In Italy, events were also moving with surprising speed. In the two months since they entered Rome, allied forces had advanced over 400 kilometres, and at dawn on Friday 4 August, South African and New Zealand units of the British Eighth Army, having cautiously moved through the southern outskirts of Florence, finally reached the River Arno. Twelve hours before, the Germans had blown up all the bridges across the river except for the Ponte Vecchio, which was too narrow and weak to carry military traffic. But each end of it had been blocked by the demolition and mining of adjacent buildings. On the north bank of the river, in the heart of the ancient Renaissance city, lay the headquarters of the Committee of National Liberation for Tuscany and the unified military command of the resistance.

It seemed clear to No. 1 Special Force that the resistance would play a far more important role in Florence than in Rome. Not only did the Arno form a vital defensive barrier for the Germans but the city lay on the direct route from Rome to the Po and was the key to the Apennines. Inside the city the resistance was highly organised and determined. In the surrounding hills, partisan groups were poised to lend their support. The battle for Florence could well be waged street by street. Conditions in the city were grim. It was packed with refugees and on the previous Sunday the electricity supply had ceased and the Germans started the forced evacuation of 100,000 people from along the banks of the Arno and other strategic points. Immediately before blowing the bridges they had forbidden civilians from going on to the streets or into the squares on pain of being shot. The city was one of extremes. It harboured a powerful resistance but was also a Fascist stronghold and contained 1,000 SS troops. Since the killing of Giovanni Gentile in April, the Germans had captured and shot several Italian agents, including a number of underground wireless operators.

Entering the city with the vanguard of allied troops was No. 1 Special Force's forward mission to Florence, headed by Major Charles Macintosh. After disembarking from the *Mutin* at Brindisi the previous September, he had served as operations officer to Holdsworth at Maryland. But after the disasters that overtook Malcolm Munthe's advanced party at Anzio, and eager to see action, he had been appointed by Holdsworth as head of the forward mission to Rome, despite the security section's pleadings that as a senior officer he was dangerously privy to too many of SOE's secrets. After Rome, he had taken on the same role for Florence. His mission was to enter the cities with, or even before, the forward allied troops, help 'friends' and round up enemies, act as liaison between the allied troops and the partisans, receive couriers from the north and infiltrate agents behind the German lines. As well, he was to establish radio contact with the base at Monopoli and, if necessary, with the missions already operating behind the lines.

Otherwise known as '5 Detachment', the Florence mission consisted of five members in addition to himself: his number two, Second Lieutenant Laurence Norris, an Italian officer, a corporal W/T operator, a machine-gunner and a driver. Their vehicle was an American 'White' scout car, which Macintosh described as 'looking like an oversized, armoured bath tub'. But it was fast, had a big 147 hp engine, and mounted in the centre, behind the driver, a steel pedestal held a water-cooled Vickers machine gun that could traverse through 360 degrees, although it was unable to cover the road directly in front of the armoured windscreen. The vehicle's main disadvantage was that it was uncovered, so offered no protection from above. 'A sub-machine gun from a high window could wipe out the lot of us,' observed Macintosh, 'to say nothing of the effect of a grenade landing in the tub.' On the other hand, it could carry all of them along with their explosives, armaments (two Bren and three tommy guns) and all their personal kit. Their entrance into the city was tricky and the sniper problem acute. But with only a couple of near misses they safely reached the river.'

Rome had offered little by way of active resistance, although Macintosh had found a useful recruit as a future liaison officer — Captain Tom Roworth, who'd been captured in Tunisia and found refuge along with a number of other allied prisoners of war in the Vatican. Macintosh had also requisitioned a couple of buildings for use as a base in Rome by No. 1 Special Force. Over the summer Gerry Holdsworth was to establish himself in the capital, leaving his number two, Richard Hewitt, in charge of the base at Monopoli.

Florence, however, was different, and was favourably to alter views of the resistance held by the regular forces. Much of this was thanks to Macintosh, who had been briefing himself intensively with the help of AFHQ on the locality and strength of the resistance in central Italy. The Italian member of the group was the Florence-born Renato Pierleoni, fresh from his work with the GAP in Rome and still on the 6,000-lire-a-month support given him since his recruitment by Salvadori in Mexico. Within four hours of their arrival he brought Macintosh together with representatives of the Communist and Action parties, as well as the leader of the Arno Garibaldi Partisan Division, Aligi Barducci, otherwise known as 'Potente'. 'They gave us the first precious information and we established the first contacts,' recorded Pierleoni. He also helped Macintosh requisition the villa of a well-known Fascist for use by the SOE team. The next morning, at nine o'clock, he also choreographed a meeting between Macintosh and all the members of the CLN living on the south bank of the Arno. One of the most urgent topics was that of communications with the partisans on the other side of the river. They had put a W/T service in place, with one of the two sets hidden in the Pitti Palace on the south bank. But for whatever reason the system failed to work.[2]

However, a solution rapidly presented itself. On the morning of Sunday 6 August, a partisan officer arrived at Macintosh's temporary headquarters announcing that he had been sent by the Tuscan Liberation Committee from across the river to make contact with the allies. His name was 'Henry Fisher', commander of the Action Party's 3rd Rosselli Brigade on the north bank. Defying German tanks and patrols in the old city, he had made his way to the Palazzo Vecchio wearing a grey civilian suit and carrying a harmless-looking parcel under his arm. Helped by a friendly policeman, he had started on the route that was to take him across the river along the secret passageway that Macintosh himself was to take the next day. Adding to the perilous nature of his mission was the fact that the Palazzo Vecchio also housed the SS headquarters for the city.

Once he reached the passageway, Fisher crawled on his hands and knees under the windows and past the unexploded charges until he reached the bridge itself. Here the floor had been largely destroyed and the beams supporting it were on the verge of collapse. He inched his way across the river. The route ended in a gaping hole above extensive rubble that he knew was mined. Untying the parcel, he took out a rope, fastened it round a beam and lowered himself to the ground. Then he sprinted across the rubble to the nearest doorway and the shelter it provided from the German machine-gunners and mortar crews opening fire on anything that moved on the south bank. The Ponte Vecchio had become a well-prepared death trap.

After making contact with Macintosh, establishing his credentials and being vouched for by partisans on the south side of the river, Fisher immediately returned across the passageway with a vital mission. 'From Brigade Signals,' explained Macintosh:

> I obtained a field telephone and some 500 yards of line, all of which fitted neatly into a medium-sized suitcase. That same afternoon, well covered by Bren guns . . . Fisher retraced his steps to a recess in the wall of the bridge which hid the rope from the other side. Once he was safely up the rope, I followed slowly in his footsteps, carrying the

suitcase. Once more the smoke from multiple small fires screened our crossings from the enemy opposite. I tied the end of the rope to the handle of the suitcase and Fisher hauled it up. He let the rope down again, waved once and disappeared into the passageway. A few hours later our telephone rang and we talked to the Partisan officers inside the SS headquarters building. It was almost too easy.[3]

In addition to providing a direct and continuous telephone link with the partisans, the secret passageway also gave those in the northern half of the city a route to travel across the Arno and meet with Macintosh. That same evening, at nine o'clock, Fisher returned with Colonel Nello Niccoli, a 54-year-old professional soldier who'd fought against the Eighth Army in Libya and was now commanding the resistance forces in Tuscany. With him came Professor Carlo Ragghianti, the president of the city's CLN, an art historian by profession. Before midnight, the first of a series of intelligence reports on the military situation, enemy troops, mining and demolition operations, and battery positions on the occupied north bank had been passed on to the allied command.

Macintosh drily recorded the events surrounding his personal crossing of the Ponte Vecchio the next day in the first of a series of daily reports he submitted to army authorities. As well as finding out if the secret passageway could be used for an undetected crossing of the river by an allied battalion, he had another reason for making the perilous journey. While prepared to accept that the Italians he had just met were on the allied side, the SOE training in security he had received at its advanced training school at Beaulieu in Hampshire demanded that he make a personal check to see things for himself. Niccoli, he noted, had asked several questions, the answers to which could also be of great use to the Germans. 'But what had jolted me,' he recalled in his memoirs, 'was to discover that "Henry Fisher" was really Enrico Fischer spelt the German way. Even if our contacts were above board there was always the possibility that the enemy had come across the telephone wire and were ready to pounce.'

Ironically, in personally checking that all the evidence fitted the stories he had been told, he breached a basic security rule himself. Crossing the bridge meant that he could be caught, and if SOE

Security had been warned in advance he knew that it would have forbidden it. 'So I told no one,' he confessed. None of the Florence mission had brought their 'L' (suicide) pills and his commando knife would be of little use. So he made sure to take with him his automatic pistol.[4] None of this appeared in his laconic official report:

On 7th reinfiltrated [Niccoli] to Northern Bank with details of Information requested by Corps. Made a personal reconnaissance to North Bank of Arno to study passage for a number of troops if necessary and made measurements for scaling ladders etc. In agreement with PWB [Psychological Warfare Branch] sent one of band leaders to Rome to make broadcast on Florence from Radio Rome and Radio London. By telephone received message from Archbishop requesting water for other side. Passed this information to [army intelligence] for action. Partizans [sic] of Garibaldi Brigade were used to clear snipers this side of Arno.[5]

The day afterwards, he received an intelligence warning from the army of a possible German raid on the bridge. 'Telephone therefore disconnected, wire taken up. German password for the day passed to other side before telephone disconnected,' he noted. But it proved a false alarm and two days later the line was in operation again. By this time Macintosh was in direct personal contact with the commander of the British 13th Corps, Lieutenant General Sidney Kirkman. Over lunch on Wednesday 9 August he briefed him on the partisans and their strength inside the city, and told him of the conclusion he'd drawn after crossing the Ponte Vecchio that it should not be used for any major crossing by regular troops. 'Having made the recommendation I then pressed for any kind of Allied crossing that would force the Germans to pull out of Florence,' he wrote. 'With the military position unchanged since 4th August, the aggressiveness of the partisans and the ever-growing hardships suffered by the population since early June were bound to lead to some sort of uprising. Without the support of Allied troops the ill-armed partisans would be wiped out and chaos would result. The general said he would discuss the situation at a meeting with General Alexander that day and asked me to dinner that evening to give me Alexander's views.'[6]

The uprising he feared soon began. At seven o'clock on the morning of Friday 11 August he was awoken to be told that the Germans were withdrawing from the city centre round the Palazzo Vecchio. Instantly, he knew that this meant that the partisans would come out into the open and that the battle for Florence had begun. A few minutes later, he was again hauling himself up the rope to cross the bridge to the Palazzo Vecchio. Inside the Uffizi, wood and fallen masonry littered the floor and shattered glass lay everywhere. 'Carried on to Questura building,' he reported, 'where met all the Committee of Liberation.' Just that morning, it had declared itself the Temporary Government of Florence. Most of its members had been living a clandestine existence for years. Privation and exhaustion were etched on their faces. The Germans had withdrawn to a line formed by the main circular roads around the city, and their nearest troops were about 800 metres away. There were approximately 3,000 partisans in the city, 900 of whom had rifles and the rest either pistols or grenades. In addition, they had forty-eight machine guns at their disposal. It was the military command that had initiated the uprising. Now its leaders, aware that they were vastly outnumbered and out-armed by the Germans, were pressing desperately for an early allied crossing of the Arno.

All Macintosh could do was promise to convey their wishes to the allied military command and urge them to avoid pitched battles and focus instead on eliminating snipers. At the end of a hectic day, he had to tell the partisans that they would simply have to look after the north bank themselves and wait a bit longer for the allies:

Gave them their orders. Returned under strong Partizan guard to this side . . . Told to report to Brigade. Reported to Brigade informed Brigadier of situation and explained urgency of sending troops to North bank. Returned to river post where by telephone passed instructions to Military Committee till 1400 hrs . . . Recrossed and examined situation. Issued new instructions to partizan leaders. Received Corps directive and instructed partizan leaders to hold canal line . . . Passed 4 tons of milk and flour through passage to Committee for distribution. Saw military leaders of Committee.[7]

Bitter street fighting followed over the next forty-eight hours, with the Germans making several counter-attacks towards the city centre, using tanks and parachute infantry. On Sunday the 13th, however, the first allied troops finally crossed the river and Macintosh moved his mission, with the exception of the wireless operator and set, to a house on the north bank. He himself took up residence in the Excelsior Hotel, choosing a fifth-floor bedroom so that he could use his hand grenades and sub-machine gun should a surprise German patrol decide to mount its grand marble staircase. Street fighting continued until the last day of August, marked by heavy sniping and continual attacks, including at least one German raid that reached the Excelsior.

By the time the battle for Florence was over, however, an exhausted Macintosh had been relieved by Major Henderson, fresh from his mission to Ancona, and had returned to Rome to report personally to Holdsworth. A week later, Henderson arranged for a formal 'passing over' ceremony for the partisans at the Fortezza da Basso, which they had captured on the first day of the uprising. In front of Lieutenant General Kirkman, close to 3,000 partisans marched past with tricolour banners flying, and the military command formally disbanded its forces.

With allied forces now in control of Florence, Allied Military Government moved in and appointed as prefect a career Italian official. The decision prompted immediate conflict with the Committee of National Liberation over the politically charged issue of the purging of Fascists. This Augean problem had been troubling liberated Italy for months. About a quarter of the population had at one time or another been members of the Fascist Party, along with at least half a million civil servants. For many, it had been a necessity, if they were to keep their jobs and feed their families. So who should be purged? Barely two weeks before, the head of the special committee dealing with the problem, Count Sforza, had issued a new decree and was working on the principle of 'leniency for the "small fry" but remorselessness for the "fat fish"'.[8] But borderline cases were inevitably tricky to decide and AMG were usually reluctant to fire officials with proven administrative abilities. Given that the prefect concerned in Florence had a Fascist past himself, the issue caused a distinct chill between the anti-Fascist resistance and the allies. This was noted with dismay by Renato Pierleoni. 'I have given the Allied authorities lists and information on fascists but up to now no steps have been taken,' he reported in early September. Unless more care was taken in future, he feared, the issue could dampen the enthusiasm of the partisans in the still occupied north.[9]

This was not lost on Macintosh or No. 1 Special Force. The fighting in Florence had put the spotlight on the possible military value of the partisans, but it was also clear that SOE could play a role broader and more important than that of merely helping mobilise them to fight. It could also play a significant part in overseeing their demobilisation and reintegration back into civilian life. At one point during the battle for the city, Macintosh had bumped into Colonel John Riepe, the American officer who headed the special-operations branch at AFHQ. Amongst much other useful advice, he had suggested that Macintosh should be more cooperative with AMG, with whom he'd had several clashes over their rough handling of partisans. Indeed, more by accident than design, Macintosh had briefly acted as senior AMG officer in the city when its commanding officer was relieved of his duties following a surprise and damaging German raid on its offices. The experience had given him a valuable insight into the dimensions of its tasks and resulted in revised rules about when and how AMG should take over from the partisans. From now on, he realised, SOE missions would inevitably be called upon to carry out duties outside their normal military sphere.

Back in Rome, Max Salvadori had been working on this urgent issue for the previous two months. A special committee of the Allied Control Commission had been created after the liberation of the city to deal with what were termed 'the patriots'. The problem was how to get them back into occupation, especially as at first they were not wanted by the army. The existence of armed civilians was an obvious threat to public order and the surrender of arms was a high priority – not least, either, because they were needed for use by the partisans still fighting in the north. So considerable effort was made in thanking the partisans for their services, separating out the bogus from the genuine, issuing them with certificates of merit and finding them work. With this end in view, General Alexander signed an address that was posted up everywhere after liberation thanking the partisans for their work and exhorting them to assist in the re-establishment of their country. 'Your first task,' he told them, 'is to assist the Allied Military Government in its duty to relieve by every means the suffering caused by the war and by the savage brutality of the Nazis and Fascists.'

Many partisans were keen to go on fighting. A few were selected for special work of one kind or another, and the rest were offered the choice of volunteering as individuals for the Italian Army. But this received a poor response, as most wished to stay with their own bands under their own officers. Many came to resent the fact that they ended up doing menial tasks for the allies rather than continuing to fight the Germans. In Florence, during the first week after liberation, only thirteen out of some 350 partisans who did not return to their homes took the chance to enrol in the Italian Army. Nor were they keen to accept other jobs. When a hundred men were needed to clean out a school for the shelter of refugees in the city, not a single partisan came forward to volunteer.[10]

The partisans, in short, were often disillusioned by their reception. 'We need camps, where the Partisans can assemble,' noted Salvadori in Rome. 'Large quantities of rations are needed, and clothing, too. Intelligent officers are badly needed, to sort out the genuine and the bogus Partisans (an exceedingly difficult job), to decide who can join the regular armed forces, who can be employed in other ways and who ought to be sent home ... Meanwhile the Partisans (especially the genuine ones) go hungry, and military operations are slowed down because there are not enough troops for the Italian front now that landings have been made in southern France.'[11] One or two exceptions were made to the rule that partisan bands should not be allowed to enlist en masse into the allied armies; the Maiella band, which had fought along the Adriatic, was integrated into the Eighth Army, and the bands of the lower Arno into the Fifth. But in general the problem of what to do with them after the fighting had passed them by remained acute.

The issue was very much in Holdsworth's mind when he sent Macintosh back to London. 'It might be to the advantage of some people in London,' he told the head of SOM, General Stawell, 'if he were to give them a talk on the problems which attend the employment of patriots as the front line moves up and over them.'[12]

Other problems also confronted No. 1 Special Force that August. In mid-July, a report commissioned by Holdsworth and sent to London had stressed that Maryland's staff, signals and transport were all under severe strain and that if operations increased in August there was a 'serious risk of breakdown'.[13] The Italian section's weekly progress report for the first week of that month drew attention to further difficulties, including unfavourable weather:

> The high priority given to the Appenine area, to the exclusion of more northern grounds during the last week in July, has proved somewhat costly. Most organisations in North West and North Central Italy have now gone without stores deliveries for two months, a fact which has not only discouraged the ever increasing resistance groups, but has also caused some of their leaders to believe that we are refusing to deliver stores for 'political reasons.'
>
> Directives have now been issued to all the main organisations explaining in detail why stores deliveries have not been effected to 'low-priority' areas, and warning those areas which are unlikely to receive many stores operations that they must make their plans accordingly and if necessary reduce their numbers, particularly in view of the coming winter which will preclude stores operations to most mountain groups . . .
>
> In the political field there are serious developments affecting the whole handling of resistance in the North . . . The main problem is an old one – whilst allowing the political committees to continue to assist and in some measure control resistance, how to prevent local political 'by-play' from interfering with the straight military problem of employment and command of the bands . . . [There is] evidence of disruption caused by communist attempts to obtain control wherever possible . . .
>
> It is hoped to solve these problems by the despatch of further B.L.O. missions to all areas of North Italy.[14]

The supply issue was to improve once the special-duties flights that had been diverted to Warsaw and southern France were re-directed to Italy. But this was not to happen until several weeks later. Meanwhile the shortage affected the number of BLOs who could be dropped as well, and the internal politics and rivalries of the resistance rumbled on.

Writing to Macintosh from Rome during the height of the battle in Florence, Holdsworth had kept him up to date on other events:

Commander Gerry Holdsworth, the founder and presiding genius of 'Maryland'.

SOE's man in Switzerland, Jock McCaffery, seen here socialising at a wartime wedding reception in Berne.

The waistcoated Teddy De Haan (centre) with other members of SOE's
mission in Berne, Switzerland, late in the war.

The talented adventurer and explorer, Andrew Croft, head of SOE's
Corsican-based 'Balaclava' mission.

The Brittany trawler *Serenini*, which Croft and his mission used as a temporary base and for training purposes.

The skipper of the *Serenini*, Lieutenant John Newton RNR, seen here with Ignace Bianconi, 'a typical Corsican... not a man to trifle with [and] ready to solve almost any problem'.

Max Salvadori in his
parachute gear, Italy 1944.

One of the many
identity cards carried by
Max Salvadori on his
SOE mission in Italy.

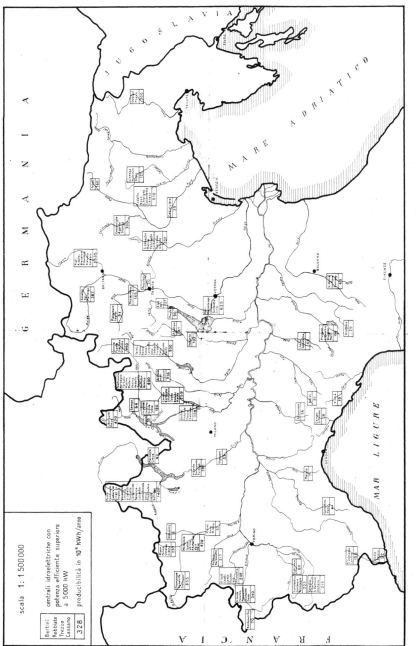

Map produced for 'anti-scorch' operations, showing major hydroelectric installations across northern Italy.

Alastair Macdonald, head of the 'Cherokee' mission (right) seen here with Pat Amoore just prior to a massive drop of supplies near Biella on 26 December 1944.

Richard Tolson (left, with pipe) takes part in a mule-handling course prior to his mission to Italy.

Hedley Vincent at his field headquarters, September 1944.

Jim Davies relaxes after the fighting stops, Italy, June 1945.

Resistance ID card used by Captain Christopher Woods ('Colombo')
during his behind-the-lines mission in the Veneto,
August 1944 – April 1945.

Harold Tilman's mission in North-East Italy, seen here in Belluno after the partisan stand-down,
May 1945. *From left to right*: Victor Gozzer, Tilman, Captain John Ross and (arms folded) 'Pallino'.

Cheerful partisans during the stand-down ceremony in Belluno, 25 May 1945.

Banker Alfredo Pizzoni ('Longhi'), wartime chairman of the CLNAI (right), with Hedley Vincent, head of SOE's mission to Milan after the liberation.

the head of the Control Commission's Patriots' Branch, Colonel McCarthy, was hard at work and Holdsworth was hoping its head-quarters could soon be established close to his own; he had recently been visited by Tarchiani – one of the anti-Fascist 'elderlies' who had landed with Munthe's group – who was hoping soon to get an important job in the Italian government (eventually he was to become its ambassador to Washington); it looked as though SOE would soon get an airfield and squadron in the Cecina district; he was planning to put in a considerable number of behind-the-lines missions in September and then 'pack up' until next spring; and, he added cryptically, 'old C and the chap who won the MC succeeded in touching down.'[15]

'Old C' was the 55-year-old General Raffaele Cadorna, who as commander of the heavily armoured 'Ariete' Division had acquitted himself well during the German descent on Rome the previous September and subsequently worked closely with the Montezemolo resistance circle in the city. His father, Field Marshal Luigi Cadorna, had been Italian commander-in-chief during the First World War. His grandfather, a hero of the Risorgimento, had led the troops that captured Rome in 1870. Even before the Central Command of the Corps of Volunteers was formed in June, the CLNAI in Milan had told Edgardo Sogno that it would be a good idea to have a profes-sional officer on the spot to improve the training and tactics of the partisans, and Cadorna's name surfaced early in the discussions.

After the liberation of Rome, the idea snowballed. Thanks to the Action Party leader in the capital, Riccardo Bauer, who by now was working closely with Max Salvadori, both Holdsworth and De Haan met the general in mid-July at the Special Force offices in the city. According to Cadorna, both were optimistic about an early end to the war, or at least the withdrawal of German forces from Italy. They also speculated about the partisans being able to occupy a large valley in the north, such as the Aosta or Ossola, for the parachuting in of troops and supplies.[16]

A few days later, Edgardo Sogno confirmed that the Christian Democrats and Liberals were also strongly in favour of Cadorna. 'It was a happy choice,' recorded Sogno who, like everyone else, was aware of the need for the general to be acceptable to all the polit-ical groupings in the CLNAI. 'His name, already connected with

Italy's history, was a banner. His past and openness with regard to political problems had helped him overcome the distrust of the left-wing parties.'[17] Sogno had just arrived after his escape from the north and was having his first meetings with De Haan, Mallaby and Holdsworth.

The security-minded De Haan was at first uneasy to learn how much the La Franchi leader already knew about their networks in the north, but decided in any case to take him into his confidence. They left De Haan's room and went next door. 'The wall at the end was covered by a curtain,' recorded Sogno. 'With a swift, clean movement De Haan pulled it back. There was a huge map of Northern Italy made up of many sheets of paper stuck together. Some pins had been placed here and there with little notes and flags. I moved closer. There were some English names on the notes. "This is our work map," said De Haan, smiling. "The flags mark the groups, to the extent that we know of . . . Now you can revise it with Mallaby." . . . The rest of the morning was spent repositioning the flags.'[18]

Once the Italian government had approved his appointment, Cadorna was taken in hand by No. 1 Special Force. At Brindisi he was given an accelerated course in parachute jumping, where he made his first practice jump into the sea. Holdsworth laid out the red carpet by introducing him to Alexander's chief of staff, Lieutenant General John Harding, and arranging for the commander-in-chief to send him a letter thanking him for agreeing to undertake his 'very difficult and dangerous mission'. He also met Colonel Riepe for a detailed discussion about the resistance situation in the north.[19]

There was a week's delay in despatching him behind the lines because the RAF was desperately trying to supply the Warsaw uprising and no special-duties flights to Italy could be laid on immediately. But on the night of Saturday 12 August, after being personally briefed for his mission by De Haan, the general was escorted to his Halifax aircraft by Henri Boutigny. Then, an hour before midnight, the plane took off, bound for a site near Bergamo, some 40 kilometres north-east of Milan. Sogno was supposed to parachute that very night to the same location, although on a different mission, and had spent several days in the same holding house as Cadorna.

As events unfolded, however, his plane was forced to turn back and it was not until several days later that the La Franchi leader arrived back behind enemy lines.

Accompanying Cadorna was a British liaison officer, Major Oliver Churchill, the 'chap with the MC' of Holdsworth's message to Macintosh. Aged 29, and with a shock of curly black hair that earned him the sobriquet 'the Black Prince', he had been studying architecture before joining the Worcestershire Regiment on the outbreak of war. He was no relation to the prime minister. However, one of his two brothers was Captain Peter Churchill, who was sent into France by SOE in 1942 and, after falling into the hands of the Abwehr along with his courier Odette Sansom (whom he was later to marry), claimed such kinship in the hope of better treatment. It was he who had recommended his brother to SOE, and when it suited him Oliver himself was also to let people assume he had connections in high places. After standard training at Arisaig and Beaulieu he was sent out to Malta and then Cairo as a conducting and training officer for Italian and Yugoslav agents before being transferred to No. 1 Special Force in June 1944. He had won his Military Cross the previous September after parachuting into Corfu on a special mission to assist the beleaguered Italian garrison that refused to surrender its arms to the Germans.

Making up Cadorna's four-man party was an Italian liaison officer, Lieutenant Augusto di Laurentis ('Ferreo'), a Sicilian-born Action Party protégé of Riccardo Bauer, and Sergeant Delle Monache ('Alfieri'), the wireless operator. Ferreo's task was to act as Cadorna's 'cut-out' contact link with Parri and the CLNAI. Cadorna adopted the *nom de guerre* of 'Valenti', and Churchill that of 'Peters'.[20]

Cadorna was given no specific orders by SOE and, contrary to frequent assertions in Italy, was not forced on the Italians by the British. But in London Roseberry told the Foreign Office that he hoped that the mission (codenamed 'Fairway') would keep the resistance high command 'on the right lines', and in his brief for it Holdsworth expressed the hope that Cadorna would be able to coordinate the military resistance and become its commander. He also made explicit that while the allies considered the results achieved by the resistance in the north outstanding, they could only support those organisations they believed would 'assist the allied plans for the destruction of the German armies in Italy' – which was why in July, he explained, some 150 tons of supplies had been sent to the Apennines. No. 1 Special Force would keep Cadorna informed of the priority areas. Yet even those not on the list could continue to provide a useful service by carrying out minor sabotage and keeping their organisations intact until later.

But Holdsworth also issued a warning. While support would be given regardless of political persuasion, wherever politics interfered with the organisation and planning of operations which formed an integral part of the allied advance, 'support will not be forthcoming from this headquarters. Examples of this political interference,' he complained, 'have occurred again and again in Central Italy and Le Marche.' For this reason, he suggested, the organisation of resistance groups in the north along political lines was 'clumsy and ineffective' and should be raised as an issue with the CLNAI leaders. Thus Cadorna's first task should be to achieve the maximum degree of internal organisation and ensure reliable leadership within each of the resistance groups. They should concentrate on receiving and conserving weapons and explosives, and while small-scale sabotage should be carried out, stores and ammunition should be preserved for the 'final effort' against the enemy that would be timed to coincide with wider operations by the allies. The ultimate object of all resistance work in Italy, he declared, 'must be to harass German lines of communication by sabotage and guerrilla warfare and eventually to impede the withdrawal of German forces from Italy in order that the allied armies may be able to get at them and destroy them.'[21]

Holdsworth's determination, backed by SOE in London, to bind the northern resistance as closely as possible to allied objectives, also coincided with a crisis in relations between McCaffery in Berne and the CLNAI – or at least, those within it claiming to speak for the partisans. On the one hand, McCaffery and Pizzoni were amicably about to conclude a complex financial arrangement, involving banks in Milan and Switzerland, for a massive 100-million-lire loan to support the partisans, split fifty–fifty between the British and the Americans and to be repaid after the war. On the other, McCaffery's long-stretched patience with the incessant complaints and sniping from Ferruccio Parri and the CLNAI's military representatives in Lugano about the alleged failures and shortcomings of SOE's support for the partisans was reaching breaking point. Finally, in mid-August, after word reached him that Parri was accusing the allies of 'ill-will' and proposing to send him a document on the subject, it snapped.

Taking up his pen and signing himself 'Rossi', he wrote the Action Party leader a scathing letter. 'You are not receiving adequate arms? I know,' it began. Then the furious McCaffery continued:

They have never had enough arms also in France, Belgium, Poland, Greece, Yugoslavia, Holland, Denmark, Norway and Czechoslovakia. But in four years I have not had complaints from anyone else but from you. And no one else has ever dreamt of speaking about Machiavellian designs on our part.

As I have said many times with regard to Italy, I have always acted as a friend. I am now also speaking as a friend . . . it is precisely for this reason that I must speak frankly.

Italy has suffered under fascism; we accept that. Italy entered the war against our wishes; we accept that too. Despite all the goodwill of you and your friends, we know very well how much Italy's involvement has cost us in terms of men, materials and effort.

Due to our very difficult but successful operations you were in a position to effect a *coup d'etat*. That it was unsuccessful was due, in large part, to the lack of preparation and of mutual trust which were among some favourable factors down there. The person writing this letter knows something about it.

You now have the possibility of finding yourself ending up alongside those to whom Italy has caused so much damage. There is no one happier about this possibility; there is no one more ready to help you. But, good God, do not now claim to direct military operations in place of Eisenhower or Alexander.

A long time ago, I said that the greatest military contribution you could make would be continuous and widespread sabotage on a massive scale. You wanted bands. I supported your request because I recognised its moral worth for Italy. The bands have worked well. But you wanted to make an army. Who asked you to do such a thing? Not us. You did it for political reasons; precisely to reintegrate Italy. Nobody blames you for this idea. However do not put our generals in the wrong if they basically work to military criteria; and above all do not try to hold us back with your political objectives.

I do not want to say any more but one last word of advice: You have friends. Do not try to lose them.

Separately, in a simultaneous note to Stucchi, McCaffery also rebutted the frequent allegation that SOE was doing less to support the partisans than the OSS. Providing the tonnage statistics for supply drops for May, June, July and August, he showed that in each of these months the British had, in fact, supplied more than the Americans. But it was not his point, he stressed, to highlight these differences. Both Britain and the USA were fighting the war together and each was doing what it could. What he really wanted to do was make sure that 'these baseless stories are finished once and for all. I would appreciate it,' he concluded, 'if the content of my letter and my comments could be forwarded to the CLNAI.' It was with the hope that direct liaison with the committee in Milan would inject some realism and greater appreciation both of the extent of allied support and of their military objectives that No. 1 Special Force was so anxious to get Cadorna and Churchill into the north as soon as possible.[22]

Alongside the strategic objectives he gave to the Fairway mission, Holdsworth also included more detailed operational instructions, relating, inter alia, to communications. While Cadorna could safely use the W/T sets at his disposal for communicating with SOE in Monopoli, because of the dangers of radio interception by the Germans he was advised to use couriers for messages within Italy. But pigeons were also available, he explained. 'Their maximum range is 300 kms. They can be dropped for immediate use for delivery of messages from occupied Italy to this HQ, or with the object of training them for local intercommunication.' There is no evidence, however, that the Italians ever resorted to this method for other than *coup de main* sabotage missions.

Like many operations, Fairway veered quickly off plan once it encountered awkward realities on the ground. It had been arranged, for example, that the mission would make a drop to a reception party organised by an Italian mission codenamed 'Anticer', which had been sent in a few months earlier and was working with a Green

Flames group close to Bergamo. The partisans had selected a well-protected dropping zone in the mountains. But Anticer's leader, 'Romolo', overruled them and instead chose a reception ground elsewhere, controlled by a band whose leader was a friend of his — presumably, Churchill reflected later, for reasons of Romolo's 'personal glory'.

It proved woefully insecure. A mere four hours after landing, a sudden Fascist *rastrellamento* forced the mission's members to abandon both their main safe house as well as a back-up and spend the whole of their first day hiding in undergrowth. In the confusion, their stores and parachutes, which had been loaded on to mules, were cut loose and abandoned in a maize field.

Cadorna and Churchill had been carrying half a million lire apiece, with another million lire dropped separately. But when the muleteers returned the next night to the maize field the million-lire package and all of Churchill's kit were missing. Other kits had been rifled as well. Romolo blamed it all on 'greedy peasants', although Churchill had his own suspicions about the local band. At least the two radio sets were intact. But this proved of little comfort because Churchill quickly concluded that the radio operator left a lot to be desired. After they finally reached their secure base in the mountains with the Green Flames, Alfieri failed for a whole month to make contact with base. Churchill attributed this to fear of being detected by the Germans and thought that the Italian's explanations were merely excuses. The operator was also extremely insecure. 'He consistently forgot to destroy the worked-on pages of his one-time pad or the workings of encoded and decoded messages,' complained Churchill. 'He mixed up true and bluff checks, having often to ask about things which, as a trained WTO, he should have known instinctively.' It was not an auspicious start for SOE's chief liaison mission with the CLNAI.[23]

Nor did it run smoothly thereafter. Holdsworth had suggested to Cadorna that after the CLNAI had been alerted to his arrival it would be safer for him to stay in the mountains and have its members visit him there. But after a week Cadorna decided otherwise and moved into Milan. He left Churchill behind him with the Green Flames. The group was known as the South Camonica Brigade and numbered about 300 well-disciplined men and boys led by a group of zealous and regular Alpini chosen for their leadership qualities and their knowledge of mountain warfare. Each of the Brigade's small bands of thirty men also had two or three Russians as well as a German deserter. The food was good and plentiful, if unvarying, and every day they had home-killed meat, polenta and milk. Everything was paid for with Green Flames coupons, to be redeemed after the war. 'As all [Green Flames] are natives of the area and do not indulge in looting,' approved Churchill, 'they get all the help they need, and more, from the valley dwellers.' He stayed with them for a month and learned a lot.[24]

But communications with Milan were painfully slow. It took seven days and several couriers for a message to pass one way, which meant that he was unable properly to do his job as liaison officer with Cadorna. Eventually, after a month in the mountains, he suggested that he should join the general in Milan. But Cadorna wrote back strongly advising against it. The city was swarming with Gestapo and SS men. Churchill would be unlikely to survive for twenty-four hours.

To the holder of the Military Cross, however, this was a counsel of despair, and he turned to Sogno for help. By this time the La Franchi leader was back behind German lines, having finally parachuted into the Biella area on 20 August with the Italian 'Bamon' mission, led by Lionello Santi ('Sciabola'). From there, along with Santi, he had made his way to Milan, one of the four major north Italian cities, with Turin, Genoa and Venice, where his network had effective cells. All were tied together by the magnetism of their leader. 'He is physically, mentally and nervously indefatigable, brave (knowing what fear is),' reported Churchill, 'and a born leader for the intelligent, independent, energetic men in his organisation.'[25] Sogno responded rapidly to his request and sent a car to pick him up. On Thursday 14 September, Churchill and his radio operator finally reached Milan, capital of the northern resistance and seat of the CLNAI.

Cadorna, in the meantime, had discovered that as well as confronting the Germans, he faced some fierce battles on the political front and there followed a long-drawn-out wrangle that was never fully resolved. At first things went well. He had a friendly meeting with Pizzoni, and was warmly received by the entire CLNAI leadership at a clandestine meeting held in a convent in the city. But after that, matters deteriorated. Ambiguity about his role had existed from the start. Was he to be a counsellor, or to act as the commander of a unified force? So far, CLNAI military affairs and the CVL (Corpo Volontari della Libertà – armed partisan units) had been dominated by the parties of the left, and especially by the dynamic Ferruccio Parri.

In Cadorna, the centrist and rightist parties – mainly the Liberals and Christian Democrats, along with the Autonomous partisan commanders with no special political affiliation – saw a useful counterweight to the Action Party leader and the left. Sogno also added his considerable energy to their views. In their turn, the leftist parties saw Cadorna, in any role other than mere counsellor, as a threat to their own position. By the first week of September, political deadlock meant the committee was unable to agree to his nomination as commander. Any allied hopes that he might emerge as the Italian de Gaulle, or more accurately as its Koenig (the commander of the Free French Forces of the Interior), were thwarted. It would take until December, after weeks of bickering and in-fighting, for the issue to be nominally resolved, and even then not very satisfactorily. Cadorna was never to have the staff and independent channels of communication that would have equipped him properly for a role of real authority.[26]

# CHAPTER EIGHT

# Looking bright

During the remainder of August six more British liaison missions were dropped to the Italian resistance. Significantly in the light of Holdsworth's brief to General Cadorna and Oliver Churchill about allied strategic requirements, half of these related to Eisenhower's needs in southern France rather than to Alexander's campaign in Italy.

On the night of 31 July/1 August, two groups were dropped to liaise with Italian partisans in Piedmont close to the French–Italian border. Four days before, Alexander had radioed the resistance leadership in Turin that the Piedmontese underground could expect an allied signal very soon, at which time it should launch 'violent and sustained' operations against the enemy. He promised to despatch more supplies and a liaison officer to coordinate plans. From this, the Piedmontese inferred that the allies were poised for a drive into the Po Valley and that liberation was imminent.

In fact, Alexander's directive was motivated by the needs of Dragoon, the landings on the French Riviera that took place in mid-August. So were the two drops, as well as a third which took place a week later. Codenamed respectively 'Ferrula', 'Donum' and 'Flap/Fin', all formed part of a plan that was sometimes referred to as 'Toplink'. This had originated within the allied supreme command in the Mediterranean earlier in the year, and then been refined later by the Special Project Operations Centre (SPOC), the unit at Massingham specially set up to coordinate French resistance activities with the Dragoon landings. The idea was designed to link Italian and French partisans for operations across the border in the High Alps, and No. 1 Special Force was brought into it only very late in the day. Alexander had been told in early July that the campaign in Italy was to be subordinated to the needs of the French landings.[1]

Ferrula was headed by Captain L. Hamilton, the *nom de guerre* of Leon Blanchaert, a 44-year-old Belgian who had fought with the Long Range Desert Group in North Africa and later escaped from a POW camp near Parma. Donum was led by Captain Pat O'Regan, aged 24, who had worked with Field Security in Syria and the Political Warfare Executive in Cairo. Both had been recruited for SOE the previous May by Major Harvard Gunn, an officer from the Seaforth Highlanders who had lived as an artist in Provence before the war. O'Regan, described by Blanchaert as a 'very plucky little Irishman', was the son of a highly respected history master at Marlborough College and had started the war as a registered conscientious objector, working with an ambulance unit in the Middle East, before joining the Intelligence Corps in search of a more active role.[2]

Flap/Fin was in the charge of 'Major Temple'. In real life, he was Neville Lawrence Darewski, the 30-year-old son of the Polish-born Herman Darewski, a well-known music-hall composer and band leader in England. His mother was the Edwardian actress Madge Temple, from whom he took his *nom de guerre*. Previously, he had headed a difficult SOE mission into Slovenia.[3]

The first two missions, trained and prepared by Massingham, were parachuted, after a flight from Blida aerodrome in Algeria, into a zone just inside France on the border with Italy. Accompanying them was Simon Kalifa, a 27-year-old Frenchman and radio operator from Constantine, provided by the Bureau Central de Renseignements et d'Action (BCRA), General de Gaulle's Free French intelligence and special operations service, together with three Italians. One, Livio Rivosecchi, had been recruited by Max Salvadori in Rome, while both Mario Nocerino and Salvatore Parisi, who were wireless operators, were SIM recruits allotted by No. 1 Special Force to Blanchaert and O'Regan, respectively, for communications with Maryland.

The Blanchaert/O'Regan missions received what Kalifa described as an 'extremely cordial' reception about 130 kilometres west of Seyne-les-Alpes, north of Digne, organised by Lieutenant Colonel Francis Cammaerts, the outstanding leader of SOE's French Section's 'Jockey' circuit, and known throughout the High Alps by his *nom de guerre*, 'Roger'. In preparation for the arrival of their mission, he had assigned his courier and effectively second-in-command, Christine Granville ('Pauline'), the challenging task of establishing contacts with the Italian partisans across the border. Granville's real name was the Countess Krystina Gizycka (née Skarbeck), a 29-year-old Pole of part-Jewish origin whose exploits with SOE in France and elsewhere have since become legendary. A local ski instructor took her on the back of his motorcycle as far up in the mountains close to the border as he could. Then she walked across the 7,000-foot-high Col de la Croix into Italy, where she succeeded in meeting up with the local Italian partisan leader, Marcellin, who had about 1,200 men under his control. A former Alpine guide and Alpini sergeant major, he was, in Blanchaert's view, a 'very fine partisan commander'. He was also reputed to be the only partisan leader to possess heavy artillery and a battalion capable of constructing fortifications and emplacements. 'He always remained a rebel,' said another member of the mission, 'an independent and indisciplined lover of liberty.'[4]

Unfortunately for SOE's plans, however, the arrival of Blanchaert and O'Regan coincided with a major German-Italian *rastrellamento* on the Italian side of the frontier and Marcellin's partisans were forced to disperse, regroup and then once again disperse. To complicate matters further, O'Regan fell briefly ill, and Blanchaert was injured in a motorcycle accident and was hospitalised for three or four weeks. By the end of August reconnaissance groups of the US Army had reached the area, but the situation was deteriorating. 'Trying our very best,' Blanchaert radioed personally to Brooks Richards at Massingham, 'but Italian partisans' position extremely difficult following strong German clean up in all sectors.'

By this time, Marcellin's group had been severely mauled and reduced in number. Lieutenant Mario Marpugo ('Michelangelo'), an American officer parachuted in to assist Francis Cammaerts, encountered the Italians at about the same time and was shocked at their condition. 'Practically no clothes or shoes – plenty of them barefoot,' he recorded, 'all of them filled with lice and sick with diarrhea, following months and months of eating just boiled sheep with no bread, vegetables, or anything else, and of course no adequate weapons.'[5]

In the end, the Italian partisans in this region were rendered largely ineffective by the Germans and in October Blanchaert flew back to Monopoli to report. From there, he was sent back to Grenoble, where he set up a base known as 25 Detachment to provide trans-Alpine support for the partisans in north Piedmont. Over the next few months, until the end of the war, he was also to handle the increasingly sensitive issue of Franco-Italian relations in the face of French ambitions to annex the Aosta Valley.[6]

O'Regan fared little better during his first month in the High Alps, and in retrospect decided that, for all his strenuous efforts, it had all been 'a waste of time'. He explained that this was largely because, despite many promises, the French – both the Maquis and the regular Free French troops once they reached the area – had failed to secure the border and thus provide a gateway into Italy for supplying the partisans there with explosives and weapons. Rivosecchi, Max Salvadori's recruit, was despatched by O'Regan across the frontier to make contact with the regional military command and obtain information about partisan formations in the Aosta Valley and elsewhere in Piedmont. He later produced a detailed chronicle of his activities which demonstrates that he was constantly on the move, evading the enemy. On returning from Turin early in September he recorded how he only just escaped a German ambush and was forced to take refuge in a local mine. He remained there for a week in the guise of a workman while waiting to cross back into France. 'In the meantime,' he wrote, 'every day I saw more and more German Alpine troops passing to reinforce those who were already covering the hills.'[7]

In mid-September O'Regan decided to cross permanently into Italy with his W/T set before the frontier finally became impassable because of German activity and set up base at Cumiana, 20 kilometres west of Turin. Here he met up with various bands, as well as an OSS mission. 'I travelled about visiting the various formations,' he recorded. 'My chief objective was to support the newly established *Comando Zona* which seemed to be the only hope, though a faint one, of uniting the bands under some administrative command, not under a centralised military command directing partisan operations, which could only end in disaster.' By the end of October, however, fighting against growing partisan disillusionment with the allies over supplies, combined with the dawning realisation that no major offensive was close, his priority turned to the problem of how the partisans would survive the approaching winter. Helped considerably by Rivosecchi, he was to serve as liaison officer with partisans west of Turin until the end of the war.[8]

Meanwhile, Darewski's mission had been parachuted close to Marsiglia, south-east of Cuneo, where it dropped to a reception committee organised by one of La Franchi's men, Major Enrico Mauri, who headed the Langhe partisan division of some three thousand men, with the task of building links with the partisans of western Liguria. Mauri was a 'Badogliano' and strongly anti-Communist – 'a striking figure of medium height and build,' wrote one British officer, 'about forty years old, with wavy hair greying at the temple ... [he was] remarkably good looking and had penetrating bright blue eyes ... he spoke carefully phrased but eloquent French.' Captain G. K. Lang, a South African war artist attached to the Flap mission, observed the following in notes on personalities he produced in his official report:

> Major MAURI: Cultured with background tradition of an officer in a crack Italian Regiment. Strong personality with a studied manner and affecting certain affectations of dress. Moves always with a personal bodyguard of picked young men who wear a green scarf, his favourite colour ... His personality has influenced the whole division who are more colourfully garbed than other bands (much the same way as the Royalist and Cromwellian fashions reflected in one way the political views).[9]

Prior to leaving Bari, Darewski and his second-in-command Captain Andrew Flygt had been given a rundown by Sogno on the situation in Piedmont and asked to tell Mauri that he (Sogno) would in due course make sure that he was introduced to Cadorna. In his official brief for the mission, De Haan ordered it to discover the character and potential of the partisans and their needs for supplies and instructors. 'No political issues,' he emphasised, 'must be allowed to interfere with the execution of this task which is a purely military one.' With him, Darewski was to take one million lire for his personal use, with another million provided for the mission as a whole. He was also reminded firmly about the need for strict radio security. One of the partisans recorded the powerful impact that Darewski's arrival had on them. 'An ambassador and military advisor of the British and Allied government had arrived among us,' testified Lucia Boetto Testori. 'He represented the official and concrete legitimation of our struggle. With him we became co-belligerents.'[10]

By mid-August, Darewski's group was safely headquartered at Prea, a small village high in the mountains. 'We stayed in this spot about six weeks doing, I think, some good work,' recorded the mission's wireless operator, Corporal Bert Farrimond, a miner by occupation, who had been able to make almost immediate radio contact with base after landing, 'organising the [partisans], getting a dropping ground ("Abram") ready, getting sorties in . . . and above all passing a lot of information back to base.'[11] But in the short run Darewski was frustrated. During the rest of August, he sent an increasing number of fruitless requests for airdrops. These were not to be satisfied until the logistics situation improved the following month. Soon after landing with Darewski, Captain Flygt started west with his own wireless operator to set up the separate 'Fin' mission with a long-established Giustizia e Libertà formation in the Val Stura. After meeting up with the main resistance leaders there, he was joined by Blanchaert soon after the Dragoon landings. But almost immediately, they were surprised by a German attack and forced to retreat up the valley. Eventually, Flygt induced the reluctant partisans to cross the border into France and seek help from the French and the Americans. He stayed with them a month, during which they received a three-plane drop of supplies, but he was then captured by the Germans in mid-September. Fortunately, he survived the war.

Three more British liaison missions were dropped into Italy before the end of August. The first, codenamed 'Ruina', was headed by Major John Wilkinson, a 29-year-old regular officer in the Royal Artillery who'd been born in Shanghai and spent his boyhood in China. He fought in France and North Africa before joining SOE in the Middle East. He had also taken part in the abortive campaigns on the Aegean islands of Kos and Leros and only escaped from the latter by swimming to the Turkish mainland, a distance of some 18 kilometres. 'He was a big blondish character and spoke no Italian,' recalled a fellow officer, 'but nevertheless bicycled around the Asiago area in civilian clothes.'[12]

The mission's other members were Lieutenant Christopher Woods and a wireless operator, Corporal Douglas Archibold. Woods, aged 21, had been commissioned into the King's Royal Rifles straight from school and served briefly in the Abruzzi with the 8th Indian Division before being recruited for No. 1 Special Force in June. With an elementary knowledge of Italian, he had been assigned as an interpreter to the Nembo parachutist battalion for Operation 'Batepits' before it was cancelled at literally the last moment. His briefing for Ruina was, in his own words, 'pretty rudimentary', along the lines of 'we don't know what's going on in there, so we want you to go in and tell us.' It was the first British mission to be dropped to the partisans in the western Veneto. Its action zone lay in the mountain areas of Vicenza and Trento, between the rivers Brenta and Adige to the east of Lake Garda.[13]

All were in uniform. They took off in a twin-engined RAF Dakota from Bari at midnight on Saturday 12 August. Three other British missions were also flying north that night: Taylor and Godwin were bound for Hedley Vincent's mission; General Cadorna, Oliver Churchill and the rest of the Fairway group were bound for Bergamo; and a third mission was heading towards Friuli in north-east Italy.

It was a clear moonlit night, perfect for a parachute drop. Uncomfortably vying for space amongst the jumble of packages on the fuselage floor were the two Italian members of a parallel mission codenamed 'Fluvius'. Major Antonio Ferrazza, a 54-year-old veteran Alpini officer, was about to make his first operational jump along with his 21-year-old wireless operator, Benito Quaquarelli. Based at an Italian Air Force meteorological station in Dalmatia at the time of the armistice, the latter had joined the Yugoslav partisans before returning to mainland Italy earlier in the year and being recruited by SIM. Their ultimate destination was supposed to be the Alto Adige, close to the Austrian border.

The dropping zone lay in a wooded mountain area on Monte Pau, on the southern edge of the Asiago plateau north of Vicenza. The air crew correctly identified the reception party's fires, and the parachutists jumped, one after another, into the void. 'I recollect looking down and seeing shapes which seemed to be houses and thinking that I was in danger of landing on a roof,' recalled Woods. But what he thought were houses were in fact huge boulders, and thus much closer than he thought. He hit the ground hard, executed a perfect parachute roll and was ready for action. Major Ferrazza, however, was less fortunate, landing badly and fracturing his hip. Carried off to a nearby sanatorium in the mountains, he was to die a few weeks later from complications of his injury.

Arrangements for the reception had been made through an Italian mission codenamed 'Pearl', which had been despatched the previous October as one of the first No. 1 Special Force Italian missions to be sent into the field. Infiltrated by sea on the Adriatic coast, it had been in more or less uninterrupted radio contact with Monopoli ever since and had previously organised the successful receptions of two or three Italian missions. Its leader, an Italian Air Force officer named Lieutenant Renato Marini, had already established contact with most of the partisan bands in the region, as well as with the Veneto Regional CLN and the Regional Military Command in Padua. Ruina arrived bringing one million lire in Italian banknotes for his mission, as well as one million for its own. The thirty or so partisans who greeted them with a shot of grappa belonged to the Sette Communi Battalion. This was a band camped out in the nearby Bosco Nero, or 'Black Forest', and sheltering in tents fashioned from parachute silk hidden amongst the pines or in tunnels dating back to First World War battles between the Italians and the Austrians. They were led by 'Cervo', a tall, broad-shouldered regular army artillery officer and a good disciplinarian of strong anti-Communist views. But, noted Woods later, 'he wasn't really cut out to be a partisan.'

Over the next few days, Wilkinson – who took the *nom de guerre* 'Freccia', or 'Arrow' – also met with most of the other partisan leaders in the area. 'Alberto', the leader of the Communist partisan brigades, was a short, dark-haired veteran of the Spanish Civil War who had spent time in French prisons. He immediately impressed the mission with his intelligence and grasp of the situation. 'Definitely a careerist,' the mission's report later recorded, 'but the most capable man of the mountain zone.' He was followed the next day by Colonel 'Cugini', a retired Italian staff officer who they'd been told in their briefing was the commander of all partisan forces in north-east Italy. However, it turned out that he was only a 'military consultant' to the regional committee and the mission's relations with the Veneto Command came to mirror, on a minor scale, Oliver Churchill's difficulties with the CLNAI on the position and role of General Cadorna. It rapidly became clear that Cugini lacked much authority – although exerting this over a vast area covered by mutually antagonistic bands of partisans, as well as stringent enemy security, would have been a superhuman task for anyone.

As part of his brief, Wilkinson had been told to strive for a centralised partisan command, and Cugini was named as the most obvious leader. 'You will probably find considerable difference of opinion between the political parties and the military leaders of the resistance organisations,' No. 1 Special Force headquarters pointed out helpfully, 'but we expect that the arrival of a British officer will assist considerably in clarifying the situation.' This, as Woods later politely put it, was 'utopian' advice and, as he also noted, the partisans were already busy 'fighting the peace'. Before August was out Giacomo Chilesotti, the leader of the Catholic 'Mazzini' brigade, also turned up. He and Alberto were the two most important resistance personalities in their area, although Chilesotti operated in and from the plains, while the mission's contacts were principally with the leaders of the mountain formations.[14]

The mission's most urgent priority was to coordinate partisan activities with Alexander's forthcoming offensive. Codenamed 'Olive', this was designed to break through the Gothic Line into the Po Valley before the winter. On D-Day, the partisans were to focus on sabotaging specifically named road networks and railways, with particular attention on the Verona–Trento, Bassano–Trento and Belluno lines. The remaining units should harass the enemy as strongly as they could by attacking and ambushing convoys, marching columns and troop concentrations. Wherever practicable, they should also descend from the mountains and occupy the valleys through which the Germans were retreating. On top of that, Wilkinson was told, there were special targets that required particularly well-trained saboteurs who would be sent in to carry out the task. To assist in creating chaos as the Germans withdrew, No. 1 Special Force would also send the mission special stores, such as samples of signposts that could be copied and placed wherever they would cause confusion.

It spoke volumes for the optimism then sweeping through the

allied high command and beyond that it was hoped that Olive would see the arrival of allied troops in the area within a couple of months. Indeed, Woods recalled later that when he was at Monopoli confidence ran even stronger than that. 'There was a widespread hope that the war might be over by the end of the year,' he noted. 'I recall myself that when we went in . . . we had been led at Base to anticipate that by October our mission might be overrun by Allied troops or that at least they might be in close contact with us.'[15]

After Wilkinson established his temporary headquarters south of Asiago, plans were set in train for the immediate infiltration of two more British missions. These were 'Simia', led by the 46-year-old Major Harold Tilman, and 'Gela', led by Captain Paul Brietsche, both of whom dropped from a Dakota on the night of 31 August/ 1 September. Tilman's mission was destined for the Belluno region, while Brietsche was allotted the area of Monte Grappa, a 6,000-foot mountain that had seen bitter fighting between the Austrians and Italians just a generation before.[16]

Tilman was a born adventurer, and already world-famous as a mountaineer. In the 1930s he'd teamed up with the legendary Eric Shipton to climb both peaks of Mount Kilimanjaro and had subsequently conquered Nanda Devi in the Himalayas, the highest peak yet to have been climbed. Two years after that, he'd led the 1938 Mount Everest expedition and had climbed more than 8,200 metres without oxygen before being driven back by bad weather. He also had a highly distinguished First World War record. As a teenager he'd fought with the Royal Field Artillery in the battles of the Somme, Ypres and Passchendaele, been wounded twice, and won the Military Cross with bar. He arrived in Italy straight from several months with an SOE mission in Albania, where he'd impressed everyone as the only person who could out-walk the mountain inhabitants of that wild and inhospitable land. Short, stocky and quiet, a man of determined opinions who kept them mostly to himself, he was to carve out a similar reputation in the mountains of north-east Italy.[17]

Brietsche, in his own way, was also an adventurer. He had worked as a farmer and gold miner in Southern Rhodesia after leaving Britain in 1935 aged 25, and had seen military service with the Rhodesia Regiment of the Union Defence Force (in effect the South African

Army) in West Africa and Abyssinia. Immediately prior to joining SOE he had been serving with the Long Range Desert Group. After receiving paramilitary, parachute and ski-mountaineering training at SOE's schools in Palestine and Syria, he'd been assigned to No. 1 Special Force earlier that month. One of his fellow officers described him as 'a cheerful good-time Charlie sort of a man and brave', while another said that he knew, or at least showed, no fear. 'He was a very good soldier,' he added, 'and always knew unerringly what to do. He was also great fun to be with.' Like Wilkinson, he had been instructed firmly that 'no political issues must be allowed to interfere with the execution of your tasks, which are purely military.'[18]

Brietsche's second-in-command, the 24-year-old Lieutenant John Orr-Ewing, had been born and grown up in Palestine and was a law student at Cambridge when war broke out. Commissioned into the Argyll and Sutherland Highlanders, he'd joined SOE the previous September and been trained at its schools in Palestine. The mission's wireless operator was Corporal William Ball, a 22-year-old from Cardiff, whose previous employment had been as a butcher's errand boy and crane driver. Tilman's wireless operator was an Italian, Antonio Carrisi, otherwise known as 'Marini'. Recruited by SIM after working on submarines for the previous twelve years, his lack of physical fitness and general torpor failed to impress his fellows.

The interpreter for this mission was Tito Vittorio (Victor) Gozzer who, wrote Tilman, had proved his worth as an interpreter while working for the Long Range Desert Group. 'He was not long and weedy,' noted the tough mountaineer, a keen observer of such physical characteristics, 'but emphatically lean, with features so clean-cut as almost to resemble the "hatchet-faced" men of American detective stories. He spoke excellent English and presumably impeccable Italian.'[19] He also had the advantage of having been born in the Piave Valley and so was familiar with the area and its strong Veneto dialect. His brother Giuseppe was recruited by the OSS and was also dropped into northern Italy, where he was chief of staff to a Garibaldini group before being caught and later killed while attempting to escape from a train bound for the Mauthausen concentration camp.[20]

Tilman's second-in-command was Captain John Ross, a gunner, who had spent the previous two and a half years in a heavy anti-aircraft regiment setting up AA defences in Iraq, Beirut, Aleppo and

Tobruk before being transferred as a staff officer to GHQ Cairo. But bored with the inaction, he'd got himself recruited into SOE. 'I attended an interview about which I remember little,' he recalled, 'except that I had to see a psychologist who asked me if I was afraid of death – reply "Yes".' He was 25 years old, and had been studying zoology at Cambridge when war broke out. All four of his grandparents were Jewish. But his father had changed his name from Rosenheim to Ross on joining the British Army in 1914, and Ross himself had been baptised as an Anglican – a typical move by many Anglo-Jewish families given the subtle anti-Semitism and more obvious anti-Germanism of English life at the time. Similarly, he had been discouraged by his family from ever referring to his Jewish heritage.

Ross left an interesting account of how he was recruited by Tilman for the mission. After some basic parachute instruction near Brindisi he was sent to the castle at Monopoli where Italian agents received their training. Here, between sunning, swimming and eating apricots plucked from the trees, he spent a few days 'rope climbing, shooting and unarmed combat with plenty of laughs'. It was then that he first met Tilman, who was recuperating after his gruelling exploits in Albania:

> He asked me if I would join him . . . Although he talked little, he could be very interesting, not just about mountaineering but he was widely read with particular enthusiasm for Jane Austen – perhaps my similar interests appealed to him. We prepared for our trip, keeping as fit as possible, carrying heavy weights on our backs over rough country and swimming regularly. Tilman used to disappear into the Adriatic distance for ages. After a while we were moved into a flat in Monopoli where Victor Gozzer joined us. Victor was an Italian Army officer, speaking excellent English with a good knowledge of English history and literature. He came from the Dolomite area and had been with the Alpini. When the Germans occupied Italy after the Italian armistice, he was taken prisoner and put on a train for Germany. He managed to escape and made his way south and joined a partisan group with escaped POW. They joined up with the Americans from Anzio and Victor claimed to be the first Italian to re-enter Rome with the Americans.[21]

Impressed though he was by his comrades-in-arms, Ross was distinctly less enthusiastic, in retrospect, about the briefing they received. 'We went down to our headquarters in Monopoli to be briefed, which was really pathetic,' he recalled. 'The staff there knew virtually nothing about the area we were going to work in . . . and they had very little knowledge of what the resistance movement was doing there and they had very little idea of the geography. They had dreadful maps and sort of pre-war picture postcards of the attractive areas, but nothing much else. So as a briefing it was hopeless.'[22] This contrasts sharply with Sogno's reaction to his briefing by De Haan shortly beforehand, where the No. 1 Special Force map room had obviously impressed him. But the difference may well be explained by the Italian's prior familiarity with the terrain.

For the Tilman mission it was a case of third try lucky. Twice already they had taken off and reached the destination only for the plane to turn back when the pilot failed to find the target. This time, along with the men of the Gela group as well as two Italian ORI sabotage instructors, they made the drop, although with only partial success, as Brietsche reported later:

> We arrived over the target area at approximately 2330 hrs, spotted the fires and correct recognition signals, and the plane began to circle. The exit was to be made in two sticks, one stick of four with Tillman [*sic*] and one stick of five with myself, in two runs. Major Tillman's party was despatched successfully, but on the second run cloud covered the target run. The aircraft then made eight runs over the target, the red light coming on twice, but on the ninth run the green light came on and my mission jumped. I landed approximately one kilometre from the fires, in a forest on the mountain side, Lt. Orr-Ewing landed about 900 yards from me, Cpl Ball landed in rocks in the vague distance, and two Italian Piat [anti-tank projectile] instructors, destined for Major Wilkinson, landed in other remote places. No bodies landed on the DZ [Dropping Zone]. My party suffered no injuries, and we found Major Wilkinson lying under and milking a cow. He stated 'Well, I warned base that this was not a body dropping ground, anyway.'[23]

Brietsche's leg-pulling apart, his report well conveys the all-too-familiar hand of fate that invariably intervened on such drops. If

the Gela group was lucky, however, Tilman's mission was less fortunate. 'I was swinging pendulum-wise and on landing went over like
a ninepin, striking a rock with the base of my spine with no ordinary
violence – a blow which even the packet of two million lire stowed
away in the seat of my Sidcot [flying] suit failed to mitigate,' he
wrote. 'Ross landed in a tree from which he had to be cut down,
Gatti [Gozzer] was all right, and Marini sprained his ankle. All of
us landed wide of the target.'

Worse was to follow. The deteriorating weather that had forced
the pilot into his eight circles of the dropping zone now began to
swirl around the mountainside, blocking out the fires from his view.
After circling again a few times, the plane finally abandoned the
effort and departed without dropping any of the missions' personal
kits or supplies – although Tilman's two volumes of Thomas Carlyle's
history of the French Revolution, which he took along to keep
himself company, somehow survived. Their owner comforted himself
with the thought that another plane would arrive in the course of
the next few nights. As luck would have it, however, four months
were to elapse before the next successful drop.[24]

The injured Tilman and his radio operator (minus his radio which
was amongst the stores never dropped) temporarily stayed put while
Gozzer and Ross left for the Belluno area. Brietsche and Ball headed
in the direction of Monte Grappa, and Orr-Ewing stayed behind for
the hoped-for drop of supplies. Fortunately, Wilkinson had a spare
radio, which he was able to give to Tilman when he departed a few
days later to catch up with Gozzer and Ross. With the corpulent
Marini still unable to carry on, he also provided Tilman with Benito
Quaquarelli as a substitute wireless operator now that the young
Italian was no longer needed by the mortally wounded Major
Ferrazza. He proved a brilliant asset. 'With the most amateurish
aerial, which the experts would view with derision,' testified Tilman,
'he would in a few moments make contact with Base several hundred
kilometres away, and pass and receive messages singularly free from
corruptions.' Ross was also impressed, noting Quaquarelli's ability
to recognise the operator at base by her touch on the Morse key.
Fortunately, these exceptional qualities balanced his personal defects,
which Tilman also recorded with feeling. 'He was idle, insubordin-
ate, temperamental, mindful of his own comfort, and extremely

touchy if any of his shortcomings were pointed out. He was like a desert sore, always there, always irritating, and quite incurable,' he added.[25]

At least the two missions had arrived, and were alive. Not all missions were so lucky. The partisans, usually impatient for action and desperate for supplies, were often quick to criticise No. 1 Special Force for failing to support them. But it was one thing to plan an operation on paper, quite another to bring it to fruition. A great deal was completely out of SOE's control, as Christopher Woods quickly found out. Shortly after landing he was sent forward to arrange the reception of another group destined for the northern mountain zone of Verona province, along with Sergeant Hancock, an escaped British POW. This was the 'Blackfolds' mission headed by Captain Jim Beatt, a regular army 28-year-old from Essex who had volunteered for special operations after demolishing the front of an old cottage while driving his heavy tank at speed through an English village during a training exercise. Other mission members were Lieutenant Chris Leng and Captain 'Roccia', who had been recruited through the ORI as an interpreter. Roccia was lucky to be alive. He had originally been assigned to a sabotage mission. But before it left, Riccardo Bauer had arrived in Monopoli and recommended him instead as an interpreter for Beatt. Shortly afterwards, all the members of the sabotage team were killed when their aircraft struck a mountain. Beatt's team never arrived in Italy either, but for different and less lethal reasons, as he explained later to Christopher Woods. 'We were to drop in an area north-west of Verona. This proved very elusive and we took off from either Brindisi or Bari no less than eight times, twice returning because of engine trouble en route, and on other flights because of no reception at the dropping zone, enemy activity, or bad weather.' Finally, in November, after the snows of winter arrived, the mission was cancelled until the spring. A similar fate befell another such mission headed by Captain Colin Irving-Bell, an Italian-speaking regular officer scheduled to drop with a nineteen-strong sabotage team to attack targets on the Brenner route, but who ended up instead being dropped elsewhere in December.[26]

That partisan operations in the Veneto would be fiercely resisted by the Germans and the Fascists quickly became clear. Ten days after landing, Woods – whose first name had led him to choose the *nom de guerre* of 'Colombo' (which also means 'dove') – set off on a reconnaissance mission to the west. But he was able to find out very little. Just days before, a severe *rastrellamento* by 10,000 enemy troops in the Posina area had totally disorganised the partisans. Even more severe German offensives were to disrupt activities in the weeks that followed. This was to be the general pattern across northern Italy for most of the next two months.[27]

The third plane heading out of Brindisi in mid-August, along with the Ruina and Fairway-Bantry groups, was carrying two British officers and a radio operator to Friuli in north-east Italy, where they linked up with a mission dropped some two months before led by Squadron Leader Count Manfred Czernin. Accompanied by an Italian wireless operator, he had parachuted into the mountains just south of the Italo-Austrian border followed a month later by his deputy, Captain Patrick Martin-Smith.

The task of the mission, codenamed 'Balloonet', was to make a reconnaissance of the frontier of the Austrian Tirol to explore the possibilities of infiltrating agents into Austria from northern Italy. It was also a clandestine mission under firm instructions to avoid all contact with the enemy and to disguise its true purpose by claiming its task was to help exfiltrate ex-allied prisoners of war to safety. Strictly speaking this was an Austrian, not an Italian, mission and would otherwise belong to the story of SOE and Austria. But its intense experience in Friuli delivered information about conditions in the area that proved valuable for some of the later missions there.[28]

Czernin was a flamboyant figure connected by marriage to Britain's Foreign Secretary, Anthony Eden. His father, Count Otto Czernin, an Austro-Hungarian diplomat, was a member of the Bohemian nobility and had been counsellor in St Petersburg on the outbreak of the First World War, the year after his son was born in Berlin. His uncle, Count Ottokar Czernin, was the last Foreign Secretary of the Austro-Hungarian Empire. His English mother, the Honourable Lucile Katherine Beckett, was the daughter of Ernest Beckett, the second Baron Grimthorpe, who owned the magnificent Villa Cimbrone at Ravello overlooking the Bay of Sorrento that had been made available to No. 1 Special Force as a rest and relaxation centre for its officers. Czernin's parents separated when he was only a year old and with his mother he returned to Italy before being sent, aged seven, to England for schooling. Something of a playboy with a penchant for Mayfair restaurants and gambling, he later admitted during vetting for SOE that he had spent a couple of years in southern Africa 'shooting and farming', four years 'travelling' in France and the United States and some six years in Italy as 'a property owner'. He took a commission with the Royal Air Force Volunteer Reserve in 1936 and after war broke out flew Hurricanes with Fighter Command during the French campaign and the Battle of Britain before being posted to the Far East as a squadron leader. Invalided out a year later, he joined SOE in September 1943 on a recommendation from Air Intelligence. In the field, where he took 'Becket', a modified spelling of his mother's maiden name, as his *nom de guerre*, one contemporary recorded that 'he wore a kind of skiing cap with a large peak that made him look as though he had transferred from Rommel's Afrika Corps.' A charmer never reluctant to embellish a story, he was disliked by Hedley Vincent, who dismissed him as 'a romancer', while Dick Hewitt, Holdsworth's deputy, thought him 'a complete bullshitter'. Nevertheless, he was exceptionally brave and his wartime medals included the DFC, the DSO and the MC.

His companions were equally outstanding. Martin-Smith was a Cambridge-educated scholarly former commando who had landed at Salerno with an intelligence unit before transferring, as a German speaker, to SOE's Austrian section at Monopoli. Major George Fielding, the officer who arrived with the August drop and was eventually to take over command of the entire mission, was also a German-speaker who had grown up in Switzerland and studied at the University of Freiburg. He had then lived for a year in the Canadian Arctic running trap lines, worked as assistant manager on an estancia in Argentina, and on the outbreak of war was a cattle-buyer in Chicago. After fighting in Crete and North Africa, he had volunteered for SOE. The mission was based on information provided by Flight Lieutenant Mott, a Lysander pilot captured on a flight to Italian-occupied French Savoy who had escaped from his POW camp and been sheltered by Osoppo partisans in Friuli, who eventually helped him escape to Switzerland. Balloonet achieved its main goal of identifying possible routes across the frontier as well as finding some trustworthy guides, although Fielding personally expressed doubts that anything could actually be achieved in Austria because of the Gestapo's grip, and all such efforts were abandoned for good with the coming of winter.[29]

More important from the Italian perspective, however, was that Czernin managed to identify a suitable dropping zone for supplies to the Friuli partisans that could also be used by Lysanders. In addition he established a successful escape route for ex-prisoners of war into Slovenia, and even managed to send a female courier successfully through German-occupied territory to make contact with Charles Macintosh's SOE group in Florence. He was also able to report on the Osoppo and Garibaldi divisions as well as the two OSS missions in the area, not to mention the behaviour, weaponry and morale of the 30,000 Cossacks deployed in Friuli by the Germans. 'When the Germans use them in action against the Partisans,' he reported, 'they are more brutal than either the Germans or the Fascists.' As for the latter, he explained, their behaviour was scarcely less horrific. 'The treatment the Partisans receive is usually that of having paraffin poured over them and being set fire to. In one particular case in Barcis, they scalped a Partisan, kicked him to death and then proceeded to burn the whole town.' Czernin's report was distributed to all those concerned with Italian operations after he left the area by Lysander in October.[30]

By the end of the summer the prospect for SOE in Italy looked bright, at least from headquarters. 'Our decision some months ago to commence the despatch of British liaison missions to all the main organisations in the field is now bearing fruit,' reported No. 1 Special Force in early September. 'Increased control from this HQ, improved morale in the organisations concerned and a general large scale increase in the effectiveness of patriot activity have resulted.' In general, it concluded, the outlook for the enemy was as bleak in Italy as in France. 'Harassed by strong patriot units and by the mass of a hostile population his efforts at an organised defence are becoming more and more difficult and, we confidently hope, will shortly become impossible.'[31]

# CHAPTER NINE

# 'Rose-tinted spectacles'

The summer's optimism about allied military progress in Italy, along with similar success in France and on the Eastern Front, opened up the prospect of a possible German collapse – or at least an early withdrawal of its forces from Italy to strengthen its other fronts. Early in August, allied planners began to focus on problems that might arise in the event of an early end to hostilities and developed a plan, codenamed 'Rankin', covering two or three different scenarios, ranging from sudden total collapse to partial and controlled withdrawal on particular fronts.[1]

Simultaneously, General Alexander's Olive offensive envisaged penetrating the defences of the Gothic Line and following through with an advance in a north-easterly direction that would force the Germans to withdraw their troops from Italy through the Veneto. This in turn would require the concentration and employment of all available allied forces and leave a void in the north-western provinces of Italy – mainly Lombardy, Liguria and Piedmont – with no allied troops left to deal with any remaining Republican Fascist units.

All this had a significant impact on No. 1 Special Force, requiring it above all to step up its missions in the north-west to help facilitate the introduction of Allied Military Government and maintain law and order during the transition from war to peace. It first learned about Rankin in early August, and within three weeks Hewitt, now a lieutenant colonel and running No. 1 Special Force in Monopoli after the departure of Holdsworth to Rome, had drafted a provisional plan outlining the tasks that British liaison officers might usefully undertake in Rankin conditions. In doing so, he drew heavily on what had been learned during the liberations of Ancona, Rome and Florence. He noted how the 'higher authorities' had lacked any policy on the disarming and dispersal of the partisans and so had turned to No. 1 Special Force officers for advice and assistance, even though this was an area outside the basic SOE charter. And while BLOs had been best placed to deal with the partisans, they had been seriously hampered by shortages of personnel and transport and lacked any formal authority to help. Politics, too, had caused problems, as they had done in the field. 'Communist infiltration particularly interfered with military leadership of the bands,' noted Hewitt, writing of Henderson's experiences in Ancona. 'This problem was not solved with the arrival of AMG who turned to our BLO to solve problems which he himself did not always understand since he was not in possession of any political brief.'

Hewitt's general conclusion was that, provided SOE officers were given the authority by the army authorities and the Allied Control Commission (ACC), No. 1 Special Force could help significantly with Rankin tasks. Military help would include preventing the Germans sabotaging basic infrastructure, assisting in the collection of both patriot and German arms, harassing the enemy withdrawal, preventing 'anti-German or anti-Fascist excesses', and arranging local armistices. On the civil affairs front, they could help restore law and order, ensure the fair distribution of supplies, find re-employment for disbanded partisans and issue them with certificates for services rendered. Politically, they could also encourage 'those trends of political thought which have the support of the Foreign Office and the State Department'. Conversely, they could discourage – 'by clandestine means' – those trends that could embarrass them. Generally, they could spread 'the democratic gospel of Western Europe'.[2]

Alexander launched his Olive offensive on 25 August. That same day, Hewitt appointed Flight Lieutenant Christopher Brock as planning officer for all Rankin matters and ordered that all relevant personnel should be assembled in the Castello di Santo Stefano for special training. Once second-in-command to De Haan in Massingham's Italian section and recently in charge of the SOE unit in Naples, Brock had joined SOE from Courtaulds textiles company in London – a favourite Baker Street recruiting ground – and had served briefly with the Royal Air Force Volunteer Reserve. To help with training, Charles Macintosh provided some specific lessons drawn from his experiences in Rome and Florence. The most important was that liaison officers already in the field would not be suitable for Rankin tasks because it would be difficult to train them over the radio, they were mostly located outside the large cities and they were likely to be biased in favour of the groups they were working with.

In Rome, Holdsworth was also busy. On the day Olive was launched, he met with Colonel Jenny, an American technical expert from the ACC, to discuss immediate post-liberation problems. He instantly communicated the gist of the discussion to Hewitt:

It appears that if the Germans succeed in totally destroying the white power [electrical] network in the north of Italy this country has just about had it politically and economically for at least ten years to come. The absence of electricity in the north during this coming winter, for example, could scarcely fail to lead to the greatest internal strife. We have been asked by A.C.C. to do absolutely anything we can to avoid the destruction of certain vital links in the electrical network.

Jenny will be sending a list of targets to be saved and I am thoroughly convinced we must do our damnedest to comply. The list will be compiled on a priority basis, but every item in it is important. It will need carefully thinking about, but won't you please get the Country Section to make signals to well located sets, earnestly requesting them to fight to the death if and when the Germans try to touch off various installations.[3]

Then, on the last day of the month, he attended a high-level meeting at the headquarters of the ACC in Rome to discuss the measures to be taken with regard to civil affairs in Piedmont and Lombardy in case the Germans withdrew before allied troops arrived. Here, he floated the radical idea of boosting the CLNAI by having it recognised as the 'forward detachment' of the official Italian Government and giving it responsibility, through its military committee, for law and order, enforced by the partisan bands to which British liaison officers were attached. Although the proposal would inevitably run into legal and political obstacles, he brushed these aside. 'Lots of time people are not very real,' he told Hewitt. 'For example, the P.M. when reminded there may be trouble in the North owing to shortage of food said "Any bread riots – you will crush them ruthlessly forthwith." It isn't on record, but the chap to whom this was said asked the P.M. what he supposed they should be crushed with; and it doesn't seem to have occurred to anyone to avoid such a situation arising by the simple expedient of having grub all teed up to send.' To his pleasant surprise the idea was welcomed. As well as strengthening the CLNAI, there was also agreement that No. 1 Special Force should send in 'as many of the right sort of chaps with communications' as it possibly could. 'They buy our proposals lock, stock, and barrel,' he reported triumphantly to Gubbins.[4]

Four days later, Hewitt issued his final Rankin plan. This envisaged an imminent German withdrawal from all of Italy except for north-east Veneto and with it the severe risk of a breakdown of public order, and even civil war. By this he meant not an attempted Communist takeover but serious conflict between the Fascist forces of Mussolini's Social Republic and the resistance as a whole.[5] As a first priority the plan called for the establishment of four missions in the regional capitals of Turin, Milan, Trento and Genoa. As a second, it foresaw fifteen or so further missions in the more important provincial capitals. With several British and Italian teams already in the field to serve as nuclei around which a network of such missions could be constructed, No. 1 Special Force began to plan for three completely new missions equipped with W/T, as well as thirteen reinforcing missions, plus five more to take over from the existing Italian groups. All of them, as both Alexander's headquarters and the Allied Control Commission agreed, 'should assume the responsibilities of ACC and AMG until the eventual arrival of Allied troops'. This meant empowering the missions to inform the local CLNs that the allied commander-in-chief considered them to be the representatives of the Italian Government and that 'it was their duty to maintain order and public services until the arrival of allied troops'. Patriots could be deployed for this purpose, and the degree of success or failure of the committees acting under SOE orders would help shape the nature and extent of the ultimate occupation.[6]

The gist of the Rankin plan was also conveyed to McCaffery in

Berne, emphasising the immediate planning required from local CLNs to prevent the destruction of public utilities such as electricity, water and gas – an issue that was to assume ever greater importance in SOE's Italian mission over the coming months under the description of 'anti-scorch' or 'counter-sabotage'. Also stressed as vital were the preservation of 'all records and repositories of intelligence', the interim replacement of Fascist officials and the temporary taking-over of police duties by partisans. In thus alerting McCaffery, Hewitt was assuming that Edgardo Sogno was then on one of his many cross-border visits to Switzerland and could be entrusted with the mission of carrying the message back to Milan. But if the La Franchi leader had already returned to Italy, he said, McCaffery should ensure through his other contacts that the CLNAI was immediately informed of the Rankin requirements.[7]

Hewitt also reorganised No. 1 Special Force, creating a new out-station equipped with W/T communications (known as 10 Detachment, or 'Compass') in Siena under Captain Pat Gibson, a peacetime investment manager and stockbroker who'd escaped from the same POW camp in north Italy as Eric Newby and worked with Roseberry in London before arriving in Monopoli to help Hewitt and De Haan organise supplies and brief the British Liaison Officer teams. It was 10 Detachment's task to liaise with the special-operations section run by an American Army colonel, John Riepe, at the advanced headquarters of the Allied Armies in Italy, as well as with the OSS, which had established an HQ in the Siena area. In addition, he reinforced the Rome outstation (5 Detachment) and in Monopoli he divided the Italian section into three parts: D (for Destruction), to carry out operations in support of the allied armies; C (for Construction), to work with the Allied Control Commission; and a Services Section, to provide common support for the other two as well as to liaise with SIM. De Haan now became principal staff officer to Hewitt for all Italian affairs and personally responsible for the coordination and direction of the work of C and D sections. Simultaneously, an urgent appeal was sent to Massingham for extra staff to cope with the new 'enormous' Rankin tasks. Among personnel requested were six field officers, twelve WTOs, three staff officers and six secretaries.

Meanwhile, planning went ahead for the despatch of the missions to Milan, Turin and Genoa — Trento having by now been dropped from the list. Darewski, who was already in the field, was chosen to head the Turin mission, helped by a back-up team under naval Lieutenant Robin Richards, who in the event was to be diverted elsewhere and replaced by Michael Lees and another Italian mission. Later, in October, its leadership was handed over to Lieutenant Colonel John Stevens, an officer with previous SOE experience in France and Greece. Lieutenant Colonel Peter McMullen, also with experience in Greece, was appointed leader of the mission to Genoa. Finally, Max Salvadori was selected to lead the mission to Milan (codenamed 'Chariton').

Holdsworth set great store on strengthening the mission to Milan and the CLNAI. 'Either Cadorna's mission must be expanded or another mission, a purely political and economical one, must be sent soonest,' he had earlier advised Hewitt. 'Such a mission would have to contain an accredited emissary for the Italian Govt, ACC and PWB [Psychological Warfare Branch] at least ...' Who it would comprise would need to be discussed, although he had floated Salvadori's name and told Hewitt he was sending Max down to Brindisi for parachute training. 'Let's get him jumped while we do some thinking,' he proposed.[8]

A few days later he broached the idea directly to Salvadori, who unsurprisingly leaped at it. Having been stewing throughout the summer with the ACC in Rome dealing mostly with 'Patriot' matters, he was now getting restless and was keen to resume a more active role. 'I can finish my parachutist's course,' he noted happily in his diary after talking with Holdsworth, 'and at the first favourable opportunity I shall be sent north into German-occupied territory. He [Holdsworth] is in a hurry because he feels that the war will be over this autumn.' Indeed, only the next day Holdsworth confided to Hewitt that he was beginning to wonder whether it would be 'necessary to continue No. 1 Special Force for more than another, say, six weeks'. His hope reflected the broader mood of optimism sweeping across all allied fronts. In the first week of September allied forces crossed into Belgium and quickly liberated Brussels, Ostend and Antwerp. American troops, having captured Liège, were within 32 kilometres of the German border. In the east, the Red Army had advanced 483 kilometres since July and had now recaptured virtually all the territory lost since Hitler's invasion. On 8 September, Sir Alan Brooke, the Chief of the Imperial General Staff, confidently told the prime minister that it seemed unlikely the Nazis could survive the winter.[9]

Salvadori received his instructions on 20 September, with orders to establish liaison with the CLNAI, pass on directives from General Alexander and the Italian government and assist in maintaining law and order and restoring public services during the several weeks it was assumed it would take allied troops to arrive in Milan. Until German forces actually began to withdraw, Salvadori was told, his task was twofold:

> The organisation of patriot organisations to protect vital installations, personnel and factories from destruction and pillaging by the Germans.

and

> Preparatory work in organising local administrative authorities and under them, the patriots, for the day when the German and Fascist administration has fallen and they are themselves responsible for maintaining law and order.

It was also emphasised that he would have no political authority himself and that he should not give official recognition to the assumption or execution of power by any party or group of patriots, that he should inform the CLNAI that the Rome Government enjoyed full allied support, and that regional and local CLNs should not question its authority. 'You should,' the directive instructed, 'give your moral support to all groups and parties which constitute a potential source of law and order, and you should withhold it from all extremist movements, whether political or military.'

The other mission heads were issued with similar instructions. The same day, in a personal letter to Roseberry about his own longer-term future, Salvadori echoed both Holdsworth's optimism about a speedy end to the fighting in Italy and the wider political concerns now troubling the allies. He himself might be tempted to stay in Italy, he told the J Section head, but he would require considerable support in the face of the 'un-British or anti-British' forces he would inevitably confront. General conditions in liberated Italy had recently been better than most people expected. But there were a couple of elements that needed to be closely watched. One was the social tension that could easily lead to sudden disorder and riots. The other was 'the still increasing popularity enjoyed by the Soviet Union', which had not been helped by some recent 'bad blunders' on the part of the allied military administration. 'A considerable amount of work will have to be done,' he concluded, 'if the UK wants to maintain a certain influence over this country after the armed forces have left.'[10]

The Rankin missions were ready for departure by 25 September. But within a matter of days the scene abruptly changed. Bad weather, along with the recent diversion of air support for the Warsaw uprising and a consequent loss of aircraft and experienced crews, had led to a serious deterioration in the supply situation for the partisans in the north. It was also now obvious that no large-scale withdrawal of German forces from Italy was taking place, and the Olive offensive came to an end that week with the allied capture of Rimini. The Eighth Army had crossed the Apennines, broken the Gothic Line, defeated eleven German divisions and penetrated the plains of Romagna and the Po Valley. But this had come at an enormous cost and the casualties, especially amongst the infantry, had been horrendous. More importantly for future progress, the promised land of the plains quickly turned into 'a green nightmare of rivers, dykes and soft water meadows', across which ran thirteen major waterways that formed formidable barriers for allied tanks. What was planned as a temporary pause was to turn into a halt that endured throughout the winter.[11]

For SOE the focus now switched back to immediate operational needs, not longer-term planning, and a mere week after Salvadori and the others received their instructions Alexander's headquarters ordered Monopoli to postpone the despatch of all its Rankin missions. The decision was welcomed in London, where Roseberry had serious reservations about the plan, mainly because it was distracting from current operations in northern Italy. But rather than abandon Rankin preparations entirely, Brock now proposed to send in the teams 'with a straightforward BLO and anti-scorch briefs until such time as they can assume their Rankin functions'.[12]

It was left to Holdsworth to summarise where things now stood in a letter to Hewitt written from Rome on 4 October:

> We are getting pretty close to the winter now and the views held by AAI [Allied Armies in Italy] concerning the cessation of organised resistance have changed more than somewhat. They seem now to be resigned to the possibility of having to batter away all through the winter with little hope of reaching Venice short of Christmas time.
>
> I know that both we and they reckon that there are numerous signs that the Germans are in the process of folding their tents in the North West. I now begin to wonder if we have been looking through rose-tinted spectacles. Just in case we have, and assuming you have not already done so, won't you meet together to consider what the various Rankin parties will have to face up to in lieu of their possible changed role and what aircraft sorties we would have to try to obtain for them so that they could discharge their duties.[13]

Meanwhile, as the high optimism of August yielded slowly to the sober realities of the battlefield, Major Oliver Churchill was struggling with his behind-the-lines mission in Milan.

As Cadorna had warned, clandestine life in the capital of the northern Italian resistance was a perilous affair, and six times in a single week Churchill had to change houses. There were frequent identity checks and the roads were stiff with roadblocks. To explain his imperfect Italian he adopted the guise of an Italian Slovene employed by the regional electricity company. He also carried with him a scrupulously forged SS *Ausweis*, or laissez-passer, because he quickly found that it was always useful to have a trump card up his sleeve. The city was riddled with informers and the Fascist police were everywhere. He lived mainly in flats provided by the La Franchi network, where a billeting officer gave out addresses and passwords to the network's senior officers without ever knowing the names of the occupants. Normally, arrangements were made through a friendly *portinaia*, or concierge, who was happy to ask no questions if four people slept in a room, or who might prepare a scratch meal or warn quickly by telephone if a raid was taking place. Alternative exits were reconnoitred, and before returning to the flat a La Franchi neighbour would always be telephoned in advance with a prearranged 'crack' signal to warn if anything suspicious had happened in the neighbourhood. Whenever he went out, he was always accompanied by a La Franchi supporter, male or female. He used live 'letter boxes' in shops or cafés to pick up or drop off messages to or from Monopoli that were transmitted by W/T sets located in the mountains. The drop he most frequently used was located in a corset shop with two separate entrances and exits. He always enciphered and deciphered these messages personally. Communications with Switzerland were handled by couriers. He always took care over his appearance. Everyone in northern Italy was well dressed – 'better than peace-time England,' he noted – and to be badly clothed was to draw dangerous attention.

Usually, he would meet with General Cadorna on the street, at a meeting place arranged with Major Ferreo, the general's highly capable liaison officer. He was often uneasy about this as he considered Cadorna's personal sense of security to be virtually non-existent. '[He] was under the impression,' observed Churchill, 'that to wear dark glasses and to keep his head over his shoulder as if every Italian was a member of the Intelligence was the best way for an agent to behave.' In case he was suddenly unable to return to the previous night's address, he always carried a clean shirt and toilet things in a small portfolio.[14]

From Milan he made two trips, escorted by Sogno, to Biella, an important textile town in northern Piedmont, where they met the local CLN and where he formed a highly unfavourable view of the Communists. 'Sciabola' (Lionello Santi) and the Bamon party had been dropped the previous month to an unfriendly reception by the local Garibaldini, who were reluctant to hand over Sciabola's stores and who – according to some sources – deliberately manhandled his W/T set so that it never worked. 'Members of the Biella CLN confirmed and added to the adverse reports given me by Sciabola,' reported Churchill, who painted a rogues'-gallery portrait of the partisan leaders. This included the second-in-command, 'Lungo', a 'smooth, soft-spoken, two-faced fanatic', and the political commissar, 'Italo', a 'cunning heartless devotee of Communism'. By contrast, he described La Franchi as by far the most important resistance move-ment and one that was active and successful by any standards. In view of the situation in Biella, he urged strongly that a senior and 'diplomatic' British liaison officer be sent there as soon as possible.'⁵

He also visited the Langhe region south of Turin, where Enrico Mauri headed the Autonomous partisans, and where he and a Justice and Liberty group had – along with other partisan forces in Piedmont that summer – temporarily established a 'free zone' republic. All told, fifteen such zones were declared during the summer for periods ranging from a few days to a few weeks. Nearly all were fuelled by the mistaken belief that allied liberation was imminent. Few if any were suitable for effective fighting against the mechanised Germans. But this did not prevent the partisans from frequently and courageously defending them.'⁶

By mid-November, however, Churchill's position in Milan was becoming precarious, and after receiving an insider tip from the police that for his own safety he should leave as soon as possible, he boarded a train to Como and slipped quietly across the border into Switzerland. Here he contacted Birkbeck in Lugano and, after a short visit to Berne to see McCaffery, crossed into France and from there was flown back to Monopoli.

During his weeks in Milan he had worked hard to bolster Cadorna's position and to resolve the ambiguity about his role. The day after his arrival in mid-September he, the general and Sogno had a constructive meeting with Parri to discuss the protection of power plants, the future planning of airdrops, and the need for the RAF to bomb the Brenner Pass. But efforts to give Cadorna actual command of the CVL quickly ran into the political quagmire. 'It was clear,' bemoaned Churchill, 'that there is NO such thing in the CLNAI as a purely military problem . . . The Communist Party and Action Party . . . were in control of the Ops. Branch of the General Command. Thus there was NO purely military HQ but one made up of men with a firmly fixed political policy.'¹⁷

A week after meeting Parri, and having rapidly gauged the internal politics of the committee, Churchill urged Monopoli to ask Alexander and the Italian Government to send a message to Cadorna simply ordering him to take control as commander-in-chief of the CVL. Three days later, after a stormy ten-hour session, the CLNAI rejected the idea and informed Rome that, by a majority vote – with the Liberals and Christian Democrats forming the minority – it preferred to stick with the current 'collegial system'. The issue was made more complicated by the fact that Cadorna himself was not prepared to force a solution on the grounds that without the full support of all parties, both at HQ and in the field, he could do nothing. Although he was as distrustful of the Communists as Churchill, the latter's unilateral action caused a shadow to fall between them.[18]

By SOE criteria, Churchill was an excellent officer. 'He is,' recorded one of his post-mission debriefers, 'one of those rare examples of an officer who combines a strong taste and an unusual ability for "O" [operational] work with a sound appreciation of the importance and value of "I" [intelligence] work. He is restless and energetic, but at the same time extremely cautious and shrewd in his judgements and observations. He can be regarded as a particularly reliable source of information.'[19]

But whether this made him an effective liaison officer with the CLNAI is another question. His transparent impatience with its politics quickly raised hackles. Max Salvadori, for one, called him 'as courageous as he was intellectually limited'. Leo Valiani, while more sympathetic, described his appearance on the scene as 'unfortunate', on the grounds that he did nothing to disguise his feelings about the CLNAI militants and did everything he could to form a 'pro-Cadorna' and 'anti-CLN' faction amongst the regular army officers he encountered. Valiani claimed that this only fuelled the suspicions of those on the left about behind-the-scenes machinations of SIM and the royalists. '[Churchill] was a brave soldier,' he wrote later, '[but] in Milan the General Command . . . took no notice of [him]. Someone had said to him that the CLNAI was dominated by "Social-Communists" and of course everyone "knows" that anyone carrying the name Churchill can only be a Conservative. In short [Churchill] came to the conclusion that all political parties of the resistance were working for the enemy.'[20]

More significant, however, is Sogno's appreciation, for the La Franchi leader was an otherwise close and sympathetic ally. Churchill, he wrote, was 'almost a caricature of the military and imperial British mentality . . . He was a sincere friend of those whom he knew and felt to be pro-British and moderate but as to Italians in general they remained for him "enemy aliens", i.e. nationals of a country which had declared and made war on Britain and was still subject to an occupation regime. As an officer of a conquering army he would never have understood why the occupying forces could and should not use their authority, and if necessary the whip, to bring into line a few anti-democratic, communist and pro-communist agitators, who reminded him of the fascists and whom he thoroughly disliked ... I myself felt compelled from time to time to argue with him to get greater flexibility and political understanding. The same often happened with Cadorna.' Sogno was not alone in finding Churchill somewhat rigid – he was later described in a message from Italy to Baker Street as 'over-difficult, self-opinionated and tiresome'.[21]

The hostile feelings between the leftist CLNAI militants and Churchill were mutual. In October he was still deploring the 'impasse' within the committee, and before the month was out he sent De Haan a scathing handwritten letter. In Malta, one of his fellow SOE officers (in contrast to Max Salvadori's estimate) had commented on Churchill's 'penetrating and terrifying intelligence combined with utterly destructive satire and contemptuousness', and to De Haan Churchill now gave full vent to his feelings. Deploying a foxhunting metaphor, he described how he and Sogno had tried to promote the groom (Cadorna) to become the master of foxhounds, only to be thwarted by the two chief hounds (Parri and 'Gallo', the Communist [Luigi Longo]. 'The rest of the pack, with one outstanding exception,' he told De Haan, 'more or less followed the other two who are part fox, one of them, and part eel, the other. The hound-fox [Gallo], with orders from outside and a boatload of ambition, is clearly thinking about tomorrow and of the day after. The hound-eel [Parri] is in an odd position, as his anti-hound-fox policy tends to turn his undeniable devotion to the cause into something limited and particular, if you see what I mean.' All he (Churchill) and Sogno sought was unity of control, for – as he rhetorically asked – 'who ever heard of a pack run by a hunt club committee without an MFH [Master of Foxhounds]?'[22]

The arguments were to rumble on until the end of the year.

As the politicians bickered in Milan, partisans in the mountains of Piedmont captured thinly held German territory bordering Switzerland and on 10 September proclaimed the creation of the 'Free Republic of Domodossola'. Lying to the north-west of Milan and west of Cannobio on Lake Maggiore, the Ossola is a broad and sparsely populated glacial valley lying in the shadow of the Alps. Domodossola, its principal town, is also the key to the Simplon Pass, linking Italy to the Swiss Ticino with a tunnel carrying the main-line railway between Milan and Geneva. It was also a vital centre for hydroelectric power. Already, it had been the scene of frequent battles between partisans and the Germans, and a severe *rastrellamento* the previous May had resulted in the deaths of at least 200 partisans as well as heavy civilian reprisals. As in the case of the Montefiorino Republic, the partisans now set up a provisional government, removed Fascist mayors and officials from office, and started passing laws and decrees. Enthusiasm ran high, and its leaders called for massive allied support. Some saw it as the opening shot in a campaign that would spark outright insurrection in Milan, and the possibility was discussed seriously by the CLNAI. Dr Ettore Tibaldi, a socialist exile in Lugano, was even conveyed in a special train from Berne to Domodossola to assume the presidency. General Bianchi in Berne managed to send some volunteer regular army officers interned in Switzerland to help. The Swiss even extended their diplomatic recognition.

But the hopes were to be bitterly disappointed. The Germans had withdrawn only to regroup, and just five weeks later a 12,000-strong force of neo-Fascist Black Brigades, Fascist militia and German troops with tanks and artillery under the command of SS General Tensfeld launched a massive drive against the approximately 3,000 partisans. Within a week they had recaptured Domodossola, and the surviving partisans, along with Tibaldi and other members of the government, fled across the border into Switzerland or retreated further into the mountains.

Bitter recriminations followed. The uprising had been largely spearheaded by Autonomous and Catholic partisans assisted by a couple of Garibaldini brigades. But once the republic had been estab-lished, the Communist, Christian Democratic and Socialist parties all rushed in representatives to set their own political mark on events and the CLNAI became deeply involved in the inevitable political wrangles that followed. When it all collapsed, some of the Catholic groups accused the Garibaldini of leaving them in the lurch. Nearly all blamed the allies for not giving them enough support. To Ferruccio

Parri, writing after the war, the episode represented 'the most obvious and painful example of Allied lack of interest in liberating certain frontier areas'.[23]

Some supply drops were made by air, but not many, and so far as No. 1 Special Force was concerned it was an uprising to hold territory they had never sought. Jock McCaffery, who was physically closest to the action, argued later that the whole enterprise was a miscalculation which he had opposed from the start as a huge provocation that the Germans were bound to crush. 'Birkbeck day in and day out, and I myself in every relevant contact or trip to Lugano,' he wrote, 'tried to dissuade the proponents of the project . . . We implored them to have patience and to increase their hit-and-run routine, the only possible one against superior military forces still far from being in disarray. It was no good . . .'[24]

Here, however, his memory played tricks on him. The idea of capturing the Val d'Ossola had first surfaced in late May amidst euphoria about the impending liberation of Rome, with G. B. Stucchi, the Lugano-based military representative of the CLNAI and successor to Damiani, as its main proposer. McCaffery's explanation for his enthusiasm, as in part an attempt to emulate the triumphs of the French resistance as well as an effort to give the Italian exile colony in Switzerland the chance of playing an active role in the patriotic struggle, rings true. What his post-war account obscures, however, is that when Stucchi first raised the idea with him he responded positively and persuaded both Roseberry and Holdsworth to give it serious thought, to the point that London agreed the uprising could be supported, with initial stores being dropped during the impending moon period. In fact, London told him, if a sufficiently large tract of land could be set up as a free zone, drops could be made from high altitude in the non-moon period. They could also find fifty or possibly more trained Italian parachutists to join the uprising. A prior condition, however, would be the establishment of a direct communication link with the partisans.[25]

Three weeks later, two Italian missions were duly dropped to the area and made radio contact back to base, with courier links established to Milan. But this did not mean that the allies were committed to the idea of a free zone as proposed by Stucchi, which went against all lessons of partisan warfare. Furthermore, as London had made clear to McCaffery from the start, any support for the project was subject to decisions on overall priorities in Italy. Over the summer, however, the project acquired a momentum of its own and — so McCaffery claimed — only when it seemed unstoppable did he decide that he had little choice but to lobby hard for the uprising and enlisted Allen Dulles and the OSS to the cause. 'We actually half-indulged in blackmail by speaking of the extremely negative reactions it would have upon all of the Italian Resistance and upon the country in its entirety if we did not do all we could to help,' he wrote.[26]

The major step he personally took was to send in Lieutenant George Paterson as an official allied representative ('observer-adviser') to the Val d'Ossola partisans. Paterson, a Canadian, had been captured in Calabria during the first airborne commando operation of the war and had spent two and a half years as a prisoner of war in Italy before escaping from a crowded boxcar transporting him to Germany and crossing into Switzerland. He'd then gone back into Italy to assist other allied POWs before being captured again, along with several other members of an escape line, and spending three months in solitary confinement with the usual torture and interrogations as an SS prisoner in Milan's notorious San Vittore prison. Miraculously, he'd escaped yet again, this time by bribing a guard to get a key cut. He had arrived back in Switzerland just a few weeks before.

Paterson made two trips to Berne to be personally recruited and briefed by McCaffery. As he later told his story, the hopes for the uprising expressed by SOE's man in Berne (whom he identified as 'John McTavish') went as follows. 'It may all come to nothing I grant you, but there is a chance it could spread . . . if North Italy were to rise in rebellion it would cut the German Army's lines of supply and almost certainly force them into surrender . . . That's why we have to do all we can to help them.' McCaffery went on to explain that while for the moment the partisans had all the weapons they needed, if the uprising 'starts to roll' they would need more and airdrops would become necessary — which was why he needed Paterson on the spot.

But there was another reason, too. How, asked McCaffery, were the partisans going to handle themselves if they succeeded in establishing the free zone? 'Will they co-operate to govern or will they break up into factions with the possibility of civil war?' he wondered. 'This may give us some clue as to what will happen in the country as a whole once Jerry is finished. The diplomats in London and Washington are interested and want reliable reports on the way it develops politically, so whoever goes in has to be half soldier and half political observer.' Even discounting some of this as cajolery and flattery by McCaffery to persuade Paterson to take on the mission, it undoubtedly reflects the reality that the allies were profoundly concerned about the likely political fallout of partisan success in Italy.[27]

A resourceful and tireless British Columbian who'd been studying forestry at the University of Edinburgh when war broke out, the 25-year-old Paterson crossed back into Italy three days before the Domodossola Republic was proclaimed, accompanied by an Italian interpreter. Waiting for him on the other side of the frontier was Colonel Monetta, formerly of the Royal Sardinian Cavalry, his designated liaison with the partisans, who were fairly well armed but short on ammunition. Soon afterwards he was also introduced to Ettore Superti, head of the local Autonomists, Armando Calzavara ('Arca') of the Green Flames and Captain Alfredo DiDio, leader of the Catholic Val Toce Division, which Paterson regarded as by far the best of the partisan groups. Vincenso Moscatelli ('Cino'), the commander of the Garibaldini, whom he also soon met, was a veteran anti-Fascist from Milan who'd recently returned from Moscow. Paterson was impressed by his drive but noted that he had 'an evil reputation for solving political differences with a bullet'. His was by far the largest partisan grouping. Little love was lost between him and the others.[28]

Apart from a single visit back across the frontier to meet up with Birkbeck and collect some 20 million lire for the Domodossola government, which he personally delivered to a delighted Tibaldi, Paterson spent the next five weeks taking part in various councils of war, urging that an effective centralised military command be established, and seeing his efforts constantly sabotaged by political acrimony. On one occasion at least, he waited for an allied airdrop that never materialised. After much wrangling, a unified command emerged that included Paterson and had Stucchi as its commander-in-chief. It made little difference, with any real unity perpetually undermined by what Paterson described as 'local party politics, distrust and jealousy, [and] the inability of Civil and Military authorities to agree on important questions such as requisitioning billets, etc.' Acting on instructions, he repeatedly tried to convince all concerned that a *rastrellamento* was inevitable. But the partisans refused to retire back to the mountains.[29]

Finally, on 8 October, the Germans launched their inevitable attack. As he accompanied DiDio and his brigade on a foray against their advance, Paterson was caught in an ambush on a mountain pass close to Lake Maggiore. Both DiDio and Monetta were killed and he himself was captured. After about five weeks in jail in Novara, he was collected by the SS and returned to the San Vittore prison in Milan, where he was to stay until the city was liberated in April 1945. Given the timing of the Domodossola uprising, Paterson concluded, the allies had been right to give it a low priority, because it was doomed from the beginning and was fatally riven by politics. But it would have been better to tell the partisans from the start that there was no hope of support instead of them 'being half-promised drops and fighter-bomber support for local attacks' that never came.[30]

Other uprisings took place that summer, encouraged if not actually ordered by the CLNAI, which was readying itself for the immediate assumption of interim political power by drawing up blueprints for civil administration and broadening the scope of local CLNs to include shopkeepers, farmers and the professional classes. It also prepared a special currency and on 14 September declared that all the orders issued by Mussolini's Fascist government were 'null and void'. Six days later, inspired by the Eighth Army's liberation of Rimini, it issued a call for insurrection throughout the Romagna. Widespread partisan attacks killed and injured hundreds of German troops, and in Bologna several daring attacks on jails saw dozens of prisoners freed. In the Friuli mountains flanking the River Tagliamento, where the Garibaldini had two fighting divisions, the 'Natisone' and the 'Nino Nanetti', and where the non-Communist Osoppo brigades enjoyed considerable popularity, a free zone was briefly established known as the 'Republic of Carnia'. But here, as elsewhere, success was short-lived. In early October the Germans, using SS and Cossack troops, launched a severe counter-attack and by the end of the month the republic was dissolved.[31]

Such counter-attacks were often accompanied by the massacre of civilians. Already in August, in the village of Sant'Anna di Stazzema near Lucca, SS troops had machine-gunned some 560 inhabitants: men, women and children. Now, following the Bologna attacks, there occurred one of the worst German massacres of the entire Italian campaign. Between 28 and 30 September near the village of Marzabotto, on Monte Sole south of Bologna, SS troops retaliated against local support for the partisans by slaughtering some 700 civilians, including the local priest, and they continued the killings for another week in the countryside around – the single worst massacre in western Europe during the entire war.[32]

Marzabotto, while the largest and the most notorious, was by no means unique – the German atrocity record in Italy far outmatched that in France. Oldham of the 'Turdus' mission in the Apennines reported one such massacre in chilling detail. In August, the local partisans killed sixteen SS troops during a firefight. As a reprisal, more than twenty villages were burned and the entire populations of two of them were killed. 'In addition to the babies of 3 months old and old women of 70 years old,' reported Oldham,

> 50 young men from the ages of 18–30, previously taken as hostages, were killed in the following manner. Having been first dragged for a few hundred yards behind a vehicle, they were lined up with a steel wire round their necks in such a manner as they had to stand upright. Then the SS shot at their legs with LMGs [light machine guns] and they died of strangulation.
>
> This atrocity in which over 400 civilians were massacred was committed by German and Italian SS. One child of seven years old escaped as she was hidden under the body of her mother and father but she was very lucky as the SS finished off the other children protected by their parents with the pistol, lifting up the corpses of their parents to do so.[33]

The killings were part of a wider and deliberate strategy adopted by the German commander in Italy, Field Marshal Albert Kesselring, who assumed full responsibility for dealing with the

partisans. He made no secret of the fact that he considered guerrilla warfare 'a degenerate form of war', and he treated those
involved accordingly. When partisan threats began to escalate in
the early summer, he had issued an order declaring that the fight
against them should be carried on with all means at the Germans'
disposal 'and with utmost severity'. He would, he said, protect any
commander who exceeded their 'usual restraint [*sic*] in the choice
of the methods he adopts against the partisans. In this connection,' he added, 'the principle holds good that a mistake in the
choice of methods in executing one's orders is better than failure
or neglect to act.' In part his orders were a reaction to the growing
number of appeals by Alexander to the partisans to assist the allied
armies as they advanced north from Rome. But this provided no
good reason or excuse. Already, long before Alexander's appeal, the
Germans had shown their brutality and ruthlessness in the massacre
of the Ardeatine Caves. Decrypted by the codebreakers at Bletchley
Park, Kesselring's order was sent to the prime minister on 20 June
1944.[34]

On 1 July, Kesselring issued yet further orders, decreeing that
where there was evidence of considerable numbers of partisans
hostages would be taken, and where Germans troops were fired on
from any village it would be burned down, with perpetrators and
ringleaders hanged in public. By the end of the month his orders
were extended to declare that all captured partisans would be shot,
as would all civilians who supplied the partisans with food, shelter
or military information, who carried arms, ammunition, explosives
or other war materiel, or who hid such weapons, or who failed to
report such materiel concealed by others, or who committed sabotage.
When it came to hostages, up to ten able-bodied Italians would be
shot for every German soldier killed.[35]

There was no letting-up of German anti-partisan action over the
summer, and the events of September produced an increasing sense
of frustration at Kesselring's headquarters. Finally, on 1 October, he
ordered a special 'Anti-Partisan Week' to make finally clear to the
partisans the extent of German power. Supply traffic was being
severely handicapped, acts of sabotage were becoming ever more
frequent and – he declared – the partisan 'pest' should be countered
with every available means and the utmost severity. This and other

anti-partisan drives throughout the autumn were to take their toll on SOE's efforts behind the lines.[36]

In the Veneto, Wilkinson's Ruina mission faced considerable frustration because of both German *rastrellamenti* and partisan resistance to the idea of a unified command. October, in Woods's own words, was 'grim', marked largely by filthy weather and the absence of allied airdrops. Partisan morale plummeted, along with their opinion of the SOE officers. 'What made us so angry,' complained Orr-Ewing and Woods later, 'was not the lack of drops, but that HQ never sent us any explanation for it, and never answered one question.'[37] Typical was the fate of what had been planned in early November as a 'fireworks day', a series of coordinated sabotage attacks throughout the Veneto to be launched in combination with Tilman and his group. But none of the explosives they had requested arrived and they simply had to abandon the scheme. Tilman himself, entrenched with the Garibaldini of the Nino Nanetti Division, also lacked supplies. 'We [were] in the field nine weeks without receiving so much as a pair of socks or spare shirt,' he lamented later, 'and we were to pass another eight weeks before this happy event occurred.'[38]

Brietsche, who had dropped with Tilman to Wilkinson's reception party, fared even worse. Two days after landing, he was despatched to Monte Grappa, where four bands of partisans were believed to be operating. The mountain — in reality more of a vast barren massif — had been the scene of a decisive battle just a generation before. Here, the Italians had finally held the German and Austrian armies after their disastrous rout at Caporetto, and the ground was still pockmarked with shell holes. Twenty-five thousand men of both sides had died in this mini-Verdun, and to the Italian partisans the mountain held semi-mythical status. Yet, when the Germans launched a massive offensive on 21 September, they rapidly disintegrated. For the next three weeks Brietsche was on the run in a cat-and-mouse chase with the enemy, desperate to keep his W/T set, but sometimes being forced to hide it and recover it later.

Finally one morning — ominously it was Friday 13 October — he spotted a German patrol labouring up the hill towards his hiding place. It was hot, the soldiers were sweating and they had their heads down. Leading them was a civilian guide. 'To get away . . .

entailed coming out through the front door in full sight of the enemy and going up an open bank at the back for about sixty yards before being able to disappear out of sight,' recorded Brietsche. 'There was no time to grab anything, but we managed to get away as no enemy happened to glance up. Their guide spotted us, but just grinned and winked and said nothing . . . [but] I lost my radio for good, and the enemy once more discovered that the British mission was still in the vicinity.' As a result, he decided to abandon the scene altogether and headed east to join Tilman. Morale was low. 'We were all completely fed up with the partisans, and considered that they were all useless and not worth working for,' he recorded, and he sought permission from No. 1 Special Force to be exfiltrated from Italy. Tilman, however, persuaded him to stay, and over the following few months he would considerably change his opinion of the partisans.[39] Not surprisingly, there was much subsequent finger-pointing over the Monte Grappa disaster, and the partisan commander 'Bruno' accused Brietsche of having wished 'to make a Verdun' of the stronghold. This is possible – his radio messages from the field no longer exist – but on the balance of probabilities it seems more likely that Bruno was the person pressing for a fortress-like defence of the position. But certainly Brietsche himself later admitted that he had made a mistake in ignoring warnings of the impending German attack. Ironically, not long afterwards, when Tilman's mission was caught in a rather similar position in Bruno's area and cornered by a German attack, it was Bruno who advocated a fight to the finish. Turning to Gozzer, he suggested that they should 'show the British how the Italians know how to die'. But Tilman's interpreter had a better idea. 'Wouldn't it be better to show them that we know how to live?' he asked. His advice was acted upon and they all took cover, and survived.[40]

To the east of these missions, in Friuli, Hedley Vincent and his Coolant mission experienced a major *rastrellamento* in late September which drove him on the run for the next few weeks. He lost the battery for his W/T set and was forced to use the electricity supply in Castelmonte, a monastery he described as 'a miniature Cassino'. It contained four houses and an inn all enclosed by a high wall with a single door forming the entrance to the village, some 600 metres up. But, he recorded, 'the monks were nervous and the population scared stiff lest we should bring the Germans up after us.' Still, he managed to send three messages back to base before he finally moved on in mid-October.

By then it was clear that the allied advance had finally ground to a halt for the year and that, as he wrote, 'we had had our fling.' After agreeing with the partisans that they should scale back operations from deliberate clashes with the enemy to acts of sabotage, and reduce their forces to a minimum, Vincent left the mission in late October and arrived back in Bari in early November. He exited via Slovene-held territory, where it was now vividly clear that territorial disputes over the border between the Italians and the Yugoslavs were becoming urgent and acute.[41]

Given the sometimes critical view by liaison officers in the field of the air support they received – or failed to receive – it is worth quoting from Vincent's tribute to the skill, perseverance and courage of the pilot who brought him out:

We were waiting on the air strip at Otok in most wretched weather for the arrival of two planes, whose E.T.A. was 2220 hours local time. There was a strong, gusty wind developing along the runway opposite to the direction in which the aircraft was to land. The sky, which two or three hours previously had been relatively clear, clouded over to ten tenths. The airfield itself was scarcely serviceable, being in places under water. The fact there was an airman seriously ill awaiting evacuation influenced the decision of the R.A.F. officer on the ground to declare the field serviceable.

When the plane finally arrived, two hours late, it pulled up with its wheels thick in the mud:

The prospects of a safe take-off did not seem rosy as the ground was so sticky as to prevent the development of sufficient speed. The pilot paced the ground in my company and decided to have a go hoping to be airborne by the time the last light of the runway was reached. Beyond this point not many yards away was a river.

The sick man was put on board with other priority passengers. All weight was reduced to a minimum and the plane took off. It was safely airborne directly opposite the last light, climbed rapidly into appalling weather which persisted for more than an hour before we broke out over the Adriatic. We touched down at Bari, most grateful for this splendid effort by the R.A.F.[42]

In the Apennines, the SOE missions also experienced mixed fortunes. Jim Davies's group in the Parma region witnessed several successful partisan actions in September and early October. These included attacks on German transports along the Parma–La Spezia highway, assaults on a couple of enemy garrisons in which some fifty Germans were killed, raids down to the plains to collect prisoners, stores, horses, cars and arms, as well as attacks on local railways. But after mid-October, he reported, 'the enemy took the offensive by sending up strong patrols which sometimes sought battle and sometimes not. We lacked ammunition and our whole main line was withdrawn apart from outposts . . .' In spite of this, he noted that morale remained good. He also tried to dispel the notion, which was gaining strength at higher levels, that the partisans should be regarded with suspicion or fear. They had great tactical potential in assisting in any future allied advance, he stressed, and about 70 per cent or more would want to go home after being liberated. Their discipline was now such, he added, 'that disorders will be unlikely'.[43]

In nearby Modena, Wilcockson also concluded that the partisans were unlikely to cause political trouble, mostly because he was convinced that the majority were more desperate to avoid service with Mussolini's Republican Army than because they had any real political commitment. He, too, as in the missions in the north-east, witnessed a distinct decline in morale as the autumn progressed. It peaked with his mission's arrival, and with it the promise of supplies, but deteriorated rapidly after mid-September. Successive entries in his after-action report paint a graphic picture of collapsing spirit.

Sept. 10th: On receipt of orders from Base the attack and occupation of Modena was arranged in conjunction with Partisans from inside the town in the event of an enemy withdrawal. On the night of the 10th the long awaited drop arrived and was found to consist of only 12 containers (one half plane load). On examination, the load was found not to contain one of the items which had been urgently requested since August 27th. This had the effect of causing the Partisan morale to slump badly, the prestige of the British Mission to reach rock bottom and the all-out effort to come to a virtual standstill for lack of supplies.

Sept. 17th. A new H.Q. was established at Quara and a new dropping ground recced and opened. The position of Partisan supplies – particularly ammunition – was now extremely critical and any offensive operations against the enemy impossible.

Oct. 13th. Despite urgent and repeated signals, we were still without a supply drop and, during the night, the enemy surrounded a partisan outpost at Manno, captured and hanged 11 of the Partisans and cut the throat of the twelfth, who had expressed a desire not to be hanged . . . The Partisans had not fired a shot and had given themselves up when the enemy set fire to the house.

Oct. 14th. Left Quara (which was occupied by enemy 2 hours later) and fled to Romanoro. The Partisans' morale was nil. They saw the approach of winter; they were without boots, ammunition and winter clothing and, in their opinion, were handicapped by a British Mission and alleged supply officer whose record to date stood at 12 containers since August 26th – a pitiful show!

Even after they moved to a quieter location and found a new dropping ground, morale stayed low. The allies were obviously no longer advancing, supplies remained critical and, worst of all, partisans who asked to cross the lines into liberated Italy in complete formations to re-equip and fight with the allies were refused permission to do so as a matter of policy.[44]

If September and October were thin on the provision of supplies, the same held true for the despatch of British liaison officers.

Early in September, Darewski's mission in Piedmont was reinforced by Captain Michael Lees, who'd previously worked with Mihailović's Chetniks in Serbia. Self-confessedly unamenable to discipline and described by Charles Macintosh as 'the most impatient and headstrong of the BLOs', the restless Lees had been recruited by SOE in Cairo from a parachute battalion and had married one of SOE's FANY signallers, Gwen Johnson, in Bari Cathedral just the month before. He parachuted in with Captain Geoffrey Long, a South African war artist, and Paul Morton, a Canadian war correspondent from the *Toronto Star*. Both had been given the job of publicising the exploits of the partisans. Lees had met Darewski on a short training course and liked him. He was, he wrote, a 'charming rather cosmopolitan person [with] a great attitude'.[45]

Darewski's headquarters lay in a mountain hut 900 metres above sea level, with views across the Piedmont plains to Turin. The Alps lay beyond, and on clear days Lees could see the snow-covered peaks of both Mont Blanc and the Matterhorn. Occasionally, he would watch as a squadron of American Thunderbolts, black specks against the white, attacked some German convoy or fortification, and he'd see small puffs of smoke climb into the air, or hear the distant rattle of automatic fire. While Darewski made frequent visits to the Committee of National Liberation in Turin and warned that the 'pro-Communist' city could cause problems unless dealt with firmly and promptly once the Germans left, preferably through the imposition of martial law, Lees helped train the partisans in discipline and weaponry and enjoyed the physical rigours of mountain life. In between times, he spent spare moments talking with Bert Farrimond, the mission's wireless operator. He was the ideal type for the job, thought Lees. A 'dour Lancashire miner in civil life,' he recorded, 'he would never give up a task as hopeless. Sometimes when conditions were bad and he had difficulty in contacting base he worked away for hours, determinedly tapping out his call signal and never letting up until he got an answer. He only complained when there was not enough to do, and then he could be very tiresome.' When Farrimond confessed that his favourite pastime was wildfowling, that he was no stranger to poaching and that he loved life in the mountains, Lees felt that he had found a kindred spirit.[46]

But the idyll was short. After only three weeks, he was assigned by Darewski to exfiltrate two members of the local CLN who'd volunteered to go to southern Italy to report on its activities to No. 1 Special Force. As there was no local airstrip available, they would have to make it out by land across the French border. Because Morton and Long had got all the material they wanted for their respective tasks, they would go along as well.

Late in September, Lees, the two Italians and the others left

Darewski's headquarters accompanied by a ragtag group of escaped British prisoners of war and downed American airmen, making their difficult way on foot towards the Ligurian coast. Finally, frustrated at their slow progress and leaving half the exhausted party in the mountains to follow on later, Lees and the Italians went on ahead and dodged or fought with German patrols before crossing the frontier into France near Menton. Back in Monopoli, Lees delivered his report on what he'd seen in Piedmont. 'The morale of the partisans is excellent,' he wrote. 'The Italians are particularly suited to this flamboyant type of work.' He also recommended that a British liaison officer should be sent to Turin as soon as possible to settle political differences dividing the resistance and to prepare the ground for civilian rule when the Germans left.[47]

Two weeks after Lees's arrival in Piedmont, Major Tom Roworth – the escaped prisoner of war who'd been recruited by Macintosh in Rome – parachuted into Friuli, close to Udine, to a reception prepared by Hedley Vincent's mission. Accompanied by Captain Richard Tolson, wireless operator Corporal Donald Laybourne and Lieutenant Alfonso Boccazzi, a young doctor from Aosta passed on to No. 1 Special Force by SIM, his mission was to establish liaison with the partisans in the mountains to the west of the River Tagliamento. One of his top priorities was to find suitable dropping grounds for both personnel and supplies. At the time of his conscription in April 1940 he'd been working as an engineer for Blackpool Borough Council ('mainly on sewage'). Tolson was a 25-year-old Sandhurst graduate in the Royal Sussex Regiment who had narrowly escaped the Germans in northern France in the debacle of May 1940 and had recently served as a chief instructor at the 10th Indian Division's battle school in Palestine. Boccazzi, who took the *nom de guerre* 'Piave', had been stationed with the Nembo Division in Sardinia at the time of the armistice.[48]

After about ten days with Vincent at his base at Attimis, Roworth and his group set off on foot to the west and waded the shallow waters of the Tagliamento on a moonless night. Eventually they reached the village of Tramonti di Sopra and established their base in the Locanda Vittoria, the hotel that had served as the Italian Army's headquarters during the retreat from Caporetto. To his dismay Roworth found Manfred Czernin comfortably installed in a farmhouse at the north end of the village. His briefing had made no mention of this, nor had it prepared him to find that the Garibaldini were stronger and better organised than the Osoppo. For a while Roworth and Tolson worked hard to mediate between the factions and Tolson liaised briefly with Victor Gozzer's brother, Beppi, the chief of staff to the local Garibaldini, before the Italian was captured during one of the frequent *rastrellamenti* and later killed. One of their principal sabotage targets was the railway line linking the area with Villach, across the border in Austria. This, explained Roworth later, 'was just as important for the Germans as the Brenner. They would send everything down there ... I personally didn't do it, but I would plan for the Italian people to blow up parts of the railway and signal boxes. We did it with the combined Garibaldini and Ossovani [Osoppo] ...'

Soon afterwards, the Germans, using some 35,000 troops, including a large contingent of Cossacks, launched their massive offensive against the Carnia Republic, forcing Roworth to retreat. Throughout October, he sent an urgent series of signals back to base requesting both ammunition and the RAF bombing of German positions. 'Was the RAF a myth?' he wondered aloud in a message of 16 October. Finally, in late October, he delivered a scathing report that firmly placed the blame for partisan failures on the allies who, he alleged, and despite firm promises, had failed to deliver supplies or to provide air support for ground operations. 'It is apparent,' he wrote angrily, 'that the Allied High Command has not taken a sufficient interest in this zone. If the Command has no intention of being interested, it should not have promised arms and materials or have sent Allied Missions to give them false hopes ...' The report was taken to Monopoli by Czernin, who was evacuated from Friuli five days later by a Lysander aircraft.[49]

Two other British missions were despatched to Italy in September. Both were conceived, not by No. 1 Special Force, but by the Czech section in London. In July, reports had begun arriving through McCaffery in Berne about Czech deserters from the German Army joining the partisans in the mountains of the far north. The news immediately caught the eye of Colin Gubbins, who had a special sympathy for the Czechs. On 1 August he proposed to an enthusiastic General Miroslav of the Czech general staff in London the formation of Czechoslovak fighting units to act with the partisans

'on analogy with the Czech effort of 1917/1918 in Siberia' – a reference to the Czech Legion that had fought against the Bolsheviks
after the Russian Revolution. This, explained Gubbins, would require
the despatch of both British and Czech officers to reconnoitre and
organise action behind the lines in northern Italy. The Czechs, as
ever keen to establish their credentials as allies, promised their
support.[50]

Having also received the blessing of SOE's minister, Lord Selborne,
Gubbins pressed for the despatch of missions as soon as possible.
The first, commanded by a former liaison officer in Yugoslavia, the
39-year-old Lieutenant Colonel Selby Cope, was dropped near Cuneo
on the night of 9/10 September, where it was received by Darewski's
mission. Cope was accompanied by Captain J. M. Havel, a Czech
officer, and Corporal Williams, a W/T operator from the Royal
Signals, and all arrived, as was customary for the British missions,
in battledress. They were also provided with cover stories claiming
they were escaped prisoners of war who were making their way to
Switzerland. Havel was the field name of Captain Rudolf Krzak, of
the Czechoslovak Army in exile. 'He has been known to SOE since
autumn 1941,' it was reported, 'and his record, including security, is
good.' Tragically, however, the next night a Halifax bomber carrying
a second mission crashed into the mountains near Biella and all on
board were killed.[51]

Through no fault of his own, Cope's mission came to nothing.
His object was to locate Czech units still serving with the Germans
and persuade them to desert and join the partisans. But five days
after his arrival he signalled that local partisans had failed to make
contact with any Czechs at all and – worse – that the Czech units
being targeted had shortly beforehand been transferred by the
Germans east to Milan. After briefly holding out the prospect that
Havel could be sent to contact them, at the end of the month he
concluded that this was simply not feasible and suggested that his
mission should return to base via France. After Michael Lees reported
on the basis of his own recent experience that this was an extremely
dangerous route, Cope and his party were eventually brought out
by a Lysander pick-up operation in mid-November.[52]

Predictably, Gubbins was profoundly frustrated by all this. 'I wish
Silica project to be pursued with energy,' he insisted in a personal

message to Holdsworth in mid-October. 'You should accord [it] necessary air priority to ensure progress.' But there was little more to be done. Intelligence about Czech units was both scanty and quickly out of date and, above all, the lack of air support that was hampering No. 1 Special Force operations generally proved an immovable obstacle here as well. Holdsworth's reply to Gubbins was brutally frank. 'It is useless to contemplate sending further personnel here with a view to their parachuting into North Italy for any purpose whatsoever,' read his personal reply to SOE's director. 'AAI [Allied Armies in Italy] who allot air sorties to us out of their bulk grant from MAAF [Mediterranean Allied Air Force] will not repeat not allow further sorties for Czech subversion.' That was that. 'It's a bloody poor show,' admitted Holdsworth to Colonel David Keswick, the head of European operations in Baker Street, 'but I can assure you it has not arisen for the want of perpetual belly-aching and fighting on the part of myself, SOM, and AAI.'[53]

From behind the lines in Milan, General Cadorna added his voice to the growing chorus of despair about the situation in Piedmont, the Val d'Ossola, the Veneto and Friuli. 'In every sector ferocious reprisals are being made on partisans and population,' he reported. 'Winter finds the formations without any clothes, socks, shoes and blankets, and everywhere there is a shortage of arms and ammunition.' Selborne himself was also becoming exasperated by the lack of support for SOE efforts in Italy and in his quarterly report to Churchill for July–August–September 1944 he noted that if adequately supplied with arms the partisans could have aided the allied armies as much as the French Maquis. Instead, he remarked tartly, 'lack of aircraft has made it impossible to supply even their minimum needs, and this has meant disaster to many an excellent group.' In June, 221 tons of supplies had been dropped, followed by 281 tons in July. The figures then fell sharply. August saw only 158 tons, followed by 185 tons in September – most of the decline being explained by the emergency flights needed to support the Warsaw uprising. This did not, however, explain a dramatic fall in October, to a mere 73 tons.

Selborne's comment reflected a concern that had been building for weeks inside both Baker Street and No. 1 Special Force about the

Italian situation, while in Berne Jock McCaffery added his voice to complain that the supply crisis was having a damaging political effect on British prestige, to the advantage of the Americans and the OSS, as well as threatening the support they could offer in the spring. 'With the present allocations of aircraft,' noted J Section in early September, 'it is impossible to do more than touch the very edge of our three-fold task of assisting the tactical plan of the Allied Armies in Italy, of supporting British Missions in building up pro-Allied feeling, and of encouraging resistance to the enemy throughout the country.' Flurries of telegrams between London and the Mediterranean focused on the problem. Selborne raised the issue directly with Air Marshal Sir John Slessor, the commander-in-chief of all RAF forces in the Mediterranean when he visited London. Gerry Holdsworth had already had 'a first class shouting match' with Slessor on the topic over the summer. And the Baker Street staff produced a brief for their minister to raise the matter directly with the prime minister.

Finally, eleven days after Cadorna's desperate plea, on 24 October Selborne despatched a passionate letter to Churchill. He pointed out that there were some 150,000 partisans in northern Italy, along with some eighteen British and fifteen Italian missions, and that general Alexander had testified to their excellent work assisting his operations. He then pleaded for an urgent rebalancing of priorities in the Mediterranean and for the diversion of some of the aircraft being used to supply Tito's partisans in Yugoslavia to Italy, especially as Tito's troops and the Red Army had at last entered Belgrade. Of the 600 tons promised for Italy by the air force in October, he lamented, so far only 45 tons had been delivered. Two days later, he returned to the charge with even greater vigour, fuelled by learning that General Wilson had just that very day decreed that Yugoslav partisan deliveries should continue to have higher priority than those to the Italians, which should be restricted to the minimum tonnage necessary for the maintenance of existing commitments. 'When you have called out a Maquis into open warfare,' he protested to Churchill, 'it is not fair to let it drop like a hot potato. These men have burned their boats and have no retreat. If we fail them with ammunition, death by torture awaits them.'[54]

It was to little avail. No one – not even Churchill – could do anything about the atrocious weather in October that caused all flights to Italy to be grounded for fourteen days out of nineteen. Nor could the prime minister, even if he wanted to, unilaterally change the broader allied strategy which dictated that Tito's partisans continue to be well supplied. Slessor himself was profoundly reluctant to risk unarmed Dakotas on dangerous routes to northern Italy with the possibility of heavy casualties in terms of lost or damaged planes and killed or wounded air crew. Moreover, it was now clear that the allied offensive in Italy had virtually come to a halt and SOE's demands seemed out of kilter with the actual need, now calculated by Alexander to be in the region of 250 tons a month.

Yet almost as quickly as it descended, the gloom began to lift when Lieutenant General Joseph McNarney, the American Deputy Supreme Commander in the Mediterranean, threw his weight behind enhanced support for Italy and when a technique of mass drops was introduced in November. By the end of that month, indeed, Holdsworth was even in a buoyant mood. 'It seemed almost months ago now, but is in fact only a matter of three weeks,' he wrote to Gubbins on 24 November, 'that we had a first class battle over the airlift to the North ... But a coordinated attack along a front stretching right from Mola [sic] to Siena has resulted in a better airlift than we had ever supposed possible.' Baker Street reflected the same new mood, and in early December Harry Sporborg, Gubbins's vice-chief, was able to tell Orme Sargent of the Foreign Office that SOE officers at AFHQ were hopeful that, given reasonable weather, the minimum tonnage of 250 tons a month might even be substantially exceeded. This indeed is what happened. The November figure ended up at 289 tons, and in December the number leaped to 737 tons. There was a temporary fall in January to 437 tons, but then February and March were to see more than 1,000 tons each – thanks largely to the diversion of the US 51st Troop Carrier Wing, equipped with Dakotas, from Yugoslavia to Tuscany.[55]

All this, of course, was no comfort to Max Salvadori who on 30 October, a week after Selborne's protest to Churchill, was waiting impatiently in Brindisi to be sent into the field after completing his parachute training course. 'The news is far from good,' he noted in his diary on 30 October. 'In [north-eastern Italy] there have been the fiercest rastrellamenti to date, with thousands of casualties among

both the Partisans and the civilians accused of helping them ...
The districts of Valdossola, the Langhe, the upper Modenese liberated by the Partisans during the summer, have been for the most
part reoccupied by the Germans. The "republics" of Montefiorino,
Alba and Domodossola have gone ... It is reckoned that before the
German offensive in October there were about 100,000 fighters in
the bands ... How many remain, no one knows. Perhaps no more
than twenty thousand.'[56]

An effort, added Salvadori, must be made to reorganise the partisans and re-establish their efficiency. The allies needed them for
their military purposes, while Italy required them for her own regen-
eration. By now, Alexander's armies in Italy had shot their bolt. The
Fifth Army had advanced to within 8 kilometres of Bologna and
then stalled, while the Eighth Army's progress had slowed dramatically in the face of continued stiff opposition from the enemy. It
was rapidly becoming clear that the campaign would last at least
until the spring. How to deal with and best employ the partisans
was now the dominating question.[57]

# CHAPTER TEN

# Winter blues

On Saturday 28 October Richard Tolson was sitting in the kitchen of an old farmhouse in north-east Italy overlooking the plain that stretches from the Alps to the Apennines. Attached to the headquarters of the southern group of the Garibaldi-Osoppo Friuli Division, he was writing up his diary. This flouted all the security rules, but was a not uncommon practice by British liaison officers often bored by long periods of inaction. 'Mists have hung about our heads for the last ten days,' he observed, 'and the snow is settling firmly and whitely lower and lower down towards the plain. The rivers, too, show great increase, for rain has been heavy and continuous, and their straightness lies white, stretched across the plain below, disappearing into the haze that wreathes the Adriatic shore. Down on the plain the Germans await their last winter of the war.'[1]

Elsewhere, other British officers were also experiencing the approach of winter. Just the week before, after ploughing his way through deep snow for several hours, an exhausted Christopher Woods had slipped and partly rolled down a hillside to within sight of a German parade ground. He'd lain there for several minutes, resting, before making his escape. Further to the east, Harold Tilman was headquartered with the Garibaldini Nino Nanetti Division on the edge of the Cansiglio forest above Vittorio Veneto. Home was a *malga*, or stone barn, where the partisans, men and women, slept together at night. Four cows quartered in the space below provided them with both milk and warmth. Early in November, a representative of the Veneto CVL paid a visit from Padua. 'Lying in the hay, the door firmly shut, with rain sweeping incessantly across the little clearing,' recorded Tilman, 'the leaders discussed the winter plans for the best part of two days. The fortunes of the partisans were at a low ebb ... warm clothing, food and shelter, were as urgently needed as arms.' So far, he had received nothing. Unable to guarantee supplies, he could only promise to stay with the partisans as long as any remained for him to work with. Finally, after long discussions, the partisans decided to reduce their numbers to a minimum and keep only the strongest and trustiest men in the mountains. On 10 November, the first snow fell.

With his keen mountaineer's eye, Tilman had already welcomed its arrival over the Dolomites to the north. 'Snow softened their jagged outlines,' he wrote, 'toned down the angry colouring, and dispelled [their] atmosphere of fierce aridity.' But aesthetically pleasing though this was, he had to admit that it meant 'everything that was evil' for the partisans. 'The once friendly mountains turned hostile overnight,' he wrote, 'shelter became a necessity instead of a luxury, movement became difficult or impossible, and tracks were an open book betraying all who made them.'[2] Hedley Vincent had already returned to base from Friuli convinced that little useful action by the partisans could be expected with the arrival of winter. Paul Brietsche was concluding much the same. 'We were all completely fed up with the partisans,' he reported later, 'and considered that they were all useless and not worth working for ... They were talking of dispersing for the winter, and I foresaw the Mission being left high and dry in the mountains.'[3]

Ironically, it was in early November that some of the long-awaited drops of supplies finally began to arrive. On 12 November, Enrico Mauri in Piedmont received a massive drop, arranged over his radio by Darewski. This one arrived in daylight. 'The day of the much awaited drop finally comes,' Mauri recorded in his memoirs. 'It is St Martin's summer [Indian summer] 12 November, sky blue as blue, hot sun; at midday the first aircraft should come ... Temple [Darewski] is impatient ... [punctually] a huge Halifax approaches Marsaglia, so low that the pilots can be seen waving ... A shower of parachutes, white, green, yellow, red, blue slowly fall to earth, like a great rain of flowers. The aircraft arrive one after another: Blenheim, Halifax, Liberator ... Fifteen in all.'[4]

Likewise, Richard Tolson at last received a couple of drops following the long drought of September and October. The first, made by more than thirty aircraft, took place on the night of 10/11 November. 'The drop last night lies scattered over three mountain ranges and will take a fortnight to collect providing the snow doesn't cover it entirely,' he wrote. 'The indifference of Div HQ now that the stuff is arriving is astonishing. Mario said that if we had another drop like that they wouldn't bother to collect it . . .' Two nights later, allied planes reappeared. 'Returning to the hotel at Tramonti di Sopra at 1.30 am this morning,' he noted, 'I was nearly knocked off my bike by a package of boots all over the bridge which crosses the Meduna. Had to go back and root out Aurelio and three men to take them in as they would have disappeared by morning. God help the RAF, they need it. This morning, first snow in Tramonti . . . Under four inches of snow the valleys are beautiful, with every fir tree tinselled and the delicate olive green thread of river running through turned to mauve at the edges where the pebbles and stones surface. Any more snow will ruin our chances of recovering the remaining containers.'[5]

Regularly, the partisans would tune in at nights to the BBC Italian service to listen for special messages that would herald the arrival of a drop or contain some other important item of news. Tilman described how this system worked and the reaction it often prompted. 'It consisted in short Italian phrases (known as "cracks") supplied by us and broadcast by the BBC on the Italian news at 4.30 pm, 6.30 pm, 8.30 pm, and 10.30 pm. One phrase was "negative", meaning no plane need be expected, and the other "positive", which meant we must stand by. For example, "Polenta e Grappa" might be the negative and "il Maggiore senza barba" the positive phrase . . . Our arrival . . . to await the coming of planes of which we had been advised, soon became a well-worn jest and was usually the occasion for the consumption of the battalion's reserve supply of "grappa", a fiery white brandy similar to the raki of Albania . . . What the partisans, or we, would have done without this bottled lightning', he added, 'I hesitate to say . . . in moments of despair or jubilation it was our unfailing solace, and for heat or cold, dryness or thirst, fullness or fasting, it was an unfailing remedy.'[6] The main point of the negative cracks was to confuse the Germans by providing cover for the positive ones. Thus on any given day positive cracks would be broadcast for all drops scheduled for that night, interspersed with a random selection of negative cracks for deception purposes. The crack phrases were invented in conversation between the mission and the partisan recipients.

But partisans and liaison officers listening to the BBC on the night of 13 November heard a very different sort of message. This one arrived *en clair* and came from General Alexander himself. In view of the change of season, he suggested, the partisans should halt large-scale military operations, save their munitions and materiel until further orders and prepare for a new phase of the struggle against a new enemy, the winter. He did not, however, preclude small-scale actions or intelligence-gathering, nor did he rule out larger operations if the situation suddenly changed and the Germans suddenly retreated. He did, however, omit any mention of the CVL or the CLNAI.

Coming amidst the severe *rastrellamenti* that were cutting swathes through the partisans, the declaration provoked strong reactions. How, critics wondered, were the partisans supposed to hibernate and conserve their ammunition in the face of every onslaught? Was this some sinister plot to emasculate the radical elements of the resistance? Ferruccio Parri, for one, later described it bitterly as 'a cold shower in a season which was already in itself physically and morally icy enough'. Alexander's staff had not consulted No. 1 Special Force about the declaration but had been guided instead by the political warfare experts. The motives were well-intentioned, but the directive was poorly drafted, came without warning or preparation and gave the partisans the impression that the allies had no further use for them. It was a needless mistake, especially as some partisan units were, as Tilman had witnessed, voluntarily scaling back their efforts already.

The SOE command was severely put out by the whole affair. 'The tragedy of this ill-conceived directive,' complained Roseberry, 'was that it was given two days after the expiry of [an] amnesty [by Mussolini's government] to "the rebels",' while an internal SOE history later recorded that 'Despair and confusion filled the minds of the Partisans and our Liaison Missions were hard put to control them and re-orientate them to this new policy. Many formations broke up and there were numerous desertions of Partisans to the Republican forces in order to ensure food and clothing for the winter.'

Charles Holland, working with the partisans in the Apennines, maintained that it 'was the worst possible thing that could have happened to us at that moment . . . it left us with a feeling that we were being abandoned.'[7] He was not the only BLO to feel that way. What they could not see, of course, was the wider strategic picture in which the Gothic Line offensive was coming to a halt and that everyone had to prepare for another winter.

However, a close examination of Alexander's motives reveals that far from containing some sinister political component – a suggestion frequently levelled by those antagonistic to the allies – they were exclusively military in character and aimed at *preserving* the partisan movement as far as possible for future operations. Indeed, on the same day the proclamation was broadcast, he wrote to General Wilson arguing that it was 'important to do everything possible to increase the dropping of supplies to partisans in Italy forthwith to enable them to make a major effort in conjunction with my offensive operation in December. I think,' he added, 'that this task should be given priority over certain bombing missions if such a course is necessary to produce the requisite air lift.'[8]

Two days after the directive, tragedy scarred events in the Langhe. Here, the Germans had waited until the lack of foliage in its heavily wooded valleys gave them the advantage in launching a major *rastrellamento* against the partisans. Neville Darewski had based himself in Marsaglia, along with Corporal Bert Farrimond, his W/T operator. On Wednesday 15 November, heavy mortar fire began falling in the neighbourhood and at 10.30 a.m. the mission hastily decided to abandon the scene. As they were loading their truck a mortar exploded just a hundred metres away. Panic set in and the driver stamped heavily on the accelerator. The truck skidded violently sideways and Darewski was crushed between the vehicle and a brick wall. Driven by the partisans to a nearby hospital in considerable pain, he died later that afternoon and was buried the next day in the local cemetery after a partisan military funeral. Shortly afterwards, his personal possessions were brought out by Selby Cope on his return to Monopoli.[9]

Just three days before, Darewski had sent a letter to Monopoli via a Lysander aircraft reporting on a trip to Turin that he'd made the previous week. It was only the last of several visits where he'd expressed his worries about Communist influence in the heavily industrialised city. 'It was an interesting but depressing experience . . .' he wrote, 'depressing because I am convinced that the real thought number one in the minds of all the [resistance] committees was "How much power can I get for my party." And then secondly "Down with the Nazis."' The financial situation was also precarious, he reported, with funds having run completely dry. Just a month before, he'd also backed an appeal by General Trabucchi, the military leader of the resistance in the city, to have martial law proclaimed as soon as the Germans left in order to prevent the seizure of power by one or another of the political parties. The Communists had already decided to take over the prefecture, he claimed, and the Socialists the city hall. Such a proposal, however, raised significant legal and political issues about relations between the allied high command, the Italian government and local CLNs. As a result, Darewski was instructed not to make any commitments. Instead, Monopoli suggested that Roseberry should refer the issue to the Allied Control Commission.

Ever since Rankin planning for Italy had begun, Roseberry had been concerned about its political implications. Far from becoming redundant following his contretemps with Dodds-Parker and involuntary return to London the previous December, as he had feared, he had been kept continuously busy with Italian affairs. 'One would have thought that J Section would have expired but it has more to do than ever before,' he confided to his protégé, Max Salvadori. 'The Foreign Office (whose southern section is almost entirely newly staffed) have to fall back on me for all information regarding personalities and parties and there is a constant coming and going with PWE [Political Warfare Executive] on the question of resistance propaganda.' Only the month before, the Foreign Office had defined British objectives in Italy as being threefold. First and most important was the need to check Communism. Second came the need to create a stable and prosperous Italy that would look to Britain in the post-war world; and third and last was the mobilisation of Italian resources and manpower for the war against Germany.[10]

As a result, Roseberry was constantly reminding Stawell and

Holdsworth of the broader political context of their operations. When the first Rankin directives emerged from Hewitt's pen in mid-September, he had expressed concern that they assumed rather than demonstrated that the local CLNs could take control when the Germans left. Yet they enjoyed no acknowledged authority from either the government in Rome or the allied commander-in-chief and would have to rely on superior force or the agreement of the local population. But this could not necessarily be counted on. In many cases civil and police authority would lie in the hands of armed Fascists, many of whom might resist. In any event, he said, in big industrial cities a large proportion of activists were 'strongly communistic'. Unless the CLNs (which were multi-party) were able to assume authority, he told Stawell, 'your missions cannot function'.[11]

At the crux of the problem were the tangled political and legal relationships between the Italian government in Rome, the allied military authorities still waging a hard-fought campaign, the CLNAI in Milan and local CLNs. However, ten days after Roseberry expressed his concerns, a sea change took place in allied attitudes towards Italy with publication of the Hyde Park Declaration. Issued by Winston Churchill and President Roosevelt from the latter's home on the Hudson River following the second Quebec Conference ('Octagon'), this recognised that Italy was now fighting on the side of the democracies and promised full Anglo-American support for the rebirth of Italy as a free and democratic nation. From now on, it declared, an increasing measure of control would be handed over to the Italian administration, provided that it could maintain law and order and administer justice regularly. To mark the change in attitude, the word 'Control' was removed from the title of the Allied Control Commission and the British high commissioner became an ambassador. The two allies also promised to help in restoring Italian industry and looked forward to the end of Fascism and the holding of free elections.

These were the hopes. Behind them lay some significant fears. Inside the Allied Commission, these mostly centred on the intentions of the partisans, who were seen as predominantly Communist, and, more specifically, on the aims of the CLNAI. When the Germans departed, would it set itself up as a revolutionary government in the north? Eyes were especially focused on north-west Italy with its big cities such as Turin, Genoa and Milan. It was assumed that the bulk of allied forces would be pursuing the Germans on their natural line of retreat into Austria through the Veneto, so there would be no significant delay in the north-east before Allied Military Government could be enforced. But in the north-west, the time lapse after German departure and before the arrival of allied troops might be as long as a week or ten days. What political forces might fill this alarming vacuum? Here the estimated number of 75,000 partisans exceeded those in the north east by 50,000. A proposal to fly in AMG officers to give advice to the British liaison officers working with the resistance in the north-west was, however, vetoed by Allied Forces Headquarters.[12]

It was against this background that Roseberry flew to Switzerland in early October to assess the situation for himself. Here, over the next four weeks, he talked with political leaders of the resistance and helped hammer out some important agreements that were to shape SOE policy until Italy was liberated the following April. McCaffery and Birkbeck brought him up to date on the CLNAI scene and stressed that something more than a merely token allied force would be necessary at the moment of liberation for Rankin plans to succeed. 'Milan is the crux,' they told him. Then he met in Lugano with delegates of all the CLNAI parties to grill them about whether local CLN would be able to assume and maintain control when the Germans withdrew. Not surprisingly, the replies were mixed. The Communist and Action Party members thought that only small allied missions would be needed to back them up. The others saw the need for a stronger force ('1,000 with armour'), to prevent civil war.[13]

But Roseberry needed some firm understanding with the CLNAI itself. To that end, Alfredo Pizzoni and Leo Valiani came across the border from Milan to meet him. They had their own reasons, too, for making the journey. Financial support was drying up, Cadorna's arrival had done little to provide direction or clarify military relations with the allies, and the recent fiasco of the Domodossola Republic had raised troubling questions about allied support for the resistance. Pizzoni, as both CLNAI chairman and resistance 'banker', was an obvious choice as representative. But Roseberry insisted that he also wanted to talk to Leo Valiani, a man whom he both knew and trusted. So far as the J Section head was concerned, the veteran anti-Fascist was 'our man' on the committee. Valiani reciprocated the respect. Long after the war he remarked that Roseberry was very intelligent and 'a real gentleman' with long professional experience who understood the difficult political problems in Italy.[14]

'Only luck and providence saved us from capture,' Pizzoni wrote after a typically perilous journey across the frontier. It was raining heavily as they set off, and in the dark they failed to make contact with their courier. Taking a risk, Pizzoni entered a bar and asked the whereabouts of a man in the area whose name he knew. When he reached the house, the man reluctantly agreed to put him up for the night. But several minutes later he returned and apologetically asked Pizzoni to leave. At the local railway station the CLNAI chairman linked up again with Valiani, and the two of them returned to Como. The next day they went back to Milan to plot another route. The following night, after their courier had poisoned a German guard dog, they dashed through the border fence beyond Como and made their way to safety, helped by complicit Swiss officials.[15]

Edgardo Sogno, who was separately crossing the frontier that same night, had a far closer shave. Indeed, since being parachuted into Piedmont two months before, he had been continuously courting disaster. With his typical frenetic energy he had tirelessly travelled throughout the north-west organising sabotage, locating dropping zones, arranging supplies, making risky visits to Milan, Turin and Biella, and generally overseeing his La Franchi network. He had also met the principal partisan leaders such as Mauri and Moscatelli, as well as Neville Darewski; attended at least two meetings of the CLNAI; helped arrange Oliver Churchill's transfer to Milan, and had more than once crossed into Switzerland to confer with the CLN in Lugano and McCaffery in Berne. In between times, in one way or another, he had managed to stay in radio contact with Monopoli. They had alerted him about Rankin tasks and told him to inform the CLNAI of what was expected by way of anti-scorch and the preservation on liberation of all Fascist intelligence records. More recently, he'd also been tasked to get up-to-date information on CLN planning in Genoa and given detailed anti-scorch instructions for the crucial Ligurian port city. Only three days before this latest crossing of the frontier, he'd had a narrow escape when a meeting of his Turin group had been rudely interrupted by the Gestapo. Only a last-minute warning meant that he'd escaped along with all the others except one, who was later interrogated and tortured.[16]

This time, accompanied by a CLNAI courier named Dino Bergamasco, he was stopped by two members of the Fascist Militia close to the border. They showed their papers, gave their cover stories and were allowed to continue. Relieved to have escaped the inspection, Bergamasco found a compromising slip of paper in his pocket, so screwed it up and threw it away. But the Militia was still searching the area for copies of a Communist leaflet that had been circulated the night before. It had previously been raining heavily, and they quickly spotted the still dry and incriminating piece of paper. Sogno and Bergamasco were arrested and taken to the nearby Fascist barracks. Here, a thorough search revealed documents sewn into the linings of Bergamasco's clothes and wallet, as well as under the insoles of his shoes. Sogno was carrying a driving licence and membership card of the Retired Officer's Union, forgeries given him by Major Marchesi of SIM in the name of Giulio Mosca. The two men were detained overnight, guarded by two Italian soldiers armed with pistols and a sub-machine gun.

At five o'clock in the morning, with the panache that made him legendary, Sogno took action. Noting that one of the guards had carelessly placed his pistol about an inch away from his hand, the La Franchi leader suddenly grabbed it and held up both of the guards. With Bergamasco holding open the door, Sogno carefully backed out. Then the two of them ran as hard as they could for an hour in the pitch dark until they reached the house of a sympathetic priest, willing to give them shelter. Four days later, after things had quietened down, they slipped unnoticed across the border.[17]

In the eyes of No. 1 Special Force, Sogno was the 'mainspring of the resistance' in the north-west. But the Germans were hot on his trail, making dozens of arrests. Peter Lee's security section had moved to Rome within a week of its liberation, and here there were serious doubts about whether Sogno should have been sent back into Italy at all. Even Pizzoni was worried. He was horrified at Sogno's indiscretions, he later admitted, stating that La Franchi had visited him repeatedly in Milan 'in the most embarrassing circumstances and even when he [Pizzoni] had taken every possible precaution not to be found by anyone'. It was scarce wonder that before long the security section was beginning to question whether Sogno was a double agent, or perhaps deliberately being let run by the Germans to help them identify his network and related SOE contacts – neither of which was, in fact, the case.[18]

After his narrow escape, Sogno made his way to Berne to confer once again with McCaffery. Meanwhile, during six days of extensive discussions in Lugano, Roseberry and the Italians cleared the air on a number of issues. On the Italian side, the most contentious were the fate of the Domodossola Republic, the shortage of airdrops, the continued allied bombing of Italian cities, and the content of allied radio propaganda that, in their view, failed to highlight the role of the CLNs. On the SOE and SIS side ('C's' man on the spot took full part in the talks), concern was expressed about the incessant internal political battles of the CLNAI, and Roseberry urged it strongly to focus more clearly and immediately on the question of how it proposed to keep order during the crucial days immediately following the departure of German forces. OSS took no part. Instead, Valiani and Pizzoni made a special journey to Zurich to brief Allen Dulles on what had happened.

Finally, Roseberry felt able to report with some confidence on the way ahead. The CLNAI, he told London, was generally accepted as the centralising body of the resistance and was administering its funds to the best advantage of the resistance, although it now needed a minimum subsidy of some 100,000,000 lire a month from outside sources. 'I am satisfied that the members are serious and honest individuals and that they are accepted as being the best available representatives of their respective parties,' he wrote. The committee, he added, 'definitely regards itself as being the agent and steward in North Italy of the Bonomi [Rome] government.' More importantly, this allegiance did not detrimentally affect its acceptance of directives issued by the allied commander-in-chief. His conclusion was that the allies should support the committee while maintaining close liaison to ensure operational control – and here a strong military commander was still required. Perhaps, he suggested, the provision of funds should be made conditional on ensuring such control.

By the time the J Section head sent his report to Baker Street,

Valiani had already returned to Milan. But Pizzoni briefly stayed on. Roseberry had also agreed that a CLNAI delegation should be sent first to Rome and then to Wilson's HQ at Caserta to reach accords with both the Rome government and allied military head-quarters. Pizzoni was a key figure and would be flown down to the south to head it.[19]

On leaving Switzerland, Roseberry made for Lyons where there were other urgent problems involving Italy to be discussed. Salvadori flew up from Brindisi to meet him. By now, he had completed several practice parachute drops ('a damned unpleasant experience') and been appointed head of all SOE missions bound for Lombardy, as well as liaison officer between 15th Army Group and the CLNAI. He'd also seen for himself the rising tempo of behind-the-lines operations being run from allied bases in southern Italy into the Balkans and central Europe, all competing for special-duties flights. His future tasks in Lombardy reflected the increasing focus on the transition from war to peace as this affected the north-west. His main job, he recorded, was 'to organise the Partisans so that they could intensify their attacks against the Germans and *repubblichini* and occupy the nine provin-cial capitals of the region at the earliest opportunity. We were to arrange for drops of arms and ammunition, medical supplies and clothing; it would be up to us to maintain public order and to see that industrial plants were not destroyed or damaged.'[20]

From his discussions with Roseberry, Salvadori highlighted two main points in his diary. The first involved Italian–French relations. 'There are influential Frenchmen who want Val d'Aosta, Val di Susa and the Valli Valdesi in north-western Piedmont annexed to France,' he recorded. The second issue, even more acute, involved Venezia Giulia and Friuli, where Tito, leader of the Yugoslav partisans, was 'fighting primarily against other Yugoslavs and Italians, and only secondarily against the Germans . . . He is a fanatical and convinced Leninist . . . [his] partisans are already refusing to allow Italian Partisans to operate east of Cividale . . . they are getting ready to pounce on Trieste, Pola, and Gorizia.'[21]

So far as the first of these matters was concerned, the emergence of autonomist elements in the Aosta Valley interested in annexation

to France had prompted concern inside the Turin Liberation
Committee as early as September. As a result, it had been agreed
that for this and other reasons no French or other forces under the
command of SHAEF (Supreme Headquarters Allied Expeditionary
Force) would be allowed to operate east of the Italian border. In the
meantime, it became clear that the French were unwilling to allow
Italian partisans who had crossed the border in order to escape
German pressure to remain inside France, still less to supply them
with badly needed food, clothing and equipment. As a result, at the
end of October No. 1 Special Force created two sub-missions, one in
Nice and the other in Grenoble. The first, known as 20 Detachment
and under the direction of Squadron Leader E. Betts, was established to support SOE operations in the western part of Liguria and
especially the province of Imperia. No. 25 Detachment, the second
sub-mission, was directed by Leon Blanchaert ('Major L. Hamilton'),
who had been operating across the French border since his earlier
despatch to France. Their task was to help receive, rearm, re-equip
and reinfiltrate groups of dispersed partisans, to establish courier
and intelligence networks across the frontier and to maintain close
liaison with allied military authorities. No. 20 Detachment also had
a naval section to carry out coastal operations, while 25 Detachment
established a forward base in the Val d'Isère.

Both were established with the agreement of the French, although
Paris later vetoed a plan to have a CLNAI mission sent to Savoy to
deal with some practical military matters concerning the partisans.
'The work of these two Missions was carried out in conditions of
the greatest difficulty,' records an internal SOE history, 'local
resources were small, there was a certain natural rivalry with OSS
and constant suspicion from the French. In order to co-ordinate the
activities of the two Missions and to reinforce SOE representation
so as to ensure the best possible relations with the French, a
Headquarters Mission to command [both missions] was established
at Avignon.' [22]

Even as Salvadori and Roseberry were discussing the rapidly esca-
lating conflict with the Yugoslavs, a replacement for Hedley Vincent
was taking the measure of the situation in Friuli. On the night of
4 November, Major R. T. S. ('Tommy') Macpherson parachuted in

to a reception party organised by the local Osoppo partisans. He was accompanied by his wireless operator, a 19-year-old sergeant named Arthur Brown. 'Quite a nice landing, though from God knows what height, as we took some five minutes to come down,' reported Macpherson in a letter from the field nine days later. 'It is snowing here and bloody cold. We are working hard to fix winter food reserves. I cannot urge strongly enough the need for boots and clothing. It is pathetic to see these boys at work in the snow & ice.'[23]

Macpherson, a 24-year-old Cameron Highlander, already had a remarkable war record. After receiving commando training at Lochailort in north-west Scotland, he had been captured during a raid on the Libyan coast in 1941 and imprisoned in an Italian camp on the mainland. There followed a failed attempt to escape from a train transporting him to Austria, a successful escape into Italy from the Austrian camp in which he was held, and his recapture by German Alpine troops. He was sent first to a Gestapo prison in East Prussia and then to a POW camp in Bromberg, Poland. From there he had finally made good his escape, boarded a Swedish ship in Gdynia and shortly thereafter landed in Kinross thanks to an RAF flight from Sweden. Following further training, two days after the Normandy landings he and Brown had been parachuted into France with a Jedburgh team to help organise a sabotage campaign that significantly delayed the transfer of German troops towards Normandy.

It was Macpherson and Brown's second attempt to reach Friuli. Their first, in a Halifax belonging to the Polish Flight of 334 Wing RAF, a few days before, had failed to locate the dropping zone. 'I landed well off the DZ,' Brown wrote later, 'could not see where I was, or the signal fires, and I launched myself into the drill of hiding my parachute and preparing for God knows what.' Fortunately, a partisan spotted him and soon he was downing a welcome glass of powerful grappa. It was the start of what proved to be a gruelling six months. In France, despite some tricky moments, the food had been good and the weather excellent. But Italy was different, as he later remembered with feeling: 'Six months of mountains, snow, temperatures at times miles below zero, deadening internecine rivalries between partisans of different political persuasions and, as time went on, an exceedingly limited geographical area for manoeuvre between hostile elements of all stripes – German, Fascist, Banda

Nera, Mongol, Cossack, Decima Mas and, somewhere in the wings, the Slovenes, Tito's partisans and the Chetniks. I must have been either very trusting or clean off my head,' he added, 'to have agreed to it.' In fact it was his trust in Macpherson, forged in France, that took him there.[24]

In turn, Macpherson later paid tribute to Brown's efforts. 'His messages, I have seen, reached Base corrupt, but not unintelligible. He was working under every conceivable technical and physical discomfort; he was not in good health; yet he kept up almost unbroken contact from the arrival of the Mission until his exfiltration . . .' Macpherson's criticisms, instead, were reserved for the wireless operators at base and the systems in use. Operators were of variable quality, he noted, and were particularly guilty of wasting time. More important, however, was the lack of continuity which meant that Brown had to deal with many different individuals. 'Better results would be obtained,' he suggested, 'if operators were assigned to work definite missions, and had some idea of the conditions [they] were working under. Continuity would be obtained, accuracy gained and time saved as the operator came to know the idiosyncrasies of his opposite number (the same, incidentally, applies to cipherers).'[25]

Not surprisingly, given his tasks in France, Macpherson's principal mission was to maintain a high-level of sabotage in Friuli over the winter. As soon as possible, instructed Holdsworth, 'you will begin to contact the groups in the plain around Udine in order to create efficient sabotage organisations on a cell basis with particular reference to the sabotage of enemy communications.' As Taylor, Godwin and Trent had not returned to base with Hedley Vincent, Macpherson inherited a trained and competent team to help him. He arrived to find the Osoppo on hostile terms with the Garibaldini. Although the latter had accepted Vincent's idea of a joint command, they had worked hard to become the dominant party and recently refused to renew the much-lauded agreement. More ominously, just four weeks beforehand, they had transformed themselves into the Garibaldi-Natisone Division, an integral part of the Ninth Slovene Corps of Tito's partisans.[26]

Relations between Slovene and Italian partisans had long been tense. In June, the Italian Communist Party had persuaded Tito to send an official mission to Milan to discuss the problem. Headed by

Dr Anton Vratusa ('Professor Umberto Urban'), a key figure in the Slovenian Titoist Front, it had persuaded the CLNAI of its benevolent intentions and the latter had duly issued orders to the Italian partisans in Venezia Giulia to organise mixed Italo-Slovene and Italo-Croat CLNs. The following month, after more talks with the Slovenes, the CLNAI signed a series of agreements, known as the Milan Pacts, that stressed the urgency of Italian–Slovene coordination, the elimination of ethnic rivalries and the principles of post-war national self-determination. To demonstrate its solidarity with the Slovenes, the committee lent the Slovene National Front some 3,000,000 lire, thanks to the efforts of Enrico Falck, an Italian steel magnate and CLNAI member who was also treasurer of the Christian Democrats.

Barely had the money been transmitted, however, than Vratusa demanded a written assurance of Italy's recognition that the Slovene littoral should be included within the borders of Yugoslavia. Then, on 14 September, Tito himself publicly demanded that Istria, Trieste and its hinterland, plus the entire Dalmatian coast become part of Yugoslavia. This open repudiation of the Milan Pacts caused a severe chill in Italian–Slovene relations and from then on the frontier dispute came increasingly to the fore. Hedley Vincent, indeed, had returned from the region to expatiate at length on the issue, and in Rome Gerry Holdsworth had sent him to brief General Wilson, Harold Macmillan and the British ambassador. 'Everyone has been keenly interested in what he has to say,' Holdsworth informed Gubbins, 'and I suggest that there will be those in London – Foreign Office chaps and so forth – who will also wish to meet him.' His report, completed by the end of November, was sent immediately to Sir Orme Sargent, the deputy under-secretary of state at the Foreign Office, who was increasingly concerned about the prospect of the Soviet domination of post-war Europe.[27]

After Macpherson had established himself he went off to interview local partisan chiefs about their objectives and needs. 'He discovered,' claimed Brown, 'that the bulk of arms and explosives sent in during the summer and autumn had been handed over to the communist, Garibaldi partisans (who evidently had wasted no time in passing them on to the Slovenes) and that the [Osoppo] had been kept on very short commons . . . That policy was changed *sine mora*.'[28]

In Macpherson's view, as he reported officially, the Slovenes 'did everything they could' to provoke the Osoppo into starting a war or, if that failed, to eliminate them along with his own mission. 'Against the Osoppo,' he later wrote, 'they used accusations of capitalism, fascism and league with the Germans [*sic*]; they arrested and deported Osoppo couriers and small detachments, carried off food dumps etc.; they reported to the Germans all the Osoppo positions, HQ and movements which they could spot; and finally with a Garibaldini detachment and with orders to liquidate the British Mission, they attacked and eliminated all members of the Osoppo HQ in the area.' Also, he reported, in the villages that the Slovene troops managed to occupy for any length of time, they decreed the Italian language illegal and 'enforced teaching, preaching, civil administration etc. in Slovene'.[29]

Four days after Alexander's winter directive, his headquarters circulated a background paper on the partisans. Written as a briefing for army officers liaising with air crews making drops behind the lines, it sought to clear away what it described as 'much tainted enemy propaganda and so much extravagant and ill-informed scribbling from this side of the line' on the subject. 'There are three Allied Armies fighting in Italy,' it declared, adding that of the partisans to the Fifth and the Eighth. It outlined the origins, politics, composition, order of battle and impact on the Germans of the partisans, along with a review of what the allies had done to support them. It stressed that it would be easy to over-emphasise the hold of politicians on the partisans given that many of the bands were non-political and that others, while nominally political, merely had leaders owing allegiance to one party or another, with the rank and file politically apathetic. It also acknowledged that although higher priority had recently been given to other theatres, which, when combined with 'execrable flying weather', had caused a sharp decrease in deliveries, plans to improve this were now in place.

'What do the Partisans really do?' it asked rhetorically, answering that allied assistance had paid a good dividend. 'The toll of bridges blown, locomotives derailed, odd Germans eliminated, small groups of transport destroyed or captured, small garrisons liquidated, factories demolished, mounts week by week, and the German nerves are so strained, their unenviable administrative situation taxed so much further, that large bodies of German and Italian Republican troops are constantly tied down . . .' it declared. 'Almost any front line troops could tell stories of Partisan assistance. Many enemy prisoners have been brought in; guides provided; intelligence supplied; enemy demolitions prevented; often bands are unofficially "taken on strength" and their fighting qualities and local knowledge are constantly proved invaluable.' It asked sceptics to consider what the situation would be like if the allies, rather than the Germans, had them to cope with. It painted a telling picture:

> Large areas over which we could never motor except in protected convoy;
> in which no small body of men would dare to camp alone; a constant
> unnerving trickle of men who just disappear from the unit; all roads
> liable to be mined; bridges blown; supply and troop trains derailed from
> coast to coast; the necessity of strong guards on every installation; the
> exhausting business of combing hills far in the rear for an enemy whose
> earth is never stopped and of whom nothing may be seen or heard but
> a sniper's bullet now and then; above all the necessity always to be on
> guard and alert for trouble wherever you are. Not an attractive prospect
> as a bonus to war's other anxieties.[30]

Whatever else this briefing accomplished by way of giving heart and a sense of urgency to air crew on their dangerous missions, it made clear that despite Alexander's directive allied supplies to the partisans would continue to flow. Almost at the same moment, however, Holdsworth was reporting to Baker Street that the Rankin missions put on hold in September would now be despatched as soon as possible. Not surprisingly, the bulk of these were destined for north-west Italy, where allied anxieties about the political intentions of the resistance ran deepest.[31]

Liguria was one focus of concern. Following the collapse of the Otto organisation the previous spring, the only direct contact with the province for most of the year had been through the mission headed by Gordon Lett in the La Spezia area. Plans to send in another British mission were severely delayed by heavy *rastrellamenti* against the partisans, as well as by the autumn bad weather and shortage of aircraft, with the result that there were several false starts. Finally however, on the night of 16 November, a mission took off from Brindisi in two Halifax aircraft. Its head was Major Duncan Campbell, a veteran of SOE operations in Greece. His instructions were to operate in or as close as possible to Imperia 'in order to assist in the restoration and maintenance of order' at the moment of German withdrawal. His team comprised eight members in all, two of whom had already been sent to Nice for infiltration across the frontier by land or sea.

Unfortunately, the first Halifax carrying Campbell and the bulk of his group failed to find the dropping zone and returned to base. The second aircraft, after circling for twenty minutes, dropped its two remaining members some 40 kilometres from the target and 24 kilometres south of Mondovi. Within a matter of days these two managed to link up with the radio operator who had been working with Lieutenant Colonel Cope and managed to make radio contact with base. Campbell and his group had to wait until 9 December, when they finally parachuted in, thanks to a daylight drop by American Dakotas from a forward airbase at Malignano, near Siena. Three days later, however, they were taken by surprise by a German patrol. All except one, who managed to escape, were captured and imprisoned for the rest of the war.[32]

Another concern was Biella, to the north of Turin. In mid-October Oliver Churchill had urged that in view of 'the political military crisis caused by the Communists there', as well as its importance as a major textile centre, a 'resolute but diplomatic senior officer' be sent to the city as soon as possible. Just a month later, on the night of 17/18 November, a British team parachuted in to a nearby dropping zone. In command of 'Cherokee' was Major Alastair Macdonald assisted by Captain Jim Bell, Captain Patrick Amoore as interpreter, and a radio operator, Corporal Tony Birch. The reception was prepared by the commandant of the local Justice and Liberty brigade, assisted by the Bamon Italian mission that had been operating in the area for several months. Amoore, the last of the party to jump, had the misfortune to land in a pigsty between two of its startled occupants. Birch succeeded in making W/T contact with base the next day. Soon afterwards, the mission was joined by a Captain 'Burns', in reality a Pole named Buryn, tasked with making contact with any Polish troops in the area.[33]

Macdonald had been a schoolmaster at Charterhouse, a journalist on the *News Chronicle* and an adviser to the British-Argentine Railway Company. Commissioned into the Intelligence Corps, he had worked for SOE on Spanish affairs before transferring first to MI5, then to the Political Warfare Executive, and then back to SOE, for which he had parachuted into the Ardèche to work with the Maquis in the Massif Central after the allied landings in the south of France. He was 37 years old. Amoore, a decade younger, had fought with the Canadians in Sicily and southern Italy before transferring to the Polish Corps as an intelligence officer for the final battle of Monte Cassino. Volunteering for SOE after the fall of Rome, he had been sent to the Brindisi battle school and attached to Macdonald's mission at the very last moment. He was given, so he later recalled, 'no briefing'. Bell was a sabotage specialist. Birch, in Macdonald's words, was a 'staunch, completely unflappable young radio operator'.[34]

The mission's first priority was to meet with the Biella CLN and the zonal partisan command to discuss supply needs and possible new dropping zones, as well as to urge that recruiting should cease and activity be kept to a minimum until more arms arrived. The arrival of the British officers also put some heart into the moderate members of the committee, who had become dispirited by the total Communist control of its affairs. Amoore noted with interest how it financed its resistance activities. It was all extremely simple. Various local textile manufacturers were taxed at a percentage of their total estimated wealth – known partisan sympathisers at a lower rate than Fascists. 'If a manufacturer refused to pay,' observed Amoore, 'he was sequestered and taken to a most unpleasant Concentration Camp situated in a tumbledown farm higher up in the Sersera Valley where there was almost perpetual snow; there he was kept until his relations or friends produced the money. There were surprisingly few cases of default.'[35] Macdonald firmly put an end to talks that had recently begun between the partisans and the SS commander in Biella about a local truce, and when he received a visit from Oliver Churchill the two of them agreed that 'a good deal of house-cleaning would be necessary' – meaning a weeding-out of some of the less competent partisan leaders.

After this, Macdonald, Amoore and Birch headed north-east to establish a permanent headquarters, while Bell went off in the opposite direction to scout out the lower Aosta Valley for suitable sabotage targets. He spent most of the next month there with the 76th Garibaldi Division and received some useful supply drops. Two days after Christmas he was reinforced by Staff Sergeant Johns, a Royal Engineers sabotage instructor, and Sergeant Bell, a radio operator from the Royal Corps of Signals. The Italian operators of the Bamon mission were, Captain Bell complained, 'of very little use'. Thanks to his expert training, however, the railway bridge at Ivrea, carrying all traffic between Turin and the Aosta Valley, was destroyed by the partisans using a minimum of explosives. It was an important target, as the enemy was using it to remove high-grade steel and munitions to Germany. One end of the bridge dropped into the river and the Germans were forced to transport the railway wagons laboriously by road. This was probably one of the most successful acts of sabotage carried out in Italy under the auspices of No. 1 Special Force, and considerable thanks were due to the local GL commander, Mario Pellizzari, whose idea it originally was.[36]

That same day, 26 December 1944, just before dark, Macdonald's mission received a massive drop of supplies from some fifteen planes on its newly established dropping ground near Monte Solivo – the largest drop, Macdonald claimed, ever made by No. 1 Special Force in Italy. In addition to large quantities of explosives, fuse wire and detonators, it also included 165 Bren guns, 80 PIAT grenade launchers, 85 2-inch mortars, 505 Sten guns, 5,725 hand grenades and ample supplies of ammunition. The amount was so large that it could not be shifted immediately and some had to be temporarily buried in a nearby cemetery until a distribution plan could be agreed with the local partisan command. The general rule was that of equality between the different Garibaldi brigades, with some provision for the Justice and Liberty Brigade. The mission itself kept back a considerable portion of the sabotage materials for ad hoc operations and for use in areas outside the Biella command zone. Inevitably, Macdonald had to mediate in disputes over who exactly should receive what.[37]

He also travelled north to investigate the desirability and possibility of establishing an allied mission in the Val d'Ossola, while Amoore went off to make contact with Moscatelli, the redoubtable leader of the partisans near Lake Orta, as well as with an OSS mission in the area. In late December, Edgardo Sogno turned up and was able to brief Macdonald on the progress of talks with the CLNAI. They made arrangements for closer liaison with Milan and agreed to set aside a portion of the large quantities of sabotage supplies being held by the mission for later use, both locally and in Turin. In general, throughout this period, partisan activity consisted mainly of minor skirmishes with Fascist and German forces. On Christmas Day, however, they celebrated by capturing the Fascist headquarters at Cigliano, taking hostage several of its troops who were enjoying the day off at the local cinema, and walking away with a number of heavy machine guns and mortars.

In the meantime, it had been decided at Monopoli to send a heavyweight team to Piedmont as the senior British mission in the region, with the aim of helping the CLNs in Turin and elsewhere to maintain order when the Germans withdrew. Early in October, the choice as leader of the 'Bandon' mission fell on Lieutenant Colonel John Stevens. A veteran who had headed the Greek section of SOE in Cairo before carrying out two operational missions in the Peloponnese, he had found himself embroiled in the virtual civil war between the left- and right-wing factions of the Greek resistance and had ended up, according to a fellow SOE officer, as 'almost the most fanatically anti-EAM [anti-Communist] officer we ever had'. He had also served briefly in France with F Section after D-Day.[38]

The ultimate goal was to have his mission located in Turin, working closely alongside the local CLN, with several sub-missions located in provincial capitals cooperating with local liberation committees. Heading its list of tasks was the protection of vital installations, personnel and factories from destruction and pillaging by the Germans. Priority targets were listed as electric power plants, ports and shipping, public utilities, stocks of food, petrol and tyres, railways and especially rolling stock, and industrial works. In addition, read Stevens's instruction, 'every effort will be made to collect and send out all intelligence of a military nature. It is the general military policy of AAI that Partisan military activities in North Western Italy should be reduced to defensive actions and that sabotage is subordinate to anti-scorch.' The instructions spelled out that while every effort would be made to supply the partisans by air, by sea and by land, owing to the shortage of facilities and the winter weather, few supplies would get through and the missions should operate on the basis of receiving no supplies. Stevens would take 3,000,000 lire with him for his own needs, and the separate sub-missions would be provided with 2,000,000 lire apiece. A later amendment to his orders emphasised that there should be no increase in the number of partisans in the field, and that any stores dropped to help them survive the winter would be defensive only. A background paper on the situation in Piedmont outlined the political dangers in Turin. Highlighting the variety of affiliations in Piedmont, including the Communists, the Action Party and a powerful royalist presence amongst many of the ex-Italian Army officers heading several partisan groups, it painted an alarming picture of what could happen at the moment of liberation. 'A concentration of Partisans on Turin, particularly of the Garibaldi formations may, in conjunction with the left wing industrial population and with strong Communist GAPs,' it stressed, 'constitute a danger of political disturbances. Every effort should therefore be made to prevent a large scale Partisan march on the city when the Germans depart.'[39]

On 18 November, three days after Neville Darewski's death, Stevens's party arrived in north Italy. Unusually, instead of landing by parachute, they stepped out of a B-25 Mitchell bomber on to an airstrip in Piedmont. This was thanks to Charles Macintosh, who the previous month had been moved to Florence to set up No. 1 Special Force's forward tactical headquarters for liaison with the Fifth Army. Here, he gradually took over operational control of all British missions in the central Apennines and established amicable relations with the local air force command. He also acquired the use of three special aircraft with which he was able to organise short-notice supply drops to the partisans as well as pick-up operations to extract various people from the field. In addition to the Mitchell, there was a Fieseler Storch, the renowned single-engined German liaison plane, ideal for very short landings and take-offs, and an Italian Nardi FN-305, a two-seater monoplane. The pilot who flew the Fieseler Storch, Furio Lauri, was an ace fighter with several decorations to his credit who had made his way to Rome after the September armistice and worked with the GL resistance in the capital.

Some of his operations involved bringing out wounded allied officers – and all were extremely hazardous. On one occasion the plane was damaged on landing and a new propeller had to be dropped in and fixed before Lauri could take off again.

The flight that took in Stevens had been organised to extract a group of downed airmen and ex-POWs. Escorted by eight P-47 Thunderbolts, the twin-engined Mitchell, flying in daylight, made its way safely to the airstrip and deposited Stevens before hastily taking off with its boarding party as the Germans closed in. Accompanying him were Captain Hugh Ballard, a South African, and an Italian radio operator named 'Occaso', who was destined for Turin. After that, however, things went badly. Stevens had expected to inherit Darewski's radio operator, Bert Farrimond. But without his knowledge, Farrimond had actually left with the party on the outgoing plane after having buried his set, batteries and charger, which were never recovered. Moreover, the Italian mission ('Pluma') with which Stevens quickly made contact was already on the run and had also buried its set, which then had to be unearthed. Stevens's own party took in one set, one battery and a hand charger. But the battery was stolen on the first day and Pluma had no batteries and no charging engine. This meant that Stevens was dependent on electric light, which was not always easy to find. Moreover, he complained, the two Italian operators 'proved anything but competent', and it took him a full three weeks before he was regularly on air back to base. Pre-war, Stevens had been a solicitor. He found working with the Italians difficult. 'Antonelli [the group's leader] plays cards,' he complained. 'Mario drinks, and Giorgio is too grand to work: all are extremely windy and spendthrift.'

Little occurred before Christmas to improve his mood. After carrying out a reconnaissance of the Langhe region, he reported that German *rastrellamenti* had split Mauri's partisans into three separate groups, that there was no agreement between them and the Garibaldini, that partisan intelligence was dangerously poor, that they were all short of money and that they were dispersed and living in hiding. 'Under such circumstances,' he concluded dismally, 'it is not possible for me to establish a command in the field, but only to inspect and clutter up [*sic*] an area which is not very healthy at present.'[40]

\*   \*   \*

There was one anomaly amongst the British missions despatched to northern Italy in this period. Targeted assassinations were a rare but not untested weapon in SOE's armoury of 'ungentlemanly warfare'. In 1942 it had facilitated the training and transport of the Czech resisters who assassinated SS Obergruppenführer Reinhard Heydrich, the Nazi 'Protector' of Bohemia and Moravia in Prague. Roseberry and Gubbins had once given serious consideration to a project to assassinate either Mussolini or Farinacci, the secretary of the Fascist Party. Earlier in 1944, Baker Street had mounted a coordinated assassination effort, codenamed 'Ratweek', aimed against Nazi security forces across occupied Europe. More recently, it had spent considerable time and effort in planning the assassination of Hitler himself. Now, early in November, it sent an officer to kill or capture a German general in Italy.[41]

The putative assassin was Major Bernard James Barton. Aged 24, he had joined the Grenadier Guards as an NCO in 1938, obtained a commission in the Royal East Kent Regiment ('The Buffs') two years later, and in 1943 took part with No. 2 Commando in operations off the coast of Yugoslavia. There, in early February 1944, he landed on the small island of Brac, and after hiding out for several days, shot and killed its German commandant. A few days later he returned with another commando patrol and killed several additional members of the German garrison, this time using grenades. For these two actions he was awarded the DSO. He also went on a German death list, to be shot if captured. He arrived in Italy bearing the sobriquet 'Lucky', or 'Killer', Barton.

He left Brindisi in a Liberator bomber on the night of 3 November and parachuted to a reception prepared by Major Wilcockson's Silentia mission near Modena. Wilcockson had been warned to expect a drop, but not that it would include any 'joes' (agents). Barton's mission, as he described it in his after-action report, was 'to kill or capture General "X," whose H.Q. was reported to be at "Y"'.[42]

The identity of General 'X' has been the subject of some speculation, although an internal history of SOE later stated that it was 'the German General commanding the German 10th Army'. This was General Heinrich von Vietinghoff. However, after interviewing Wilcockson many years later, the British historian Richard Lamb claimed that the putative victim was in fact General Max Simon, the

Waffen SS general responsible for a civilian massacre outside Florence in August 1944, and that he was deliberately targeted in revenge. Had Barton perhaps revealed that to Wilcockson, who in turn told Lamb? With all the parties now dead, it is impossible to say. In any event, such speculation is redundant, because Hewitt's recommendation for the bar to Barton's DSO states explicitly that he was parachuted to the Appenines 'with the task of killing or capturing' von Vietinghoff, thus confirming the internal SOE history. It is no wonder, therefore, that General Alexander took a close personal interest in the project from its start and was kept informed throughout of its progress.[43]

It is also clear that wherever von Vietinghoff's headquarters was actually based, its whereabouts, as given to Barton, was based on faulty intelligence. In fact, he almost immediately had to start asking for more details. After staying the first night with Wilcockson, he moved on to Johnston's mission at Ligonchio. Here, while waiting for the latter to provide a guide, he put together a small operational squad consisting of a former POW to act as an interpreter (Barton spoke neither Italian nor German), an Italian parachutist and a German-Italian who claimed he could pass as a German – but only three days into the mission, he dropped out.

Barton and the others left the mountains, descended to the north Italian plain at Reggio and took to bicycles. Riding at night, they had several narrow escapes, especially as Barton was wearing his British Army uniform and openly carrying his specially silenced Sten gun, slung across his shoulder. Within a couple of days the Italian parachutist, out on his own, was arrested by a German patrol and was never seen again. In Modena, the remaining pair picked up a guide and, still on their bikes, made for the general direction of Ferrara. Here they spent a month hiding from Fascist patrols and trying to get more accurate information about their target. 'We tried every channel there was open to us,' reported Barton, 'but [received] no clue as to the General's whereabouts ... one report said that General "X" was on the Western front, but there was nothing to confirm this. Strangely enough,' he added, 'everyone seemed to know where Kesselring was ...'[44]

Shortly before Christmas, after considerable hardship and further narrow escapes, Barton decided that General 'X' must be north of the Po, so headed towards the Verona-Venice area. But after being told by a partisan contact that it would take some five or six weeks to get firmer intelligence, he decided to abandon the mission and instead return to base with the information he had gleaned about partisan movement on the plains. After a couple of weeks with a Garibaldini group near Modena, he made his way back to Wilcockson's HQ, walked through the American lines to Florence, and from there was flown back to Brindisi and No. 1 Special Force headquarters at Monopoli. The report he delivered soon afterwards painted a grim picture of life in the towns and cities on the plains, with civilians constantly being terrorised by the Fascists or Germans and being strafed and bombed by the allies.

To help anyone following in his footsteps, he also drew up a list of basic rules for survival. They should never remain static, and one night and a day in the same house was ample; they should try to avoid being seen by children, but if they were they should pretend to be a German; they should be aware that the partisans were easily over-confident; they should trust no one, as there were spies everywhere; the poorer the house the safer they were, as rich houses were invariably Fascist; women working in the fields were usually safe; if a farmer saw them and later returned with food, they were probably okay, but if he did not produce food they should 'go away very quickly'; any farm with young men walking around was probably safe, as they were almost certainly deserters from the army or evading labour service in Germany and hence in as bad a spot as themselves; they should always cycle around with a pistol and, if challenged, ride up to the sentry and shoot first: a pistol, he wrote, 'is the best weapon for a cyclist.' Finally, he recorded, if they once stayed and ate in a house they would be safe. The inhabitants, he declared, would 'not tell the Germans as their house would be burnt down'.[45]

Meanwhile, on the political front, the CLNAI disputes were finally being resolved. Following the meeting with Roseberry in Switzerland, an Italian mission visited Caserta, the headquarters of General Sir Henry Maitland Wilson, the supreme allied commander in the Mediterranean, between 15 and 26 November. It comprised Pizzoni ('Longhi'), Ferruccio Parri ('Maurizio') and the Communist, Giancarlo Paietta ('Mare'), the second most senior Communist of the committee.

For the Italians, the journey crossing the Swiss frontier was another cloak-and-dagger affair. 'C's man in Geneva provided them with false British and French passports and Pizzoni became 'Captain Collins', an escaped prisoner of war. Then the SIS man drove them in his Buick to the French frontier, with their bags following in the car of the American vice-consul. Sogno, although not yet a member of the CLNAI, was far too important to leave behind and accompanied them as a 'technical military expert'. Once they were safely on French territory, the American drove them to the SOE office in Lyons from where they were flown by military aircraft via Marseilles to Naples. Their arrival on free Italian territory proved a shock, however. Far from the joyous welcome they expected, the local prefect gave them what Pizzoni described as a 'glacial' reception, showed no interest at all in their perilous lives in German-occupied Milan, and instead complained at length about his problems in getting the local trams back into service.[46]

Fortunately, things picked up in Monopoli. Here, during several meetings with the top No. 1 Special Force figures such as Hewitt, De Haan, Brock and Boutigny, they found both genuine curiosity and sympathy. They also established some crucial common ground, including the vital importance of gaining proper recognition for the committee. In Rome, they met Holdsworth and Harding, Alexander's chief of staff, without whose support then and later, declared Pizzoni, the Italians would have received substantially less than they actually did. 'They are two men,' he wrote later, 'who deserve particular recognition from the liberation movement of northern Italy.'[47]

After that, the mission moved on to Caserta and an amicable meeting chaired by Wilson in his office on 23 November – his last day as supreme commander in the Mediterranean before handing over to Alexander. Besides the Italians, Major General Stawell as head of SOM was present, as were Gerry Holdsworth and Hedley Vincent. Pizzoni reported that there were some 90,000 partisans, described the challenges they faced from the Fascists as well as the Germans, and strongly urged that the CLNAI be given formal recognition by the allies as well as by the Italian government. He also stressed that while he had heard rumours of possible allied financial support, amounting to 100,000,000 lire a month, this would not be enough; a more appropriate figure would be 160,000,000.

For his part, in what Pizzoni considered 'a very able presentation', Holdsworth reported that the CLNAI 'much regretted' Alexander's recent proclamation and aired some complaints about the quality of allied broadcasting to the partisans. It was unprofitable, he declared, 'to lay restraint upon Partisans operating some distance from their homes [and] necessary, in order to maintain Partisan Formations in being and at a high-level of efficiency to conduct active operations at all times.' Wilson pointed out that there were limits to what could be done over the winter, but promised to help the partisans as much as he could to enable them to carry on. He also went out of his way to ask about partisan plans for anti-scorch operations. To this, Pizzoni replied that already essential machinery parts were being hidden in the countryside but that more arms were needed to defend industrial plants against attacks by tanks and armoured cars.

The meeting concluded with a draft agreement for allied recognition of the CLNAI, reciprocated by its acceptance of allied military directives and a willingness to do its best 'to maintain law and order and to continue the safeguarding of the economic resources of the country until such time as Allied Military Government is established'. Once that happened, the CLNAI would immediately hand over all the authority and powers it had assumed. To finance the deal, the allies agreed to subsidise the committee and the partisans to the tune of the 160,000,000 lire a month requested by Pizzoni. Holdsworth was exultant when he reported to Gubbins the next day. 'The effect of this in the North will I am sure be enormous,' he wrote. 'Those who are already up to their neck in the resistance movement will be encouraged, waverers will see which way the wind blows, Fascists will become more fearful than ever before. Adequate sums of money will be provided by the proper source, that is to say by the Italian Government, and, in broadest terms, law, order and anti-scorch will be brought more under control than at present is possible.'[48]

To celebrate the new spirit of cooperation, the delegation was invited to dine with Alexander in Siena. Pizzoni, seated to his right as guest of honour, dared to explain over soup how disastrous the proclamation of 13 November had been. Only after the ribs alla milanese had been consumed, however, did Alexander reply. 'You have to realise,' he gently told Pizzoni, 'that I am a soldier and not a politician.' With that, recalled the CLNAI chairman, 'he led me to understand that it was possible he had made a mistake.'[49]

Two weeks later, on 7 December in the Italian capital, the CLNAI signalled its formal acceptance of the terms of what became known as the 'Protocols of Rome'. Parri later described the scene at the Grand Hotel: 'On the one side, imposing and majestic as a pro-consul, Sir H. Maitland Wilson, on the other the four of us. A glass of something, a word or two, a hand-shake, and then the signing. I ask myself if whenever the British pro-consuls sign agreements with some sultan of Baluchistan or the Hadramut it is not a little the same.'[50]

The power of the allied purse undoubtedly helps explain the CLNAI's agreement to the vital political terms of this deal. 'Trust that Parri visit will facilitate solution of financing CLNAI,' Dulles informed the OSS chief, 'Wild Bill' Donovan, reporting from Berne on the discussions. 'We are extending no further aid now and ZULU [SOE] is also holding up financial aid pending result of this visit . . .'[51] In turn, Parri admitted that in the end he had swallowed many serious doubts. There had been fierce and heated debates within the committee about whether to accept such allied direction. 'Let it be enough to say,' he wrote, 'that at a certain moment we asked ourselves if it suited us to sign. But we signed. What we had obtained was too great, too important, to be jeopardised by other considerations.'

Three weeks later, on 26 December, a bilateral accord between the CLNAI and the Bonomi government saw the committee offi-cially recognised as 'the organ of anti-Fascist parties in enemy-occupied territory', and 'delegate of the Italian government'. This helped appease the acute Foreign Office worries about a possible attempted seizure of power by the Communists when the Germans left Italy. These had recently reached a crescendo because of events in Greece, where British troops were battling Communists on the streets of Athens. Ironically enough, however, Oliver Churchill, who had finally left Milan and returned to base to report on his experi-ences, did *not* think that another Greece was likely in Italy. He certainly believed the Communists would make a bid for power. But, as he told the officer debriefing him, 'this will not come to very much, and . . . the CLNAI will ultimately be able to assert itself.'[52]

Nonetheless, Foreign Office fears continued. 'I am very much afraid that, if we are not careful,' wrote Sir Orme Sargent, 'we shall be building up in northern Italy with arms and money a rival Italian government which, like the EAM [the Communist Greek resistance] will challenge both our authority and that of the Italian government when we occupy Northern Italy. If Field Marshal Alexander feels it essential for his military operations to make use of this Resistance Movement, we hoped at any rate to bring them as far as possible under the direct control of the Italian government instead of allowing them to evolve as an independent political authority . . .'[53]

This, finally, had been achieved. It was now largely up to No. 1 Special Force to deliver the goods. Fortunately, by this time the air situation had considerably improved and the tonnage of airdrops was improving, helped by the policy of mass drops recommended by the RAF. More important, however, was the use of forward air bases in Tuscany which finally became available in late November. The first sortie flown for No. 1 Special Force from the Malignano airfield near Siena took place on 22 November. But this was a small field surrounded by hills and suitable only for daylight flights. It was not until January 1945 that operations could be transferred to a better, larger field near the coast at Rosignano, from which both day and night operations by four-engined aircraft as well as Dakotas could be flown. But in all these matters, No. 1 Special Force was not master but subordinate to the decisions of the military authorities.

Despite the overall improvement in supply drops in November, in some areas the drought continued until late December. 'The period 15 November to 26 December, when the first sortie arrived, was one of the worst,' reported Brietsche from the north-east. 'There was absolutely nothing to do except wait for aircraft that never came. We had very few arms, were still wearing the clothes we landed in during August, and the food position was foul. To make things more cheerful,' he added sardonically, 'sorties were being dropped to the enemy. We were in a constant state of alarm, and in quite filthy conditions. Snow was about eight feet deep, and we did all our manhandling of stores and food at night. It was impossible to carry out any action against the enemy, as we had to spend time dodging them.'[54] By now, Richard Tolson had left Roworth's group to become

Brietsche's second-in-command. At least, he wrote in his diary, they made the best of the festive season. On Christmas Eve, they and the partisans enjoyed a great feast, consumed vast quantities of wine and sang each other songs. His own contribution was a rendering of 'It's a long way to Tiperary'. The partisans also celebrated by capturing an 18-year-old Fascist and, after enjoying their Christmas dinner, shooting him. Two days later, allied planes finally appeared and dropped a generous supply of food, clothes, arms and ammunition.[55]

The picture for No. 1 Special Force as the year ended was best summed up by Brock in a letter he drafted for Stevens in the field. 'As we anticipated,' he wrote, 'the Winter has proved too much for some of the partisan formations, particularly the weaker ones, and those living in the high mountains. Some Divisions have disbanded while others have moved down into the foothills and plains and have transformed themselves into GAPs where possible. This is inevitable as we cannot hope to feed and clothe *all* the Partisans. What is important,' he concluded, 'is to retain wherever possible a skeleton organisation which can be used as a basis for expansion in the Spring if this proves necessary. Meanwhile, the emphasis remains on "I" [intelligence] on small scale sabotage activities, and on anti-scorch work.'[56]

On the wider political front, however, Salvadori struck a more positive note. 'Parachute operations are to be stepped up . . .' he noted in his diary on 28 December from Rome, where he had helped draft the terms of the Protocols, 'I was very moved to meet Parri. To the Allies and to most Italians he is one of the leading spirits of the Resistance. To me he is infinitely more — he stands for democracy in its best sense, the expression of a positive idea of freedom . . . Pizzoni is quite different . . . patriotism once made him a fascist and now makes him a sincere and reliable anti-fascist. He has brought into the CLNAI the nationalist element without which the Resistance of the north could never have become a popular movement. Parri and Paietta are fighting a political war, Pizzoni and Sogno are fighting as patriots. Their co-operation is in itself a sign of political maturity and the best thing that could happen to Italy.'[57]

CHAPTER ELEVEN

# Action stations

On 4 February 1945, at about nine o'clock in the evening, Max
Salvadori boarded a DC-3 at the USAAF base at Rosignano, about
80 kilometres south-west of Florence, bound for a special mission
to Milan. Briefed by both 15th Army Group and No. 1 Special Force,
his task reflected a new mood of caution in dealings with the resistance. It took place against the backdrop of a winter that had taken
a heavy toll on the partisans. 'Enemy activity has continued to be
forceful . . .' noted No. 1 Special Force, 'communications with the
field have been irregular and many missions have been forced to
change location frequently and to live and work in conditions of
extreme hardship.' Decrypts by Bletchley Park in January suggested
that more than 70,000 partisans had surrendered.[1]

Meanwhile, the allied armies remained where they had halted
in December, on a line that stretched from south of La Spezia in
the west to the southern shores of Lake Comacchio in the east. But
at least No. 1 Special Force had advanced. Having its headquarters
in Monopoli so far south of the front line had long been recognised
as a disadvantage. First Ancona, then Rome, had been considered
as alternatives. In the end the decision was made for Siena, a mere
64 kilometres away from its tactical headquarters (TAC HQ) at
Florence and close to those of the Allied Armies in Italy. The move
began early in February and took several weeks, during which the
separate Maryland mission ceased to exist and was amalgamated as
a country section within SO(M), while all facilities such as training,
signals, finance and security were pooled, leading to a considerable
saving of personnel and the elimination of duplication of effort. At
the same time, General Stawell was replaced as head of SO(M) by

Colonel Louis Franck, a Belgian banker and formerly SOE's chief liaison officer in Washington. Gerry Holdsworth, who had left for London before Christmas, was formally replaced as head of No. 1 Special Force by his long-standing and hard-working deputy Dick Hewitt, who had been doing most of the detailed work in Italy anyway. Although Holdsworth returned briefly to Rome as liaison officer with the Allied Commission, he now faded from the scene, exhausted by his strenuous work for SOE since the start of the war. An internal history of the Italian section records that while the amalgamation with SO(M) was not very popular within Maryland, one of its beneficial results was the sidelining of 'tired and inefficient' officers. 'The shake-up was fortunate in its timing, and justified by its results,' it records. As this was almost certainly written by Roseberry, no fan of Holdsworth, its meaning is clear. So is the fact that without Holdsworth's charismatic presence, drive, determination, as well as ability to motivate people, Maryland might never have got off the ground in the first place and the military never have accepted the resistance as an important factor in their planning.[2]

Rosignano had now become the principal airbase for special-operations flights. Hitherto these had taken place mostly from Brindisi thanks to the efforts of 301 Polish Squadron of the RAF, using Halifax bombers, and 15 Special Bomb Group of the USAAF, flying Liberators supplemented from Bari by Dakotas from RAF Transport Command. These heavy aircraft had operated both day and night. But, as learned the hard way by many British liaison officers, the planes had been considerably handicapped by being based so far south and having to fly 800 kilometres or so to their dropping zones through varying bands of weather. Flights had also taken place from Malignano, but this was surrounded by hills and could only be employed in daylight for flights to the Apennines. The advantage of Rosignano was that it could be used round the clock and could service the missions of western Liguria and Piedmont at short range. The aircraft used belonged to the US 64th Troop Carrier Group using Dakotas, which were later supplemented by Liberators of the 2641st Special Group.[3]

Despite the Rome Protocols, allied fears about the political situation in Italy had increased over the winter, not least because of some radical proposals emanating from within the CLNAI to transform itself into an extraordinary government that would proclaim a republic and socialist programme between German withdrawal and the arrival of allied forces. These anxieties found high-level political expression in a speech delivered by the prime minister in the House of Commons on 18 January. At any time, declared Churchill, 'the cities of Turin and Milan and other centres of industry and activity [will be freed]. A large population of all kinds of political views, but containing great numbers of violent and vehement politicians in touch with brave men who have been fighting in maintaining a guerrilla war in the Alps, all these will be thrown ... hungry upon the fragile structure of the Italian Government in Rome, with consequences which cannot be accurately foreseen and certainly not measured.'[4]

In preparation for the endgame in Italy, the first three months of 1945 saw an intensified effort by No. 1 Special Force to increase the number of its missions in the field and to reinforce those that were already there. In the north-west, fears focused on the growing influence of left-wing and Communist resistance in cities such as Milan, Turin and Genoa. In the north-east, they worried about Tito's ambitions for the annexation of Italian territory.

These anxieties, especially over the latter, surfaced the same day that Salvadori took off for his mission in a directive to 15th Army Group issued under the name of Lieutenant General John Harding, chief of staff to Field Marshal Alexander, who by now had been promoted as supreme allied commander in the Mediterranean, leaving General Mark Clark as commander of the Allied Armies in Italy. The directive modified existing policy towards the resistance and specified the types of supplies to be provided in different regions of Italy. Broadly speaking, it sought to discourage indiscriminate armed expansion of the resistance, encourage sabotage and demolitions designed to assist both anti-scorch and allied military operations, maintain the morale of partisan forces by supplying them with the maximum percentage of non-warlike stores such as boots, food and money, and prepare for the post-liberation period.

So far as particular regions were concerned, the north-west was to receive the maximum of 'non-warlike' stores. Ammunition was to be provided only for weapons already supplied, and an 'absolute minimum' of arms would be dropped sufficient to replace losses or when considered absolutely essential to permit the partisans to carry out their assigned missions. 'It will be borne in mind,' declared the directive, 'that all warlike stores to those regions will only be issued on a selective and controlled basis when you are confident that they will be used solely for action against the enemy.' This covered Piedmont, Lombardy, Liguria and Tuscany. By contrast, in Emilia, Venezia and the Veneto, higher priority was to be given to warlike stores, given that here the partisans would be situated along enemy lines of communication when the German armies withdrew. But in Venezia Giulia, it insisted, *no* warlike (or even non-warlike) stores were to be issued to *any* Italian partisans operating under the command of the Slovene Corps of the Yugoslav Army of National Liberation. The overriding consideration here was that special operations 'must be so controlled that Italo-Yugoslav frontier problems which already exist will not be aggravated, *even if this involves forfeiting a military advantage*' [author's italics].

That the problem of arms in the hands of partisans at the moment of liberation was becoming a matter of major concern is evident in simultaneous discussions about when and how the partisans should be required to hand them in. The general conclusion was that in every location this should take place roughly a week after the arrival of allied forces. To help the process, the handover should be accompanied by ceremonial stand-down parades and the handing-out of certificates testifying to patriotic service to every partisan surrendering a weapon. It is possible that No. 1 Special Force played a significant part in determining this change of policy regarding the types of supplies to be delivered to the partisans. 'I recall that 1SF wrote a paper, I think on their own initiative, and probably largely drafted by Peter Lee's security section,' writes Christopher Woods, 'drawing attention to the possible political threat of communist dominance of the partisan movement.'[5]

Salvadori's specific directive was multifold and reflected the new priorities: to encourage the CLNAI and the resistance in the northwest to coordinate partisan and GAP activities as far as possible with allied forces; to see that supplies were distributed regardless of political colour; to encourage the CLNAI to set up organisations in every province able to take over public administration as soon as the Germans departed; and to ensure that all necessary steps were taken to protect industrial plants and power installations from sabotage. 'Having prepared the first draft of the Caserta agreements,' wrote Salvadori later, 'I was aware of the responsibilities of the CLN and of the functions entrusted to them by the allied command and by the Italian Government.'

In addition, he was to nip in the bud any efforts by individuals or groups to make any kind of local agreements or truces with the Germans, to keep an eye on Yugoslav or French manoeuvrings on the eastern and western borders, and – perhaps the most challenging of all – to do everything possible to maintain harmony among the parties of the CLNAI. Salvadori himself, however, placed the greatest emphasis on the question of ensuring that supplies were distributed regardless of political orientation. Here, his target was not so much the resistance, but lay closer to home. 'Many liaison officers,' he noted in his diary, 'have shown a tendency to identify themselves with the Partisan group to which they are attached, and ignore the others, often sending disparaging remarks about them.' This could have applied to any one of several of the BLOs who, often isolated in the field and sometimes speaking little or no Italian, came to be more dependent than was desirable on a particular partisan group.[6]

Salvadori's immediate destination was a dropping zone in the Langhe controlled by Mauri's partisans. Clambering aboard the plane with him were two other British liaison officers. One, Major Adrian Hope, was a middle-aged ex-Indian Army veteran from Johannesburg who'd been seconded to British forces the year before and whose task was to join up with Stevens in Piedmont as head of a 'Bandon II' mission. He spoke, as another member of the group recalled, with 'the clipped tones' of a BBC radio announcer. The other was Captain John Keany, a 28-year-old Irishman who, like thousands of his compatriots, had ignored Eire's neutrality by signing up with allied forces. Three radio operators made up the rest of the group. One was an American-Italian from New York bound for a nearby OSS mission. The US agency employed a large number of such agents for secret work in Italy. Another was Corporal Millard, a dark and curly-headed professional from the regular army, and the third was Salvadori's own radio operator, Sergeant Bill Pickering of the

Royal Signals. A 21-year-old from Oldham in Lancashire, the eager Pickering had escaped from his job as a grocer's junior clerk by altering his birth certificate and enrolling in the army at the age of 17. Trained by SOE's radio experts at Fawley Court in Henley, he had seen service with Massingham in North Africa, landed at Salerno to work with Malcolm Munthe's group in Naples and survived the Anzio debacle. A tough and resilient character, he was typical of many of SOE's radio operators.[7]

The group had already spent over two weeks at the airfield waiting for suitable weather, and it seemed that they were about to suffer another exasperating delay when the air crew failed to see any lights over the landing zone. However, when the plane circled again, the signals were spotted and they jumped into the darkness. Several seconds later Salvadori landed in snow and found to his alarm that he had sunk too deep to get up. 'From somewhere above me,' he recalled, 'came a voice: "Quick! Germans!" Quick, hell! Stuck in the snow with all the impediments, how could I be quick?' Fortunately, the agile Pickering had landed close by. Digging 'like a demented terrier sensing a rat', the radio operator managed to rescue him. Then he and the rest of the group were taken by Mauri's partisans to temporary safety deep in the woods. Before long, Pickering and Keany found themselves being hidden by a farmer and his wife just outside the village of Monesiglio a mere 350 metres from German troops. 'We slept in the house overnight,' recalled Pickering, 'and every day just as dawn was breaking we would move into a small wooden shack about 200 metres above the house where the farmer's wife would cover us with dry leaves. She would come up twice a day to bring us food. Every evening after dark we would come down to her home and operate the radio from the attic ... Many of her neighbours had had their houses burned down and their menfolk killed for such acts, but this did not deter her or her husband in any way from helping to rid Italy of the enemy.'[8]

Not long after, leaving Keany and Pickering, who spoke little Italian, to make their way by a more roundabout route, Salvadori set off on his own towards Milan. Dependent as he was on local partisan commanders to provide guides and transportation, and constantly dodging German *rastrellamenti*, the journey took him more than a month. His first stop was Turin, where he was shocked to discover how seriously the Gestapo had weakened the resistance leadership: of the four CLNAI representatives he had met in Rome shortly before, two had already fallen into German hands. From the Piedmontese capital he was driven to Milan, where he immediately made contact with the CLNAI and local resistance.

Clandestine life here was also perilous, and he quickly became aware that the Germans were on the track of the underground leadership. He arranged for several hideouts, told no one where he was living, never took the trams or met anyone in a public place and stayed in after dark. 'I met many people,' he wrote later, 'but psychologically I was alone ... and ... always on the run.' Nonetheless, he was able to attend several secret meetings of the CLNAI to discuss liaison questions and pass on to AFHQ his own detailed estimates of how missions in the region should be strengthened to deal with the crucial end-of-war tasks. Of all the CLNAI parties, he noted, the Communists stood out as the most disciplined and efficient, if not the most popular: 'a hundred per cent Stalinist,' he wrote. His communications with headquarters were frequent, if difficult, mostly via couriers to Switzerland or by W/T sets belonging to various allied services such as SOE itself, the OSS and SIS. Pickering and Keany, with their own radio set, never made it to Milan. Just three days after Salvadori arrived there, Keany was killed in a German ambush, and as a result Pickering stayed in the Langhe awaiting further instructions.[9]

The north-west was also proving to be dangerous terrain for the Cherokee mission in the Biella area. On 17 January, on a reconnaissance trip to locate a new dropping zone, its leader Alastair Macdonald was captured by a German patrol. Fortunately, neither his second-in-command Pat Amoore nor the radio operator Corporal Birch was captured, but they were forced to spend almost the whole of the next two months on the run from a lengthy and determined German round-up. On one occasion they had to spend five nights living in a hole in the wall of a church at Azeglio, where the priest took care of them. After that, moving to higher ground, they rarely settled. 'We were obliged to move to new hideouts every night and sometimes twice in 24 hours,' recorded Amoore, 'as enemy agents infiltrated into the Partizan [*sic*] Formations somehow succeeded in obtaining the general location of members of the Mission. This necessitated at one stage cutting off all contact with Partizan H.Q. and relaying contents through couriers and cut-outs.'

The bleak midwinter also witnessed at least one episode of bitter in-fighting between rival partisan factions. The commander of one of the battalions, who employed the battle name 'Biscotti', also served as the official executioner for the zonal command, and on several occasions had shot Fascist and German officers in plain clothes in the streets of Biella. 'The mere mention of the name of Biscotti,' recalled Amoore, 'made the Fascists turn pale . . . On one occasion two of the Black Brigades made the owner of a cake shop remove a notice with the word "Biscotti" and substitute "Biscottini".' But 'Biscotti' consistently refused to join the Communist Party and so was denied higher command. Instead, during the intense German *rastrellamento* that winter, he formed a Socialist unit of his own, without the approval of the zonal command. It was a fatal step. Shortly afterwards his headquarters was pinpointed by the Germans and in their surprise attack he and his brother were killed. 'There is very little doubt,' wrote Amoore, 'that the particulars of their location and strength were communicated to the Germans . . . by elements in the Zone Command, following the usual Communist methods of getting rid of superfluous elements.'[10]

Even before Salvadori's mission left for the field, SOE had been made acutely aware of the special perils facing the political resistance leadership at this late stage of the conflict with the news of the arrest in Milan of Ferruccio Parri. After meeting with allied leaders in Rome and Caserta, the Action Party leader along with Sogno and Pizzoni had stopped off in Lyons and Upper Savoy to discuss troublesome matters relating to the status of the Aosta Valley and the position of Italian partisans who had been forced across the border into France. Then, on Christmas Day, he and Sogno hiked over the mountains, took a small boat across Lake Maggiore and caught trains to Milan and Novara respectively. Six days later – on New Year's Eve – Parri was arrested with his wife in his lodgings, surrounded by a mass of papers. Ironically, the Germans had arrived to arrest someone else. Fortunately for Parri, however, they were aware of his political importance and quickly transferred him from the dreaded San Vittore prison to more comfortable quarters in the

Hotel Regina. Here they treated him well in the hope that they could later use him as a pawn in eventual armistice negotiations.[11]

This was the most dismaying in a series of damaging arrests inflicted on the resistance over the winter. Before leaving northern Italy in early December, Oliver Churchill had reported that numerous detentions had taken place in Milan and Turin, and later that month the leaders of the Turin La Franchi organisation were all rounded up. Indeed, SOE's security section was becoming seriously alarmed about the German penetration of the entire La Franchi network. While recognising Sogno's position as the mainspring of the resistance in the north-west, it also argued that his continued activity and presence were becoming a liability rather than an asset. When he, Parri and Pizzoni were in Rome, Lee's section had even given them a special briefing on the acute security threat to resistance networks, in the hope that this might prevent further disasters. 'It is certain,' read a subsequent security section report, 'that the Germans had traced their every movement, including their journey to liberated Italy and their activities there.' That the dangers were neither inflated nor imaginary was amply demonstrated by Parri's arrest. Barely a month later Luciano Bolis, the Action Party's secretary and regional inspector, was arrested in Genoa – yet another calamity. Unlike Parri, however, Bolis was brutally tortured and cut his wrists in a vain attempt to commit suicide. Then, to cap it all, Sogno himself was captured in a brave but rash attempt to rescue Parri.[12]

Lee and his section were not the only ones to be concerned about the security of the Italian resistance. In Berne, Jock McCaffery was both worried and suspicious. 'Victory as well as spring was in the air,' he wrote later, 'and it made for over-enthusiasm and undue exposure . . . most importantly there had been a great deal of infiltration. It was this last, obviously, which was most worrying.' Urgent steps were taken to improve direct W/T communication with SOE units in the field, establish new courier lines to and from Switzerland, change the hideouts and meeting places of the leading resistance figures, move all suspected dropping grounds, and then – in McCaffery's words – 'find those most indicated as penetrators and kidnap them'.[13] This search produced perhaps the most extraordinary cloak-and-dagger episode in the entire history of SOE's Italian operations.

The most likely source of penetration was a double agent. Two people ranked high on the list of candidates. One was Commendatore Valerio Benuzzi, an ambiguous figure whose name subsequently appeared in a post-war list of OVRA members, who was working closely with Colonel Rauff, the SS commander in Milan, but who had also helped many resistance members escape to Switzerland and had cooperated with the Swiss Red Cross. Lee's security section described him as 'a very sinister character'. The other suspect was Ugo Osteria, who for years had also worked for OVRA but who claimed now to be wholly committed to the resistance. Both were clearly taking out insurance on an allied victory. A third man, Stefan Porta, a CLNAI courier, also came under suspicion.

The plan, as developed by McCaffery, was to lure them to Berne, drug them, smuggle them by car into France and then fly them to Rome for interrogation. It was bothering him considerably that the widespread wave of arrests had affected the La Franchi organisation worst of all and that the Communists appeared to have escaped completely. His suspicions, perhaps fuelled by his personal Catholicism and anti-Communism, had grown to the point where he suspected that there existed – as he confided by telegram to Baker Street – a 'vast communist plan including (a) elimination of opponents by means of arrests and (b) understanding with enemy so that they remain in sole military and political control.' Baker Street approved his plan. Roseberry too was worried that something sinister might be going on, although he was more inclined to give credit to the Communists' long experience of clandestine work and their better regard for security to explain how they had largely survived unscathed. Also, as he pointed out, the ability of both the Fascist and German counter-intelligence services should not be discounted. As a precaution in case things went wrong, both General Cadorna and Leo Valiani were removed from the occupied north for the duration of the operation.[14]

After extensive preparation, including several rehearsals, the plan, codenamed 'Boykin', was successfully carried out on the evening of Wednesday 28 February. The three men were lured separately to Berne on the pretext that McCaffery needed to see them urgently for consultation. Once in his house, they were drugged by a sleep-inducer in the soup and strong-armed upstairs, where they were bound to beds. Only Benuzzi put up a fight but he was quickly over-powered by the deputy SIS officer in Geneva who, along with Teddy de Haan and John Birkbeck, had been mobilised to assist. Once securely bound, all three were given a powerful anaesthetic, bundled into two cars and driven across the French frontier to Lyons. 'Ugo, Benuzzi and Porta trapped beautifully and taken doped and hand-cuffed into France,' reported McCaffery triumphantly in a telegram to Baker Street the following day. Two days later the three Italians were in Naples, from where they were taken to Rome for interro-gation. Porta was quickly cleared, as eventually was Ugo. But prolonged questioning provided unparalleled first-hand information about German and Fascist intelligence operations. It also laid to rest the notion of a Communist conspiracy.[15]

The same day the three Italian suspects arrived in Rome for their interrogation, Max Salvadori finally reached Milan. His mission was only one prong in SOE's broader strategy to exert as much direction as possible over the resistance in the north-west to ensure close co-operation with the allied armies and an orderly transition of power when the Germans withdrew. Lieutenant Colonel John Stevens had already been sent to Piedmont in November, and in early January a similarly senior mission ('Clover') was also dropped into Liguria. This was headed by the 30-year-old Lieutenant Colonel Peter McMullen, with Major Basil Davidson as his second-in-command. McMullen had had almost a year's experience behind the lines in Greece as a liaison officer to nationalist groups in the Peloponnese, while Davidson, a journalist by profession, was a Section D veteran who had run subversive propaganda in Hungary, spent over a year with Tito's partisans in Bosnia and – unlike McMullen – spoke fluent Italian. They seemed an unlikely pair. McMullen was the conservative-minded scion of a wealthy Hertfordshire brewing family, the latter a self-professed left-wing radical of passionate anti-Nazi convictions and often scathing opinions about the real or imagined reactionary views of SOE's top brass. But the two liked and respected each other and got on well. Their radio operator, Corporal George Armstrong, had worked with Davidson in Yugoslavia. Accompanying them was an Italian officer of Russian extraction, Lieutenant Elio Wochiecevich, who had previously worked as a courier for TAC HQ out of Florence.[16]

The trouble-free drop by DC-3 took place on the night of 17/18 January after lengthy briefings by No. 1 Special Force and a military update at Fifth Army headquarters near Florence. The landing zone had been arranged by an OSS team on the slopes of Monte Antola, north-east of Genoa, and a separate American special-operations team was dropped at the same time and place. The area concerned was the 6th Partisan Zone, which included the provinces of Genoa and parts of the provinces of Pavia and Alessandria. All in all, it consisted of three partisan divisions and a mobile brigade amounting to some 2,000 to 2,500 men.

The British mission was greeted by a small group of partisans. 'One,' recalled Davidson, 'was a large man in a rumpled wind jacket, civilian trousers and ski boots. "Miro," he said; and we had his name already as the commander of the zone. Another was of much the same age, rising fifty, and this was Marzo, the zonal chief of staff. Neither had any marks of rank or even uniform save for a red scarf, but both were armed.' They were Garibaldini, and friendly. Most of the fighters under their control were aged about 20 or so and only about 10 per cent of the partisans in the zone were supporters of the Action Party.[17] Michele Campanella, another member of the partisan command, was deeply impressed by the arrival of the mission. 'The three British officers adapted immediately to our way of life,' he recalled, 'resting and sleeping fully dressed on the ground (at first, unlike us, they had slept in the sleeping bags, but these they soon abandoned), eating wherever possible mostly sweet *polenta* made from chestnut flour or chestnut cakes, living with lice, putting up with the cold, the hunger and the continual heavy wear and tear, both physical and psychological. We all maintained our dignity and there was great mutual respect.'[18]

For all HQ's concerns about Communist influence, McMullen saw no evidence that this would affect relations with the allies. 'Miro', the commander, was typical of his kind. A veteran anti-Fascist since the 1920s, he had spent several years in the Soviet Union, fought with the Republicans in Spain, led Ethiopian guerrillas against the Italians, helped the Maquis in southern France and (as a native of Trieste) fought with the Istrian partisans. He spoke Italian, French, German, Russian and Serbo-Croat. 'He is a man,' reported McMullen, 'of no mean culture and is gifted with an amazing physique.' He and the other zonal command leaders were Communists of long-standing conviction, but they were, he emphasised, 'by no means crude hotheads [and] understood their absolute need for collaboration with the Allies and with non-communist elements among the Italians themselves.' All this was to help significantly when the moment of liberation arrived.[19]

Relations with the OSS on the ground were also good, despite the fact that in Italy it had been impossible to arrive at any overall agreement on spheres of influence or distribution of tasks between the Americans and No. 1 Special Force, and no such thing as an OSS/SOE joint planning staff existed. The result was that both in the field and at rear headquarters the two allied agencies were working independently. But, as sometimes happened elsewhere, McMullen reached a private ad hoc agreement with his local OSS opposite number. 'To some extent,' noted McMullen, 'this private arrangement was blessed by both our commands.' The Americans looked after supplies, while the British took care of intelligence, tactical planning, liaison with the CLN and the Regional Command, and political affairs generally.[20]

Beyond the standard Rankin briefing covering the final phase of the war, McMullen had been given a priority directive by 15th Army Group, along with other missions in the Apennines, to gather intelligence on the enemy order of battle, movements and intentions. Only secondarily was he to encourage the partisans to carry out 'sharp, stinging attacks' on enemy columns and command posts, while preparing the partisans for an all-out effort when the final allied offensive began.[21]

The mission had originally been conceived the previous September as part of Rankin planning, when optimism about an early end to the campaign was riding high and the partisans were on the offensive. By the time it arrived, however, the winter had taken its toll, as McMullen graphically described in his after-action report. It was typical of other BLOs' reports at the time, as the weekly assessments of No. 1 Special Force also made clear.

The general position in the area . . . into which we had been dropped and in which, for various reasons we decided to make our headquarters, was bad. Enemy drives had been very successful in disrupting the internal organisation, confidence, and morale of all these formations; the season was winter, and a cold winter with deep snow at that; there was little or no prospect of the long-expected Allied offensive . . . We found there-fore that the Zone Command had decided to cut its losses for the rest of the winter season, to cease its previous (and by no means unsuc-cessful) attempt to hold an occupied area in the mountains around Monte Antola free of the enemy, and to revert to the sketchiest form of partisan warfare until better times should come . . . they had already anticipated Army Group directive [*sic*] to cut formations to minimum size by sending home all those who had weakened during the recent drive, and who grumbled at winter conditions. The comparatively few who remained were all the better for that.[22]

The infiltration of the mission coincided with the final phases of yet another *rastrellamento*, but its arrival provoked the Germans to continue their offensive. 'The enemy's flagging interest,' recorded McMullen drily, 'was apparently whipped up to new efforts by the exaggerated stories he then received of waves of Allied parachutists landing in the mountains. He came after us and after one or two hurried and undignified withdrawals we kept moving at almost daily intervals for two or three weeks.' Fortunately, they were able to keep well ahead of the Germans. Thanks to this, as well as the outstanding efforts of Armstrong, they were able to maintain wireless contact with base and send back a large volume of traffic.

The *rastrellamento* continued until the middle of February. But the arrival of the mission had put new heart into the partisans and by the end of the month morale was on the rise and the problem soon became the number of Germans being taken prisoner. Another factor making for improved morale, noted McMullen, was the changing attitude of the local peasantry to the resistance:

The men in the [partisan] formations were almost all from the towns, almost all from Genoa; they had little knowledge of, or interest in, peasant ways, and the peasants responded by resenting their intrusion and the additional dangers it meant for them. This lack of sympathy was occasionally acute; on the whole, it seems to have decreased as the Spring approached and, in the end, there was even cordiality.[23]

The whole of Liguria was too large for McMullen's mission alone, so several other sub-missions were also sent in. That led by Captain Robert Bentley to western Liguria ('Saki') had enormous difficulties in even getting started. Briefed by Holdsworth in October to infiltrate Italy from southern France with the help of 20 Detachment in Nice, he first opted for a land crossing over the Alps but was forced to turn back by severe weather. There followed several attempts by sea, but it was only during the first week of January, in a speedboat operation commanded by Lieutenant Robin Richards, that his party succeeded in landing close to Bordighera. His main partisan contact was 'Curto', commander of the 1st Ligurian zone operating along the Franco-Italian border. Bentley described Curto, a veteran anti-Fascist and Communist trained in Russia, as a 'born leader – calm, cool, intelligent and daring', although he was poor at administration. The partisans were desperately short of arms, suffered constant *rastrellamenti*, and morale remained low until March. Several attempted sea operations failed and, thanks partly to effective German direction-finding operations, the mission was kept on the run for weeks. Bentley's after-action report records a litany of near disasters, *rastrellamenti* and frustrations – the first arms drop, for example, only reached them in late March. Food was very scarce and medicines even scarcer or unobtainable. 'The terrorised population,' added Bentley, 'with few exceptions gave little help . . . because of their fear of reprisals.' The German forces in the area consisted of the 34th Infantry Division, which was well up to strength, and with little by way of military action it was able to concentrate most of its attention on hunting down partisans, burning villages and carrying out reprisals. 'It can generally be said,' Bentley reported, 'that all captured partisans were inhumanly tortured before being killed. A large number of innocent people were either burnt alive or massacred as hostages; others were eliminated on the least suspicion.' Only in April was the Saki mission able to accomplish anything of much significance.[24]

All members of the sub-mission headed by Major Campbell ('Clarion') to Liguria had been captured early by the Germans except for Captain Irving-Bell, who succeeded in reaching Stevens's headquarters before he, too, fell into enemy hands near Savona. He was replaced by Major V. R. Johnston (on his second mission) and a radio operator, who were able to make contact with the local CLN and remain operational through the liberation. The mission was also later reinforced by Captain J. R. Gordon, Lieutenant Robin Richards, Captain Murphy of the Royal Army Medical Corps, and a team of six commandos. Already in place when McMullen arrived in Liguria was the Blundell mission near La Spezia headed by Gordon Lett.[25]

The most important of the Ligurian sub-missions, though, was that headed by Captain Stephen Hastings to the adjacent 13th Partisan Zone lying to the north of the coastal mountain range. Here, in McMullen's words, partisan formations 'had waxed fat on a land which, compared with the mountains to the South, was flowing with milk and honey; their size had grown with an afflux of every sort of idler and vagabond; and they steered unhandily towards the winter with a mass of baggage and tophamper [*sic*] that simply invited rastrellamenti.' German drives over the winter had duly decimated them, and by February the local command was riven by personal quarrels. McMullen's arrival prompted them to ask him for help in repairing it.[26]

On Monday 19 February, the 23-year-old Hastings was dropped in from a DC-3 flown by an American crew to take on the task. The Eton- and Sandhurst-educated son of a Rhodesian farmer, he had served with the Scots Guards at Tobruk and taken part in an SAS raid on Benghazi before joining SOE to participate in the landings in the south of France. He ended up in liberated Paris. Accompanying him were Lieutenant Giorgio Insom, an Italo-Russian, as interpreter, and Sergeant 'Chalky' White of the Signal Corps as his wireless operator. They were met by McMullen and Davidson before heading off north for the Piacenza area and the headquarters of the 13th Zone.

Here, in the small village of Groppallo, they found its commander, Colonel Marziolo, a professional soldier aged about 50. The atmosphere was gloomy and suspicious. Partisan resistance, as elsewhere, had collapsed. Marziolo had only recently been appointed and his position was being jealously undermined by his predecessor. The Italian spoke bitterly of the devastation wrought by the Germans. 'I was shown a photograph of 20 or 30 grinning German soldiers grouped round the body of a woman they held naked and spatch-cocked between them,' wrote Hastings, 'while a NCO posed above her body with a long dagger ready to strike; another of a girl, her hands tied behind her, hanging on a meat hook like the carcass of a pig. They had died in the *rastrellamento*. When, they repeatedly asked, would we be able to bring the aeroplanes?'[27] Over the next few weeks Hastings and his mission succeeded in welding the various partisan units – Communist, Action Party, Christian Democratic – into a coherent force, establishing an intelligence network and organising supply drops, the first of which arrived on 23 March. Shortly afterwards, thanks considerably to Hastings's efforts, the CLNAI ordered the detention of Marziolo's troublesome predecessor and a major source of disruption was removed.

By this time, a second mission had arrived, led by Captain B. W. S. Irwin, to be followed later that month by another ('Insulin'), comprising Captain Charles Brown of the Intelligence Corps, Flight Lieutenant Frederick Rippingale, and Corporal Bradley (W/T). Rippingale's task was to find suitable landing grounds for the small Lysander aircraft that SOE used for drop-off and pick-up operations – now becoming more common across northern Italy. Brown focused on collecting intelligence, anti-scorch, minor sabotage and Rankin preparations. 'The latter was discussed and planned in detail,' he reported, 'and the Mission found cooperation from all sides. Attacks on enemy garrisons, petrol and ammunition dumps, transport and communication were stepped up from now on and results were reasonably satisfactory, especially between Via Emilia and the Po, where the crossing came in for quite a lot of attention.' Although Rippingale had limited success in finding landing strips, by early April the partisan division to which Brown was attached was 'in fair shape,' he thought, 'to make a start in something like co-ordinated action . . . All were glad of a British Mission in their area and political problems had not cropped up.'[28]

In addition to McMullen's mission to Liguria, January 1945 also saw the return of Michael Lees and his wireless operator Bert Farrimond to the Reggio area, followed by that of Jim Davies to Modena at the end of the month to replace Ernest Wilcockson as head of the Silentia mission. By now Macintosh's TAC HQ in Florence, operating in close coordination with the Fifth Army, had assumed control of the missions in the northern Apennines and was in direct W/T and courier contact with them. Over the winter it concentrated on developing an intelligence network based on the British and Italian missions and passing information on to 15th Army Group, which found it invaluable in building up a picture of the German order of battle. Exfiltrated agents and couriers also provided valuable information. At the request of 15th Army Group a number of Italian missions were sent into cities in the Po Valley and Apennines to transmit intelligence received from partisan networks.

So far as active partisan resistance was concerned, however, No. 1 Special Force painted a generally gloomy picture of the partisan position in this area close to the front line, with constant and determined *rastrellamenti* by the Germans. 'Partisan activity,' noted a report issued just days before Davies's return, 'has been reduced to a minimum.'[29] This was due both to the general allied directive to lie low, and to heavy anti-partisan activity by the Germans. A Wehrmacht communiqué making claims that were clearly extravagant, if not fantastic, nonetheless reflected the increased tempo of enemy anti-partisan activity:

> Fascist-Republican Units as well as units of the Army, of the S.S., and of the police, commanded by the senior ranking S.S. and Police officer and General plenipotentiary of the German Army forces in Italy, Senior Group Leader of the S.S. and General of the S.S., Karl Wolff, completed the mopping up of large areas of Northern Italy. In bitter fighting in the mountains, extending over several weeks, the bands lost several thousand dead. Over 80,000 members of bands were compelled to lay down their arms. This action has cleared the greatest part of Northern Italy from the terrorism of armed bands.[30]

Lees had scarcely arrived before being driven out of his operational zone by a *rastrellamento*. Finding the partisans 'little more than a rabble', he spent the next few weeks knocking them into shape. Given his orders to concentrate on gathering intelligence from the front line and on carrying out sabotage attacks on the main roads, he persuaded them – contrary to guerrilla orthodoxy – to establish a safe area and defend it from all attacks. Such a permanent headquarters, he reasoned, would provide a known and certain destination point for the large number of couriers, all women, who were bringing in intelligence, as well as a safe jumping-off point for sabotage. To carry out the latter he created a squad of some thirty men under the command of a former Alpine Division officer, Glauco Monducci ('Gordon'), while in command of the intelligence service he placed a 21-year-old partisan named Giulio Davioli, who rejoiced in the battle name of 'Kiss'. Lees also established a strict and centralised distribution for supplies to ensure they were handed out equitably and according to need. He had been dismayed to find on his arrival that the Garibaldini were going about unshod and in rags while members of the Green Flames brigade had as many as four pairs of boots apiece. As a result of his decision, he reported, 'the Mission was soon on the best of terms with all the Garibaldini [brigades] who had previously been very Anglophobe.'[31]

Early in February Lees also received a mission codenamed 'Cisco Red II' led by Captain Neil Oughtred, who had previously served with No 2 Commando in Yugoslavia. Oughtred's task was to establish an advanced base in the north-east Apennines from which to organise a courier and intelligence service to the Po Valley, with a view to developing a resistance movement there. Once he and his wireless operator, Sergeant Ted Fry, had laid the groundwork they were to be followed by a main party led by Major James Barton, whose first mission, to assassinate General von Vietinghoff (or possibly General Simon), had ended in frustration. There also remains a question mark over the real objective of this second one. Oughtred's official operation instruction refers only to Barton's earlier encounters with resistance groups on the Ferrara plain and suggests that resistance could be increased there if arms and direction were supplied. Yet after the war Oughtred claimed far more for it. 'We were,' he wrote, 'to be joined by [Barton] (being personally somewhat unpopular with the Germans) with a view to causing maximum inconvenience, hopefully terminal, to a German general resident in those parts and, thereafter, to see what we could do with the local population.' If this, indeed, *was* Barton's target on his second mission, then it, too, misfired, for he never made contact with Oughtred who, early in April, was ordered to close down the mission and join up instead with Charles Holland's group near Parma.[32]

In March, Lees became involved in what he later described as 'one of the most ambitious, organised and daring operations carried out by the resistance forces' in Italy. As the time for the spring offensive approached, all those involved began to discuss how best to direct the partisans in front of the Fifth Army. Charles Macintosh, in charge of TAC HQ in Florence, remembered as follows:

> It was decided that apart from calling for an 'all-out' guerrilla and sabo-tage effort to coincide with the Army attack we would try and create chaos in the German communications system by attacking not only roads, railways and bridges but also enemy headquarters, telephone lines, wireless stations, etc.

Largely thanks to 'Kiss' and his female intelligence network, but also making a reconnaissance of his own, Lees had learned that an important German headquarters was based at the Villa Rossi situated on the edge of Albinea, a suburb of Reggio Emilia. Further investigation suggested that it was known as 451 Headquarters and controlled all German divisions west of Bologna to the coast and up to Genoa.

Immediately Lees began to make plans either to attack it or to murder the German officer in command, General Feuerstein. 'We made one attempt to do this,' he reported in somewhat confusing language, 'but as we were ambushing him on his journey to church, he being a devout Roman Catholic, we were fooled by a changeover to Lt. Gen Hauk who was apparently not so devout and did not go to church on the route to [sic] which a reception was waiting for him!'[33] Lees then turned elsewhere for help. At about this time Macintosh asked if he could make use of a squadron of SAS troops to assist in attacking enemy communications. He replied enthusiastically that he could. The first group was parachuted to him in early March under the command of Major Roy Farran, a decorated veteran of the North African desert campaign with a maverick reputation.

Farran had arrived in Italy the previous December after a visit by three senior SAS officers to prepare the ground for joint operations with SOE. The first major one, codenamed 'Galia', was coordinated with Lett's Blundell mission and helped partisans of the First Ligurian Division over the winter in several useful harassing attacks against the Germans. The second, codenamed 'Cold Comfort', involved an SAS group dropped to the 'Ruina' mission – against its strong advice because of the severe winter weather – in February 1945, and resulted in a failed attempt to block the Brenner Pass by causing a landslide. The third was Farran's effort with Lees, code-named 'Tombola'. Each of these operations played an important part in the life of the SOE mission concerned.[34]

Contrary to explicit orders, Farran jumped with his men, claiming later that he did so to preserve their trust – although at the time he persuaded the American air crew to say that he accidentally fell from the plane while helping despatch the men. He and Lees then created a mixed battalion consisting of about 100 Italians, seventy Russians (mostly deserters from the German Army) and fifty SAS men. The target of their operation would be the Villa Rossi and an adjacent building, the Villa Calvi. The mission was approved by TAC HQ, whereupon aerial photographs of the target were dropped to Lees, and the date of 27 March agreed upon.[35]

At this point things began to go wrong. AFHQ soon decided that the operation should be postponed until it could be properly coordinated with the forthcoming allied spring offensive and Macintosh signalled accordingly to Lees. For reasons still obscure the message was ignored, either because Lees had closed down his radio – which he later vigorously denied – or because the signal arrived after the force had left, or because (as Farran later claimed) it was couched in only the vaguest of terms. Jim Davies, who was sent to reinforce the stop order, arrived after a long trek by foot and bicycle only to find no one present at Lees's HQ. In any event, the attack went ahead using a hand-picked force of 100 men armed with automatic weapons rushing the two villas in the dead of night. In a typical flourish, Farran had arranged for a bagpiper to be present. But even his valiant efforts to paralyse the enemy with a powerful rendition of 'Highland Laddie' proved to no avail. The British force encountered fierce resistance, failed to penetrate upstairs to the general's quarters, and after ten minutes Farran was forced to sound the retreat, leaving the two villas engulfed in flames. The casualty rate was high. Some thirty Germans were killed, plus three of the SAS party and a few of the partisans. Lees himself was seriously wounded and had to be evacuated a few days later by small plane. General Hauk, it transpired, had not even been present in the Villa Rossi at all on the night.

Farran escaped disciplinary action because of the important role assigned to his SAS squadron in the forthcoming allied offensive. Given Lees's injuries, no disciplinary action was taken against him either by No. 1 Special Force, although it was clear he had made himself unpopular with his superiors. Recalling much later that prior to the attack he had received signals from base to the effect that neighbouring missions, especially that of Davies in Modena, had warned of impending *rastrellamenti*, Lees told how he had informed Florence that he and Farran were not concerned, that their positions were strong and that they were at war to fight. 'I also seem to recollect being reproved for making life difficult for others,' he said, 'specifically I recollect sending the cable "rastrellamento balls" when they kept on about it. I think this made me very unpopular . . .' Because of his injuries, however, he was replaced as head of mission.[36]

Nearby, Jim Davies had found the Modena partisans still 'in hibernation', and it was not until March that active recruiting resumed following the creation, largely at his own instigation and with the support of the Modena CLN, of a provincial partisan command. 'In spite of the fact that many members of the committee were later imprisoned for periods up to a fortnight,' he reported, 'the committee continued to function in a most energetic manner, not only regarding the reorganisation of the provincial CVL, but also in making anti-scorch preparations and general plans for maintaining public life when the enemy withdrew, and for co-operation with AMG.' By the end of March, the Modena partisans were poised to make significant attacks on the Germans the moment they withdrew. Davies also succeeded in sending back numerous intelligence reports on the enemy order of battle that proved of considerable value to Alexander's headquarters in Caserta. This was largely thanks to his radio operator, Corporal Charles Barratt, and to his second-in-command, Captain John Stott of the Intelligence Corps, who before the war had worked as a tea merchant in Berlin and who excelled in interrogating captured Germans.[37]

In the north-east, Harold Tilman's group in the Veneto had by now linked up with the Belluno partisan division. He, John Ross, Victor Gozzer and the wireless operator 'Pallino' spent most of January holed up in the frozen mountain landscape as they prepared to reconnoitre a suitable dropping zone. Their hideout was a cave reached by a precipitous path on a mountainside. 'We lived in this awful place with three partisans for about three weeks,' recorded Ross. 'I cannot remember what we did during the days except squat by a miserable fire – the wood we could gather was mostly green ... The nights were remarkably cold and miserable.'[38] At the end of January they began their five-day journey north, led by a local Italian guide and sheltering at nights with resistance sympathisers. Again, they stayed in a cave while they finally located a dropping ground in the Val di Gares, a region dominated by snow-covered peaks up to 3,000 metres.

It was a reasonable spot, recorded Ross, although uneven and surrounded by steep tree-covered slopes. They radioed details back to base, and waited. In the meantime Tilman skied and read his tattered old edition of Carlyle's history of the French Revolution. Victor Gozzer wrote poetry, and Ross did some sketching and tried to learn more Italian. Finally, on 13 February, they received news that supplies were coming. In order to preserve secrecy they had made no preparations. They consequently had to rush to the dropping ground, summon helpers to collect loads of wood, dig holes in a metre of snow and prepare fires in them. 'These were lit with the aid of petrol as soon as the plane was heard,' Ross remembered, 'and Pallino signalled to it with a huge headlamp and battery brought from a vehicle. There was an answering signal from the plane,' he went on,

and then it circled around our steep and hidden valley for, to us, a worryingly long time before accurately dropping its load. The containers whistled down for some time before the 'chutes opened – a few 'chutes did not open but no one was hit by the bomblike containers; there were also a number of kitbags with 'soft' contents. Inevitably some containers landed on the steep mountain sides but fetching them was no problem for the locals. Everyone worked hard and the loads were taken away on sledges and hidden near Forno. As soon as possible, the supplies were taken down to Belluno for distribution – Sten guns, Brens, explosives, mines and clothing – hidden beneath loads of wood in lorries. Regular deliveries of wood were going to the Germans from all over the area, for fuelling transport. Four nights later we had another drop by two planes, equally successful. These drops were made by the American Air Force. I don't think they had ever made such difficult drops before and the crews were awarded medals for their achievements.[39]

In late March, Tilman returned to the adjacent Nino Nanetti division headquartered on the edge of the forest above Vittorio Veneto. By now, the snows had melted, the number of partisans had grown considerably and they were well supplied. The Nanetti, noted Tilman,

were now very strong. A short time before they had ambushed and wiped out a party of the Black Brigade of the Fascist Republican Army. These men had just arrived from Venice, and were sent up the Cansiglio motor-road under the mistaken impression that the partisans were no longer a force to be reckoned with. Twenty were killed in the first volley, the rest captured and subsequently shot. This may seem cruel, but there was really no alternative. The guarding and the feeding of prisoners were extremely difficult, but, in spite of this, Zone H.Q. had set up a prisoner of war cage for a limited number. They actually succeeded in exchanging a few German prisoners for partisans, but there was no market for Fascists.[40]

Tilman's memoirs also provide a valuable description of the partisan zone headquarters' activities which were typical of many others during this final phase of the struggle:

In addition to maintaining close liaison with the civil side of the movement through the C.L.N. and the general supervision of affairs in the zone, they dealt with higher appointments, discipline, and the boundaries of brigade areas. These last were sometimes troublesome, because there were now three independent brigades directly under the command of Zone who had to be kept in step with the Garibaldi formations. Political jealousies were a fruitful source of headaches for Zone H.Q. For example, a good but over-zealous battalion of one of the independent brigades caught and hanged a woman spy out of hand, whereupon the Communist party, professing to be grievously shocked at such brutality, demanded the offender's instant trial as a war criminal. The Intelligence branch at H.Q., as well as collating information received from the two divisions, had its own agents, one of whom was a sergeant-major in the S.S. at Belluno. Contact was maintained with divisions by a daily courier service of girls on bicycles, and less frequently with regional Command at Padova which also sent round its own inspector once a month. Funds were received from the Central Committee at Milan through Padova and re-allocated to divisions and independent brigades. For the two divisions only general directives were issued and the plans co-ordinated. Each division had already made and submitted its own plan of action in case of an enemy withdrawal or collapse.[41]

Nearby, in the western Veneto, the Ruina mission suffered a heavy blow when its commander, Major John Wilkinson, was killed in an ambush in early March, shortly after the disaster experienced by the SAS Cold Comfort operation that resulted in the death of its leader, too, after he was captured by the Germans and later shot in Bolzano. For all its efforts, the SOE team that had parachuted on to the Altipiano di Asiago the previous August had achieved disappointingly little. Virtually no supplies reached it before the onset of winter, and January and February were hard months with plenty of snow that made movement extremely difficult. In addition, their many attempts to create a unified partisan command for the mountain zone were constantly frustrated by political divisions between the local Garibaldini commander and his non-Communist rivals. 'In our bit of the Veneto, a traditional Catholic area,' records Christopher Woods, 'we were made increasingly conscious that, while the Allies were concentrating on winning the war, for the partisans winning the peace was of at least equal and in some respects greater importance, and that on this internal front there was an uncompromising struggle for post-war political power. Our mission comprised two partisan formations: a *Garibaldini* division led by a professional communist with no local connections, and the other having indigenous leaders of strong Catholic persuasion. John Wilkinson's strenuous efforts to persuade them to co-operate under the aegis of the regional CLN in Padova to the extent of forming a joint command never succeeded.'[42]

Ironically, when the long-awaited airdrops finally began to arrive in early February, they came in such volume that they proved counterproductive, as Captains Orr-Ewing and Woods complained in their after-action report. 'They came in such quantity,' they noted, 'that they defeated their own ends, because the enemy could not help but notice it, and he turned his full attentions on the area, with the result that much was lost.' Indeed, Wilkinson's two juniors were harshly critical of the RAF for constantly using the same dropping zones, even when asked not to, because closely adjacent zones often served different partisan brigades. The result was that supplies often went to a group that did not need them, while another remained deprived. Moreover, they added, 'the security of receiving a drop was not helped by the RAF's unnecessary habit of circling over the D.Z., signalling continuously, and on one or two occasions with his lights ablaze. This was particularly harmful in our area when there was nearly always a garrison within 3 kilometres of the D.Z.'

Their complaint was a rare explicit criticism of the RAF by British liaison officers. It was not unusual for officers behind the lines to become frustrated over airdrops, especially when the wrong sorts of supplies were delivered, or when none came at all, or when weather conditions were perfect over the dropping zone but the skies remained empty because of poor conditions at base or en route (of which the reception party was ignorant). But few of them ever recorded their criticism so strongly. Undoubtedly it reflected a combination of factors: the inevitable frustrations associated with air supplies, their disappointment at falling short of their principal goals to unify the partisans, the particularly challenging conditions of their zone of operations – populated as it was with numerous German garrisons – and possibly also their shock and anger over the death of their commander.[43]

One who *did* echo their anger, however, was another BLO in the north-east, Major Tom Roworth, who operated in the plains around Udine until he was withdrawn in February. Drops, he complained, had shown 'a remarkable degree of inefficiency on the part of the air forces, at least 50% of the material being lost or, worse still, falling into the hands of the enemy. This,' he added, 'included at least four operational personnel being dropped to the enemy.'[44]

But this complaint paled alongside Roworth's damning indictment of the political gulf that had developed between the Osoppo and Garibaldini partisans, effectively halting any military cooperation.

Since October, when a major German *rastrellamento* had inflicted a heavy blow on the partisans, the latter had barely managed to defend the territory they held in the Val Tramontina. The civilian population, terrified of reprisals, had done little to help. The partisans' political divisions he blamed mostly on the Communists, whom he accused amongst other misdemeanours of refusing to accept sabotage instructions from his own specialised team and instead preferring to run a school for political indoctrination. He also held them responsible for launching a violent anti-British and anti-American campaign and stimulating a corresponding pro-Russian and pro-Slovene feeling. Furthermore, he accused Garibaldini brigade leaders of stealing British supplies during a *rastrellamento* in December and of abandoning the battle before the organised resistance came to an end. As a result, he had concentrated his efforts on working with two of the Osoppo divisions in and around Udine. '[They] are now co-ordinated,' he reported in late February, 'and work well together with a combined chief of staff ... Their complete force is 6,000 and I forecast an increase this spring in operational work.' He also noted the creation of two Lysander pick-up zones as well as considerable success in transmitting intelligence to base concerning bombing targets. Most significant of all, however, was his observation that local resistance to Slovene territorial aims was producing a spread of Italian nationalist sentiment in the area. This, he suggested, required a major allied effort at conciliation between the Italian and Yugoslav governments if it was not to lead to a serious deterioration in relations.[45]

Political divisions between Garibaldini and Osoppo, and between Slovene and Italian, also seriously troubled Major Tommy Macpherson's Coolant mission operating in the same general area. From the start, sabotage had been its principal task, and despite both the severe winter weather and successive German *rastrellamenti* it continued unabated. One of those involved was an escaped prisoner of war, a New Zealander named Frank Gardner, who went by the *nom de guerre* of 'Franco Rossi'. Gardner had jumped from the train deporting him to Germany and taken shelter with a courageous Italian family near Udine. Supplied with material by Macpherson, he carried out some spectacular operations as well as the assassination of an SS officer implicated in a civilian massacre. Some of the letters that Macpherson wrote to him in the field have survived. One of them, dated 13 February 1945 in reply to letters from Gardner reporting on some recent sabotage successes, gives a flavour of his work. After offering the New Zealander any medicine or money that he needed and apologising for not being able to provide him with a battledress or any coffee or tea, Macpherson continued:

The war's going pretty nicely and Jerry seems to be getting ready to pull out of Italy. Your information is very valuable and so is every railway action. About the factory job. I know about the Gemona one that you did with Nino and a damned good job it was but I was wondering if you managed to knock out the silk factory at Maiano that we spoke about. I'll try to get the RAF to take a crack at the one at Marcento. Thank you very much for the butter and eggs and drink sent up with Nino. Very welcome as ever. Ref. the silent pistol: it's out on a job just now, so not immediately available. But you are pretty well off for silent weapons. I have no stock of Sten Ammo here, but have sent off for it right away and 250 rds [rounds] will be ready by the time the next courier comes up.

Six days later, he followed up with another:

Many thanks for your letter . . . A very nice list of successful actions – well done. Be careful on the railway with these new civvy guards – Max will tell you about them. You'll have to work in with some of them and make believe to tie them up, or something like that. We want very much to get the one remaining steam engine at Gemona, and to stop electric trains by blowing down and keeping down the pylons of the high tension line, which are more important than the electric brackets on the railway. I can't get sticky bombs, as they are apt to explode in a drop. For land mines, we generally make our own with a box, 10lbs of 808, and a couple of pressure switches with a board balanced across them to make the pressure . . . Will you lend Max a couple of Stens for a day or two? There is a bird that he is going to have cleaned up.

Both of these letters he signed 'Rosquiggle'.[46]

Macpherson's hands-on direction of sabotage operations had already revealed itself in January, when, equipped with a genuine

ID card from the Todt Organisation as well as a bicycle, he had started spending more time on the plains around Udine in order to supervise more closely the sabotage operations being carried out by the 3rd Osoppo Brigade. Coolant's highly successful sabotage campaign, like all but one branch of its intelligence service and all of its propaganda, rested heavily on the Osoppo. Their main advantage was the support of the clergy and other leading members of the community. But in early February their morale was badly shaken.

The hostility of Slovene partisans who were operating east of the River Tagliamento, an area to which they had staked a firm claim, had long been apparent. They took prisoner Osoppo patrols on the pretext that they were Fascists, cut their courier lines and threatened to attack Osoppo HQ. To Macpherson's protests they simply replied that they had their orders and that if he opposed them they were perfectly ready to eliminate the British mission as well. To these verbal threats they added physical intimidation, as Macpherson reported with typical *sangfroid* on 1 February:

> The SLOVENES, as expected, surrounded the OSOPPO HQ the other day, with lots of malice aforethought and automatic weapons. A fairly sticky battle looked like developing, but I managed to persuade the SLOVS to be good boys and go home. Their reaction seems now a desire that the Huns clean us up. Last night they left a series of signposts 'Alla Brigata Osoppo' extending from 200 yds from the nearest Cossack garrison to 350 yds from our door. Fortunately our patrol found them first, but the game is sure to be tried in other forms.[47]

A week later, indeed, the game took a murderous turn. On Wednesday 7 February, in the early afternoon, a force of some hundred partisans of the Garibaldi-Natisone Division, which had placed itself under the command of the 9th Slovene Corps, arrived at the Osoppo command post near the small village of Porzus, close to where Macpherson and Brown had parachuted in just months before. The command post was occupied by about twenty Osoppo. The Garibaldini claimed they were on the run from the Germans and were seeking shelter. The Osoppo guards lowered their guns, only to be overpowered and disarmed. One who made a run for it was shot on the spot. This was the beginning of a slow-motion massacre that was to last for another week. The Osoppo commander was Francesco de Gregori, known as 'Bolla,' a man whom Macpherson considered to be by far the most competent he had met. After accusing him of collaboration, the Garibaldini broke his jaw and most of his teeth, then hanged him. Two of his staff, including a woman claimed by the Communists to be a German spy, received similar treatment. Over the next few days the remaining seventeen Osoppo guards, all witnesses, were taken in batches into the nearby woods and shot. Only one of them survived to tell the tale.[48]

Bolla's brutal murder was a bitter setback for the Coolant mission, as it eliminated an important link in Macpherson's command, intelligence and communications chains. It also dealt a shattering blow to Osoppo morale, as he later reported:

> A critical period followed, when the Mission, at the time of the heaviest enemy reaction, had to force the surviving leaders out of their mood of passive despair. Their position looked very gloomy. They counted seven enemies – GERMANS, RUSSIANS, REPUBLICANS, SLOVENES, GARIBALDI, civilian spies, and the winter itself. The allied armies were still on the wrong side of Bologna, their most able leader had been murdered by their 'Allies,' their troops had to be dispersed.[49]

It was to take considerable effort by Macpherson to rally the Osoppo and make them an effective force by the time the allied offensive began. It also took much of his energy to prevent full and open warfare breaking out between the two rival factions in the aftermath of the affair. Nor did it help that Corporal Micky Trent was killed, allegedly by an enemy patrol, while being escorted by a Slovene guide on a mission to the headquarters of the Ninth Slovene Corps.[50]

If 'allies' were proving difficult, the enemy was continuing to make life hard. In late February Cossack troops entered the valley where Macpherson and Brown were hiding, in what proved to be the beginning of yet another general *rastrellamento*, this one involving some 5,000 enemy forces assisted by the Fascist Black Brigades. Hiding in a narrow cave on Monte Ledis, Macpherson and Brown along with some of partisans suffered three freezing nights with very little food. On 27 February, Brown noted as follows:

Cossacks start climbing M. Ledis, looking for us. It is around four o'clock. Light not good. We decide to make a run for it, but it means traversing back across the ice-field in full view. As we emerge from the cave, they start firing. So far, only five or six of them, but more coming round on the west side. Machine guns firing in the valley. I have a US marlin sub-machine gun, Macpherson has his carbine – both useless for this kind of fighting. We are three hundred metres higher than they are ... Macpherson now over ice field and is potting with his carbine; like a peashooter at that range and the same unconvincing noise ... Thank God they are rotten shots. On the far side I start jogging down to where Macpherson is firing from behind a boulder as though at a grouse butt. I am lumbered with gear, with the Marlin now slung. I put my hand back to steady it on my shoulder and get my thumb in the trigger guard. It fires merrily away, frightening the life out of me. Now dusk. Cossacks get fed up fighting and retreat to valley. We move higher.[51]

At dark, Macpherson and Brown decided to spread the risk by splitting into two parties, one to go along the valley floor, the other along the crest of the mountains, and then meet up at the cabins that served as their headquarters. Macpherson took the valley route, Brown the high road. Eventually they joined up as planned and gradually the partisans, too, began to return. In March they started making their presence felt again with more aggressive action. New radio equipment was dropped to the mission and planning began in earnest for the final phase of the campaign.

The gloomy January predictions for the partisans across northern Italy had not come to pass: abnormally fine weather for February allowed over 900 tons of stores to be supplied to them. The Germans soon began to feel the effects, and on 26 February Field Marshal Kesselring sent a message to his army commanders and the SS warning them that:

Activities of the Partisans in the Western Apennines and along the Via Emilia, particularly in the area of Modena, Reggio and Parma, and [south-west] of them, as well as near Piacenza, have spread like light-ning in the last ten days. The concentration of the Partisan groups of varying political tendencies into one organisation, as ordered by the Allied High Command, is beginning to show clear results.[52]

Not surprisingly, Hewitt's weekly reviews were soon exuding a new-found spirit of optimism about the partisans' morale, achievements and potential. 'There has been a considerable quickening of resistance activity,' he reported on 15 March. 'All over the North there is evidence that formations are beginning to look towards the time (which they hope will not be long) when regular and vigorous action may be resumed.' Three weeks later a report to the German high command by Kesselring's chief of staff painted a picture of increasingly serious partisan activity in which many vital German supply routes were only usable in convoy and were 'to some extent completely in Partisan hands'.[53]

At the end of March, General Mark Clark broadcast a special message to the partisans that made it clear the time for action was approaching and they should now prepare themselves. 'Your bands,' he told them, 'which contain only the finest examples of Italian soldiers, proved by their ability to resist the enemy through the hard winter, should now be so reorganised as to be ready at a moment's notice to undertake the tasks which are ahead.' He also urged them not to take on new recruits or to form new bands. 'Quality is what is necessary,' he stressed, 'rather than quantity. The aim is to consolidate compact highly disciplined and trained groups for efficient action: and remember also,' he added, 'that there will be many who, the nearer the end approaches, will try to join the winning side with suddenly-acquired enthusiasm.' Left unstated was his concern that the armed resistance could easily spin out of control and suddenly transfer itself from the credit to the debit side of the allied ledger. It was now No. 1 Special Force's task to ensure, as best it could, that this did not happen.[54]

# CHAPTER TWELVE

## 'This is the end'

In the end, liberation came rapidly to northern Italy. The allied armies launched their final offensive along the Gothic Line on 9 April and only twelve days later Bologna fell to forces of the Polish II Corps. The exploitation of this victory was, in the words of the official historian of the military campaign, General Sir William Jackson, 'like the bursting of a giant cascade firework'. Forty-eight hours later allied troops crossed the Po and began their sweep towards the Alps. That same day they also entered Modena, and Reggio Emilia, Parma, Mantua and Verona all fell in quick succession. Genoa was reached by Fifth Army forces on 27 April and Turin, Venice and Milan were all entered on 30 April. Meanwhile, long-standing secret negotiations for the capitulation of German forces in Italy had culminated the day before at Field Marshal Alexander's headquarters in Caserta with the signing of unconditional surrender, to come into effect at noon on 2 May. This agreement also covered Mussolini's Italian Republican army under the command of Marshal Graziani.[1]

The Italian dictator himself was captured by partisans on 27 April near Dongo on Lake Como, huddled in the back of a German Army truck heading for the Swiss border. The following day, along with his mistress Clara Petacci, he was shot by a special resistance squad sent from Milan. Their bodies were then driven to the city and hung head downwards from the roof of a garage in the Piazzale di Loreto, to be kicked, spat upon and jeered at by the local populace. By the time the German surrender was publicly announced the whole of northern Italy, including the all-important port of Trieste, was occupied by the allies, except for some remote Alpine areas and parts of

Venezia Giulia under the control of Yugoslav forces. Two days later, all remaining German armies surrendered and the war in Europe was finally over.

SOE's part in these events was significant. In many cities, towns and villages of the north, partisans seized power as the Germans left and before allied forces arrived, which meant that control of the administrative machinery passed into the hands of the local CLNs. What might happen then had for months been the stuff of nightmare for allied planners, as their imaginations ranged freely from civil war between Fascists and partisans at one extreme to outright seizure of power by Communists at the other. That none of this happened owed much to the presence of SOE and OSS liaison officers on the spot, the political agreements reached by allied headquarters and SOE with the CLNAI, and the work of forward detachments of experienced No. 1 Special Force officers attached to the advanced units of the allied armies. This is not to mention also the policy of the Communists, which thanks to Stalin's larger strategy for post-war Europe was to ditch revolution and exploit instead the emerging structures of a democratic Italy.[2] Militarily, victory was certainly assured in Italy without the partisans. But the fact that the latter sought readily to assist allied troops and ensured them a friendly reception was important and reassuring. Politically, however, the resistance counted for much more. 'It was a political gain,' writes W. J. M. Mackenzie in his official history of SOE, 'that in every town and village Committees of National Liberation emerged at once as a provisional organ of government, with the co-operation of all political parties, the allegiance of a vast majority of the populations, and the habit of command.' Thanks for this went in considerable part to the efforts of SOE.[3]

By 1 April, 125 British officers and men had been sent into the field by No. 1 Special Force, along with ninety-two Italians. A number of the British personnel had been infiltrated behind the lines only during the previous four weeks, either as reinforcements for existing missions or as replacements for casualties. Additionally, a number of small two-man Italian missions had been sent into cities of the Po Valley and the Apennines, mostly to gather tactical intelligence in areas where British liaison officers could not operate in uniform and where even long-established partisan organisations were finding it difficult to operate thanks to intensified enemy counter-measures.[4]

Typical of the SOE officers infiltrated during this final phase was Major Robert Readhead, who arrived to take over command of the Cherokee mission in the Biella area after the capture of its leader, Major Alastair Macdonald. He was accompanied by an Italian officer, Marco Folchi-Vici, who used the cover name Mark Terry, and subsequently the mission was reinforced by several Polish officers briefed to secure desertions by young Poles conscripted into German units, which they did with some success. From carrying out an impressive amount of sabotage, its activities had recently shifted towards anti-scorch, which itself included sabotage in the form of measures taken to obstruct the Germans in their efforts to attack infrastructural key points. Captain Jim Bell, the mission's sabotage expert, carefully reconnoitred the Val d'Aosta, where many of Italy's most important hydroelectric power stations were located, to ensure that the local resistance was well supplied with weaponry to protect itself against German attack. In late March, after three planes had dropped a load of arms that he distributed to the local Garibaldini, Bell outlined to their leaders an extensive plan for the defence of the valley. 'At the moment of the enemy withdrawal I was to close the valley by mines which were already prepared,' he reported, 'and the partisans were then to eliminate all the enemy between Carema and Breuil thus occupying all the stations and then to hold them as long as possible.'[5]

This focus on hydroelectric plants dated back to February, when two experts with experience gained elsewhere in Europe had flown out from London to produce a special SOE counter-scorch plan. They had concluded that with the limited time and resources available it would be impossible to save the entire economic and social infrastructure of north Italy. As a result, a list of priority targets was drawn up and coordinated with the military needs of the allied armies and the post-hostilities requirements of the Allied Commission. This gave the highest priority to electricity generating and transformer stations, and lists and maps were prepared for each of the three main areas of occupied Italy – the north-east, the north-west and the Apennines. Meanwhile, the delivery of supplies to missions was adjusted to include the special requirements for the

arming and equipment of anti-sabotage teams. In areas such as the
Val d'Aosta, Val Maira, Genoa and Venice that were not already
covered, missions were infiltrated with a view to securing particularly important areas (the port installations of Genoa and Venice,
for example, being declared vital for supplying the allied armies
both in Italy and Austria). A special leaflet about the importance of
anti-scorch was dropped to partisans along with regular supplies,
and special messages were broadcast on the subject over the *Italia
Combatte* radio programme. By the time liberation came, it had
become the primary concern of the missions operating in the areas
where vital targets were to be saved.[6]

The breakneck pace of events during this final allied offensive is
well captured in the series of special situation reports sent by SOM
HQ to Baker Street in London. Codenamed 'Freeborn', and
numbering twenty in all, they summarised reports that came pouring
in from missions in the field. The first was despatched on 25 April:

> Owing rapid progress in Apennine Battle Zone, all missions controlled
> by Macintosh at 5th Special Force Unit now overrun after making solid
> contribution to allied advance and having considerable success in anti-
> scorch measures. Following reported from sets (a) Carrara no repeat no
> excesses by partisans and no evidence of purge or bloodbath (b) Bologna
> no repeat no disorder. Partisans being (?) used (?) as guards, electricity
> and water functioning 24 hours after fall. Anti-scorch appears have been
> effective although orders received late.[7]

One of the first missions to be overrun was Silentia under the
command of Major Jim Davies, who had taken over its control from
Major Wilcockson in late January. He and his second-in-command
Captain John Stott had recently spent much of their time organising and improving their sources of intelligence. Some was couriered
from the military resistance command in Bologna, but their most
reliable and concrete information came from interrogating deserters
and prisoners of war of whom they always had a good supply. All-
out activity in support of the allied advance by the 1st Modena
Mountain Division with which Davies was liaising began on 13 April.
Constant raids and sabotage on Route 12 south of Modena succeeded
in totally blocking its use by the Germans for withdrawing their

forces. But when the order came from base on the night of 20/21 April to march on Modena itself, Davies was disappointed by the failure of three of the division's brigades to attack the enemy lines. This was not, he believed, a deliberate rejection of allied orders. Instead it was 'because partisans are incapable of a tactical plan of that nature involving real leadership, timing, fire and movement etc. And they would not go in against machine guns and risk the casualties . . . Under a good leader,' he added, '20 partisans can cooperate in a scheme, but lack of military discipline and training gives them too much inclination to consider the risks.' He also blamed the rapidity of the allied advance and the shortage of time to organise.

The next night, however, the 2nd Modena Division proved more effective. 'Partisan activity and pressure in and around Modena increased when the enemy started withdrawing,' he reported. 'Partisans occupied the first objectives against opposition that night and on 22nd the Allegreti and Tabacchi [brigades] seized the Questura, Santa Eufermia gaol, power stations, Fascist federation offices, tobacco factory, the Maserati works and the Accademia where a strong force of Fascist and German officers and men were contained. The city was under control and orderly apart from a few snipers when the first American columns entered on the evening of 22nd April.'

The mission itself entered Modena on 28 April, and two days later the official parade and disarmament of the partisans took place with some eight to nine thousand partisans turning in their arms. In the fighting for the city they had lost thirty-seven killed and twenty-seven wounded. As for the all-important anti-scorch campaign, reported Davies, it 'really worked because the Germans were too disorganised at the last moment and their policy to destroy all public utilities before withdrawal could not be enforced' – a pattern that was to be repeated elsewhere across most of northern Italy.[8] In nearby Parma, Captain Charles Holland's Toffee mission had likewise focused most of its more recent efforts on intelligence-gathering, as well as benefiting in March and April from ample supplies dropped by some eighty aircraft. On 22 April orders came to move all available partisans northwards for the occupation of Parma city. Three days later resistance forces entered its suburbs and that night, at around 10 p.m., the first American tanks arrived on the scene. The next day Holland, accompanied by Captain Jim Beatt from TAC HQ at Florence, entered the city.[9]

That same evening, a Freeborn telegram to London carried a report by an SOE officer bringing dramatic news from inside the vital port city of Genoa. 'Partisan formations closing in from all sides ...' it read, 'General Meinhold surrendered unconditionally with 7000 troops under him to CLN ... situation calm and curfew imposed and all public utilities intact.' Less than twenty-four hours later, advance units of the Fifth Army entered the city.

Only two days before, the SOE mission headed by Peter McMullen, based with partisans in the hills north-east of the city, had ordered all-out action throughout Liguria. Earlier in the month it had been reinforced by a parachute drop bringing in Naval Lieutenant Robin Richards, Captain J. R. Gordon, and two radio operators. A few days after that, Captain Murphy of the Royal Army Medical Corps also turned up from La Spezia with some useful medical intelligence. At about the same time an Italian officer, Lieutenant Quattrocolo, was dropped for courier duties. A team of six commandos also arrived and McMullen set them the task of catching prisoners for interrogation to get intelligence about German forces. Until then the task had largely been carried out by German-speaking Basil Davidson, his second-in-command. 'I used to have them brought in one by one, their eyes blindfolded,' wrote Davidson, 'and then would cock my pistol and put it on the table with a clump; but this was to save precious time more than anything else, and none of them was beaten or otherwise tortured or shot.'[10]

The taking of Genoa, in McMullen's words, was 'an achievement which astonished no-one, perhaps, more than those who carried it out'.[11] The general insurrection began on 24 April, by which time the SS had already left and American forces were still some 50 kilometres to the south. Resistance forces quickly seized control of the major public buildings but both the port and the surrounding heights remained in enemy hands. The day before, the city's CLN, in accordance with allied policy, had rejected an offer by the German commander, General Gunther Meinhold, not to damage the city in return for a promise of an unimpeded withdrawal. Four partisan brigades in the mountains began a march on the city and Davidson, along with his radio operator George Armstrong and 'Attilio' (Amino Pizzorno), the newly appointed zonal partisan commissar, drove into the city centre to report on events by radio to No. 1 Special Force. Inside the monastery of San Nicola they found the CLN in full session. After testifying to what was happening in the hills that ringed the city, Davidson and Armstrong stayed the night. The next morning, setting his radio transmitter on a bed with an aerial poking out of a window, Armstrong tried to reach base. Frustratingly, he could not get through. It was ironic. Here, where they were safe from enemy direction-finding units and could transmit all day and night, they were unable to make contact. Cursing the bad luck, Davidson was suddenly summoned by the CLN leaders. 'The Germans have surrendered,' they told him. 'To the CLN, to us.'[12]

It was true. Only hours before, after heavy fighting, Meinhold had suddenly surrendered to the president of the CLN, all too aware that any attempt to leave the city would suffer from relentless attack by partisans along the route. 'The document was there on the table,' wrote Davidson later. 'I read it in the yellow light of a chandelier, two copies, one in Italian and the other in German. I hope I said something appropriate.' According to Michele Campanella, another of the partisans who entered the city and was sporadically present at this and other CLN meetings, Davidson simply told them: 'You have all been marvellous.'[13] Later, after he had succeeded in making radio contact with base and transmitting the report that was forwarded to London, Davidson witnessed the investiture of the new prefect in Genoa at a ceremony in which, for the first time, all the members of the CLN actually met in one place and recognised each other. Just as the ceremony was closing, three German garrisons still holding out in the city in defiance of Meinhold's surrender orders attempted to link up. This caused momentary panic until partisans were hurriedly rushed in from outlying areas and managed to quash the enemy. When General Almond, the commander of US forces, arrived at the Hotel Bristol to congratulate the CLN on its contribution to the liberation, Davidson acted as his interpreter. All in all, some 7,000 German troops and an equal number of Fascist forces surrendered to the partisans in Genoa. McMullen and Davidson urged that SOE should quickly spread the news. 'Mission considers essential broadcast report on events in Genoa last few days,' SOM told London. 'Change over by CLN has worked admirably and most anxious hear BBC repeat BBC say so. Propaganda urgently required and mission is providing dropping ground . . . Partisan success most remarkable and worthy.'[14]

In western Liguria, German withdrawal was also swift and sudden and the partisans hardly had time to get into action. Ventimiglia, Savona and Imperia were all occupied after only sporadic fighting. 'Great welcome and anti-scorch most repeat most successful,' reported Captain Bentley of the Saki mission. 'Power and water plants saved and functioning. Harbours state property and dumps all saved. Law and order reigning. CLN repeat CLN cooperating and working very well. Whole zone expected be cleaned by tonight.' In Acqui, Major V. R. Johnston, dropped in late March to replace the captured Captain Irving-Bell near Savona, held an unsuccessful meeting about surrender on 26 April with the local German commander, General Hildebrand, but that same evening heard that Savona was in partisan hands. The next morning he reached the city at 9 a.m., went straight to the Prefettura, and called a meeting of the CLN for that same afternoon to discuss the demobilisation and disarmament of the partisans – of whom there were some 5,000 in the town – as well as the re-establishment of law and order. 'As a governing body in the first days of liberation,' he reported, 'they coped fairly well with the most immediate problems and collaborated in every way with our Mission.' Although damage had occurred to some railways and roads, all the major power stations fell intact into allied hands.[15]

To the allies' relief, they also found the port in Genoa largely undamaged and could make almost immediate use of it for military needs. Its fate had long been of great concern and No. 1 Special Force had alerted its missions in the area to several priority directives: the port itself; road and rail communications linking it with the rest of Italy; power stations providing electricity to the port and city; and all public utilities. As a result, McMullen had discovered a good deal of information about German demolition preparations for the port through Robin Richards, who had been dropped specifically to handle naval aspects of the mission. Thanks to excellent contacts amongst the dock workers, Richards soon determined that potentially the most damaging of the preparations involved the many kilometres of quays, along which depth charges had been buried and cemented every few metres. Demolition charges had also been placed in the outer breakwater protecting the port from the weather. As a result, he made sure that plans were laid for pouring cement into the pipes left protruding above ground along the quayside for the insertion of primers. Likewise, he put plans in motion to cut the undersea cables that were to be used for setting off the depth charges on the outer breakwater. For this, an Italian diver was recruited in the south and flown in a captured Fieseler Storch to a nearby landing strip prepared by partisans.[16]

Another threat to the port was represented by the *Aquila*, the 24,000-ton former passenger liner *Roma* that had been converted into Italy's first aircraft carrier and was berthed in the harbour. She had already been damaged by allied bombing, and resistance sources reported that she was being prepared as a blockship to be sunk across the entrance to the port. SOE accordingly made plans to sabotage this effort by sinking her instead at her moorings. On 1 April, Captain Edgar Chavasse, who had passed through the paramilitary training course at Monopoli, was sent by Gerry Holdsworth and Hedley Vincent to Florence to help develop the plan. Dated a week later, it envisaged using two two-man human torpedo boats (known as 'Chariots') which would penetrate the harbour and attach limpet mines to the *Aquila*'s hull. The Chariots would be carried by Italian fast torpedo boats from Leghorn to about 3 kilometres offshore and would then make their own way to the ship. After they had fixed limpet mines they would return to their parent ships. If for any reason they were unable to do that, McMullen provided precise details of two safe houses in Genoa that the crews could use with confidence, along with exact route maps on how to reach them. As the plan required the full cooperation of the Royal Italian Navy, Chavasse travelled to Taranto to brief the Italians and oversee the assembling of an assault team.

This was led by Captain 'Forza'. Ironically, three years before, he had been awarded the Medaglia d'Oro for helping sink the British battleship *Queen Elizabeth* and her sister ship, HMS *Valiant*, in Alexandria Harbour by using an earlier Italian version of the Chariot, the Maiale, or 'sea pig'. On 13 April, he left Bari by air and, accompanied by Chavasse, set off on his night-time cloak-and-dagger mission on 18 April. The SOE officer later summarised events as follows:

A copy book attack was carried out from about 4 miles outside the port and the MTSMs brought the Chariots close in to the mole. The Chariots got in undetected but, due to an enormous amount of weed and barnacle growth, were unable to make the limpet charges adhere to the hull. These had to be left on the bed of the harbour beneath the target's heel . . . In due course the charges exploded but only damaged the "Aquila" rather than sinking her.[17]

Robin Richards, however, officially reported the operation slightly differently, noting that one of the two torpedo boats failed to enter the harbour at all because of mechanical problems and that the charge laid by the other damaged the *Aquila* so lightly that she was moved four days later by the Germans in the planned attempt to sink her as a blockship. But that attempt, too, failed, and when Richards and McMullen entered Genoa on 27 April it was to find the liner still afloat across the harbour entrance. That night, however, the wind carried the ship away and only the next morning was she moored fast in a position to do no harm.[18]

Hewitt was delighted with the anti-scorch results in Genoa. Describing them as 'beyond the most optimistic expectations', he attributed them to the hurried nature of the German withdrawal and surrender, prompt partisan action and the 'waverings' of General Meinhold — possibly on orders from SS General Karl Wolff — to refrain from demolitions. Liberation achieved, the various CLN parties worked harmoniously together and shared out various administrative positions. Allied Military Government was quickly established, although informal partisan tribunals continued to deliver rough and ready 'justice' to Fascists and over the next four weeks several hundred bodies were deposited by night in various places around the city and its suburbs. At the instigation of Davidson, resistance members hunted out enemy spies still hiding in the city, many of whom were equipped with portable two-way radios.[19]

A spectacular resistance parade took place on 2 May, and weapons were handed in by the partisans. But most of these were obsolete, and thousands remained unaccounted for. Throughout Liguria several partisan bands were deliberately kept armed to help the allies in mopping-up operations which helped, in McMullen's view, to ensure a more rapid return to normal conditions. Along the border with France, disarmament of the partisans was also delayed in view of French designs on parts of Italian territory – exemplified by their advancing beyond the frontier as far as Imperia three days after its liberation. Here, they exacted revenge for the Italian advance on Nice in June 1940. 'They made themselves thoroughly unpopular,' reported Captain Bentley, 'requisitioning cars, removing stores from harbours and acting in a most unfriendly manner towards the population. A few partisans were disarmed, and it was only through a very firm hold on the partisans that no incident occurred.'[20]

South of Genoa, Major Gordon Lett, who since the previous summer had been working with partisans in the Rossano Valley above the naval port of La Spezia as head of the Blundell mission, was now attached as liaison officer to the US 92nd Division. Tasked with organising partisan support for its advance, he personally entered the city ahead of allied troops after it had been liberated by the local resistance. 'Where is the acting Prefect?' he asked when his jeep finally drew up in the city's Piazza Verdi. 'Will someone ask him to come here?' At this, wrote Lett in *Rossano*, his invaluable memoir of life with the partisans,

> The excitement increased. There were cries of 'Inglesi! Inglesi!' and still more flowers were showered upon us. Men jumped on to the vehicle and wrung our hands, while women embraced us hysterically. There was something theatrical about the scene – the half light of approaching night, the sea of upturned faces, the flowers, the noise, and the majestic building of the *Prefettura* looming overhead. It only lacked Verdi's music to complete the opera. At length a tall figure could be seen struggling through the crowd.
>
> 'I am the acting Prefect,' shouted the newcomer. 'Welcome, welcome!'

If this was a scene to be repeated elsewhere throughout northern Italy, so was the following, witnessed the next day by Lett from an upper window of the Prefecture where he had spent the night.

> I was suddenly awakened in the middle of the morning by the sound of running feet in the street outside the window. The curtains were still drawn; I pulled them aside and looked out on to the square. An angry roar began and grew louder and louder as a crowd converged on the

Piazza Verdi from all directions, surrounding a man in civilian clothing whom they had recognised as a member of the *Brigata Nera*. I saw what was about to happen, and could do nothing to prevent it. The miserable wretch screamed as the crowd closed in on him, and then disappeared beneath their feet. As suddenly as it had begun, the yelling ceased. The crowd melted away, as if ashamed of what they had done, dazed by the fact that, after twenty years of despotism, they had the power to do it. A gory mess of human flesh lay in the square, bathed in the bright sunshine, and I turned away from the square duly sobered by my first taste of mob violence. By the time the American advance guard arrived that evening, the Piazza Verdi was clean again.[21]

Hardly had the news about Genoa reached London than a third Freeborn report delivered the breaking news from Milan: 'Voice of Max repeat Max heard here from Free Milan on frequencies 495 to 500 metres at 18.20 G.M.T.' Max, of course, was Salvadori, SOE's liaison officer with the CLNAI. Since arriving in the Lombard capital he had devoted much of his attention to anti-scorch preparations and initiated lengthy discussions with representatives of industry about Lombardy's industrial production and its power plants. As a result he was convinced that the armed resistance in the province was neither large nor strong enough to protect the factories. Instead, he argued, it should organise sit-down strikes by the workers. 'If the Technische Truppen [German destruction units] find in the factories thousands of workers, they will think it over twice before shooting them in order to reach the machinery . . .' he told No. 1 Special Force. 'I will meet again the representatives of the clandestine trade unions and will further discuss the problem with them. Through a flourishing system of bribery,' he added, 'the industrialists have succeeded until now to save most of their industry . . .' He was also at pains to make clear to the resistance that the allies could not approve of any local deals struck with the Germans whereby the partisans would not hinder their withdrawal provided the Wehrmacht spared the plants. Unconditional surrender, he insisted on firm instructions from No. 1 Special Force, was the final aim of the allies. He also persuaded his superiors to increase the number of missions in the area between the River Sesia and Lake Garda.[22]

For many of his communications Salvadori relied on the radio set of an Italian mission operating near Bergamo with a Green Flames partisan group. Codenamed Anticer, it had been parachuted behind the lines over a year before as one of the dozens of Italian missions that played such a vital part in SOE operations. Its radio operator, a 29-year-old Milanese named Giovanni Carnesecchi, had been trained by No. 1 Special Force in southern Italy. He was a good and reliable operator and maintained regular contact with base until the end of the war. 'If Anticer's set works properly,' Salvadori reported shortly after arriving, 'it will be convenient to me as there is now a regular courier service twice a week between the Green Flames and Milan.' Over the weekends he typed up lengthy reports for SOE that were taken by couriers – mostly female – to Birkbeck in Lugano. He was also making use of an SIS set in Turin and another near Bergamo, as well as relying on messages conveyed via the SOE missions led by McMullen and Manfred Czernin.[23] Earlier that month, Czernin had been parachuted into Italy a second time, on this occasion to work with partisans north-east of Milan. For all his flamboyance he was carrying out valuable work with partisans around Bergamo and in due course was to enter the city, transmit direct to base from the Questura and accept the German surrender there.[24]

On 29 March Salvadori attended the first full-dress meeting of the CLNAI to be held in Milan since Parri's arrest. He took only a limited part in its discussions and was careful merely to advise, not to give orders. In this and subsequent meetings he helped clarify allied policies on issues ranging from supply drops and border rela- tions with the Yugoslavs and French to negotiations with the enemy. In turn, he provided No. 1 Special Force with information it demanded about events inside the occupied north. 'Besides signals and reports concerning the VDLs [Corps of Volunteers] and the CLN,' he recalled, 'I remember being asked to find the whereabouts of Parri and of Sogno . . .; to check on rumours concerning the willingness of the SS commander to negotiate a German surrender in Italy, something involving also a high ranking member of the archbishop's [of Milan] entourage; and to check on preparations [by Mussolini] in Valtellina for a last stand.'[25]

Meanwhile, he continued his contacts with leading politicians, trade union leaders, bankers, industrialists, as well as leaders of the

military resistance, often meeting as many as sixty people a week.
One of them was General Cadorna. After months of political wrangling, including threats and counter-threats of resignation and
dismissal, Cadorna had finally clarified his status as commander of
the CVL in late February with a compromise that involved him
accepting the CLNAI as his superior so long as he was not given
military directives that conflicted with those of the allies. Salvadori
was relieved to see him back in Milan after several weeks away in
Switzerland and southern Italy. 'His absence had been causing us
concern,' he recalled, 'and his presence was indispensable now that
events were moving quickly – with Parri away and Cadorna absent,
[Luigi] Longo was in command of the [CVL] and that meant a free
hand for the communists.' On 21 April, the day Bologna was liberated, Salvadori ensured that his mission's anti-scorch plans were
activated.[26]

Four days later, as allied forces approached the city, Salvadori –
now a lieutenant colonel awarded the Military Cross for his services
in southern Italy – attended what proved to be a crucial meeting of
the ruling committee of the Italian resistance, held secretly in the
Collegio dei Salesiani convent on the Via Copernico. The end of the
war and of the Fascist dictatorship was imminent. Railwaymen
had already stopped work and orders for a general strike had been
issued along with instructions to the workers to remain inside their
factories to block any attempts at demolition by the Germans.
Rumours of approaches by high-ranking Fascist and Wehrmacht
representatives to the allies were rife. An increasingly desperate
Mussolini, who was in Milan after fleeing from his headquarters at
Salò on Lake Garda, had expressed a wish to meet with the CLNAI
to discuss a possible deal.

'In the large, bare, shuttered room whose approaches were watched
by silent black-cassocked figures, there were seven of us,' recalled
Salvadori. 'Our hearts were heavy with emotion and a burden had
been lifted from our spirits. We knew that this was no ordinary day.
The end was at hand . . .'[27] What precise role Salvadori played in
the discussions that followed remains opaque. But what emerged
clearly were some firm directives, including the orders for a general
insurrection, a demand for unconditional surrender by the Germans
and Fascists by 6 p.m. that day, and the immediate transfer of all

civil and military power to the CLNAI and the various regional and local CLNs. Most drastic of all, however, was the ousting of Alfredo Pizzoni as the committee's chairman and his replacement by Rodolfo Morandi, a Socialist. The ground for this had been prepared at a meeting a week earlier and sprang from the left's conviction that the eminent banker was not the right person to stand up to what it believed was an impending showdown with the allies over the power of the CLNAI. The coup was easily executed. Pizzoni was in Berne that day, meeting in McCaffery's absence with De Haan, following two weeks' intensive discussions in the south with Italian and allied officials, including both Alexander and Holdsworth.[28] The initiative to replace him came from the Socialist representative backed by the Communist and Action Party members. The Liberal representative offered only weak resistance before also agreeing. The Christian Democrat decided to accept the majority decision in order to preserve unanimity.

The Action Party member concerned was none other than Leo Valiani, the long-time protégé of J Section and, in Roseberry's eyes, 'our man' on the CLNAI. As recently as March he had travelled to Berne with General Cadorna to talk with McCaffery and Dulles, followed by a meeting with Roseberry in Lyons, to help assuage allied fears about the strength and intentions of the Communists in the north and the likelihood of a replay of events in Greece. But Valiani's loyalties to SOE were always tempered, and he was now first and foremost an Italian and veteran anti-Fascist. Pizzoni had done excellent work and he was shocked and embittered by the brutal manner of his removal. But it symbolised the powerful political hurricane now sweeping across northern Italy as anti-Fascists sought to seize the moment to create a reborn Italy.[29]

One further decision by the committee that day was to have momentous consequences. This was the decree to establish popular courts of assize, tribunals of war and commissions of justice. 'Members of the Fascist Government and the hierarchs of Fascism . . . are to be punished with the penalty of death,' it declared. By implication, this ordered the execution of Mussolini. That same evening, the dictator and his entourage fled the city and headed north. When news of his capture by partisans reached Milan, General Cadorna raised no objection to suggestions that he be shot. The final decision was made by the Insurrectional Committee of the CLNAI, which included Valiani. 'Having refused to give himself up on insurrection day,' he later wrote, 'Mussolini by his own action became an outlaw.'[30]

Salvadori, likewise, had no qualms about the dictator's fate or that of the other Fascist hierarchs who were also executed in Dongo, and held firmly that this should be an Italian, not an allied, decision. Indeed, if they were going to do it, he advised the committee at one point, they should do it quickly before the allies arrived. 'To many people in Italy and abroad,' he wrote later in justification, 'this was a brutal act of civil war. They were wrong. The Dongo executions were the punishment for crimes which until then had gone unpunished, crimes committed twenty, twenty-five years before by the order of the fascist leaders, when thousands of people were assassinated to open the road to power for the fascists. The executions at Dongo were punishments for the greatest crime of all — that of robbing the Italian nation of its liberty.'[31] Thus, both of SOE's closest contacts with the CLNAI gave the green light to Mussolini's death at the hands of his fellow Italians.

At about 1 p.m. Salvadori left the meeting to go to lunch. Life still appeared normal with plenty of German and Fascist troops around, shops open and public transport running. Then, about an hour later, the streetcars disappeared from circulation. 'The number of German and Republican uniforms was rapidly decreasing,' he reported. 'Shops were closing down. At 16.30 I saw the first patrol of GAP on bicycles, apparently unarmed and with no badges ... At 17.00 hours I saw a truck hoisting a red flag. At 18.00, passing near Piazzale Baracca I saw crowds of civilians looting two German trucks ... I saw car after car, loaded with people and baggage, all streaming towards Como and Valtellina ... when I reached my lodging I told my host: "This is the end."' Somehow, he found time to draft a message for a courier to take to Czernin for radio transmission to base. 'Situation still under control,' it read, 'but possibly not for long.'[32]

Next morning, as Fascist troops evaporated, a Socialist Party member was proclaimed mayor of the city and the CLNAI moved its offices to the Prefecture. Salvadori, the only allied representative in the city, took possession of an office next door and hoisted the British and American flags. That evening he made a short broadcast which was relayed from the BBC in London at 22.20. He spoke of the courage and sacrifice of the partisans and praised the spirit of collaboration that had characterised the work of the CLNs. 'I express my admiration for those who fought and my grief for those who fell,' he concluded. 'I hope that as the resistance movement has been able to fight united during these months of struggle soon it will be able to remain united in carrying out the work of administration entrusted to the Committee of National Liberation until the arrival of the Allied Military Government.'[33]

Two days later, Hedley Vincent reached the city to assist Salvadori. He arrived in dramatic fashion, parachuting on to the city's racecourse with five Italians and a complete W/T station after a two-hour flight from the air base at Rosignano. Within hours he met Salvadori and signalled to base that he hoped soon to secure an aerodrome for the landing of reinforcements. There was a palpable sense of urgency to his message, and both he and Salvadori pressed for the early arrival of allied forces in view of the massive preparations being made in the city for the 1 May Labour Day celebrations.[34] By now, Lieutenant George Paterson, captured the previous summer during the collapse of the Domodossola Republic, had been released from the San Vittore prison and was also helping the SOE team in the city. Birkbeck had already arrived from Lugano. Life was slowly returning to normal and in the event, despite Vincent's fears, there was little disorder. At about noon on 29 April the first American patrol, including tanks and jeeps, appeared in the city centre. Some German troops had barricaded themselves in the Hotel Regina and Vincent, along with an American officer, successfully urged them to surrender. AMG officers had also by now arrived and the next day, with the official entry of US troops into the city, they took over the administration of Milan and the province of Lombardy.

That evening, Salvadori handed over his responsibilities to Vincent whose role, once AMG was installed, was to serve as the senior British representative to 15th Army Group, advising on the disarmament and disbanding of the partisans as well as seeing to the liquidation of SOE interests in Lombardy, a subject on which he had been thoroughly briefed by No. 1 Special Force. His takeover, explained Hewitt, would enable Salvadori to concentrate his own efforts as 'a political watchdog and cabinet maker'.[35]

In summing up his mission, Salvadori considered that his most important success had been in insisting that all resistance groups agree on three fundamental points: no compromise with the enemy; acceptance of the military orders of the CLN military command, based on the orders of the allied headquarters; and the use of non-violent general strikes. It was also fortunate, he pointed out, that the Germans and Fascists had overestimated the number and the strength of active patriots in Lombardy and thus decided to leave the province rather than turn it into one of their last strongholds in the country. The abrupt collapse of the Germans had also meant that little damage was done to the economic infrastructure. '[It] took place so rapidly, during the night of 25/26th April,' he told No. 1 Special Force, 'that the enemy lacked the time to do any damage to points of economic interest.'[36]

The same Freeborn report about Salvadori's broadcast over the Free Milan radio station also brought news of the mission headed by Stephen Hastings. Following the order for 'all-out action' on 5 April, Hastings had implemented his 'Guireza' mission's plans for the sabotage of enemy communications and successfully cut the Via Emilia to the east and west of Piacenza. Orders to take and hold the city came on 23 April and two days later the attack was well under way by partisan forces, who were only 3 kilometres from the town.

At this point there arrived on the scene Captain Hugh McDermot, one of No. 1 Special Force's liaison officers with the Fifth Army, who had driven up the Via Emilia ahead of the advanced allied forces in order to reconnoitre the resistance scene. He was a member of one of two Special Force Staff Sections [SFSS] travelling with both the Fifth and Eighth armies to liaise at all army levels on matters concerning the resistance. Administered by No. 1 Special Force, but operationally controlled by the army, they also provided mobile forces mounted in jeeps or scout cars, for the special tasks of making contact with the resistance and British liaison officers, and for carrying out reconnaissance. McDermot brought news to Hastings of the approach of the US 135th Infantry Regiment, and together they went back to report to its headquarters. It was obviously necessary. 'No one seemed to know that the mountains, and indeed all of the approaches to Piacenza belonged to the Partisans,' recalled Hastings. 'I briefed the American Colonel as best I could and was glad to be released. We managed to maintain a liaison with them from then on.' This Hastings–McDermot encounter was only one of dozens that throughout this final campaign ensured necessary liaison on the ground between allied forces and the resistance.[37]

As Piacenza was occupied by some 500 SS troops with ten armoured cars and several 20 mm guns, Hastings asked for help from American forces. After first refusing because they needed their tanks elsewhere and were content, so they told him, 'to leave Piacenza to the partisans,' they relented the next morning and released three Sherman tanks. The partisans, now joined by the forces to which Captain Brown's Insulin mission was attached, then attacked. 'Partisans fighting house to house but very tired,' reported Hastings to base. Finally, they entered the city shortly after dawn on 28 April. The enemy armoured cars hurriedly disappeared and were followed in short order by the SS and Fascist forces.

Hastings then found himself negotiating between CLN officials, partisan military commanders and Allied Military Government in the shape of an American major who, despite an Italian name, knew neither Italian nor Italy. Hastings's autobiography amplifies the brief and neutral language of the official report that recorded what happened next:

'We ought to have an election,' said [the major], looking earnestly at his regulations. I have to confess I vetoed the election. It would have to be contrived. This was no time for a sudden outbreak of democracy. So far as I was concerned the only people with any claim to authority were the Partisan commanders because they had done the work, because they were my friends, and because anyway they had the guns. I would try to arrange a selection of those who seemed most deserving and [the major] could work it out for himself. We commandeered an office in the Palazzo del Commune, a splendid gothic edifice from which the Farnese family once ruled the town. Word spread and a large crowd filled the anterooms. I had warned our partisan chiefs to position themselves as near to the door as possible. Once we had [the major] in position behind an imposing desk, we opened the doors enough to let in one at a time. The rush was sensational. When we had roughly the requisite number of dignitaries we heaved them shut. A line of grinning panting

heavily armed aspirant Mayors and Questure stood facing [the major].
Somehow we sorted it out without too much ill feeling and some firm
advice from us. That was the election.[38]

The day that Max Salvadori handed over to Hedley Vincent in
Milan also saw the entry of the first allied troops into Turin, where
Colonel John Stevens was the senior British liaison officer in
Piedmont. After several months behind the lines he had returned
briefly to base in March, but on 2 April he was parachuted back
into the Langhe with his second-in-command, Major Derek Dodson,
who like him had seen service with SOE in Greece. A week later,
dressed in civilian clothes, Stevens drove into Turin, passing safely
through seven roadblocks on the way. Dodson, along with the
mission's radio operator, set up base with a group of partisans about
20 kilometres east of the city.

Stevens found the military command of the resistance in 'a parlous
state'. The commander of the partisans, General Trabucchi, as well
as his chief of staff, had been arrested, and his successor was charming
but, in Stevens's view, incompetent and before long he replaced him.
He was dismayed to find that the only order issued so far had been
that at a given signal all the partisans were to march on Turin. As
this was contrary to 15th Army Group instructions, Stevens robustly
rescinded it. He was also horrified to learn that police functions were
to be handed over to partisans with no experience of police work,
so he ensured that they were bolstered by a number of Carabinieri.
Better news emerged from a meeting with Captain Pat O'Regan,
who was based with partisans to the west of the city. It turned out
that O'Regan had acquired a first-rate source of intelligence in two
Austrian signallers based at German military headquarters, and as
a result he was able to provide Stevens with copies of all the enemy's
operational signals. He also had a source in the SS headquarters in
the city. Thanks to this, Stevens was relieved to learn that the
Germans had no knowledge of the false name he was using nor
the address at which he was staying.

On 24 April he received news that the Germans intended to withdraw from the city and immediately ordered a general partisan
mobilisation. Two days later, with a general strike in full swing,
fierce street-fighting broke out and Stevens ordered that some two

thousand partisans be infiltrated into the city to bolster the already substantial defences of Turin's factories. Little German damage to the city's industry occurred. The enemy's plans for the destruction of the railway yards were captured and as a result railway workers were able to cut the detonator leads. Plans to blow up the Simplon Tunnel had been foiled earlier when partisans blew up the wagons carrying the necessary explosives.

At dawn on 27 April partisans launched an attack on the city. 'Partisans now occupying outskirts Turin,' reported Dodson by radio a few hours later. 'Fascists possibly some Germans still hold centre firing at all movements.'[39] Heavy fighting continued in the centre until German troops began withdrawing that night, leaving behind only a small force of Republicans, and by noon the next day the city was completely in partisan hands. Amongst them was Major Mauri, who rushed the men of his Langhe Division to the city to take part in its liberation. Accompanying him was Sergeant Bill Pickering, who after being separated from Max Salvadori had worked as a radio operator for the Chariton mission with partisans in the Cisterna area, where amongst other things they had secretly prepared a landing strip for the evacuation of downed allied airmen and the reception of small Lysander planes.

He had already taken part in the liberation of Asti and witnessed the irresistible desire of the partisans for action, even against allied orders. Trying to stop the partisans from liberating the city, Pickering explained to a forgiving SOE officer, had 'been like King Canute's efforts to stem the tide'. In Turin, he participated in the final rounds of house-to-house fighting as Fascist forces desperately fought for their lives. 'From time to time,' he wrote later, 'a car would flash by with a Republican soldier firing a machine gun out of its window. It reminded me of scenes from gangster movies, but these were real bullets pinging into the brickwork behind us.' Gradually, the shootings petered out and civilians began to emerge cautiously on to the streets.[40]

Fighting continued on the outskirts of Turin until allied troops arrived, and on 2 May General Ernst Schlemmer, commander of the German 75th Corps, surrendered all his forces in Piedmont to Pat Amoore in Biella. The Cherokee mission had established its headquarters there and Amoore had been awaiting Major Readhead's arrival to finalise the tentative contacts he had already made with Schlemmer's headquarters to discuss the issue. 'I was taking my first bath in five months,' Amoore recalled,

> when the formal conclusion of [Readhead's] surrender negotiations was pre-empted by my being summoned urgently to the *Albergo Principe*. There I found that Oberst Faulmuller, the Chief of Staff of the German 75th Army Corps, had arrived with a white flag and a document signed by Schlemmer offering immediate and unconditional surrender. But he was still reluctant to surrender to the partisans. So in the event it was my signature that was finally appended to this historic document, on behalf of the British Cherokee Mission. The third participant in the ceremony was Colonel John Brett, from the US armoured group whose spearhead had just reached Biella, and which had astonished the crowds in the streets as they saw unmistakably Japanese heads belonging to the US Nisei units popping out of the tank turrets. He took a quick look at the surrender document, had a brief word with his ADC, and said: 'That's OK by us, go ahead.'[41]

By this time Stevens had firmly attached himself to the Piedmont CLN in Turin and, with O' Regan and Dodson, was handling much of the civil administration. 'On 28 April,' he reported, 'I ordered shops and banks to be opened and the tram service to be re-started as from 29 April, as it was essential to restore normal life as quickly as possible.'[42] One of those who arrived to help was Captain Jim Beatt, from Charles Macintosh's TAC HQ at Florence, who had been accompanying the forward elements of the advancing allied forces in a Dingo scout car, helping them make contact with No. 1 Special Force missions and Italian partisan headquarters as they entered Bologna, La Spezia, Reggio Emilia, Parma, Piacenza, Milan and Novara. On his arrival in Turin, Stevens requested him to assist with the urgent task of keeping the population fed. 'Stevens . . . asked me to escort 5 trucks with Italian drivers to Vercelli to bring back rice for the civilian population,' Beatt recalled. 'At times we were under fire from the north bank of the Po, still under German control. The following day he sent me some miles from Turin to recover 50 million lire which all in notes had been dropped in a few days previously in large green bags. I was able to strap these over the engine at the back of the Dingo and eventually got back to Turin, but on one occasion I had to get some bullocks to pull us across the river where the bridges were blown.'[43]

To his considerable relief Stevens found that thanks to excellent collaboration between the parties of the CLN, the political situation never got out of hand. May Day, a potential trouble spot, passed quietly and the next morning the city's factories were back at work. The situation was helped by the fact that the electricity supply remained uninterrupted and that some three hundred Carabinieri arrived to keep order. This did not, however, prevent the spontaneous purging of Fascists. Some thousand or so were killed in the first week of allied occupation.[44]

On 5 May, with AMG established, Stevens handed over his responsibilities to the regional commissioner for Piedmont, regretting only that the disarming of the partisans was not proceeding more rapidly. French territorial ambitions in Piedmont were also causing him concern, and he had even taken steps to speed up the arrival of American troops to forestall a possible French incursion into Turin. Elsewhere in Piedmont French troops annexed three communes close to Nice, and on 18 May they organised a pro-French demonstration in Aosta. Only in June, after high-level political protests to General de Gaulle from London and Washington, did French forces pull back.

Hydroelectric installations had largely escaped damage or destruction. This was down to the efforts of Readhead's Cherokee mission, assisted by two further SOE teams that arrived in March and April. The first of these, known as 'Clarinda' or 'M4', was under the command of Major William McKenna and had a purely anti-scorch brief. Because of problems with his W/T set he soon began transmitting from the set being used by Cherokee's demolitions expert, Captain Bell, and the two of them met up on 18 April to coordinate anti-scorch plans. By this time the 'Clarinda II' mission had also arrived, led by Captain George Morton, a former instructor at SOE's Beaulieu training school who went by the battle name of 'Smith'. All three of them met with local partisan commanders on 22 April to finalise preparations. Four days later, a group of twelve Germans dressed in civilian clothes were caught by partisans trying to get into the power station at Breuil and — so Morton reported to

Siena – were shot. West of Aosta, German efforts to carry out demolitions were thwarted by Alpini forces who decided that at this late stage of the war protecting Italian assets was preferable to following German orders.

As elsewhere, the rapidity of the German surrender also blocked other demolition plans, and General Schlemmer kept to a promise to the partisans not to carry any out. From Freeborn Situation Report No. 10, Baker Street learned in the early hours of 29 April that the liberation of Aosta was imminent. In fact, by the time they received the message the town had already been entered by partisan forces. But the situation remained tense because of the nearby presence of French forces and the latent threat of the annexation of territory. Robust intervention by Morton helped defuse the situation and the arrival of US forces on 4 May was greeted with relief by the Italians and put paid to any French ambitions. Three days later Allied Military Government officers set up office there, and SOE's mission was over.[45]

Once the major north-western cities of Turin, Milan and Genoa were free, partisans across the Veneto to the east were called upon to launch a massive campaign of harassment against enemy forces now steadily retreating towards the border with Austria. In the words of Hewitt's final report on No. 1 Special Force, they 'rose against the enemy banishing him from the towns and occupied places, clearing the roads, and liberating whole tracts of country through which the armoured columns of the allies drove on without hindrance to complete the liberation of the North.'[46] This final campaign was extremely short, and the time between orders being given and the arrival of allied forces varied between a mere two and six days. British liaison officers scrambled hard to stay ahead of the game but were often overtaken by events, while well-laid plans for action by the partisans were sometimes brushed aside in their long pent-up impatience to get at the enemy, Fascist or German. Allied troops occasionally arrived unexpectedly on the scene before plans could even be implemented.

Freeborn telegrams continued to capture the pace of events. Report No. 12 received in Baker Street on the afternoon of 29 April carried the following paragraph covering No. 1 Special Force missions in the region:

(A) Reports from Simia rpt Simia +Fluvius? rpt Fluv?ius? rpt Fluvius Tabella Gela rpt Tabella Gela tell of continued liberation by partisans of localities in mountains and plain. March on Udine rept Udine expected begin tonight. (B) Padova freed by Eighth Army (C) Cottrell rpt Cottrell reports today CLN rpt CLN Venice has agreed with enemy that Germans will quit today and not rpt not carry out any demolitions. No more fighting. Partisans control town. Entrance to Lagoon partly closed. Cottrell hopes secure chart of mine fields. Germans also surrendered in Mestre, rpt Mestre.

Venice, like Genoa, was another Italian port the allies were keen to capture intact. But by now their eyes were mainly focused on capturing Trieste to the north-east, which was far more important as a port to service their future needs in Austria. 'The place we want to get to most of all is Trieste,' Lieutenant General Sir John Harding, Alexander's chief of staff, told Lieutenant General Sir Bernard Freyberg, commander of the 2nd New Zealand Division that formed the spearhead of the Eighth Army advance. As a result, his troops bypassed Venice in their headlong chase of the Germans and left the city to the resistance.

The British liaison officer there, Captain Cottrell, had already discussed anti-scorch tasks with the CLN. The Germans had mined the Mestre–Venice causeway and major quays, and had prepared blockships, but the CLN claimed it could mobilise some 2,500 men of whom more than 1,000 were armed. On the night of 27/28 April Cottrell advised the CLN that the time was ripe for an uprising and this was ordered for dawn. While the Fascist authorities, including the commander of a Black Brigade, surrendered unconditionally, the Germans refused to do so and their commander threatened to bombard the city from the mainland and the Lido. Heavy fighting followed until midday when the Germans finally requested a truce. Three hours later it was agreed that enemy personnel would be allowed to leave the city, taking with them only their personal weapons, in return for which no demolitions would be carried out. Cottrell spent that night at enemy headquarters, refusing to let them leave unless the commander handed over a chart of the minefields. Finally, at 5 a.m., he obtained the chart and the enemy left the city by barge. Cottrell described the whole affair as a gigantic bluff. 'The

Germans were scared stiff,' he reported, 'and could have wiped the Partisan forces off the map at any time they liked.' None of the Italian warships in the port was sunk, and no attempts were made to sink the blockships. Thus, when a squadron of 12th Lancers turned down the causeway at 4 p.m. that day to be the first allied troops to enter the city, Venice was handed over in good working order.[47]

Inland, in the western Veneto mountains, the Ruina/Fluvius mission, now being run after the death of Major John Wilkinson by Captains Orr-Ewing and Woods, found that despite orders from base 'it was almost impossible to keep the men in check . . . and from early April [they] were in action.'[48] From 25 April, the final all-out effort began and the partisans took prisoner or killed thousands of German troops, occupied towns, villages and factories, attacked and destroyed enemy lines of communication, and liberated most of the area before the first allied forces arrived. Christopher Woods joined partisans who fought their way into the industrial town of Schio, where the Germans eventually surrendered to the partisans at the town hall. Here, too, the British mission set up its final headquarters. Unfortunately, the partisans let the Germans – parachute troops – retreat with their weapons. As they passed through a small village, someone took a potshot at them and in retaliation they shot sixty-four of its inhabitants – men, women and children – and then burned down their houses with many of them still alive inside.[49]

After liberation, Allied Military Government rapidly moved in and Orr-Ewing stayed on briefly to assist. In both the provinces of Verona and Vicenza, things soon settled down to a normal life. The primary remaining problem was caused not by militant partisans but by enemy forces in the heavily wooded hills, who proved reluctant to surrender. For three or four weeks after the liberation, he reported, there were 'small bands of Huns, Russians and Fascists . . . [who] would not surrender to the partisans and who would make occasional inroads to find food'. In Trentino – the largely German-speaking province annexed from Austria at the end of the First World War – trouble likewise continued for about a month. The occupying American forces had herded some 10,000 German troops into the area, where they simply took over several villages, threw out the inhabitants and made themselves at home stealing food and other possessions. Despite urgent pleas by the two SOE officers virtually no attempt to stop them was made by the American commander before the end of May. 'It can hardly be wondered at,' noted Woods, who was the only member of the mission to have had any contact with the area, 'if in the meantime the civilian population considered themselves worse off than they had been previously under German occupation.'[50]

On 28 April orders from 15th Army Group were passed to No. 1 Special Force missions beyond Venice to do everything possible to cut the German lines of communication running north and south. In the Belluno zone partisans quickly occupied towns and villages and took prisoner hundreds of German troops. From a vantage point above the main road leading north from Vittorio Veneto towards Belluno Harold Tilman noted the sudden cessation of German traffic. Twenty-four hours later partisan leaders were in contact with General Scholl in the town encouraging him to surrender, but according to a Freeborn report he remained 'recalcitrant'. Tilman, who was now linked up with a squadron of the 27th Lancers and a motorised company of the Rifle Brigade, found himself briefly caught up in a vicious small battle just south of the town during which RAF planes accidentally strafed them and caused several injuries, one death and terminal damage to a number of vehicles. Finally the Germans gave up and by noon the next day the stubborn remnant in Belluno had also laid down their arms.

Tilman and two of the senior partisans rode into the town on a motorcycle. 'I should like to report,' the legendary mountaineer wrote later, 'that we were wrenched from the cycle by an enthusiastic crowd, borne shoulder high to the Piazza del Duomo, and there crowned with laurel wreaths to the prolonged deafening cry of "Viva's" of the assembled multitude. We were too soon for that. The streets were nearly empty, most of the people wisely remaining indoors until the situation cleared.' Instead he found partisans guarding an ever-increasing number of bewildered German troops, while in the Prefettura the newly elected prefect, CLN, and the mayor were already establishing civilian administration.[51]

Meanwhile, Tilman's second-in-command John Ross had missed most of the action because of the sheer speed of events. Ten days before, he had headed to a site 16 kilometres north of the town to take delivery of a drop. After several days waiting in vain in bad weather he heard the dramatic news filtering in from the town, as he hastily noted in the diary he should not have been keeping:

> Low cloud and rained all day. Poor sched as battery low. Staffeta arrived at night with mail including Simia Flash plan from Clinton. Huns surrendering from Belluno with many small garrisons. Everywhere great news. Himmlers [*sic*] peace offer. No message and busy night. New battery arrived.[52]

The next day it both rained and snowed all morning and he abandoned the notion of waiting for a drop and decided instead to return to Belluno. On the way down he ran into the staff of the partisan division. 'I was rather bad-tempered with them about attacking garrisons instead of roads,' he scribbled, 'they said they have no explosives — balls!' Eventually he reached Belluno and met up with Tilman. When Allied Military Government was established under what he remembered as 'a rather fuddy duddy elderly English Colonel', he helped it settle various problems between it, the partisans and the local population. 'The AMG expected the partisans to be a wild and disorganised lot who brandished arms but had done little — as they had found in the south of Italy,' he recalled. 'They did not realise that the partisans in the north were thoroughly responsible men who had planned local government to take over when liberation arrived.'[53]

Also in the Veneto, one of the last-minute British arrivals was Captain Arthur Radley who landed near Cansiglio by Lysander in early April with his radio operator on an airstrip 'of epic proportions' prepared by the partisans, to work with the Garibaldini Nino Nanetti Division. Having earlier served as British liaison officer to a brigade of Italian partisans driven by a German *rastrellamento* across the border into France, he came to join Captain 'Bertie' Lingen, who had replaced Paul Brietsche as head of the Gela mission. Brietsche and his deputy Richard Tolson, whom Radley was replacing, were taken out of the field by the same small plane.

Radley later recalled two powerful memories of his mission. The first was of the flight that took him right over the German-occupied areas north of Venice in full daylight but without a single anti-aircraft or fighter attack – a clear sign of allied air superiority. The second was that while 8,000 German troops surrendered to the partisans along with 1,000 pieces of equipment, the Royal Air Force proceeded to 'shoot up' all the vehicles thinking they were still in German hands. 'Thus perished,' wrote Radley, 'all the prospective Division booty – and we were even attacked by bombs at our HQ; the British mission was understandably not exactly popular.'[54]

On the day allied forces were given their orders to make 'at top speed' for Trieste, Major Tommy Macpherson's Coolant mission near Udine implemented its action plan to target German telephone and telegraph communications and cut their withdrawal routes, especially along Routes 13 and 54 heading north towards Villach and Klagenfurt. Crossing points over the River Tagliamento were also attacked. By this time the Germans were heavily reliant on horses for pulling their equipment and the animals offered easy and effective targets for the partisans because once they were shot the Germans had no choice but to abandon the equipment.

But motorised transport also proved vulnerable. 'Olmo', commander of the 4th Osoppo Division, personally directed a flying squad detailed to destroy enemy patrol vehicles. 'He watched a column of twenty heavy enemy tanks,' wrote Macpherson, 'and attacked their petrol supply with such determination that 6 surrendered, 7 were caught stationery by British artillery directed by the Partisans, and of the remainder only 2 managed to reach Austria.'[55] Around Carnia, both Osoppo and Garibaldi divisions blocked the Monte Croce pass over the border to Lienz. Twice the Germans managed to reopen it, and twice the partisans succeeded in blocking it again. Here, Russian (mostly Cossack) forces were thick on the ground and Macpherson had a fruitless meeting with one of their emissaries to discuss unconditional surrender. On 30 April, however, some 500 Russian Georgians went over to the partisans, joined in the fight on the Monte Croce road and lost some fifty dead.

By this time Macpherson was based in Gemona, having joined in an attack on the town when the partisan offensive began. His

W/T operator, Arthur Brown, begged to go along but received what he succinctly described as 'a very short answer'. Instead, from the heavily camouflaged mountainside cabins that served as their hideout, he recalled events from his reconstructed radio log for 28 April:

Party of Germans appears in the valley just 50 yards below our position. Almost no warning. Remaining four of us man the ramparts. Party turns out to be a dozen German prisoners sent back under partisan escort to bring us and the stores down. Watch while I send off Macpherson's traffic to base. Load up and start down. On the way, stop and tune into the BBC to find out where things have got to. Germans straining their ears to hear. Beckon them over and let them listen to the news in Italian. Pathetic gratitude. Seems odd. Share their cigarettes with them (glad to share anybody's). Continue march to strongpoint on saddle above Gemona. Set up shop. Heavy fighting in the town, a mile down the hill. Contact base and go down to Gemona. The road is under fire from SS in caverns on neighbouring hill, fortified for last stand ... Shells going both ways. Houses blazing in the middle. Macpherson has taken over Gestapo HQ, but is not there. Battle for town seems to be going on in the next street. Find a load of propaganda against the British. All about British atrocities against the Sepoys during the Indian Mutiny. Do not believe it. Spend the night.[56]

Fighting in the town continued the next morning but died down later and the partisans insisted on a 'booze up'. Brown tried in vain to control them and ended up himself that night in an inn halfway between the town and the hideout:

Wake up next morning to find six bodies outside house, shot by partisans – Mongols, Cossacks, one fascist; all identified to me by the lady of the house who kicks each one by turn and recites his crimes ... Up to strongpoint to take sked. Partisans have vanished again. Go to Gemona, find Macpherson and pass on decoded traffic. Go with Nino to view Mongols and Cossacks and their families in a cage around a factory – looks like a couple of thousand of them.

Macpherson meanwhile was keeping in touch with events in Udine over a special telephone line laid by the Elettrica Friulana. So he knew immediately when the city was liberated on 1 May by

partisans, both Osoppo and Garibaldini (some of whom were operating under Slovene control), after the Germans were taken off
guard by a feint on the south side of the city. The surprise attack
delivered valuable dividends. 'Anti-scorch of the electric substations,
the telephone exchange, the city buildings, and the main entrance
bridge, was 100% successful,' he was able to record.[57] Heavy fighting
between partisans and the retreating enemy forces continued until
allied troops began arriving in large numbers. Even then, battle
continued and a fierce counter-attack briefly forced advanced British
vehicles to withdraw. 'The position was critical,' wrote Macpherson,
who was in the thick of it. 'The Partisans were not exactly encouraged by the departure of British vehicles . . . We were attacked by
two heavy tanks, by approx. 1100 Russians and Wehrmacht, and by
800 SS [who] coming from the West [had] broken in and were
fighting in the cemetery at the entrance to the town itself . . . I fully
expected we had had our day.' Fortunately, a lucky shot from a
captured gun hit one of the German tanks and they decided to withdraw, a counter-attack pushed the enemy troops back a few hundred
metres, and the most advanced SS spearheads captured a 'pub'
and – in Macpherson's words – 'got very drunk'. By nightfall Gemona
was once again securely in partisan hands, though elsewhere they
were forced to make tactical retreats, such as briefly abandoning
Osoppo in order to escape being overwhelmed.

Four days later Macpherson was able to get to Udine to see for
himself that the partisan town command and the CLN had everything in hand and were ready to receive AMG. One of the reasons
he had been making so many urban visits over the previous few
weeks, as he explained later to Arthur Brown, was that he was
instructed 'to make sure there was some provincial and urban government ready to take over on liberation other than the Communists'.[58]

Entering Udine the day it was liberated was one of the dozens of
Italians dropped by No. 1 Special Force on missions behind the lines.
Paola del Din was a blonde, steely-grey-eyed 21-year-old native of
the city, and a fourth-year student at Padua University. Her father
was a regular army officer now languishing in a British POW camp
in India and her brother, Renato, had been killed the year before
during an Osoppo attack on Tolmezzo, capital of the Carnia region.
Taking the battle name 'Renata', she had started working as a partisan

courier and in the summer of 1944 was asked to undertake a mission to SOE in Florence. She accepted, and was taken to the nearby headquarters of Manfred Czernin and Patrick Martin-Smith. Here she was given several documents with the single instruction to take them to their destination but without running any more risks than necessary. She was not to cross the lines but to wait until she was overrun by allied troops. Given 13,000 lire for expenses, she had made a perilous journey and safely delivered the documents along with a letter of introduction from Czernin. At first, no one believed her story but after a thorough grilling she was declared a bona fide agent. 'This girl is extremely capable . . .' noted her interrogator. 'She wishes to return to her area [and] is quite willing to work for us.'[59]

This she did. After parachute training she joined the 'Bigelow' mission led by Gianandrea Gropplero di Troppenburg, a former pilot officer cadet otherwise known by his battle name of 'Freccia' [Arrow], who after the armistice had gone to Rome and taken part in armed activities of the Action Party. Finally, after ten abortive sorties, the party was dropped from a Dakota 8 kilometres north of Udine on the night of 9 April, when the final allied offensive opened. Shortly afterwards di Troppenburg and his radio operator 'Secondino' were captured by Cossack troops and beaten and tortured before being dramatically rescued by their comrades. 'We had to find somewhere for Freccia and Secondino to stay as one was wounded in the thigh and the other in the head,' Paola explained. Worried that if kept in the countryside they would fall victim to yet another round-up, one evening just before curfew she and two other partisans took Freccia by car to Udine and the house of a Red Cross worker, who, along with her family, had helped looked after, and hidden, many wounded partisans.[60] She also recovered a radio set, thus enabling Secondino to re-establish contact with base. Over the next two weeks she acted as a courier supplying messages for the two secret transmitters working in the area. After entering Udine, Paola carried out various tasks for the mission until it was disbanded on 20 May. When the final uprising began she had pleaded for a machine gun, hoping to avenge her brother. But the request had been met with a firm refusal.

The announcement of the German surrender made little immediate difference to Macpherson's work. Many enemy units simply ignored the order, or claimed that they belonged to the Balkan Army Group, so were not covered by it, and continued to head towards the Austrian frontier. Allied forces now had instructions to continue the advance where possible but to commit no hostile act and to parley everywhere. Frequently, however, they encountered SS strong points which heavily sniped at them. Rather than disobey orders the British forces were 'most helpful', explained Macpherson, for example in allowing partisans 'to "steal" temporarily such useful toys as flamethrowers, etc., with which extensive and successful "winkling" was carried out.' Finally, on 9 May, Eighth Army forces crossed the frontier into Austria.

In some ways, however, the most important and delicate part of the Coolant mission's work remained. It was tasked with maintaining security on the main routes through the mountains to Austria against threats from the snipers and stay-behind enemy resistance groups, and anti-sniping patrols continued until the end of the month when the last of the enemy resistance groups in the area, led by a Fascist, was cleaned up on 29 May. Coolant also had to maintain control of the partisans and see to their disarmament and disbandment. This, quite apart from the administrative arrangements for over 20,000 men, meant keeping good relations with them, locating their dumps of hidden arms and finding them immediate and useful work. 'Successful cajolery on the one hand, and intelligence and direct action on the other, led to the voluntary or compulsory surrender of an estimated 90% of existent weapons in the area. As a result,' wrote Macpherson in his official report at the end of July 1945, 'this most troubled political area has since been relatively free of violence and (outside Trieste) intimidation.' He also stressed how vital it was to find the partisans jobs: 'The partisan must be sure of a small *immediate* gratuity and of an occupation: indigent and idle ex-partisans are criminals in the making,' he stressed. It was also vital to give them full recognition of a job well done. 'This last,' he wrote, 'is achieved by the maximum of pomp and ceremony, on a day of public holiday, at their "stand-down parade".' In Coolant's case, this was greatly helped by the presence on the day itself of Lieutenant General Sir Richard McCreery, the commander of the Eighth Army.[61]

These various tasks kept the mission busy until far later than envisaged by No. 1 Special Force. Elsewhere across the north demobilisation of the partisans proceeded fairly rapidly following liberation and once political tensions along the French frontier had dissipated. At the request of Eighth Army, however, Macpherson remained in Udine for six weeks after the liberation, and the official ceremonial disarmament of the Osoppo and Garibaldini only took place on 24 June. All was made more uncertain and difficult by the tangled political and diplomatic crisis that erupted between the West and Yugoslavia over the future of Venezia Giulia following the liberation of Trieste. For a while it even seemed that another war could break out, and on 16 May allied troops in the area were placed on standby. Fortunately, however, thanks to high-level intervention by London, Washington and Moscow, the crisis was resolved before the end of the month.[62]

Late on the afternoon of 4 May a column of allied cars, prominently marked with the Union Jack and Stars and Stripes, passed through a barrier across the road in the middle of the Italian town of Rovereto in Trentino north of Verona, and entered German-controlled territory. When the battle lines had frozen two days before, General von Vietinghoff was still in his headquarters in Bolzano, which was where the allied mission, consisting of some twenty officers and men in battledress, was now heading. It was also the headquarters of SS General Karl Wolff, the supreme SS and Police Chief in Italy, who had been mostly responsible for German anti-partisan activities in the north. The allied mission was led by three senior officers, Lieutenant Colonel Threlfall of SOE, Colonel Russell Livermore of the OSS and Lieutenant-Colonel S. H. White of the Allied Commission. Its task was to discuss disarmament and other issues related to the partisans. Armed German patrols guarded the road, German troops stared as they passed by and anti-tank guns still pointed down the highway towards them. Just before midnight, they finally reached their destination.

The next morning they met the local representative of the CLNAI, Dr Bruno de Angelis, and explained that one of their aims was to disarm the partisans and prepare the way for AMG. De Angelis proved friendly and cooperative, said that he too would like to see the partisans disarmed, but pointed out that this would be difficult while the Germans themselves kept their weapons. Once they were deprived of them, however, he was certain that the partisans would 'give up their weapons like lambs'.[63]

In the meetings that followed Threlfall found the Germans extremely nervous yet contemptuous of the partisans, using their presence as an excuse to keep their weapons and delay implementation of the surrender terms, and at times declining to surrender to their units. Wolff, he reported, was 'most glib and suave ... a man of admirable manners, great charm, and ... full of pretentions [*sic*] of goodwill.' But his SS staff proved reluctant to provide sensitive information – such as the fate of missing allied officers – and only when American troops raided Wolff's headquarters did they finally come clean about an OSS officer who had been murdered while under interrogation in the town.

Continuing attacks by the partisans were unhelpful. Only the day before the mission arrived, street-fighting between the resistance and the Germans had left about eighty people wounded or killed. In addition an SS column on the march in nearby hills was attacked by partisans and reacted by burning down a large number of houses and killing some twenty-seven Italians, by no means all of whom were partisans. In turn, the partisans took sixty-seven prisoners. When Threlfall received a formal request from the Germans for their return he received an evasive reply from a CLN representative. 'So I asked him off the record whether [they] were still alive,' reported Threlfall. 'He looked at me, shrugged his shoulders, and said "You know, they were all S.S. men and had done terrible things in the neighbourhood." We thought the best action in this case was no action at all, and we therefore did not reply to the original German request.'[64] Partisans also continued to sabotage German telephone lines until it was explained to them that these were now being used by allied forces. Then, only a few days into the mission, several trucks arrived bringing 120 partisans from Milan. 'They were very much excited and were itching for a fight with the Germans,' reported Livermore. Only after much persuasion and the production of written orders did they eventually agree to leave. All of this made the mission's task more difficult, as did simmering resentment among the town's population over the billeting of Germans in hotels and private residences, some of them the homes of partisans.[65]

Over the ten days it was in the town, however, the mission managed to solve some, if not all, of the partisan questions. Threlfall and his colleagues succeeded in getting them to hand back to the Germans several military vehicles they had seized but that were needed for the implementation of the surrender terms, and in return the Germans handed over a number of Italian civilian vehicles they had requisitioned or stolen. But when regular allied troops finally arrived on the scene they lacked any definite orders about disarming the Germans and this, in turn, delayed that of the partisans. Ten days after the surrender, the town was still being patrolled by SS men armed with tommy guns. This bizarre situation ceased abruptly just before the mission left, but it meant that it was not possible for it to hold any of the disarmament parades for the partisans that by now had taken place in most of the rest of northern Italy. The mission did, however, acquire valuable documentary intelligence about what the Germans knew of the partisans, their order of battle for dealing with them and the anti-partisan directives issued to their forces. The considerable friction that had existed between the regular army and the SS was also confirmed. But whether SS or army, concluded Threlfall, 'all of them were alike in showing the blandest ignorance of or indifference to the war crimes of the German forces, and all were united in trying to put across to us the old story of the correct, soldierly and honourable German officer.'[66]

On 4 May — the day that the Threlfall/Livermore mission reached Bolzano — the penultimate Freeborn report was despatched to London. 'In all areas mopping up,' it noted, 'police work and disarmament proceeding rapidly. Relations with Army and AMG ... excellent in all areas. Many missions engaged with partisans on quote tidying up unquote after surrender.' The next night the final message, No. 20, was received by Baker Street: 'All Pulpit missions now installed,' it began, 'and liquidation proceeding well.'[67]

Plans had been put in place well before liberation to carry out a rapid and comprehensive liquidation of all SOE interests in Italy, a process that involved settling all claims on the British Government for services rendered on behalf of SOE by its agents there, as well as an appreciation of whether each person concerned would be suitable for further employment by the allies. To help assess the claims, a special committee of senior SOE officers, representing finance, security and the country section, was formed by SOM headquarters with the title of SOELIQ (MED). Within No. 1 Special Force, a special liquidation section was created to gather all the relevant information and to make and implement recommendations. In order to speed up the process, four special missions, codenamed 'Pulpit North', 'Pulpit East', 'Pulpit South' and 'Pulpit West', were sent to Italy even while liberation was under way. The advance party of Pulpit North was the group led by Hedley Vincent that had parachuted on to the Milan racecourse the day before the city's liberation. The other Pulpit missions were sent by road and moved in with the forward allied troops to Padua, Genoa and Turin respectively.

'Liquidation' involved the final paying-off of individuals, providing them where necessary with a completely new outfit of civilian clothing and accessories and with rations to assist their return to civilian life, and giving them a 'Patriot's Certificate' produced by the Allied Commission along with a special letter of attestation from No. 1 Special Force, recommending them for awards (either British or Italian). It also annulled any outstanding charge against individuals recruited before the Italian surrender, awarded suitably inscribed gifts to 'special high grade agents or prominent personalities who had assisted Maryland's work but could not be expected to accept financial reimbursement', and either helped them in finding work or in obtaining permission to go abroad. The liquidation of volunteers recruited by SIM was carried out by SIM itself, and close liaison was maintained with the OSS, SIS, MI9 and other agencies to ensure that responsibility for Italians who had also worked for one or more of these organisations was properly shared. A complex and detailed task involving hundreds of cases, it had not been entirely completed by the time that SOE was wound up early the next year. For Italians recommended for British awards there was a bitter pill to swallow. All were rejected on the blanket political ground that the British public would not stand for any awards made to nationals of a former enemy of Britain.[68]

Discussions about the post-war future, if any, for SOE had been under way for months with no resolution in sight. Exasperated by the delay and keen to mark one of SOE's undoubted successes, Major

General Gubbins flew out to Italy shortly before the German surrender to visit the various British missions and confer with top officials in Rome and Caserta, including Field Marshal Alexander. VE Day found him in Siena, where he attended a moving ceremony of thanksgiving in the courtyard of the SOM headquarters. Margaret Pawley, one of the dozens of FANYs who had worked both there and at Monopoli, was among those present. It was extremely hot and everyone sweltered in their service dress and gloves. An out-of-tune piano had been carried out to the courtyard. 'Despite being outnumbered,' she recalled, 'the soprano singing of the FANY predominated over that of the tenors and basses. General Gubbins gave an address. Perhaps it was because many of us had cause to remember countless friends and relations who had not survived to this day,' she added, 'that the ceremony did not appear particularly joyful. I heard one senior officer remark "you'd think we'd lost the war and not won it."'[69]

For Gubbins personally the event indeed carried an especially sombre meaning, as his beloved elder son Michael now lay buried in Italian soil after being killed on his SOE mission the year before. Gerry Holdsworth had bent his best efforts to find where Michael had been temporarily interred, basing his researches on what turned out to be a mistaken map reference made by the padre involved. 'We have now been five times to the general area and have seen absolutely everyone who can help us with the exception of the Padre, who we are now trying to trace,' he wrote in a personal letter to Gubbins six months after Michael's death. 'The main difficulty is that the area has not been cleared of mines yet and we cannot make a thorough search.'[70]

All this gave special poignancy to the order of the day that Gubbins issued to all ranks at SOM as Europe celebrated victory. In recognising their contribution, he repeated the words used by Field Marshal Alexander in the message that he had recently passed to the chairman of the CLNAI. 'I would be pleased,' he had written, 'if you would convey to General Cadorna and all the subordinate patriot commanders and units my admiration and gratitude for the successful part which they have played both in the destruction of the enemy and the preservation of installations and plants vital to the future life of Italy. I have noted also with particular pleasure the efficiency and speed with which the CLNAI has been able to turn from these military achievements to the equally important task of restoring in conjunction with my Allied Military Government officers civil administration in liberated Italy.' To this, Gubbins added that he had personally seen Alexander just the day before and been thanked for the important contribution made by the Italian patriots to his operations by their capture of so many towns behind the enemy lines and the number of prisoners they had taken.[71]

Two days after Gubbins's VE Day appearance in Siena, Sir Noel Charles, the British ambassador in Rome, sent a telegram to the Foreign Office based on reports from his political adviser in the north. 'After successful patriot insurrections in Milan, Turin, Genoa and other northern towns and withdrawal of German and Fascist troops,' he enthused, 'law and order were preserved to a remarkable degree.'

He was more specific in a message he sent to the prime minister the next month expressing his broad satisfaction with what the CLNAI had accomplished by way of anti-scorch and maintaining law and order, and he singled out two individuals for special mention. The first was Alfredo Pizzoni, who since being ousted as chairman of the CLNAI had been serving as head of its finance commission and exercising what the ambassador described as 'a moderating influence'. The second was Max Salvadori. For the SOE officer's liaison work with the CLNAI the ambassador had nothing but the highest praise. 'As a former political prisoner of the Fascists,' he told Churchill, 'he had the confidence of all parties and he did not hesitate to use his influence fully and courageously in pressing the unity of the Committee and in securing the carrying out of their undertakings.'[72]

Despite these generally confident reports, however, anxiety simmered beneath the surface about the legacy of the armed resistance for the future of Italy. Liberation had been followed by widespread killings that left hundreds dead on the streets of cities and towns throughout the north. 'Total of unidentified bodies at the mortuary since the liberation of [Milan] now amounts to over 400,' reported the ambassador only five days after sending his upbeat message about law and order. 'Sinister feature of these killings is that all identification marks have been carefully removed before shooting. It is therefore difficult to say whether the victims are Fascists executed by Partisans or Partisans executed by Fascists or just victims of personal vendetta.' The telegram was considered sufficiently important to be given War Cabinet distribution.

Against this backdrop, with post-liberation euphoria rapidly fading, AMG starting to take hold, the political direction of the country as yet unclear and the future of the monarchy still in doubt, it seemed possible to Sir Noel Charles that if the left-wing parties that had dominated the CLNAI did not gain power legally they might resort to violence and turn the partisan bands into action squads of the kind used by Mussolini himself on his seizure of power. Such fears were heightened by the knowledge that in spite of the official disbandment and disarmament of the partisans, the process remained incomplete. 'Though in many places they amounted to as much as one weapon per known "patriot",' writes C. R. S. Harris in his official history of the allied military administration in Italy, 'they did not include anything like the total number of arms which the partisans had managed to secure, or . . . more than a few of the more modern and efficient weapons which had been secured through Allied sources.'[73]

The ambassador's fears were still potent when he visited London in July for personal discussions with the Foreign Office, where he told the deputy under-secretary, Sir Orme Sargent, that he was in 'desperate need' of some clandestine weapon to combat internal Communism in Italy as well as Russian propaganda and other tendencies hostile to British policy. SOE, he pointed out, 'could provide the means'. After finding Sargent unsympathetic, however, he went to see Gubbins in Baker Street. He was disturbed that SOE was pulling out of Italy entirely, he confessed. 'Could we not keep some [SOE] personnel there to help him?' Gubbins reported him as asking. The permanent under-secretary, Sir Alexander Cadogan, was away at the Potsdam Conference and Gubbins agreed to raise the issue with him when he returned. 'We must keep our eyes open for suitable personnel,' he told his senior staff. 'I mentioned De Haan and Salvadori to Sir Noel Charles who approves strongly of both of them. Please examine their positions; they must not be out posted without my prior agreement.' After meeting with Gubbins on his return to London Cadogan reacted favourably, although it was neither of the two men mentioned who was finally chosen. Instead, it was the officer once described to Gubbins by Holdsworth as 'one of the very best SOE all-rounders' and one of the few thoroughly trained and temperamentally attuned country section officers that No. 1 Special Force had, Hedley Vincent. That autumn Vincent was appointed chief information officer in Milan. Within months, SOE had ceased to exist. Gubbins's own appointment as CD was terminated on 1 January 1946, and four weeks later the organisation itself was folded into SIS. Along with it went several veterans of its campaign in Italy, who were thus able to put their hard-won experience to continuing use.[74]

On 20 June 1945, after the dissolution of the central command of the armed resistance and the introduction across the north of Allied Military Government, Ferruccio Parri was appointed as Italy's first post-war prime minister. The Action Party leader had played a prominent part in the underground struggle and his elevation to the post symbolised the high prestige that the resistance enjoyed. His relations with SOE had been close, if at times fractious, and in early September he was invited to the British embassy in Rome, where Hedley Vincent presented him with a specially inscribed cigarette case approved by the SOE liquidation committee. Parri was extremely moved by this informal gift, reported one of those present, 'and was almost in tears.' He was *not*, however, presented with a plaque that had been the object of some considerable behind-the-scenes controversy. Its precise design and inscription has not survived. But its theme can be guessed at from what happened when, invited to approve it by Lieutenant Colonel Jack Beevor, the ambassador Sir Noel Charles took an instant dislike to it on the grounds that it carried 'the unfortunate implication that the only people to represent the spirit of resistance were those who were dropped by parachute whereas there is a strong feeling in N. Italy (whether or no it is justified is another matter) that Italian resistance was to a large extent spontaneous.' As a result the idea was abandoned and a chastened Beevor took the plaque back to London. 'Quite wrong,' scribbled Gubbins when a note on the affair reached his desk, 'but too late now!'[75]

That Italians preferred to believe that their resistance was spontaneous and owed little or nothing to allied support is not surprising given the urgent need – after more than twenty years of Fascist dictatorship, foreign occupation and a devastating war waged on its soil – to see the birth of a new, democratic and self-made Italy. A similar process took place in France, where the creation of the Gaullist resistance myth helped restore the nation's pride. The episode is, of course, highly ironic, because of all the resistance voices who had consistently and continually demanded of SOE more and more supplies Parri's had been the loudest and most strident – to the point of finally provoking McCaffery's angry outburst in the summer of 1944 pointing out his unreasonableness and urging him not to risk losing his friends.

The psychology of this is uncomplicated; those who rely on others frequently distance themselves once they have shaken off their dependency. It is more interesting to ask who was dependent on whom in this story of SOE and Italy. The answer is that it was largely a tale of mutual interdependence. Without thousands of Italians to help it SOE would have been powerless to act. From the returning anti-Fascist exiles at one end of the spectrum to royalist SIM officers at the other, they all put their practical skills and energies at SOE's disposal to help it produce one of its most impressive campaigns in Europe during the Second World War. This was all the more remarkable given that this cooperation meant casting aside the enmity that had existed between Britain and Italy since Mussolini's declaration of war in June 1940 and the armistice of September 1943. Some British liaison officers infiltrated behind the lines were still carrying vivid memories of fighting the Italians in North Africa and even having been captured by them. At best their attitude towards the erstwhile enemy was wary, and at worst it was even contemptuous. Yet almost without exception they changed their minds when confronted at first hand with the courage and determination of those who risked their lives to help them. 'The strong prejudice I had against the Italians was completely changed,' confessed one BLO, 'after I had seen their patience in adversity and their endurance in the hardships of a winter which they spent hunted like animals through the frozen Alps.'[76]

It was not just partisans, of course, who demonstrated their willingness to assist SOE to help liberate their country. It was also the peasants who helped feed and shelter the British missions knowing full well that this could cost them their lives and those of their family too; the Italian naval crews who risked their lives on highly perilous clandestine sea missions; the dozens of Italians who were sent on missions behind the lines; the officers of the Italian armed forces, including SIM, who helped recruit and train them; and, of course, the vast army of those in the north who organised and ran the political and armed resistance. Some of them were unlikely but highly important figures in a clandestine war. Who, for example, can fail to be struck by the image of the middle-aged and portly banker Alfredo Pizzoni stumbling and struggling breathlessly across the heavily guarded Swiss-Italian frontier at night in order to make contact with SOE's man in Berne, Jock McCaffery? And not just once either. As soon as it became physically possible, Italians provided SOE with just about all the assistance they could muster.

In return, SOE provided the maximum help it practicably could to the Italian resistance, given the often conflicting demands on its limited resources and the dictates of broader allied strategy, not to mention the moral support it offered by simply sending missions behind the lines at all. Many a partisan was to testify that the very arrival of a team of British officers and men helped lift morale and convince the often dispirited resistance that it was worth continuing the fight. And fight they did, to the point that when the climax of the liberation struggle came in April 1945 they made a significant contribution to the military campaign. There were many mistakes along the way in the story of SOE and Italy, and the route evolved by trial and error rather than as the result of some early grand design. But this is typical of all such campaigns and should not detract from its substantial success.

In his report on the activities of the No. 1 Special Force missions in that final month of the struggle, its second and last commander, Lieutenant Colonel Dick Hewitt, readily and rightfully accepted that the partisan movement would have existed even without their assistance and that the allies would have won the military campaign if they had not been in the field. Nonetheless, he highlighted six major contributions that they had made to victory. First, they were able to tell the patriots what military action the commander-in-chief required and when, what anti-scorch measures were needed and what administrative measures AMG requested to help the liberated territories return as quickly as possible to normality. Second, the missions provided an invaluable network of wireless communications which enabled the orders of the military authorities to be passed to the resistance and thus created a degree of coordination which, in the military field alone he thought, was 'probably without parallel in history'. Third, they made possible the constant and equitable delivery of supplies to the partisans. Fourth, they provided all forms of intelligence to help not just the military authorities but also the Allied Commission and the politicians and diplomats to prepare for the future. Fifth, by their very presence and example they encouraged and got the best from the patriots in all their undertakings. And lastly, he wrote:

> They proved beyond all doubt to the Italian nation the fact that the Allies appreciated the help that the patriots could give, that we understood their sufferings and problems and were prepared to share them, that we wished to assist them in their fight against the enemy which for them was represented by their past as well as by the ever-present Nazi-Fascists, that we recognised in their struggle an act of spiritual expiation as a direct military contribution to the cause of the Allied armies, and that our wish to see a new, united, and prosperous Italy as early as possible was as dear as their own.[77]

This was clearly a hope rather than an obvious reality, but a wide body of evidence from many sources confirms the truth of his other conclusions. No. 1 Special Force's work in Italy was one of SOE's most notable successes and it left an important legacy to that nation which has been too long forgotten but that deserves to be both remembered and honoured.

# Notes

## Abbreviations

| | |
|---|---|
| *1SF&IR* | *No. I Special Force and the Italian Resistance*, Federazione Italiana Associazioni Partigiane (FIAP)/Special Forces Club, 1990. |
| COS | Chiefs of Staff. |
| FO | Foreign Office files in The National Archives, Kew (TNA). |
| HS | SOE files, TNA. |
| IWM | Imperial War Museum. |
| NARA | National Archives and Records Administration, Washington, DC. |
| *ODNB* | *Oxford Dictionary of National Biography.* |
| PREM | Prime Minister's files, TNA |
| WO | War Office files, TNA. |
| Woods Archive | The SOE files of Christopher Woods, now deposited with the Cabinet Office.. |

*Introduction* *pp. xiii–xxiii*

1. For the origins of SOE, *see* M. R. D. Foot, *SOE in France*, pp. 1–10; David Stafford, *Britain and European Resistance, 1940–1945*, pp. 10–50; Mark Seaman, 'A new instrument of war: The origins of the Special Operations Executive', in Mark Seaman (ed.), *Special Operations Executive*, pp. 7–21. • **2**. For a popular general history of SOE, *see* M. R. D. Foot, *SOE: The Special Operations Executive, 1940–1946* (1999). For a recent scholarly survey, *see* the special volume of the journal *Intelligence and National Security*, 20 (Mar. 2005), edited by Neville Wylie. • **3**. W. J. M. Mackenzie, *The Secret History of SOE*, p. 546. • **4**. Dominick

Graham and Shelford Bidwell, *Tug of War*, pp. 394–5. • **5**. For a favourable account of the contribution of the Italian forces to allied victory following the armistice of Sept. 1943, *see* Charles T. O'Reilly, *Forgotten Battles*, and Richard Lamb, *War in Italy, 1943–1945*. • **6**. M. R. D. Foot, *SOE in France*, and *SOE in the Low Countries*; Charles Cruickshank, *SOE in the Far East* (1983) and *SOE in Scandinavia* (1986). I am profoundly grateful to Mr Woods for passing on to me his substantial files on SOE in Italy and for his unstinting and generous cooperation throughout this project. The Woods Archive, now deposited with the Cabinet Office, contains detailed information on Italian missions, whether mentioned in this book or not, including correspondence with individual Italians who worked with SOE. • **7**. W. G. F. Jackson, *The Mediterranean and Middle East*, vol. 6, pt 2, pp. 119 ff. • **8**. For an account of the origins of the official military histories and the Edmonds histories of the First World War and the controversies they generated, *see* Andrew Green, *Writing the Great War*. For the Butler quote, *see* his article 'The British Official Military History of the Second World War', *Military Affairs*, 22/3 (Autumn 1958), pp. 149–51. For a more critical view of official histories, however, *see* John Connell, 'Official History and the Unofficial Historian', *Journal of the Royal United Services Institute*, 110/640 (Nov. 1965), pp. 329–34. • **9**. Mark Seaman, 'A Glass Half Full – Some Thoughts on the Evolution of the Study of the Special Operations Executive', *Intelligence and National Security*, 20/1 (Mar. 2005), p. 28. • **10**. For an invaluable discussion of the fate of the SOE archive, *see* the article by Duncan Stuart, a former official SOE Adviser, '"Of Historical Interest Only": The origins and vicissitudes of the SOE Archive', in Seaman (ed.), op. cit., pp. 217–29; *see also* Christopher Woods's unpublished paper, 'Towards a History of SOE in Italy', presented to the symposium 'Reflections on Bologna 1987' held at the IWM 28 Sept. 1990. The quotation in the text is from Patrick Whinney, *Corsican Command*, p. 9.


*One – 'Of capital and urgent importance'*                              *pp. 1–26*


**1**. C. J. C. Molony et al., *The Mediterranean and Middle East*, vol. 5, pp. 255–324; Rick Atkinson, *The Day of Battle*, pp. 197–216. • **2**. Charles Cruickshank, *SOE in Scandinavia* (1986), pp. 64, 188–91; *see also* Munthe's own memoirs, *Sweet is War*, and his obituary in the *Daily Telegraph*, 11 Dec. 1995. Also Andrew Croft, *A Talent for Adventure*, p. 140. • **3**. D. A. Macdonnell, 'Brief Record', unpublished and undated typescript in Coolant file, Woods Archive. • **4**. Initially 'Blood'; approved by AFHQ with a War Establishment of 16 officers and 39 other ranks. *See* WD 19/375 in HS 7/238.

Massingham's main signal plan with Vigilant was codenamed 'Thunder' and that for Vigilant to Massingham codenamed 'Snow'; those for use between Vigilant and its outstations were codenamed 'Typhoon', 'Tornado', 'Storm' and 'Hurricane'. The signals plans from Vigilant to work to Massingham also included 'Lightning', 'Hail', 'Fog', 'Mist' and 'Wind'. • **5**. For SOE's efforts in Italy prior to Sept. 1943, *see* Christopher Woods and Rod Bailey's forthcoming official history of SOE's role in the war against Fascist Italy. *See also* Salvadori's personal file, HS 9/1305/6. • **6**. Max Salvadori, *The Labour and the Wounds*, p. 146; J to D/Mil, 2 July 1943, in HS 9/1305/6. • **7**. Salvadori, op. cit., pp. 142–6, where he refers to Roseberry as 'Major Alp' (Roseberry's mother's maiden name). For a brief published summary of SOE's achievements in Italy 1940–43, *see* Christopher Woods's essay, 'SOE in Italy' in Mark Seaman (ed.), *Special Operations Executive*, pp. 91–7. • **8**. For a comprehensive history in English of the Italian anti-Fascists, *see* Charles Delzell, *Mussolini's Enemies*. Most if not all of the exiles who came over from the USA were supported by rich Italo-Americans, in particular Max Ascoli, who had held the chair of philosophy at the University of Rome before leaving for the USA in 1932. He later founded *The Reporter*, a leading American journal of liberal thinking. • **9**. Adrian Gallegos, *And Who Are You?*, pp. 51–2. • **10**. Major Malcolm Munthe, 'Report on Operations "Brow" and "Vigilant"', being a resume of activities of G.Topo [graphical] Liaison Unit att 8th Army and of Special Force att 5th Army', Mar. 1944 (hereafter Munthe Report), pp. 12–13, in Vigilant file, Woods Archive. • **11**. Salvadori, op. cit., p. 161; Gallegos, op. cit., p. 52. • **12**. Nigel Nicolson, *Alex*, p. 209. The armistice of 3 Sept., for example, contained clauses in which Italy promised to use its best endeavours to deny to the Germans facilities that might be used against the United Nations and (clause 9) that it would employ 'all its available armed forces' to ensure prompt and exact compliance with all provisions of the armistice. The far longer instrument of surrender signed on 29 Sept. made Italy's forced cooperation far more explicit. For the full texts, *see* Michael Howard, *Grand Strategy*, vol. 4, pp. 672–3 and 674–81. • **13**. *See* Howard, op. cit., pp. 515–38; Elena Agarossi, *A Nation Collapses*; and Molony et al., op. cit., pp. 208–16. • **14**. Joyce Lussu, *Freedom Has No Frontier*, p. 125. • **15**. Richard Lamb, *War in Italy*, p. 21. • **16**. As, for example, graphically recounted in the bestselling novel by Louis de Bernières, *Captain Corelli's Mandolin* (1994). Some units of the Italian pre-armistice army itself were guilty of atrocities against civilians, most notoriously in East Africa and Yugoslavia. • **17**. Agarossi, op. cit., pp. 104–5. • **18**. Peniakoff was a Belgian émigré of Russian extraction. For his account of the entry into Brindisi, *see* his *Private Army*, pp. 347–9. • **19**. For Mallaby and 'Monkey' *see* Christopher Woods, 'A Tale of Two Armistices', in K. G. Robertson (ed.), *War, Resistance and Intelligence*, pp. 1–17. Mallaby was awarded the Military Cross for his Monkey work, HS 6/777–780 contain the bulk of the Monkey/armistice signals. He had *not*, as claimed by Lamb, op. cit., p. 15, been dropped specifically to speed up the negotiations. • **20**. Douglas Dodds-Parker, interview 1983, IWM Sound Archive, no. 12301; *see also* his memoir, *Setting Europe Ablaze*, pp. 118–35. For Massingham, *see also* Foot, *SOE in France*, p. 32, and the article by David Thomas in *Intelligence and National Security*, 11/4 (Oct. 1996), 'The Massingham Mission: SOE in French North Africa, 1941–1944'. The article by Tom Wales in *Intelligence and National Security*, 20/1 (Mar. 2005), pp. 44–71, 'The "Massingham" Mission and the Secret "Special Relationship": Cooperation and Rivalry between the Anglo-American Clandestine Services in French North Africa, November 1942–May 1943', also provides much useful material. • **21**. Christopher Woods, 'SOE in Italy', in Seaman (ed.), op. cit., pp. 97–8. • **22**. Alexander papers, in WO 214/36, quoted in Agarossi, op. cit., pp. 81–2. • **23**. Sir William Deakin, as quoted in Roger Absalom, *A Strange Alliance*, p. 15. For Alexander's view of the armistice, *see* Nicolson, op. cit., p. 211, and for the wider SOE–SIM accord *see* Lt Col. Cecil Roseberry, 'History of the Italian Section', in HS 7/59. • **24**. For the full text of the directive, dated 10 Dec. 1943, *see* Ministero Della Difesa, *L'azione dello Stato Maggiore Generale per lo sviluppo del movimento di liberazione*, pp. 149–54. Messe had been released from a POW camp in the USA and brought back to Italy to replace Ambrosio. • **25**. She also provided five further signals plans, all with the names of jewels: 'Turquoise', 'Ruby', 'Pearl', 'Emerald', and 'Marcasite'. For the Roseberry–Castellano–SIM discussions, *see* WD 19/395 in HS 7/238 and WD 42/513 in HS 7/263; also, Giuseppe Castellano, *Come firmai l'armistizio di Cassibile*, pp. 32–5. For the signals plans brought to Brindisi by De Haan's group, *see* Margaret Pawley, *In Obedience to Instructions*, pp. 77–8. • **26**. Harold Macmillan, 'Extracts from Report on Mission to Italy 14–17 September 1943', in Harold Macmillan, *War Diaries*, pp. 219–22. For Badoglio's lack of even a typewriter, *see* C. R. S. Harris, *Allied Military Administration of Italy, 1943–1945*, p. 108, fn. • **27**. *See* 'OSS/SOE Activities in Italy', 30 Sept. 1943, in 'AFHQ History of Special Operations in the Mediterranean,' 24 July 1945, Annex B, pp. 1–2, in HS 7/170. • **28**. Malcolm Munthe, *Sweet is War*, p. 168. • **29**. Salvadori, op. cit., p. 163. • **30**. *See* Derrick Scott-Job, *Maryland and No. 1 Special Force Signals*), pp. 3–4. Scott-Job had arrived carrying the various signals plans detailed in note 4, above. • **31**. *See* Valiani's personal files HS 9/1569/4 and HS 9/1516/1. For Pierleoni, *see* his file HS 9/1187/2, and AM161 to AM10 [Salvadori to Holdsworth], 11 Sept. 1944, in the Salvadori Papers, in the IWM. • **32**. *See* Adolphus Richard Cooper, *Born to Fight*. His personal file (HS 9/347) contains a reference to 'Adolphus Cooper@Adesto@Lebrun@de la Grange@Duval 13/3/23 to 14/7/24'. • **33**. Personal file HS 9/347, based on interview at Hotel

Victoria, 13 Mar. 1941. *See also* Q2 to D/Per, 27 June 1941, for his convictions.
• **34**. Gallegos, op. cit., p. 55. For 'little dogs and gigolos', *see* Lussu, op. cit.,
p. 146. • **35**. Cooper, op. cit., p. 194. • **36**. Munthe, op. cit., p. 170; Gallegos, op.
cit., p. 62. • **37**. Henri J. Boutigny, 'Operations in Sicily and Southern Italy August–
September 1943', in *1SF&IR*, vol. 2, p. 317. • **38**. Alastair Horne, *Macmillan, 1894–
1956*, p. 200. • **39**. J to AJ3 [Salvadori], 13 Sept. 1943, in the Salvadori Papers.
• **40**. I am grateful to Christopher Woods for the above. For the strategic thinking
behind the Italian campaign, *see* Howard, op. cit., vol. 4, pp. 560–71.

*Two – Maryland: 'All in all, it did us well'*                        *pp. 27–51*

**1**. Winston Churchill, *Closing the Ring*, p. 166. • **2**. Martin Clark, *Mussolini*, pp.
297–306; R. J. B. Bosworth, *Mussolini*, pp. 403–4. • **3**. Quoted in Munthe Report,
p. 16, Vigilant file, Woods Archive. • **4**. For Croce's politics, *see* Denis Mack Smith,
'Benedetto Croce: History and Politics', *Journal of Contemporary History*, 8/1
(Jan. 1973), pp. 41–61. Along with the majority of Liberals in the Italian parliament, Croce had voted full powers to Mussolini in 1922. • **5**. Malcolm Munthe,
*Sweet is War*, p. 171; *see also* Munthe Report, pp. 16–17. Gallegos's own account
is to be found in his *And Who Are You?*, pp. 62–7. Croce's account can be found
in the diary extracts published in his *Croce, the King and the Allies*, pp. 14–17.
Vigilant reported Croce's rescue on 16 Sept.; *see* WD 42/287 in HS 7/263. • **6**.
*See* Munthe Report, loc. cit.; also WD 42/282, 287, and Croce, loc. cit. Minor
discrepancies occur between these various accounts. For example, Croce claims
that he was rescued on 15 Sept., not 16 – as stated in MASS telegram of 20 Sept.
1943 in WD 42/287, in HS 7/263 – and this seems most likely. • **7**. Croce diary,
20 Sept. 1943, op. cit. Cf. MASS 3018, 20 Sept. 1943, in WD 42/288: 'Taking no
action their end exploit Croce rescue owing local security diffs but LDN cd play
it their end if they thought desirable.' • **8**. Munthe Report, p. 14; *see also* his
*Sweet is War*, p. 169. Vigilant is reported in MASS 3059 as wanting 'all information' on Pavone; *see* WD 42/288, in HS 7/263. • **9**. For the SOE–OSS accords,
and wartime relations generally, *see* Jay Jakub, *Spies and Saboteurs*, pp. 48–60,
90–91, 193, although he does not deal with Italy in any detail. • **10**. Donald
Downes, *The Scarlet Thread*, p. 152. • **11**. Croce diary, 22 Sept. 1943, op. cit. • **12**.
Croce, op. cit., p. 22. *See also* MASS 3171 in WD 42/290, HS 7/263. • **13**. Munthe
Report, pp. 19–20. • **14**. *See* MASS 3127–8, 26 Sept. 1943, quoted in WD 19/404–
5, HS 7/238; LDN 534 and 543 of 27 Sept. in WD 42/288, HS 7/263; MASS
3142 in WD 19/404, HS 7/238; MASS 3183 of 29 Sept. for 'on very dangerous
ground indeed'. *See also* MASS 2998 of 19 Sept. in WD 42/464, HS 7/264. 'Tel
sent THUNDER asking if it had been poss contact SIM offr for sabotage collab

and presuming when planning ops as REGENT using Its they were bearing in mind risk of It High Command finding out and complaining about "pol exiles".' • **15**. Max Salvadori, *The Labour and The Wounds*, p. 168. • **16**. 'Record of a meeting held at Brindisi, 4 October 1943, 16.15–17.00 hrs', in Salvadori Papers. • **17**. Foreign Office–SOE Meeting of 9 Nov. 1943, HS 8/197. • **18**. For British policy towards Badoglio, *see* Sir Llewellyn Woodward, *British Foreign Policy in the Second World War*, vol. 2, pp. 501–12; Churchill, op. cit., pp. 162–74; David Ellwood, *Italy, 1943–1945*, pp. 19–48; Harold Macmillan, *War Diaries*, p. 266. • **19**. Salvadori, op. cit., p. 170. • **20**. *Ibid.*, p. 173. • **21**. WD 42/295 in HS 7/263. *See also* Charles Delzell, *Mussolini's Enemies*, pp. 310–11. • **22**. Munthe Report, p. 20. • **23**. Munthe, *Sweet is War*, p. 175; Norman Lewis, *Naples '44*, p. 46; Joyce Lussu, *Freedom Has No Frontier*, p. 147. • **24**. Munthe Report, p. 15. • **25**. Lussu, op. cit., pp. 58, 130. • **26**. *Ibid.*, p. 143; and Salvadori, op. cit., pp. 166–7. • **27**. *Ibid.*, p. 167. • **28**. *Ibid.*, p. 169. • **29**. Leo Valiani, *Tutte le strade conducono a Roma*, p. 44. • **30**. For Koestler's friendship with Valiani (whom he calls 'Mario'), *see* his *Scum of the Earth* (1941), pp. 9–10, 78, 138–9; for Valiani's encounter with him in London, *see* Valiani, op. cit., pp. 21–2, 44. The airdrops on 18/19 Oct. and 12/13 Nov. 1943 were codenamed 'Mountview' I and II, respectively. • **31**. Adolphus Richard Cooper, *The Adventures of a Secret Agent*, pp. 195–8. But nothing more can be gleaned from the official files of what happened to the mission. • **32**. For this operation, codenamed 'Arnold', *see* WD 42/293, 474, in HS 7/263–4; Salvadori, op. cit., p. 176; Munthe Report, p. 22, and his *Sweet is War*, p. 176. Also, for the later Arnold attempts, *see* HS 6/825. • **33**. HS 6/902; *see also* Gallegos, op. cit., pp. 69–96. • **34**. HS 7/169; and letter from Laming to Woods, Woods Archive. • **35**. Edgardo Sogno, *Guerra senza bandiera*, p. 225; Stawell note, 14 Dec. 1944, in Holdsworth's personal file HS 9/729/2; and the anonymous obituarist in the *Special Forces Newsletter*, 1986. In SOE files he is usually identified by his Massingham designation as 'AM10'. • **36**. *See* Charles Cruickshank, *SOE in Scandinavia* (1986), pp. 33–46. • **37**. For the descriptions of Mary Holdsworth, *see* Patrick Howarth, *Undercover*, p. 180, and David Stafford, *Secret Agent*, p. 62; for Holdsworth, Section D and the Helford Flotilla, *see* Brooks Richards's official history, *Secret Flotillas*, pp. 99–101, 595, 610. Richards was Holdsworth's second-in-command. • **38**. *See* Charles Macintosh's book about SOE in Italy, *From Cloak to Dagger*, pp. 16–25; and D. A. Macdonnell, 'Brief Record', p. 7, Woods Archive. • **39**. For Laming and Scott, *see* their personal files, HS 9/22666/A. For Renton, *see* Peter Wilkinson, *Foreign Fields*, pp. 193–4. • **40**. HS 7/170. 19 Sept. 1943 is given as the date the Maryland codename was assigned to Holdsworth's mission. *See also* Dodds-Parker Bigot message to AFHQ, 18 Sept. 1943, 'Move into Windsock [Italy] of Advance Headquarters SOE, North Africa', in WO 204/10239. • **41**. Sir Douglas Dodds-Parker, 'The SOE and Military Operations in Italy', in

*1SF&IR*, vol. 2, p. 15. But he mistakenly claimed that the discussion took place in Brindisi, whereas 'Maryland' as a title appears in official documents prior to his arriving there. *See also* his similar account in his memoirs, *Setting Europe Ablaze*, pp. 145–6. • **42**. W. J. M. Mackenzie, *The Secret History of SOE*, p. 77. • **43**. Laming to Woods, Woods Archive. • **44**. Major Peter M. Lee, 'Special Operations Executive', IWM Sound Archive, ref. 7493/10/7. *See also* Robin Richards transcript, *ibid.*, ref. 27462/2837–2918. • **45**. Dodds-Parker, op. cit., p. 144. • **46**. *See* Donaldson (AM84) to Lee (AM80), 19 Jan. 1944, 'With SOE in Italy' in HS 8/885. • **47**. Letter from Holdsworth to Charles Macintosh, 12 July 1973, in Holdsworth file, Woods Archive; also quoted in Macintosh, op. cit., p. 30. For Apulia at the time, *see* Margaret Pawley, *In Obedience to Instructions*, pp. 80–81.

*Three – No. 1 Special Force*                                   *pp. 52–86*

**1**. Eric Newby, *Love and War in the Apennines*, pp. 48–55; for his (Slovene) wife's account of these events, *see* Wanda Newby, *Peace and War*. • **2**. Orders issued by 15th Army Group on 23 Sept. 1943 to 'A' Force, the title assumed by MI9 in Cairo. For Simonds and the full story of MI9, *see* M. R. D. Foot and J. M. Langley, MI9, especially pp. 89, 156–65; also Roger Absalom, *A Strange Alliance*, pp. 11–25. • **3**. WO 218/81; HS 7/172. • **4**. Christopher Soames, quoted in Foot and Langley, op. cit., p. 163. Absalom's book provides an excellent analysis of the relations between the allied escapers and the (mostly rural) Italian population. • **5**. *See* e.g. the account by Anthony Deane-Drummond, one of the participants in SIMCOL, in his *Return Ticket*, pp. 184–93. • **6**. Reference in Maryland naval box, Woods Archive. • **7**. Laming to Woods, 8 Apr. 1990, Woods Archive. • **8**. WD 20/3, in HS 7/239; HS 7/170. • **9**. HS 7/61. • **10**. SOE mission Pearl, a codename of the signal plan and the first in a gemstone series produced at Massingham for working to their W/T station. The operation is also referred to in records as 'Acomb/Seaweed', the former possibly an SOE operational code-name, the latter either naval or ISLD. • **11**. SOE missions Ruby and Marcasite. Operational codename Quintet, probably naval: it also involved picking up POWs for SIMCOL. • **12**. GAH to Brooks Richards, 28 Nov. 1943, in Holdsworth file, Woods Archive. • **13**. Max Salvadori, *The Labour and the Wounds*, p. 184. • **14**. *See* David Stafford, *Camp X*, pp. 56, 152. • **15**. Quoted in Christopher Woods, 'SOE in Italy', unpublished history in Cabinet Office records, pt 1, chap. 7, p. 5. • **16**. For the SOE FANYs in Italy, *see* Margaret Pawley, *In Obedience to Instructions*, pp. 74–141; much of the following material also draws on correspondence between former FANYs and Christopher Woods, in FANYs box in the Woods Archive. • **17**. Peter Lee, IWM Sound Archive, ref. 7493/10/8, p. 84.

• **18**. *See* Cooper's personal file HS 9/347, especially D/CE2 to H.H., 14 Apr. 1943, and H.H.'s reply, 16 Apr. 1943. • **19**. For details, *see* M. R. D. Foot, *SOE in the Low Countries*, especially pp. 76–197, 223–97. • **20**. 'AM84' to 'AM80' [Donaldson to Lee], 19 Jan. 1944, in HS 8/885, quoted in Christopher Murphy, *Security and Special Operations*, p. 58. • **21**. 'Report to the Director of Special Operations, Mediterranean Area, from Deputy to Head of the Division of Intelligence, Security, Liaison and Personal Services, S.O.E., H.Q., London', 28 March 1944, in HS 8/846. *See also* Murphy, op. cit., pp. 59–68. For Lee's views and recollections on Maryland, *see* his letters to Woods, 26 Nov. 1993 and 13 Jan. 1994, in Security box, Woods Archive, and 'Special Operations Executive', in IWM Sound Archive, ref. 7493/10/8, pp. 80–82. For his reactions to the Spanish Communists and American recruits, *see* T. C. Wales, 'The "Massingham" Mission and the Secret "Special Relationship": Cooperation and Rivalry between the Anglo-American Clandestine Services in French North Africa, November 1942–May 1943', *Intelligence and National Security*, 20/1 (Mar. 2005), pp. 58–9, while for Dodds-Parker's view of the Spaniards, *see* IWM Sound Archive, ref. 83. • **22**. HS 6/875, quoted in Murphy, op. cit., p. 64. *See also* J. G. Beevor, *SOE*, pp. 119–20. • **23**. Murphy, op. cit., pp. 67–8. • **24**. For the quotation from Gubbins, *see* his 'SOE and the Co-ordination of Regular and Irregular War', in Michael Elliott-Bateman (ed.), *The Fourth Dimension of Warfare* (1970), p. 95. For Gubbins more generally, *see* Wilkinson and Astley, *Gubbins and SOE*, and the entry by M. R. D. Foot in the *ODNB*. • **25**. Cecil Roseberry, 'History of the Italian Section', p. 15, in HS 7/59. • **26**. *See also* WD 42/469–470, in HS 7/263. For Gubbins's Mediterranean tour, *see* Wilkinson and Astley, op. cit., pp. 142–63. Roseberry's scathing comments about both the reorganisation and some of the individuals involved may be found in his 'History of the Italian Section', p. 19, as well as in the comments he made dated 9 Jan. 1946 on an anonymous 'Report on SOE Operations in Italy' (in the Woods Archive): 'Its omission of or glossing over of failures, disabilities, and handicaps reduces its value . . .' he argued. 'S.O.M. was an ineffective and expensive figurehead as far as Italian affairs were concerned . . . the principal success of Maryland derived from the untiring, enthusiastic work of a body of junior officers who aimed at attainable objectives and in their own words "outwardly submitted to but in practice disregarded the hot air expelled at the top".' For CLNAI chairman Alfredo Pizzoni's comment about Roseberry, *see* his notes on a meeting he had with him in London on 14 Nov. 1947, in the Woods Archive: '*Rosberry venne . . . a conflitto con l'ambiente Holdsworth, fu silirato e mandato a Londra.*' For Holdsworth's view of Roseberry, *see* his letter to De Haan of 20 Apr. 1945 in Holdsworth file, Woods Archive. • **27**. Peter Simpson-Jones, *Nine Lives, or The Felix Factor*, pp. 88–9. The *Eduardo* is referred to in the files as FPV 2031. • **28**. A translation of his report dated

Rome 5 June 1944 using his cover name Giorgio Mancinelli can be found in
the Salvadori Papers. • **29**. Simpson-Jones to Woods, 6 July 1997, in Vigilant
file, Woods Archive. • **30**. Operation 'Alnmouth'. For the comment on Simpson-
Jones by Croft, *see* Croft to Woods, 6 Mar. 1989, Woods Archive. • **31**. Patrick
Whinney, *Corsican Command*, p. 114. For Whinney's wartime career details, *see*
Brooks Richards, *Secret Flotillas*, pp. 339–40. • **32**. Andrew Croft, *A Talent for
Adventure*, pp. 178, 189; Whinney, op. cit., p. 68; Brooks Richards, op. cit.,
p. 648. For the Brooks Richards/Croft/Dickinson meeting, *see* AC 189, and for
details on procedures and methods regarding inter-service cooperation, *see*
'Minutes of Special Operations Meeting 8 December [1943] Bastia, Corsica', in
WO 204/10240. Fisher Howe's report on his time with Balaclava can be found
in RG 226/99, box 18, folder 100A in the National Archives, Washington, DC.
He was recalled to OSS London, however, before active operations from Bastia
began. Balaclava also had a base at Calvi, on Corsica's west coast, and used the
rugged and deserted beaches to the south of it for training exercises. Further
details on all these sea operations may be found in Brooks Richards, op. cit.
• **33**. Croft, op. cit., p. 177. For biographical details, *see ibid.*, *passim*, and the
entry by Alexander R. Glen in the *ODNB*, 2004. • **34**. Whinney, op. cit.,
p. 56. • **35**. Croft, op. cit., p. 203; also Andrew Croft, 'Clandestine Sea Operations
from Corsica to Enemy-occupied Italy (December 1943–July 1944)', in *ISF&IR*,
vol. 2, pp. 325–30. • **36**. Whinney, op. cit., pp. 59–60. • **37**. Croft, *A Talent for
Adventure*, p. 186; Whinney, op. cit., pp. 56–62. • **38**. *See also* Major Andrew
Croft to Lt Richards RNVR, 4 Dec. 1943, 'Report on Operation
"Valentine/Cunningham"', in Croft Papers. I am most grateful to Andrew Croft's
daughter, Julia Korner, for letting me consult these. Croft's log for 2 Dec. 1943
also contains the details; *see* Croft Papers. • **39**. Adolphus Cooper, *The Adventures
of a Secret Agent*, p. 211. • **40**. Croft's log, 30 Dec. 1943, in Croft Papers. • **41**.
*Ibid.*, 3 Jan. 1944. • **42**. Croft to Holdsworth, 'A.J.4's Party', 28 Jan. 1944, in Croft
Papers. • **43**. Cooper, op. cit., p. 221. • **44**. Croft to Holdsworth, loc. cit. 'Fiammetta'
was Maria Ciofalo, who had originally been recruited by Vigilant. Later in 1944
she was dropped into the Veneto as a member of Operation 'Whitehorse', one
of only two Italian women to be parachuted behind the lines in Italy, and
returned through the lines on foot. The other was Paola del Din (*see* Chapter
12). • **45**. Croft, *A Talent for Adventure*, p. 190. • **46**. 'BALACLAVA operations to
Italy for MASSINGHAM and MARYLAND.' Note prepared by Brooks Richards for
Andrew Croft, no date, Balaclava file, Woods Archive. *See also* Croft, *A Talent
for Adventure*, p. 192. Cavallino ('Sirio') survived imprisonment first by the
Germans, then the Russians, returning to Italy in 1946 and subsequently rising
to the rank of general. Conforti's recollections can be found in his 'The British
Missions and Clandestine activity in Genoa', in *ISF&IR*, vol. 1, pp. 187–93. The

principal official files dealing with operations out of Bastia are to be found in
WD 20 (HS 7/239), HS 7/169; AC 178, 180, 181, 182, 183, 184, 185, 188; AC
193, 194; HS 8/828; HS 6/878. • **47**. *See* note by Brooks Richards, loc. cit.
• **48**. Brooks Richards, *Secret Flotillas*, pp. 654–5; Croft log, 6 Aug. 1944, in Croft
Papers.

*Four – The Swiss connection*                                           *pp. 87–106*

**1**. Leo Valiani, *Tutte le strade conducono a Roma*, p. 74. • **2**. Alfredo Pizzoni, *Alla
guida del CLNAI, passim.* • **3**. For the anti-Fascist resistance background, *see*
Charles Delzell, *Mussolini's Enemies*. For Valiani's journey to Switzerland and
his meeting with Parri, *see* Valiani, op. cit., pp. 74 ff., and his correspondence
with Woods in 1989, Woods Archive. • **4**. Quoted in Neville Wylie, *Britain,
Switzerland, and the Second World War*, p. 266. • **5**. W. J. M. Mackenzie, *The
Secret History of SOE*, p. 340. • **6**. *See* David Stafford, *Britain and European
Resistance, 1940–1945, passim.* • **7**. J. M. McCaffery, 'No Pipes or Drums', his
unpublished memoir is in the IWM, p. 14; Mackenzie, op. cit., pp. 95, 383. For
an excellent case study of SOE–SIS relations, *see* Ian Herrington, 'The SIS and
SOE in Norway 1940–1945: Conflict or Co-operation', *War in History*, 9/1 (2002),
pp. 82–110. • **8**. McCaffery, op. cit., p. 14; Christopher Woods, 'SOE in Italy,'
pt 1, chap. 5, sect. 5, p. 1. For Dansey and his Z network in Switzerland *see*
Anthony Read and David Fisher, *Colonel Z*, pp. 238–9 and 270, as well as M.
R. D. Foot's entry on Dansey in the *ODNB*; for Vanden Heuvel and Philby, *see*
Christopher Andrew, *Secret Service*, p. 358. • **9**. McCaffery, op. cit., pp. 2, 8, 107.
• **10**. *Ibid.*, p. 30. • **11**. Woods's interview with Jellinek, June 1992, Woods
Archive. • **12**. West, the British air attaché, as quoted in P. R. Reid, *Winged Diplomat*,
p. 171. • **13**. McCaffery, op. cit., p. 80. • **14**. *See* Dulles to Algiers, tel. 58–61, 29
Sept. 1943, in Allen Dulles, *From Hitler's Doorstep*, p. 135. The 1995 biography
of Dulles by Peter Grose, *Gentleman Spy*, makes it clear that in comparison to
gathering intelligence from Germany, Italian resistance enjoyed a far lower
priority for Dulles. • **15**. Woods, 'SOE in Italy', pt 1, chap. 4, p. 32. • **16**. *Ibid.*,
pt 1, chap. 5, pp. 1–6. • **17**. J. M. McCaffery, 'The History of the Berne Post',
Sept. 1945, in HS 7/199; *see also* his 'No Pipes or Drums', as well as the article
'007 Operazione La Malfa', in the Italian magazine *L'Espresso*, 19 Mar. 1989,
pp. 188–93, based on the memoir and an interview with McCaffery's widow,
Nancy. His pre-armistice activities relating to Italy can be followed more closely
in Christopher Woods and Rod Bailey's forthcoming official history. *See also*
Wylie, op. cit., pp. 48–9, 184–9, 266–99. McCaffery features in SOE files as 'JQ'
and in his dealings with the Italians gave himself the cover name of 'Rossi'.

In his communications with London he refers to Caracciolo as 'Philipps', La Malfa as 'Green' and Olivetti as 'Brown'. For his reference to Silone, *see* his memoir, p. 122. The reputation of Silone, whose real name was Secondino Tranquilli, has suffered considerably since the revelation in the late 1990s that for most of the 1920s he had acted as an informer for the secret police. *See* Mauro Canali, 'Ignazione Silone and the Fascist Political Police', *Journal of Modern Italian Studies*, 5/1 (2000), pp. 36–60. • **18**. 'Report on SOE Operations in Italy', p. 90, Woods Archive. • **19**. McCaffery, 'History of the Berne Post', p. 3; Berne Diary 3855/3856, 3867/3873, in the Woods Archive. *See also* WD 42/245, 246, 247, 279, 280, in HS 7/263. For Sarfatti, *see* WD 42/414, 415, 416, and for other reports from or about Almerigotti, *see* WD 42/418, 419, 436, loc. cit. The underwater operation was codenamed 'Uvula'. • **20**. McCaffery, 'No Pipes or Drums', pp. 174–5. • **21**. *See* Pietro Secchia and Filippo Frassati, *La Resistanza e gli alleati*, pp. 20–25. For relations with Damiani etc., *see* WD 42/287, 290, 303, 304, 305, 306, 307, in HS 7/263. • **22**. HS 6/780, and WD 42/247, 280, in HS 7/263. • **23**. *See* WD 42/349 of 10 Oct. 1943 (HS 7/263), reporting that 'JQ in clinic with nervous exhaustion', and WD 42/350, 351 for more related messages. WD 42/348, 349, 350, 351, 360, 380 contain details of the requests and provision of additional personnel, etc. For McCaffery's testimony about Hall and Birkbeck, *see* Cecil Roseberry. 'History of the Italian Section', in HS 7/59, and for his own account of the breakdown, *see* 'No Pipes or Drums', pp. 30–31. • **24**. WD 42/359, in HS 7/263. • **25**. WD 42/311–13, 319, in HS 7/263; McCaffery, op. cit., p. 73. For the Italians' views, *see* Secchia and Frassati, op. cit., pp. 33–4, and Valiani, op. cit., pp. 88–9. • **26**. Valiani, letter to Woods, 25 May 1989, in Woods Archive, which contains some minor differences from the account he gives in *Tutte le strade*, p. 74. For 'twice weekly contact' between the CLNAI and McCaffery, *see* his letter to Woods of 30 Aug. 1989, loc. cit. • **27**. For Dulles's views, *see From Hitler's Doorstep*, pp. 135, 245, 585. *See also* his tel. 985–8, 4 Nov. 1943: 'sincerely hope invasion rendered said agreement null and void.' For McCaffery's views about American methods, *see* WD 42/362, in HS 7/263. • **28**. Probably because, before Pearl Harbor, West had been the 'cut-out' for intelligence enthusiastically passed on by the anglophile US military attaché in Berne, General Barnwell ('Barney') Rhett Legge. *See* McCaffery, 'No Pipes or Drums', p. 18. Legge would give material to West with a request for him to pass it on to 'Bateman' – unknown to him, this was SOE, i.e. McCaffery. West had grown up in Milan and attended the University of Genoa. • **29**. WD 42/338–9. • **30**. WD 42/339 ff. • **31**. According to Roseberry, SIM claimed to have no documents in Brindisi to verify the details. Instead, the revelations all came out 'in conversation'. In his post-war memoirs, McCaffery admitted that as a complete dilettante he had been well and truly taken in by

Klein, but also claimed that it was he himself who had finally exposed the
penetration, which was not the case. *See* McCaffery, op. cit., pp. 29, 176; also
WD 42/420, in HS 7/263. • **32**. *See* Berne to London, 26 Oct. 1943, Woods
Archive. • **33**. *See* Massingham to London, 26 Oct. 1943, Woods Archive; also
WD 42/308, 446, 449, in HS 7/263, 264. • **34**. WD 42/325, 332, in HS 7/263;
also McCaffery, op. cit., p. 164. Damiani to McCaffery, 31 Dec. 1943, complains
that the results 'up to now have been pretty negative' and continues to protest
about the lack of arms drops; *See* Secchia and Frassati, op. cit., pp. 60–61. In
addition to the 3 million lire promised via McCaffery, SOE also authorised
Maryland to provide 5 million lire. *See* WD 42/302, in HS 7/263. • **35**. Max
Salvadori, *The Labour and the Wounds*, p. 178. • **36**. McCaffery, 'History of the
Berne Post', p. 4. • **37**. Roseberry, op. cit., p. 4. • **38**. Edgardo Sogno, *Guerra
senza bandiera*, pp. 179–82. For 'star turn', *see* Christopher Woods, 'No. 1 Special
Force', in *iSF&IR*, vol. 2, pp. 35–45. *See also* Sogno's 'Report on Activities
5 December 1943–25 July 1944', dated Monopoli 29 July 1944, in his personal
file. • **39**. HS 7/60; London to Berne, 4287 of 1 May, and 4290 of 2 May, in
HS 6/783.

*Five – Behind the lines*                                                *pp. 107–132*

1. For details of the campaign, *see* the official history by C. J. C. Molony et al.,
*The Mediterranean and Middle East*, vol. 5, especially pp. 585 ff.; *see also*
Matthew Parker, *Monte Cassino* (2003). • **2**. Max Salvadori, *The Labour and
the Wounds*, p. 175. • **3**. Salvadori, op. cit., p. 179; Munthe Report, p. 22. • **4**. For
Salvadori's mandate, *see* AM10 [Holdsworth] to AJ3 [Salvadori], 'Re-Organisation
of J section', 30 Dec. 1943; and Salvadori's report to Holdsworth entitled 'Survey
of the activities of AM161 [Salvadori] from October 6, 1943 to April 6, 1944',
both in Salvadori Papers. • **5**. Munthe Report, p. 22; his *Sweet is War*, p. 178;
and William Pickering, *The Bandits of Cisterna*, pp. 92–100. • **6**. Munthe Report,
p. 24. He provides an even fuller account in *Sweet is War*, pp. 180–83. Gubbins
lies buried in the military cemetery at Salerno. • **7**. Peter Wilkinson and Joan
Bright Astley, *Gubbins and SOE*, p. 169. • **8**. The operators already at work were
(signal codenames) Pearl (Padua), Opal (Cingoli), Ruby (Macerata), Marcasite
(Ascoli), Jet and Radley (Genoa), Rudder (Rome) and Rutland (La Spezia).
• **9**. For another such example, *see* the 'Bigot – Top Secret' paper prepared by
Holdsworth on 26 Apr. 1944, ref. MN/461, under the title 'No. 1 Special Force
Participation in Future Military Operations', which explicitly links the poten-
tial resistance effort in Italy to 'D-Day for ANVIL'. *See* WO 204/1990. • **10**. To
JQ [McCaffery] Personal from AD/E [Mockler-Ferryman], tel. 4581 ff., 1 Jan.

1944, in HS 6/775, and 'Italy. Appreciation by SOE', 10 Jan. 1944 [Plans/440/1956], in HS 6/781. For Mockler-Ferryman, *see* the entry by M. R. D. Foot in the *ODNB*. • **11**. *See* e.g. Parri to Damiani, 25 Feb. 1944, in Secchia and Frassati, *La Resistenza e gli alleati*, pp. 68–71. Successful airdrops were as follows: Valentine 6/7 Jan.; Valentine 1, 20/21 Jan.; Audley and Audley 1, 17/18 Feb.; Aldwinkle 17/18 Feb.; Aldwinkle 1, 20 Feb.; Afpuddle 20 Feb.; Abergwili 13/14 Feb.; Abram 13/14 Feb.; Abram II, 20 Feb.; Alston 14/15 Feb.; Alston 1, 15/16 Feb. For grievances against Parri by activists in Piedmont, *see* McCaffery to London, 3869–70, 16 May 1944, in HS 6/783. • **12**. E.g. LDN 4099, 31 Mar. 1944, in HS 6/782; and McCaffery to Damiani, 10 Jan. 1944, quoting allied source as complaining that 'we cannot but deplore that CLN persists in its attitude of internal strife instead of concentrating all its forces in chasing Germans from Italy and overturning Fascist Republic'; in Secchia and Frassati, op. cit., pp. 62–3. • **13**. LDN 4044, 24 Mar. 1944, in HS 6/782. 'The Day' is ambiguous; it could be referring to Anvil or to Alexander's Spring Offensive in Italy. • **14**. For organisational details, *see* 'Report on S.O.E. Organisation in Southern Italy', 21 Feb. 1944, in HS 6/775. Sir Peter Wilkinson's memoir, *Foreign Fields*, provides an excellent account of the Clowder mission. For the burgeoning of resistance in the Balkans following the Italian surrender, *see* Phyllis Auty and Richard Clogg (eds), *British Policy towards Wartime Resistance in Yugoslavia and Greece* (1975), *passim*. • **15**. W. J. M. Mackenzie, *The Secret History of SOE*, pp. 406–7; J. G. Beevor, 'History of HQ SOM', 27 July 1945, in HS 7/62. • **16**. Christopher Woods, 'No. 1 Special Force', in *1SF&IR*, vol. 2, p. 38. • **17**. *See* LDN 4287, 1 May 1944 ('Main lines for Sogno to follow . . .'), and LDN 4321, 7 May 1944, in HS 6/783; also Maryland 1751, 5 May 1944, and London to Berne 4318, 6 May 1944, in HS 6/783. • **18**. *See* Holdsworth's 'Bigot – Top Secret' paper of 26 Apr. 1944, referred to in note 9, above. • **19**. W. G. F. Jackson, *The Battle for Italy*, pp. 203–52. • **20**. From a paper produced by Roseberry in January 1945 as a contribution to a broad survey commissioned by Baker Street to demonstrate SOE's achievements, pp. 63–4. • **21**. Salvadori, *The Labour and the Wounds*, p. 186. • **22**. LDN 4442, 28 May 1944, forwarding MARY [49], in HS 6/773. Gubbins ('C.D.') to AM10, 5 June 1944, in Rankin file, Woods Archive. • **23**. For the use of BLOs, *see* 'Advance Force 133: Summary of Discussions during visits of Lt. Gen. Gammell, Maj.Gen Stawell and Brig.Gen. Caffey, 26 Feb–5 March 1944, Appendix G', in HS 3/151; Maryland tel. 110, 26 May 1944, and London to Maryland 969, 31 May 1944; Gubbins ('CD') to AD/H, 31 May 1944 – all in HS 6/773; report of 12 Jun. 1944, in WO 204/9905; WO 106/3964. • **24**. *See* typescript account headed 'EJT's Italian Escape' by Michael Todhunter, 2004, in Woods Archive; also pp. 5–8 of the Todhunter/Coombs report, a copy of which is also to be found in FO 371/43876.

• **25**. Charles Delzell, *Mussolini's Enemies*, p. 377. • **26**. Delzell, op. cit., p. 373; Salvadori, op. cit., p. 182. Parri reported at length on many of these operations in early May. *See* Berne (McCaffery) to London 3740–41, of 3 May 1944, in HS 6/783. • **27**. Quoted in Richard Lamb, *War in Italy, 1943–1945*, p. 59. For a graphic account of the incident, as well as the climate of fear that dominated Rome between the Anzio landings and the liberation, *see* Raleigh Trevelyan, *Rome '44: The Battle for the Eternal City* (1981). • **28**. Quoted in Delzell, op. cit., p. 379. • **29**. Alfredo Pizzoni, *Alla guida del CLNAI*, pp. 70–71, provides his version of the visit. • **30**. Dulles to Algiers, 319–21, 20 Mar. 1944, in Allen Dulles, *From Hitler's Doorstep*, p. 245; and *ibid.*, 376–8, 14 Apr. 1944, p. 604. The broader question of SOE–OSS operational co-operation remained unresolved, however, and Dulles complained about it to his superiors in Algiers. Confusion would continue, he said, until SOE and OSS could agree on separate fields of operation inside Italy. 'This matter,' he wrote, 'seems to have been taken over more and more by Zulu [the British] in spite of the fact that the Italians greatly desire help from us . . . Until orders are given to ZULU SOE concerning our working together with reference to the material each of us should drop, proper coordination at this end is extremely hard to attain.' Dulles to Algiers, 774–6, 18 July 1944, in Dulles, op. cit., p. 336. • **31**. Pizzoni, op. cit., pp. 71–2, gives his summary of McCaffery's complaints. For McCaffery's agenda, *see* his telegrams to London 3479–80, 31 Mar. 1944, in HS 6/782. • **32**. Berne telegrams 3479–80, 31 Mar. 1944, in HS 6/782. • **33**. Berne to London, 3479–80, 82–6, 31 Mar. 1944, in HS 6/782. • **34**. Renzo De Felice, 'Introduzione', in Pizzoni, op. cit, p. 22. • **35**. *See* De Felice, loc. cit., pp. 9–34; and Max Salvadori, *Resistenza ed azione* (1951), p. 228, quoted *ibid.*, fn. 3, p. 32. • **36**. Pizzoni, op. cit., p. 75; for the post-war SOE assessment, *see* his personal file HS 9/1192/8. • **37**. For protests by Damiani and others against the new arrangements, *see* Secchia and Frassati, op. cit., p. 81, and for Parri's response of 16 Apr. 1944, *ibid.* pp. 82–3. For further exchanges between Pizzoni and McCaffery to iron out the details, *see* McCaffery to Pizzoni, 28 Apr., Pizzoni to McCaffery, 12 May, McCaffery to Pizzoni, 20 May, and McCaffery to Pizzoni, 31 May, *ibid.*, pp. 83–9. • **38**. Pizzoni to McCaffery, 13 June 1944, in Secchia and Frassati, op. cit., p. 93. • **39**. *See* AM161 [Salvadori] to AM2 [?], 18 May 1944, 'Activities of AM161 from May 7th to May 16th', in Salvadori Papers. Also, his 'Report on Trip to the West Coast 7 April–21st April 1944', 27 April 1944, addressed to Holdsworth, in his personal file HS 9/1305/6. Not surpris-ingly, none of this appears in Salvadori's published post-war memoir, *The Labour and the Wounds*. • **40**. Salvadori, 'Rome Report', 17 Aug. 1944, in Salvadori Papers; Delzell, op. cit., pp. 384–8. • **41**. Delzell, op. cit., pp. 389–401. • **42**. *See*, for example, London to Berne 4307, 4 May 1944, and McCaffery to London

3869–70, 16 May 1944, in HS 6/783. For Sogno's account, *see* his *Guerra senza bandiera*. • **43**. Maryland 914 to London, 6 June 1944, in HS 6/773.

*Six – 'Squeezing the juice'*        *pp. 133–157*

**1**. The SOE Clowder mission was targeted at penetrating Austria from Slovene-held territory. Major Charles Villiers (alias 'Major Buxton'), who had been dropped in May, arranged Vincent's reception. *See* Peter Wilkinson, *Foreign Fields*, p. 189, for an authoritative account by Clowder's principal protagonist. • **2**. *See* Hargreaves article, noted below. • **3**. Vincent's report on his mission of Nov. 1944 is in WO 204/7301. Somewhat confusingly, his mission is sometimes referred to as 'Sermon', although this in fact was the operational codename for the dropping of the mission. Taylor, Godwin and Trent were dropped on the night of 12/13 Aug. 1944 in an operation codenamed 'Sermon II' and hence are sometimes referred to in the files as the 'Sermon II party'. Accounts of the mission by Taylor, Godwin and Hargreaves can be found in their separate short articles in *ISF&IR*, vol. 2, pp. 137–43, 175–9, and 167–70, respectively. 'Trent' was later killed in action. • **4**. Vincent Report, p. 7. • **5**. Donald Macdonnell, 'Brief Record', typescript in Woods Archive, p. 12; for Vincent's view of Macdonnell, *see* note attached to his report. • **6**. Harry Hargreaves, IWM Sound Archive, ref. 12158, reel 4. • **7**. Vincent Report, p. 7; Godwin, loc. cit., p. 177. • **8**. Hargreaves, IWM Sound Archive, ref. 12158, reel 5. • **9**. Vincent Report, pp. 6–8. • **10**. *Ibid.*, pp. 380–84. For details on the allied advance and the discussions about Istria, *see* W. G. F. Jackson, *The Mediterranean and Middle East*, vol. 6, pt 2, pp. 71, 210–11. • **11**. Godwin, loc. cit., p. 177. • **12**. Vincent, Report, p. 12. • **13**. Captain G. C. Lloyd-Roberts, as quoted in Major E. L. Tulloch of No. 1 Special Force to Holdsworth, 3 Dec. 1944, in HS 6/812. • **14**. Vincent, Report, p. 11. The drop took place on the night of 19/20 Sept. 1944. • **15**. *See* the extensive file on Rutland in the Woods Archive, including correspondence between Woods and Azzari. • **16**. Johnston's mission was codenamed 'Envelope', the name of the signal plan operated by Everitt. The codename of the Italian mission to which they were dropped was 'Rutland', headed by Domenico Azzari, alias 'Candiani', which had arrived in the area the previous October after landing near La Spezia. The team of six Italian saboteurs was codenamed 'Highwater' and was headed by Antonio di Marco ('Dick'). The W/T plan to be operated by Lazzari's group but left behind was codenamed 'Bonding', and the drop operation was codenamed 'Akeld', hence the group is sometimes referred to as the 'Akeld/Bonding' mission. Soon afterwards, however, it began to operate using another plan codenamed 'Blundell Violet', and was instructed to join up with Lett's group. For details, *see* the interrogations reports of both Lazzari and 'Bianchi' – his wireless operator – dated 18 Apr. 1945, in their personal files, as well as in the Akeld/Bonding file in the Woods Archive. In general, *see* Johnston's report on his mission in WO 204/7296. • **17**. As reported to London by No. 1 Special Force on 26 June 1944, HS 6/817. • **18**. Charles Delzell, *Mussolini's Enemies*, pp. 417–18; Richard Lamb, *War in Italy 1943–1945*, pp. 221–4. • **19**. Mario Nardi, 'The Partisans of the Modena Division and No. 1 Special Force in the Republic of Montefiorino', in *1SF&IR*, vol. 1, p. 402. • **20**. *See* WO 204/10238 and, for the Alexander/Maitland Wilson exchange, WO 214/37; also HS 6/776 and HS 6/844. The army's codeword for this operation was 'Albergo' and that for the infiltration of the advance force was 'Batepits'. The Italian Ministry of Defence's official history of the Italian Armed Forces' assistance to the national liberation movement, *L'Azione dello Stato Maggiore Generale per lo sviluppo del movimento di liberazione*, contains an account of it on pp. 143–5, while pp. 182–3 contain the text of the directive sent to Johnston's Envelope mission. For dissent within SOE over the Nembo drop, *see* AD/H to C.D., 1 Aug. 1944, in HS 6/776. • **21**. Wilcockson interview with Christopher Woods, 7 Oct. 1992, in Silentia file, Woods Archive. • **22**. *See* Davies's obituary in the *Daily Telegraph*, 17 Apr. 2003, while for Wilcockson *see* his 1992 interview with Woods, loc. cit.; Holland's personal file is in HS 9/730/2. • **23**. *See* Tulloch, loc. cit., in HS 6/812. • **24**. *See* Davies's 'Report on the Parma Mission for August, September and October', 21 Nov. 1944, in WO 204/7298, as well as 'Two Missions to the Apennines', in *1SF&IR*, vol. 2, pp. 229–36. For some other, Italian, eyewitness accounts of the *rastrellamento*, *see* the articles by Osvaldo Salvarini and Gino Beer in *1SF&IR*, vol. 1. *See also* Charles Macintosh, *From Cloak to Dagger*, pp. 97–9. • **25**. Mario Nardi, 'The Partisans of the Modena Division and No. 1 Special Force in the Republic of Montefiorino,' in *1SF&IR*, vol. 1, pp. 402–3; Macintosh, op. cit., p. 97. • **26**. Davies's letter to Charles Macintosh, 19 Sep. 1973, in Davies folder, Envelope file, Woods Archive; this is probably the source for Macintosh's judgement. *See also* Davies's interview with Woods, 17 Nov. 1989, loc. cit. • **27**. Johnston Report, pp. 8–9. • **28**. For his services in Italy during the war Gorlon Lett was awarded the DSO, and afterwards served briefly as British vice-consul in Bologna. In 1955 he published a memoir entitled *Rossano*, which remains a classic and powerful account of life with the Italian Partisans. • **29**. Charles Holland, 'Toffee: A British Mission to the East Cisa Area (1944–1945)' in *1SF&IR*, vol. 2, pp. 272–9. Hayhurst was to spend nine months in the Apennines and could claim the longest period of continuous service as a British radio operator behind enemy lines in Italy. At the end of the war he was awarded the British Empire Medal. Holland was the longest-serving BLO in Italy, and emerged with an MBE and MC. • **30**. *See* the report by Major C. Holland, MBE,

on his mission (Envelope Blue), in HS 6/844; also the two on Silentia by Major
J. T. M. Davies, MC, MBE, in HS 6/791; and letter from Christopher Woods to
Frank Hayhurst, 6 Feb. 1993, in Woods Archive. Woods himself had been briefed
to fly in with the Nembo Battalion and was ready to go when the operation was
cancelled. As the result of a navigational error an Italian mission using the
signal plan 'Turdus' that was destined to link up with Johnston, led by Captain
Roberto Battaglia, had dropped into the area in which Oldham and 'his' partisans were operating, and shortly afterwards was placed under his control. *See*
Oldham's 'Report on the Activities of the "Turdus" Mission July–December
1944', in WO 204/7301; also his undated memoir, 'Some experiences of an
escaped P.O.W.', in the Woods Archive. • **31**. *See* article by Wilcockson, 'With
the Partisans of the Modena Area', in *1SF&IR*, vol. 2, pp. 243–4, • **32**. Henderson's
mission was codenamed 'Elevator', and the drop operation, 'Breaker'; it also had
a SIM codename, 'Nox'. *See* HS 7/184; HS 6/779. • **33**. HS 6/789. • **34**. HS
6/794. • **35**. *See* Scott to Holdsworth, 16 July 1944, in Holdsworth file, Woods
Archive. • **36**. AM161 [Salvadori] to AM93 [Charles Macintosh] in Salvadori
Papers. For Holdsworth's instructions for his first mission to the Marche, *see*
'Operational Instruction No. 1 to Captain M. W. Salvadore', 21 June 1944, in
Salvadori Papers. • **37**. Max Salvadori, *The Labour and the Wounds*, pp. 189–90.
• **38**. *Ibid.*, p. 191. Salvadori's book *La Resistenza nell'Anconetano e nel Piceno*
(1962) contains details of Italian missions sent in by No. 1 Special Force and
active in that area. • **39**. HS 6/829; HS 8/828. • **40**. Scott to Holdsworth, loc.
cit. • **41**. 'Assistance to Italian Patriots', 1 July 1944, in HS 6/779. For communications, the *coup de main* teams were each equipped with two homing pigeons,
one to be released on arrival and the second on completion of the assigned act
of sabotage.

*Seven – 'On the right lines'*          *pp. 158–177*

**1.** *See* typescript note by Macintosh headed 'No. 1 Special Force-Forward Missions',
in Florence Mission file, Woods Archive, as well as his memoir, *From Cloak
to Dagger, passim*. Norris was wounded by sniper fire ten days later and evacuated back to the UK; he was awarded the Military Medal. For the allied advance
to Florence, *see* W. G. F. Jackson, *The Mediterranean and Middle East*, vol. 6,
pt 2, pp. 84–118. • **2**. 'Florence Report by Renato [Pierleoni]', in Salvadori Papers.
For his monthly salary, *see* AM161 [Salvadori] to AM10 [Holdsworth], 11 Sept.
1944, loc. cit; also his personal file, HS 9/1187/2. • **3**. Macintosh, op. cit., p. 58.
• **4**. *Ibid.*, p. 62. • **5**. *See* Macintosh daily report, 8 Aug. 1944, in 'Florence Mission',
report by Lt Col. R. T. Hewitt to Commander RNVR Comd No. 1 Special Force

[Holdsworth], 24 Aug. 1944, WO 204/7295. This same document contains partisan reports about the situation on the north bank. • **6**. Macintosh daily reports, 9 and 10 Aug. 1944, *ibid.*; and *From Cloak to Dagger*, p. 61. • **7**. Macintosh daily report, 11 Aug. 1944, loc. cit. • **8**. Charles Delzell, *Mussolini's Enemies*, pp. 397–8; also C. R. S. Harris, *Allied Military Administration of Italy, 1943–1945*, pp. 147–50, 173–4, 206–10. • **9**. Renato Pierleoni, 'Florence Report', Rome, Sept. 1944, loc. cit.; Harris, op. cit., pp. 187–90. • **10**. Harris, op. cit., p. 183. • **11**. Max Salvadori, *The Labour and the Wounds*, pp. 191–2. • **12**. *See* 'Role of 1SF in Rankin/Italy', 19 Aug. 1944, in HS 6/794; also, Holdsworth to Stawell, 25 Aug. 1944, in Holdsworth file, Woods Archive; and Macintosh, *From Cloak to Dagger*, pp. 64–5. • **13**. G/Plans to DH London, tel. 2249, 12 July 1944, in HS 6/790, recommending (without result) that its base should be moved to Ancona. The idea foundered on the lack of suitable accommodation. • **14**. Progress Report, Italian Section, 6 Aug. 1944, in WO 204/10238. • **15**. Holdsworth to Macintosh, Rome, 16 Aug. 1944, in Florence Mission file, Woods Archive. • **16**. The meeting took place on Saturday 15 July. *See* Raffaele Cadorna, *La Riscossa* (1948), p. 113; for discussions about his appointment, *see* Berne tel. 3869, 16 May 1944, in HS 6/783, and Holdsworth to Alexander, 31 July 1944; also Delzell, op. cit., pp. 413–14. • **17**. Edgardo Sogno, *Guerra senza bandiera*, p. 257. • **18**. *Ibid.*, pp. 255–6. • **19**. Alexander to Cadorna, 3 Aug. 1944, quoted in Pietro Secchia and Filippo Frassati, *La Resistenza e gli alleati*, p. 124; for Cadorna's pre-drop training, *see* Cadorna, op. cit., pp. 115–18; also, HS 6/862. • **20**. *See* Churchill's personal file, HS 9/316/3, as well as Richard Lamb, *War in Italy, 1943–1945*, pp. 136–7. For Peter Churchill, *see* M. R. D. Foot's entry in the *ODNB*. There was a third brother, an airman, shot down over Sicily. • **21**. 'G. A. Holdsworth to Fairway Mission. Operation Instructions', 3 Aug. 1944, in HS 6/862, an abbreviated version of which is reproduced in Secchia and Frassati, op. cit., pp. 125–7. Also, Roseberry to A. R. Dew, Foreign Office, 9 Aug. 1944, in FO 371/43872. For a refutation of the idea that the British foisted Cadorna on the Italians, *see* Massimo de Leonardis, 'Britain and the Italian Partisans', in *1SF&IR*, vol. 1, p. 50. • **22**. For the full text of McCaffery's letter to Parri ('Maurizio'), which is undated but which arrived in Milan on 16 Aug., *see* Secchia and Frassati, op. cit., p. 99. For the McCaffery/Pizzoni financial discussions, *see ibid.*, pp. 95–7; and for McCaffery to Stucchi of 14 Aug. 1944, *see ibid.*, p. 98. • **23**. 'Fairway Report by Major W. O. Churchill, M.C., 29th December 1944', in WO 204/7296. • **24**. *Ibid.*, p. 7. • **25**. *Ibid.*, p. 11. For the Bamon mission, *see* Eugenio Bonvincini, 'The Bamon and Cherokee Missions in the Biella area', in *1SF&IR*, vol. 1, pp. 113–22. Bonvincini's personal mission was to report on the political and military situation in Upper Piedmont. All members of the Bamon mission were recruits for the ORI section specifically created to work with No. 1 Special Force.

• **26**. Cadorna, op. cit., p. 140; Delzell, op. cit., pp. 414–15; Secchia and Frassati, op. cit., pp. 127–30.

*Eight – Looking bright*                                             *pp. 178–195*

**1**. For Alexander's radio message to Turin, 27 July 1944, *see* Charles Delzell, *Mussolini's Enemies*, p. 415. For Toplink, *see* A. R. Funk, *Hidden Ally*, pp. 80–82, and for the creation of SPOC, *see* his pp. 32–6. WO/204/1993 contains more on the Toplink plan, e.g. Adv AFHQ to AFHQ, 'Top Secret Bigot Anvil', 12 July 1944: 'SAC directs study urgent means coordinate action Italian Resistance Groups with ANVIL [*sic*] to interdict possible German moves W[est] through Maritime Alps.' Anvil was renamed Dragoon in mid-July. • **2**. More on O'Regan's life may be found in the O'Regan Papers in the Liddell Hart Archive at King's College London, and for Gunn, *see* Funk, op. cit., p. 80. For Blanchaert, *see* his interview with Christopher Woods in Milan, 2 May 1989, in Donum file, Woods Archive. • **3**. The story of Darewski's mission to Slovenia has been well told in John Earle's *The Price of Patriotism*. • **4**. Funk, op. cit, pp. 80–82; for a biography of Christine Granville, *see* Madeleine Masson, *Christine* (1975), as well as Marcus Binney, *The Women Who Lived for Danger*, pp. 49–110; for Marcellin, *see* Rivosecchi's testimony in 'The Mixed Crosse Mission', in *ISF&IR*, vol. 1, pp. 151–7. For Kalifa's description of the reception, *see* his report (by 'Paradisier'), 3 Oct. 1944, in his personal file. • **5**. 'Message 8 via Barodo', 26 Aug., in Hamilton/Blanchaert/25 Detachment file, Woods Archive. For Marpugo's report, *see* RG 226, E91, box 19, NARA. • **6**. *See* Chapter 12. • **7**. 'Report on the activities of Rivosecchi, Livio', 2 June 1945, in Ferrula/Donum file, Woods Archive, p. 2. Rivosecchi later cooperated closely with Blanchaert in setting up an important courier service for supplies between Grenoble and the Italian partisans. • **8**. 'Report by Captain P. O'Regan', 22 June 1945, in HS 6/846. • **9**. WO 204/1992; Michael Lees, *Special Operations Executed*, p. 156. • **10**. Memo to Major Darewski from GSO II Italian Section (De Haan), 6 Aug. 1944, in HS 6/861. Lucia Boetto Testori, 'The Temple Mission to the Langhe', in *ISF&IR*, vol. 1, pp. 163–5. • **11**. Handwritten note by Farrimond dated 21 Nov. 1944, in HS 6/861. *See also* his interrogation report, 28 Nov. 1944, loc. cit. • **12**. John Ross, MC, unpublished memoir 'Italy 1944–1945', in IWM, Dept of Documents, ref. 06/18/1, p. 7. For an account of the Aegean Islands episode and German atrocities against members of the Italian armed forces, *see* Richard Lamb, *War in Italy, 1943–1945*, pp. 125–9. • **13**. For his account of the Ruina mission, *see* Christopher Woods, 'Genesis of a Mission in the Western Veneto', in *ISF&IR*, vol. 2, pp. 113–19, as well as the privately printed short memoir produced by his family, *Petrol and Sawdust*, kindly given to me by Mr Woods. • **14**. Memo to Major Wilkinson from GSO II Italian Section (De Haan), 9 Aug. 1944, in HS 6/848. • **15**. 'Plan "W", Directives for Major Wilkinson', 1 Sept. 1944, in WO 204/7295. Pearl was also known to No. 1 Special Force variously as 'Barograph' and 'Baffle' or 'Baffle Blue', and to SIM as 'MRS'. For Woods on the allied optimism of Aug./Sept. 1944, *see* his letter to Ettore Damini, Jan. 1998, in Gela file, Woods Archive. For other examples of similar optimism, *see* Ross, op. cit., p. 5, and H. W. Tilman, *When Men and Mountains Meet*, p. 153. • **16**. Simia was also known as Operation 'Beriwind 1', and Gela as Operation 'Bitterroot'. • **17**. Roderick Bailey, *The Wildest Province: SOE in the Land of the Eagle* (2008), pp. 75–6. For biographies of Tilman, *see* Tim Madge, *The Last Hero, Bill Tilman*, and the entry by Chris Bonington in the *ODNB*. • **18**. For the descriptions of Brietsche, *see* Ross, op. cit., p. 18, and Richard Tolson, quoted in Christopher Woods's letter to Ettore Damini, Jan. 1998, in Woods Archive. For his instructions, *see* the Operation Instruction to Capt. Brietsche, 31 Aug. 1944, in HS 6/854. • **19**. Tilman, op. cit., p. 156; Vittorio Gozzer, 'Encounters in the Piave Valley and Elsewhere', in *ISF&IR*, vol. 1, pp. 237–41; also HS 6/808. • **20**. More in Laurence Lewis, *Echoes of Resistance*, p. 66. • **21**. Ross, op. cit., p. 4. • **22**. Ross interview, IWM Sound Archive, ref. 27077, 1445–551. *See also* his 'The British Mission to the Veneto (August 1944–May 1945)', in *ISF&IR*, vol. 2, pp. 127–30. • **23**. Captain P. N. Brietsche, 'Report on Mission "Bitterroot" Signal Plan "Gela" and "Gela Blue" in Area Asiago, Piave, Cansiglio from 31 August 44 to 25 April 1945', reproduced in Ettore Damini (ed.), 'Documenti Militari Britannici d'Archivio (Pro-SOE) sul Movimento Partigiano in Italia, 1944–45', pp. 48–73, privately produced typescript, in Woods Archive. • **24**. For Tilman's account of the drop, *see* Tilman, op. cit., pp. 152–9. • **25**. Tilman, op. cit., p. 161 and Ross, op. cit., p. 8. Both refer to him as 'Pallino'. • **26**. More details on its many efforts may be found in the Blackfolds file, Woods Archive. Irving-Bell's abortive operation was codenamed 'Cedartown', and he eventually dropped to the Clarion mission. • **27**. *See* the report on 'Ruina/Fluvius' by Captains Orr-Ewing and Woods, June 1945, in HS 6/848. • **28**. For the broader background of the attempts to infiltrate these Austrian missions through northern Italy, *see* Peter Wilkinson, *Foreign Fields*, pp. 190–95. • **29**. For Patrick Martin-Smith's exploits in Friuli, *see* his book, *Friuli '44* (1991). Some of Fielding's papers are to be found in the IWM. For Czernin's brief, *see* the operation order dated 1 May 1944 in HS 6/850, while on his life *see* Norman Franks, *Double Mission*, as well as correspondence in the Woods Archive. For the travails of the whole Austrian enterprise, known as Clowder, *see* Wilkinson, op. cit., pp. 207–11. • **30**. *See* Czernin's report on 'The Situation in the field in the CARNIA/FRIULI zone', in WO 204/7298. *See also* his 'Report on British

Mission in Frontier Area of North-East Italy', in HS 6/850. • **31**. Progress Report, Italian Section, 3 Sept. 1944, in HS 6/902.

*Nine – 'Rose-tinted spectacles'*                                           *pp. 196–228*

**1**. Rankin planning for the Mediterranean began as early as 6 June 1944, the day allied troops liberated Rome. *See* e.g. 'Appreciation by HQ SOM of Functions of SOE/OSS (SO) Units and Request for Necessary Directives', of that date, in WO 204/10240. This file also contains the AFHQ Instructions for Special Operations in *all* occupied countries in the Mediterranean Theatre of Operations, 20 Sept. 1944. • **2**. 'Role of No. 1 Special Force in Rankin/Italy', 19 Aug. 1944, in HS 6/794. • **3**. Holdsworth to Hewitt, 26 Aug. 1944, in Woods Archive. • **4**. Holdsworth to Hewitt, 1 Sept. 1944, and Holdsworth to Gubbins, 2 Sept., in Holdsworth file, Woods Archive. *See also* WO 214/37 and HS 6/797. The key document here is the paper of 19 Aug., cited above. Further Rankin planning documents can be found in the same file. Hewitt formally took over as commander of No. 1 Special Force in Jan. 1945 after Holdsworth returned to the UK. Macintosh's advice drawn from his Rome and Florence experiences can be found in his memo of 1 Sept. to Hewitt (AM93 to AM2) entitled 'Rankin Plans (B and C)', in HS 6/797. • **5**. *See* SOM to London 2528, 6 Sept. 1944, in HS 6/794. • **6**. For the broader context of allied planning for the administration of Italy, *see* C. R. S. Harris, *Allied Military Administration of Italy, 1943–1945*, pp. 265–83. • **7**. 'Outline Plan by No. 1 Special Force to cover sudden Rankin B conditions in North Italy', Lt Col. R. Hewitt, 2 Sept. 1944; SOM to London 2528, cited above; and Maryland 1448, 6 Sept. 1944 – all in HS 6/794. The messages reproduced by Pietro Secchia and Filippo Frassati in their *La Resistenza e gli alleati*, pp. 133–4, show that McCaffery did as requested. • **8**. Holdsworth to Hewitt, 1 Sept. 1944, in Holdsworth file, Woods Archive. • **9**. Max Salvadori, *The Labour and the Wounds*, p. 191; Holdsworth to Hewitt, 6 Sept. 1944, in Holdsworth file, loc. cit. For the high optimism about allied progress (but regarded sceptically by the prime minister), *see* Max Hastings, *Armageddon* (2004), p. 15. • **10**. Operation instruction to Major M. W. Salvadori from Commander G. A. Holdsworth DSO, RNVR, 20 Sept. 1944, in WO 204/7293; and Salvadori to 'J', 20 Sept. 1944, in Salvadori Papers. • **11**. W. G. F. Jackson, *The Mediterranean and Middle East*, vol. 6, pt 2, pp. 229–30, and – for the 'green nightmare' – his *The Battle for Italy*, pp. 277–8. • **12**. Brock to Hodgart, 28 Sept. 1944, HS 6/797. *See also* 'J' to AD/H, 2 Sept. 1944, in HS 6/794. • **13**. Holdsworth to Hewitt, 4 Oct. 1944, in Holdsworth file, loc. cit. • **14**. Interrogation Report on Churchill by Major Follies, 27 Sept. 1945, in HS 6/862, p. 3. For

more on Churchill's stay in Milan, *see* his Fairway report, in WO 204/7296.
• **15**. *Ibid.*, p. 8; also, 'Interrogation Report on William Algernon [*sic*] Churchill,
alias Major Peters alias Pietri, Antonio, alias Tonino, alias Kravic, Giulio, of the
above operation [Bantry/Fairway]', 3 Jan. 1945; and, for his recommendation re
Biella, his handwritten note to McCaffery, 11 Oct. 1944, all in HS 6/862. • **16**.
Charles Delzell, *Mussolini's Enemies*, pp. 416–17. • **17**. *See* Churchill's Fairway
report, p. 2. • **18**. *See* the exchanges between Churchill and Pizzoni, the CLNAI
and Rome, and Cadorna and Churchill between 24 and 27 Sept. 1944, in Secchia
and Frassati, op. cit., pp. 143–6. • **19**. 'Interrogation Report on William Algernon
[*sic*] Churchill', 3 Jan. 1945, in HS 6/862. • **20**. Leo Valiani, *Tutte le strade
conducono a Roma*, p. 187. • **21**. Sogno, 'Mission RRR: Signal plan Fairway',
Fairway/Bantry box, Woods Archive. For Salvadori's view of Churchill, *see*
Secchia and Frassati, op. cit., p. 143, fn. 47. *See also* Edgardo Sogno, *Guerra
senza bandiera*, pp. 264–5, and Valiani, op. cit., pp. 187–8; Churchill's personal
file, HS 9/316/3. • **22**. Handwritten letter of 20 Oct. 1944 to 'My dear Teddy',
in HS 6/862. • **23**. *See* F. Parri and F. Venturi, 'The Italian Resistance and the
Allies', in *European Resistance Movements, 1939–1945* (1964). • **24**. John McCaffery,
'No Pipes or Drums', pp. 207–8. • **25**. *See* tel. 4449 to Berne, 28 May 1944, in
HS 6/773; also tel. 905 to Maryland, 24 May, and tel. 67 from Maryland, 27
May, loc. cit. • **26**. McCaffery, op. cit., p. 209. The two Italian missions were
codenamed 'Beacon' and 'Canopy'; *see* HS 6/811 for their reports. • **27**. John
Windsor, *The Mouth of the Wolf*, pp. 141–2; Roy McLaren, *Canadians Behind
Enemy Lines, 1939–1945* (1981), pp. 174–6; Roger Absalom, *A Strange Alliance*,
p. 97. For the commando raid on which Paterson was captured, *see* Anthony
Deane-Drummond, *Return Ticket*, pp. 11–46. • **28**. Windsor, op. cit., p. 156.
• **29**. *See* Paterson's report of 23 May 1945, Woods Archive. • **30**. *See* Paterson's
report, p. 9. For the OSS role in the uprising, *see* Max Corvo, *The O.S.S. in Italy,
1942–1945*, pp. 202–04; also Delzell, op. cit., pp. 433–5. • **31**. Delzell, op. cit.,
p. 427. • **32**. James Holland, *Italy's Sorrow*, pp. 290, 385; Richard Lamb, *War
in Italy, 1943–1945*, p. 68. • **33**. 'Report of the Activities of the "Turdus" Mission
July–December 1944', by Major A. J. Oldham, MC, p. 10, in WO 204/7301.
• **34**. *See* F. H. Hinsley, *British Intelligence in the Second World War* (1988), vol.
3, pt 2, appendix 2, p. 886. • **35**. Lamb, op. cit., pp. 64–6, and Holland, op. cit.,
p. 386. *See also* Albert Kesselring, *The Memoirs of Field-Marshal Kesselring*,
pp. 224–33. This message, too, was decrypted by GC and CS. *See* Hinsley, op.
cit., p. 887. • **36**. For Kesselring's directive, 1 Oct. 1944, *see* 'AFHQ History of
Special Operations in the Mediterranean', 24 July 1945, Annex F, in HS 7/170.
'Enigma' decrypts throughout the autumn and winter reveal the heavy losses
being inflicted on the partisans. Hinsley, op. cit., pp. 888–91. • **37**. *See* their
after-action Ruina report, in HS 6/848. • **38**. H. W. Tilman, *When Men and*

*Mountains Meet*, p. 187. • **39**. Captain P. N. Brietsche, 'Report on Mission "Bitterroot" Signal Plan "Gela" and "Gela Blue" in area Asiago, Piave, Cansiglio from 31 August 44 to 25 April 45', pp. 10–11, reproduced in Ettore Damini (ed.), 'Documenti Militari Britannici d'Archivio (Pro-SOE) sul Movimento Partigiano in Italia, 1944–45', in Woods Archive. • **40**. Christopher Woods's communication with the author, 6 Aug. 2010. • **41**. *See* Vincent's report on his mission, 29 Nov. 1944, in WO 204/7301. • **42**. Vincent to Holdsworth, 13 Nov. 1944, in Holdsworth file, Woods Archive. • **43**. *See* Davies's report on Envelope Blue mission, 21 Nov. 1944, in WO 204/7298. • **44**. *See* Wilcockson's report on the Silentia mission, 19 Feb. 1945, in WO 204/7301. • **45**. Michael Lees, *Special Operations Executed in Serbia and Italy*, p. 156; Margaret Pawley, *In Obedience to Instructions*, p. 133; Charles Macintosh, *From Cloak to Dagger*, p. 148. • **46**. *See* HS 6/795, HS 6/798 for messages of 20 Sept., 20 and 21 Oct., and 3 Nov. 1944, containing Darewski's warnings about Turin. For Farrimond, *see* Michael Lees, op. cit., p. 91. • **47**. Michael Lees, 'General Report on Area Piedmont covered by Flap Mission,' 8 Oct. 1944, in HS 6/860. Morton and Long produced reports of their own; *see* WO 204/1992 for Long's, and HS 6/861 for Morton's. The drop for this operation (codenamed 'Barston II'), took place on the night of 4/5 Sept. 1944. Morton, Long and the rest of the party also made it back safely by paying a fisherman to row them along the shore from Italy into France. • **48**. *See* the instructions for Operation 'Bergenfeld', 26 Aug. 1944, in HS 6/849. The signal plan was 'Tabella'. In the field, Roworth took the name 'Major Nicholson', and Boccazzi that of 'Taboni' or 'Piave'. For Tolson, *see* Laurence Lewis, *Echoes of Resistance*, pp. 63–4. • **49**. *See* Roworth, 'Report on the zone of operation "Bergenfeld" North Italy', 24 Oct. 1944, in WO 204/7301. The Tabella mission was reinforced in mid-October by Captain M. W. L. Prior, Captain Pat Mosdell and Corporal C. Ridewood (Operation 'Bigwig'). For more on Roworth, including edited extracts from his radio signals, *see* Lewis, op. cit., pp. 64–71. • **50**. *See* HS 4/5 and HS 6/902. • **51**. Cope's mission was codenamed 'Silica South'. The doomed mission, consisting of Major Whitaker, Captain Hajny and a Czech operator named Nocar, was codenamed 'Silica North'. For Cope's report, *see* HS 4/80; *see also* HS 4/5 and HS 4/33 for more details. • **52**. *See* Cope's report, as well as report of Force 139, 22 Sept. 1944, in HS 4/32, and memorandum by Brock (AM161), of 18 Oct. 1944, on 'Subversion of Czechs', in HS 4/33. • **53**. CD [Gubbins] to AM10 [Holdsworth], 17 Oct. 1944, in HS 4/32; 'Punch' to CD, 20 Oct. 1944, HS 4/80; CD Personal from AM10, 20 Oct. 1944, in HS 4/53; Holdsworth letter to Keswick, 26 Oct. 1944, in Holdsworth file, Woods Archive. • **54**. For Cadorna's message of 15 Oct. 1944, *see* Brock to Holdsworth, 26 Oct., in WO 204/2000; for Selborne to Churchill on 26 Oct., *see* CAB 80/88, and for his quarterly report, *see* PREM 3/408/1. • **55**. *See*

HS 6/776; HS 6/902; HS 8/898; HS 8/197; FO 371/43877; and W. G. F. Jackson, op. cit., pt 3, pp. 384–5, 409–12. For 'the first-class shouting match' and 'first-class battle', *see* Holdsworth's letters to Gubbins, 9 Aug. 1944 and 24 Nov. 1944, in Holdsworth file, Woods Archive. • **56**. Max Salvadori, *The Labour and the Wounds*, pp. 196–7. • **57**. For 'shot their bolt', *see* W. G. F. Jackson, *The Battle for Italy*, p. 281; and vol. 6, pt 2, of his *The Mediterranean and Middle East*, pp. 286–91.

*Ten – Winter blues*                                                           *pp. 229–260*

**1**. Tolson diary, entry for 28 Oct., in Woods Archive; *see also* correspondence between Tolson and Woods 1990–96, loc. cit. • **2**. For Woods, *see* his *Petrol and Sawdust*, p. 33; H. W. Tilman, *When Men and Mountains Meet*, pp. 187–8. • **3**. Brietsche, Bitterroot report, p. 9. • **4**. Enrico Martini Mauri, *Partigiani penne nere*, p. 174. • **5**. *See* Tolson diary, entries for 11–15 Nov. 1944, loc. cit. • **6**. Tilman, op. cit., p. 185. • **7**. *See* 'Report on SOE Operations in Italy', p. 137, with Roseberry's scribbled comments, Woods Archive; Holland, quoted in Laurence Lewis, *Echoes of Resistance*, pp. 76–7; and Brietsche, 'Bitterroot report', p. 24. But after the war, Jim Davies defended the decision as 'honest and realistic'. *See* his 'Two Missions in the Apennines,' in *1SF&IR*, vol. 2, p. 233. Alfredo Pizzoni also condemned the directive; *see* his *Alla guida del CLNAI*, p. 124. For a measured discussion, *see* Massimo de Leonardis, 'Britain and the Italian Partisans', in *1SF&IR*, vol. 1, pp. 51–2. • **8**. Alexander to Wilson, 13 Nov. 1944, in WO 214/37. • **9**. For Testori, *see* Lewis, op. cit., p. 62. • **10**. 'J' to '161', 22 June 1944, in Salvadori Papers; for the Foreign Office views, dated 11 May 1944, *see* Sir Llewellyn Woodward, *British Foreign Policy in the Second World War*, vol. 2, p. 538. • **11**. 'J' to SOM 5078, 16 Sept. 1944, in HS 6/776. • **12**. C. R. S. Harris, *Allied Military Administration of Italy, 1943–1945*, pp. 230–35, 251–2, 265–75. • **13**. HS 6/795. • **14**. *See* Valiani's personal files HS 9/1569/4 and HS 9/1516/1, as well as his interview with Christopher Woods, 2 May 1989, in Woods Archive. • **15**. Pizzoni, op. cit., p. 84. • **16**. *See* e.g. Maryland 'for JQ for Sogno', 6 Sept. 1944, in HS 6/794; Maryland 677, 12 Oct. 1944, in HS 6/795. • **17**. *See* Sogno's account of his arrest and escape on the Swiss border on 21 Oct. 1944, in HS 6/814. • **18**. Pizzoni quoted in 'Security in North West Italy. Appreciation of the Situation as at 20 January 1945', p. 10, a detailed security section commentary on La Franchi's activities from Aug. 1944, in HS 7/170. • **19**. Roseberry, 31 Oct. 1944, in FO 371/48878. For Pizzoni's detailed account, *see* op. cit., pp. 88–96; Valiani provides his account in his *Tutte le strade conducono a Roma*, pp. 214–15. *See also* Pietro Secchia and Filippo Frassati, *La Resistenza* *e gli alleati*, pp. 106–07, and HS 6/795. • **20**. Max Salvadori, *The Labour and the Wounds*, p. 195. • **21**. *Ibid.*, p. 199. • **22**. 'Report on SOE Operations in Italy', pp. 162–4, Woods Archive; 'Special Operations (AFHQ) Franco-Italian Border and N.W. Italy 1944–1945', in HS 7/170; SOM to London, 29 Nov. 1944, in HS 6/814. *See also* FO 371/43877/8. • **23**. Letter dated 13 Nov. 1944, in HS 6/851. • **24**. *See* Arthur Brown, 'A Jedburgh in Italy', typescript kindly lent to me by Sir Thomas Macpherson. For the latter's account of his campaign in France, *see* David Stafford, *Secret Agent*, pp. 224–35. • **25**. Macpherson's report on Coolant mission, 30 July 1945, Appendix B, p. 53, in WO 204/7301. Macpherson's first report on his mission contained strong criticisms of Vincent's previous work in the area, but these do not appear in his final report, apparently as the result of an instruction. *See* Gubbins to Macpherson's brother, Colonel P. Macpherson, 25 Sept. 1945, in possession of Sir Thomas Macpherson. • **26**. Operational Instruction, 16 Oct. 1944. • **27**. *See* FO 371/43878, and Holdsworth to Gubbins, 24 Nov. 1944, in Holdsworth file, Woods Archive. • **28**. Brown, op. cit., p. 4. • **29**. Macpherson, Coolant report, 30 July 1945, p. 18, in WO 204/7301. For the Milan Pacts, etc., *see* Charles Delzell, *Mussolini's Enemies*, pp. 444–7. • **30**. HQ Allied Armies in Italy, 'The Partisan Movement in Italy: An Introduction', written 15 Nov. 1944, circulated 17 Nov. 1944, in WO 204/7283. • **31**. *See* Maryland 414 from AM10 for AD/H and J, dated 11 Nov. 1944, in HS 6/796. • **32**. *See* Campbell's instructions for the Clarion mission, dated 24 Sept. 1944, in WO 204/7293, as well as his correspondence with Woods in the Woods Archive. *See also* the reports on Clarion by R. A. Clark and W. Banks, in HS 8/810. The other members of the ill-fated mission were Captain Irving Bell, Sub Lieutenant R. A. Clark, Petty Officer 'Eddie' Cauvain, Corporal John Stevens and wireless operator William Banks. Captain Bentley and Corporal Millington were the two men sent to Nice. *See also* 'British Missions in Liguria', in No. 1 Special Force Weekly Review, 19 Dec. 1944, in FO 371/49797. • **33**. *See* HS 6/798, and Macdonald's and Amoore's reports on the Cherokee mission, 25 May 1945, in HS 6/840. *See also* Eugenio Bonvincini, 'The Bamon and Cherokee Missions in the Biella area', in *1SF&IR*, vol. 1, pp. 113–22; Amos Messori, 'Sabotage in the Biella area', *ibid.*, p. 141; and Alastair Macdonald, IWM Sound Archive, refs 11887 and 8671. • **34**. *See* Alastair Macdonald and Patrick Amoore, 'The Cherokee Mission in the Biella Area', in *1SF&IR*, vol. 2, pp. 69–75. • **35**. Amoore, Cherokee report, 16 June 1945, pp. 12–13, in HS 6/840. • **36**. *See* Bell's mission report of 22 June 1945 in HS 6/841. • **37**. Macdonald and Amoore, op. cit. • **38**. C. M. ('Monty') Woodhouse, quoted in Phyllis Auty and Richard Clogg (eds), *British Policy towards Wartime Resistance in Yugoslavia and Greece* (1975), p. 271. Stevens also served briefly in France with F Section, July–Aug. 1944. • **39**. *See* 'Operation Instruction No. 2 to Lieutenant-Colonel Stevens, OBE', from Commander G. Holdsworth,

DSO, RNVR, 28 Oct. 1944, in HS 6/795 and HS 6/796. For the 'Situation in Piedmont' report, 15 Nov. 1944, *see* HS 6/812. • **40.** *See* Stevens's report to Commander SO(M), 22 Mar. 1945, in HS 6/856, and No. 1 Special Force Weekly Review, 30 Dec. 1944', in FO 371/49797. For Macintosh's account of the landing operation, *see* his *From Cloak to Dagger*, pp. 111–15. In charge of supplies and operations at TAC HQ was Captain Jim Beatt, whose earlier mission to the Veneto had been cancelled after six abortive attempts. • **41.** For the assassination of Heydrich and SOE's role in the operation, *see* Callum MacDonald, *The Killing of SS Obergruppenführer Reinhard Heydrich*. For Ratweek and the plan to target Hitler, *see Operation Foxley*, and for the Roseberry/Gubbins discussions about Farinacci and Mussolini, *see* HS 7/265. • **42.** Report on Operation 'Cisco/Red' by Maj. B. J. Barton, DSO, MC, as circulated by Lt Col. R. T. Hewitt, 13 Jan. 1945, in WO 204/7301. • **43.** Richard Lamb, *War in Italy, 1943–1945*, pp. 224–5 and HS 7/61. For Alexander's personal interest, *see* De Haan to Pleydell-Bouverie of SO(M) Liaison Staff, 'Secret and Personal', 14 Jan. 1945, in HS 6/859. It is worth noting that Jim Davies claimed in January 1945 that Barton told him his target was von Vietinghoff. *See* Lamb to Davies, 14 July 1992, in Woods Archive. • **44.** Barton's report, loc. cit., p. 3. • **45.** *Ibid.*, p. 7. *See also* Oreste Gelmini, 'The Stone Mission and the Partisan Command of the 2nd Bassa Modena Zone', in *iSF&IR*, vol. 1, pp. 393–4. Gelmini headed the partisan group with which Barton (aka the 'Stone Mission') stayed. • **46.** For Sogno's account of this meeting, *see* his *Guerra senza bandiera*, pp. 320–22. • **47.** Alfredo Pizzoni, *Alla guida del CLNAI*, p. 115. • **48.** Holdsworth to Gubbins, 24 Nov. 1944, Holdsworth file, Woods Archive. • **49.** Pizzoni, op. cit., p. 124. • **50.** Quoted in F. W. D. Deakin, 'SOE and the Italian Resistance 1941–1945', undated paper, p. 29, Woods Archive. There is a small problem with this scene in that by then Wilson had left for home to take up his appointment as head of the Joint Staff Mission in Washington. Perhaps Parri meant Alexander, or else confused it with an earlier encounter with Wilson. • **51.** Dulles to Donovan, tel. 667, 10 Nov. 1944, quoted in Allen Dulles, *From Hitler's Doorstep*, p. 396. • **52.** 'Interrogation Report on William Algernon [*sic*] Churchill', 3 Jan. 1945, in HS 6/862. • **53.** FO 371/43878, 10 Dec. 1944. • **54.** Brietsche, Bitterroot report, p. 11. • **55.** Tolson Diary, loc. cit., p. 15. • **56.** Brock to Stevens, 21 Dec. 1944, in HS 6/856. In the end, the letter was considered too sensitive to send to the field and its contents were conveyed verbally to Stevens by another officer. 'Intelligence became one of the few things we could do in the depths of winter,' notes Christopher Woods of the Ruina mission in a communication with the author, 29 Aug. 2010. • **57.** Salvadori, op. cit., pp. 200–01.

1. No. 1 Special Force Weekly Review for Italy for the week ending 11 Feb. 1945, dated 18 Feb. 1945, in FO 371/49799. *See also* the 15th Army Group review of special operations for January, dated 12 Feb. 1945, which describes it as 'an exceptionally quiet month so far as Partisan activity was concerned'. WO 204/1994. On the decrypts, *see* F. H. Hinsley, *British Intelligence in the Second World War* (1988), vol. 3, pt 2, p. 890; and for the military situation *see* W. G. F. Jackson, *The Mediterranean and Middle East*, vol. 6, pt 3, pp. 112–33. • **2**. *See* Margaret Pawley, *In Obedience to Instructions*, pp. 96–8 for the staggered move of wireless operators and coders. She herself left the south on 13 Mar. 1945. For the internal history, *see* Cecil Roseberry, 'History of the Italian Section', in HS 7/59. *See also* Peter Wilkinson and Joan Bright Astley, *Gubbins and SOE*, p. 201, and Woods to Brooks Richards, 24 July 1995, in Woods Archive. • **3**. For a short while, supply-dropping operations continued to be flown from Brindisi, and Malignano continued to be used for some flights until the end of the campaign. For further details on the US contribution, *see* Maj. Harris G. Warren, *Special Operations*. • **4**. Quoted in Charles Delzell, *Mussolini's Enemies*, p. 477. • **5**. The text of the directive, dated 4 Feb. 1945, can be found in 'AFHQ History of Special Operations in the Mediterranean', 24 July 1945, Annex O, in HS 7/170. *See also* Speedwell to SOM, tel. 7257, 1 Feb. 1945, in HS 6/776, and W. J. M. Mackenzie, *The Secret History of SOE*, p. 554. For radicalism within the CLNAI, *see* Delzell, op. cit., p. 475. On the handing-over of arms, ammunition and explosives at the end of the war, *see* HQ 15th Army Group memo 'Partisan Problems in N. Italy', 25 Feb. 1945, in WO 204/2000. For the claim about No. 1 SF's influence on the change of policy, *see* written communication to the author by Christopher Woods, 6 Aug. 2007. • **6**. Max Salvadori, *The Labour and the Wounds*, pp. 201–05. *See also* his essay 'Mission to the CLNAI', in *1SF&IR*, vol. 1, pp. 473–6. • **7**. For a lively account of his service with SOE, *see* William Pickering, *The Bandits of Cisterna*, as well as his 'The British Mission to Piedmont', in *1SF&IR*, vol. 1, pp. 85–8, and his interview in IWM Sound Archive, ref. 12012/4. Hope's Bandon II mission is sometimes referred to in the files as 'M11', its radio signal plan. *See* HS 6/842. • **8**. *See* Pickering's essay on the mission in *1SF&IR*, vol. 2, pp. 85–8. • **9**. Pickering, *The Bandits of Cisterna*, pp. 63–80. For Salvadori's weekly reports from Milan to No. 1 Special Force, *see* 'Mission to Lombardy Feb–May 1945', in Salvadori Papers. Keany was replaced by Hope, who in turn was accidentally killed in April: for the circumstances, *see* Pickering, op. cit., pp. 152–3. For Salvadori 'alone . . . and always on the run', *see* his 'Mission to the CLNAI', loc. cit., p. 475. • **10**. Amoore report on the Cherokee mission, 16 June 1945, p. 24, in HS 6/840. • **11**. Delzell,

op.cit. pp. 470–71. • **12**. 'Security of North West Italy: Appreciation of the Situation as at 20 Jan 45', in HS 7/60. For Bolis, *see* Delzell, loc. cit. For Sogno's account of his attempt to rescue Parri, *see* his *Guerra senza bandiera*, pp. 319–24. • **13**. John McCaffery, 'No Pipes or Drums', pp. 216–18. • **14**. Berne tel. 4610, 17 Feb. 1945, and London to Berne, 18 Feb. 1945, in HS 8/886. • **15**. Berne tel. 905, 1 Mar. 1945, loc. cit. Also e.g. Interrogation Report on Osteria, Ugo Luca, in HS 6/802. and report by Captain Lake on Boykin, in HS 6/823. • **16**. For Davidson's account of the mission, as well as the rest of his time with Section D and SOE, *see* his *Special Operations Europe*, *passim*. McMullen gave a brief account of his mission ('Clover II') in a letter to Charles Macintosh dated 14 Apr. 1974, in the Clover file, Woods Archive. • **17**. Davidson, op. cit., p. 214. • **18**. Michele Campanella, 'The British Mission to Liguria', in *ISF&IR*, vol. 2, pp. 173–6. • **19**. McMullen Report (*see below*), pp. 19–20. 'Miro' was Antonio Ukmar, a railwayman by occupation. • **20**. *Ibid.*, p. 15. • **21**. 'Report by Lt. Col. R. P. McMullen, D.S.O., M.B.E., Commander of the Allied Military Mission Liguria and Western Emilia', 23 May 1945, in HS 6/843. For his original briefing in Sept. 1944, *see* Holdsworth's Operation Instruction, 25 Sept., in WO 204/7293. His mission was known variously as 'M12' or Clover II. • **22**. McMullen Report, p. 10. • **23**. McMullen Report, p. 11. • **24**. For Bentley's operational instructions and his after-action report, *see* HS 6/847 and HS 8/828. The IWM, Dept of Documents, possesses the transcript of an interview with Bentley entitled 'Allied Mission with the "Formazione Garibaldine" in the Imperia Region', ref. 08/48/1. The details of Bentley's operation can also be followed via the log kept by Captain M. Lam, the intelligence officer of 20 Detachment at Nice, between 1 Jan. and 4 May 1945, also in the IWM, Dept of Documents, ref. 08/49/1. • **25**. For Johnston's mission ('Cotulla III') *see* HS 6/838. • **26**. *Ibid.*, p. 11. • **27**. Stephen Hastings, *The Drums of Memory*, pp. 120–21. • **28**. 'Report by Captain C. Brown, Int. Corps with Report on Landing Grounds by F/Lieut. F. L. Rippingale', 27 May 1945, in HS 6/835. • **29**. No. 1 Special Force Weekly Review, 21 Jan. 1945, in FO 371/49798. • **30**. Quoted in 15th Army Group Report on Special Operations in Italy, No. 2, Jan. 1945, p. 2, in WO 204/1994. • **31**. Michael Lees, Draft Mission Report, p. 6, in Envelope II file, Woods Archive. *See also* the 'Report by Lt. Fritz Snapper, attached to the Envelope Mission', 15 June 1945, in HS 6/844. • **32**. For Oughtred's operation instruction, *see* Hewitt to Oughtred, 22 Jan. 1945, in HS 6/863; *see also* his after-action report, 30 May 1945. Oughtred's reference to an assassination target appears in a brief memoir of his mission he wrote in the 1980s, to be found in the Woods Archive. It is possible that he conflated the goals of Cisco Red I and Cisco Red II. Macintosh in his *From Cloak to Dagger*, p. 151, refers to Barton's mission without mentioning any assassination. • **33**. Lees, Draft Mission Report,

p. 8. • **34**. For details of Cold Comfort, *see* WO 218/206, 208. • **35**. For Farran's reasons, *see* his *Operation Tombola*, pp. 9–10, 18–19. • **36**. For 'rastrellamento balls', *see* Laurence Lewis, *Echoes of Resistance*, p. 102. The basic official source for the operation is to be found in WO 218/215, but there exist many other accounts. Farran left his own in his memoir, *Operation Tombola*, and Lees in his, *Special Operations Executed*. Charles Macintosh's more critical view can be found in his *From Cloak to Dagger*. *See also* Lees's 'The attack on Villa Rossi and the Flap Two Mission to the Ellero Valley', in *ISF&IR*, vol. 2, pp. 217–21. Lees remained convinced for the rest of his life that he had been made a scape-goat by TAC HQ for its failure, first, to seek Mark Clark's orders for the attack to proceed, and then to halt it in time. He also claimed that Davies never made the alleged trip to his HQ to stop the operation. *See* his letter to Christopher Woods, 11 Apr. 1989, in Woods Archive. • **37**. 'Interim Report on Organisation and Activities of Modena Partisans, February–April 1945', by Major J. T. M. Davies, MC, MBE, RE, of Silentia mission, in HS 6/791; on Stott, *see also* Macintosh, op. cit., pp. 136–7. • **38**. John Ross, 'Italy 1944–1945', in IWM, Dept of Documents, ref. 06/18/1, p. 23. Details of the Simia mission may be found in HS 6/808. • **39**. *Ibid.*, p. 26. • **40**. Harold Tilman, *When Men and Mountains Meet*, p. 214. • **41**. Tilman, op. cit., p. 215. For a tally of raids and ambushes carried out by the Nanetti and Belluno divisions as reported by Tilman to No. 1 Special Force in February, *see* its Weekly Review, 25 Feb. 1945, in FO 371/49799. • **42**. Christopher Woods, communication with the author, 18 Aug. 2010. • **43**. *See* 'Report by Capt. J. E. H. Orr-Ewing and Captain C. M. Woods' on the Ruina/Fluvius mission, especially pp. 10 and 18–19, in HS 6/848. *See also* inter-view with Orr-Ewing, IWM Sound Archive, ref. 26757. • **44**. Report by Roworth on 'Bergenfield' mission between 24 Oct. 1944 and 24 Feb. 1945, p. 2, in FO 371/49802. • **45**. *Ibid.*, p. 13. His report was circulated by Roseberry to the Foreign Office. • **46**. I am grateful to Sir Thomas Macpherson for making these copies available to me. The story of Frank Gardner's exploits with the Italian partisans is told in a book by Florence Miller entitled *Signor Kiwi*, privately published in New Zealand in 1995. • **47**. Letter from Macpherson to Captain Alan Clark, 1 Feb. 1945, in HS 6/851. Macpherson urged in vain for immediate 'high-level intervention' if (partisan) military activity was to be preserved. He was informed that this was not possible and that if he did not get satisfaction from the local Slovene commander he should withdraw his mission to the Slovene 9th Corps, which he never did. *See* G-3 Special Operations memo-randum headed 'Slovenes and Osoppo', 3 Feb. 1945, in WO 204/7297. • **48**. For Macpherson's view of Bolla, *see* his field letter to 'Major Nicholson' (Roworth), 7 Feb. 1945, in HS 6/851. For 'a slow motion massacre', *see* 'Death at Porzus' by Arthur Brown in the *Special Forces Newsletter*, Autumn 1998, p. 7. A film on the subject shown at the Venice Film Festival in 1997 caused considerable controversy as it stirred up long-forgotten and suppressed memories. One of the victims was Guido Alberto Pasolini, brother of the famous post-war Italian film director Pier Paolo Pasolini. Some 50 of those responsible for the massacre were brought to trial in Italy in 1952, with 41 of them being sentenced to terms of imprisonment. The three ringleaders were sentenced to 30 years imprisonment, but they and six others were sentenced *in absentia* as they could not be found in Italy. • **49**. *See* Macpherson's report, 30 July 1945, p. 14, in HS 6/853; capital letters in the original. I am grateful to Sir Thomas Macpherson for providing me with information about his mission. • **50**. On Trent's death, *see* Macpherson's report, 25 Feb. 1945, in WO 204/7301. Arthur Brown, however, recorded on 16 Jan. that 'word received from Porzus that Micky executed by the Slovenes about a week earlier'. *See* his memoir, 'A Jedburgh in Italy', p. 9. • **51**. Brown, op. cit., p. 11 – reconstructed by him from his surviving log and other notes. • **52**. Quoted in Macintosh, op. cit., p. 146. For February's excellent flying weather, *see* the 15th Army Group's 'Report on Special Operations in Italy – No. 3, February 1945', 21 Mar. 1945, p. 1, in WO 204/1994. • **53**. W. G. F. Jackson, *The Mediterranean and Middle East*, vol. 6, pt 3, p. 415. • **54**. 'No. 1 Special Force Weekly Review for Week Ending 11 March 1945', 15 Mar. 1945, in FO 371/49800. For Clark's broadcast and its rationale, *see* HQ 15th Army Group G-3 Section 'Special Operations – March 1945', 19 Apr. 1945, in WO 204/1894.

*Twelve – 'This is the end'*　　　　　　　　　　　　　　　*pp. 293–336*

**1**. For 'Operation Sunrise', the secret negotiations conducted between Allen Dulles of the OSS and General Wolff, *see* Dulles's *The Secret Surrender* (1967). Coincidentally, SOE's Dick Mallaby had also met with Wolff following his capture in Feb. 1945 while crossing into Italy from Switzerland, when he quick-wittedly saved himself by pretending to be an envoy exploring a possible surrender. For this, *see* Christopher Woods, 'A Tale of Two Armistices', in K. G. Robertson (ed.), *War, Resistance and Intelligence*, pp. 1–17. For 'the bursting of a giant cascade firework', *see* W. G. F. Jackson, *The Mediterranean and Middle East*, vol. 6, pt 3, p. 322. • **2**. For Communist strategy in Italy, *see* Joan Barth Urban, *Moscow and the Italian Communist Party*, pp. 184–212. • **3**. W. J. M. Mackenzie, *The Secret History of SOE*, p. 557. *See also* C. R. S. Harris, *The Allied Administration of Italy, 1943–1945*, pp. 295–316. • **4**. FO 371/49797. Almost 30 British officers were despatched by No. 1 Special Force to northern Italy in March and April alone, including many not named elsewhere in the text, such as: Major B. J. Barton (Evaporate – his second mission), Captain R. H. Pearson

(Herrington), Major D. G. Leach (Bandon), Captain J. M. L. Farran (Cherokee), Captain J. C. Stewart (Toffee), Captain H. A. R. King (Bandon), Major F. H. Cardozo (Ruga), Captain R. Neale (Cherokee) and Captain E. C. G. Harlow (Bandon). • **5**. Capt. J. Bell, Report on Mission [M6 – Cherokee], 22 June 1945, p. 16, in HS 6/841. *See also* the report, 3 June 1945, by Staff Sergeant Johns, Royal Engineers, a sabotage instructor with the mission, in HS 6/840. For Polish officers, *see* Alastair Macdonald and Patrick Amoore, 'The Cherokee Mission in the Biella Area,' in *1SF&IR*, vol. 2, pp. 69–75. • **6**. 'Report on No. 1 Special Force Activities during April 1945', pp. 28–34, in Salvadori Papers. • **7**. Cypher tel. 5272 from SOM to London, 25 Apr. 1945, in HS 6/796. • **8**. *See* Davies's interim and final reports on the Modena partisans of May 1945, in HS 6/791; also WO 215/218 and WO 204/7299. *See also*, for the failure of the partisans to attack on the city, SOM to London tel. 5318, 27 Apr. 1945, in HS 6/796. • **9**. *See* report on Envelope Blue (Toffee), by Major C. Holland, MBE, 31 May 1945, in HS 6/844. • **10**. Basil Davidson, *Special Operations Europe*, p. 242. • **11**. McMullen's report, 23 May 1945, in HS 6/843. For the events in Genoa, *see also* the report by Captain Gordon, op. cit. • **12**. Davidson, op. cit., p. 266. • **13**. Michele Campanella, 'The British Mission in Liguria', in *1SF&IR*, vol. 2, p. 177. • **14**. SOM to London, tel. 5239, 27 Apr. 1945, in HS 6/796. • **15**. SOM to London, tel. 5312, 27 Apr. 1945, loc. cit.; and report by Major V. R. Johnston, MC, on Cotulla III, 9 June 1945, in HS 6/838. • **16**. Robin O. Richards, 'The Liberation of Genoa', in *1SF&IR*, vol. 2, pp. 105–06. • **17**. E. F. S. Chavasse, 'Operation "Toast" – Genoa April 1945', typescript in Clover file, Woods Archive. This also contains the official directive for Operation Toast dated 8 April, details of the safe houses prepared by McMullen, and other related material. • **18**. Robin Richards's mission report, 20 May 1945, in Woods Archive. • **19**. Campanella, op. cit., p. 177. • **20**. *See* C. R. S Harris, op. cit., pp. 300–03; Hewitt's 'Report on No. 1 Special Force Activities During April 1945', pt 5: 'Anti-Scorch', pp. 32–4; McMullen's report, para. 17, and Captain R. C. Bentley on the Saki mission, p. 12, in HS 6/847. • **21**. Gordon Lett, *Rossano*, pp. 194, 197. For more on Lett, *see* his report on the Blundell Violet mission, 5 Apr. 1945, as well as that of his successor, Major Henderson, 2 June 1945, in HS 6/830. Henderson's report carries some fairly severe implicit criticisms of Lett's handling of the mission. • **22**. Salvadori, Reports Nos. 4 and 6 to No. 1 Special Force, 25 Mar. 1945, 6 Apr. 1945, in Salvadori Papers. *See also* his Report No. 3, 18 Mar. 1945, covering his conversation with a representative of the Edison factory in Milan. • **23**. *Ibid.* *See also* Salvadori's 'Mission to the CLNAI', in *1SF&IR*, vol. 1, pp. 473–6. • **24**. For Czernin's exploits on the 'Chariton IV' mission, *see* Norman Franks, *Double Mission*, pp. 124–46, and Mario Invernicci, 'No. 1 Special Force in Lombardy', in *1SF&IR*, vol. 2, pp. 229–32. For his report from the Questura, *see* Freeborn

Report No. 8, SOM to London, tel. 5346, 28 Apr. 1945, in HS 6/796. • **25**. Salvadori, op. cit., p. 476. • **26**. Max Salvadori, *The Labour and the Wounds*, p. 222; Charles Delzell, *Mussolini's Enemies*, pp. 485–6. • **27**. Salvadori, op. cit., p. 224. • **28**. For details of these discussions, *see* Alfredo Pizzoni, *Alla guida del CLNAI*, pp. 155–89. • **29**. Salvadori, Report No. 9, 30 May 1945, Salvadori Papers. • **30**. Leo Valiani, *Tutte le strade conducono a Roma*, p. 350. *See also* Delzell, op. cit., pp. 535–44 and Roberto Battaglia, *Storia della Resistenza Italiana*, p. 546. • **31**. Salvadori, *The Labour and the Wounds*, p. 227. • **32**. Salvadori, Report No. 9, pp. 3–4, and typed note to Manfred, 25 Apr. 1945, in Salvadori Papers. Delzell, op. cit., p. 525. • **33**. Salvadori, Report No. 9, pp. 6–7. • **34**. *See* Freeborn Situation Report No. 12, 29 Apr. 1945, in HS 6/796. • **35**. Hewitt to Vincent, 24 Apr. 1945, and Hewitt to Salvadori, 25 Apr. 1945, both in Salvadori Papers. • **36**. 'The Chariton Mission and anti-scorch in Lombardy,' Appendix 1 of Salvadori, Report No. 9, p. 6. • **37**. Stephen Hastings, *The Drums of Memory*, p. 129. For the work of the Special Force Staff Sections, *see* Hewitt's report, pt 6, pp. 35–6. McDermot belonged to 5 SFSS. The section attached to Eighth Army was known as 6 SFSS and included members of the Clowder mission. • **38**. Hastings, op. cit., pp. 130–31. *See also* SOM to London, 5312 and 5329, 27 Apr. 1945, in HS 6/796, as well as correspondence between Hastings and Gervase Cowell and C. M. Woods in the Woods Archive. *See also* the report by Captain C. Brown of Insulin, 27 May 1945, in HS 6/835. • **39**. SOM to London, 5323, 27 Apr. 1945, loc. cit. • **40**. William Pickering, *The Bandits of Cisterna*, pp. 158–60. Following the accidental death on 17 Apr. of Major Adrian Hope, he was temporarily replaced by Captain Powell and then permanently by Major R. V. Lea. • **41**. Alastair Macdonald and Patrick Amoore, 'The Cherokee Mission in the Biella Area', in *ISF&IR*, vol. 2, p. 75. • **42**. 'Report by Lieut. Col. J. Stevens and Maj. D. Dodson, Bandon Mission', 10 June 1945, in HS 6/856. • **43**. Notes on Beatt in Woods Archive. • **44**. *See* Freeborn Report No. 8, in HS 6/796, in which Stevens reports on 'excellent relations with Turin CLN'. • **45**. For Morton's report of 8 June 1945 on the Clarinda II mission – sometimes referred to as 'Incisor' – *see* FO 371/49803; Freeborn Report No. 10, in HS 6/848, and the correspondence of both Morton and Sergeant Williams, his W/T operator, with C. M. Woods in 1992–3 in the Woods Archive. Details of McKenna's mission can be found in WO 204/7298, and in HS 6/786, HS 6/841, HS 6/845 and HS 6/866. • **46**. Hewitt's report, p. 7. • **47**. *Ibid.*, pp. 30–31. For the Harding–Freyberg exchange on Trieste, and the entry into Venice, *see* W. G. F. Jackson, op. cit., pp. 325–6. • **48**. Report on 'Ruina/Fluvius' by Capt. J. E. H. Orr-Ewing and Capt. C. M. Woods, June 1945, p. 10, in HS 6/848. • **49**. *Ibid.*, p. 14. The atrocity was reported to the War Crimes Commission. • **50**. *Ibid.*, Appendix A. • **51**. H. W. Tilman, *When Men and Mountains Meet*, pp. 223–4; also Freeborn Report No. 15, 30 Apr. 1945, in HS 6/848. • **52**. John Ross, diary extracts in 'Last days of the

War', in IWM, Dept of Documents, ref. 06/18/1, p. 3. • **53.** John Ross, 'Italy 1944–1945', in IWM, Dept of Documents, ref. 06/18/1, p. 33. • **54.** Testimony by Arthur Farrand Radley to the Bologna Conference 1987, in IWM, Dept. of Documents, ref. 03/20/1. • **55.** Macpherson, report on Coolant mission, 30 July 1945, p. 34, in HS 6/853. • **56.** Arthur Brown, 'A Jedburgh in Italy'. Brown notes in a footnote that he later learned the atrocity allegations against British forces in India were 'too dreadfully true'. • **57.** Macpherson, Coolant report, p. 38. • **58.** *Ibid.*, pp. 43, 45, and letter to Arthur Brown, 27 Feb. 1987, lent to me by Sir Thomas Macpherson. • **59.** Interrogation Report of 17 Aug. 1945 in HS 6/808, quoted in Marcus Binney, *The Women Who Lived for Danger*, p. 277. • **60.** Paola del Din, 'A Young Partisan Returns to Friuli by Parachute', in *1SF&IR*, vol. 1, p. 269. For Bigelow, *see also* di Troppenburg's contribution to the same volume, 'The Bigelow Mission', as well as that of Dumas Poli, the radio operator, *ibid.* pp. 277–81, 289–93. • **61.** Macpherson, Coolant report, p. 66 (manuscript page missing from TNA copy), kindly lent to the author by Sir Thomas Macpherson. • **62.** For the post-liberation period and the frontier problems with both France and Yugoslavia, *see* C. R. S. Harris, op. cit., pp. 295–355. • **63.** *See* Colonel H. M. Threlfall, '15th Army Group Mission to German C-in-C South West, May 1945', p. 1, in Bolzano Mission file, Woods Archive. • **64.** *Ibid.*, pp. 3–4. • **65.** Livermore Report, 31 May 1945, in 'AFHQ History of Special Operations in the Mediterranean', 24 July 1945, Annex S, p. 3, in HS 7/170. • **66.** *Ibid.*, p. 6. • **67.** SOM to London, tels 5475 and 5525, 4 and 5 May 1945, in HS 6/796. • **68.** *See* the 'Report on SOE Operations in Italy', written anonymously but possibly by a Maryland officer and circulated for comment in Nov. 1945 to Colonels Keswick and Roseberry, chap. 23, pp. 185–9, in Woods Archive. • **69.** Margaret Pawley, *In Obedience to Instructions*, p. 155. • **70.** Holdsworth to Gubbins, 9 Aug. 1944, in Holdsworth file, Woods Archive. • **71.** Quoted in J. G. Beevor, *SOE*, pp. 144–5. • **72.** Gubbins to Wilkinson from Siena, undated, noted in Woods Archive, and Gubbins to Lord Selborne, 6(?) May 1945, in HS 6/902; Sir Noel Charles to the Foreign Office tel. 774, 11 May 1945, in WO 106/3965A; and his message to the prime minister, 13 June 1945, in FO 371/49771, quoted in F. W. Deakin, 'SOE and the Italian Resistance 1941–1945', undated paper, pp. 33–4, Woods Archive. • **73.** Sir Noel Charles to Foreign Office, 16 and 18 May 1945, WO 106/3965A; and Harris, op. cit., p. 355. • **74.** CD 8196 to AD/H, 21 July 1945; Gubbins to Charles, 9 Aug. 1945, and Cadogan to Charles, 3 Sept. 1945, in HS 6/776; for Holdsworth on Vincent, *see* his letter to Gubbins of 24 Nov. 1944 in the Holdsworth file, Woods Archive. • **75.** Lt Col. J. Beevor to CD, 14 Sept. 1945, in HS 6/776. • **76.** Sir Thomas Macpherson, letter of 1 August, 1946, Macpherson Papers. • **77.** 'Report on No. 1 Special Force Activities During April 1945', 3 June 1945, p. 46.

# Illustrations and maps

10. Alistair Macdonald, head of the 'Cherokee' mission (right) seen here with Pat Amoore just prior to a massive drop of supplies near Biella on 26 December 1944.
    SOE files, The National Archives.

11. Richard Tolson (left, with pipe) takes part in a mule-handling course prior to his mission to Italy.
    SOE files, The National Archives.

12. Hedley Vincent at his field headquarters, September 1944.
    The Vincent family papers; Roger Vincent.

13. Jim Davies relaxes after the fighting stops, Italy, June 1945.
    Jim Davies's papers; Peter Davies.

14. Resistance ID card used by Captain Christopher Woods ('Colombo') during his behind-the-lines mission in the Veneto, August 1944–April 1945.
    Christopher Woods.

15. Harold Tilman's mission in North-East Italy, seen here in Belluno after the partisan stand-down, May 1945. *From left to right*: Victor Gozzer, Tilman, Captain John Ross and (arms folded) 'Pallino'.
    The John Ross papers, Imperial War Museum.

16. Cheerful partisans during the stand-down ceremony in Belluno, 25 May 1945.
    The John Ross papers, Imperial War Museum.

17. Banker Alfredo Pizzoni ('Longhi'), wartime chairman of the CLNAI (right), with Hedley Vincent, head of SOE's mission to Milan after the liberation.
    The Vincent family papers; Roger Vincent.

### MAPS

Italy, 1943–1945 © Reginald Piggott
British Missions in Northern Italy at 1 April 1945 © Reginald Piggott

# Select bibliography

Absalom, Roger, *A Strange Alliance: Aspects of escape and survival in Italy, 1943–45*, Firenze, Olschki, 1991.

Agarossi, Elena, *A Nation Collapses: The Italian surrender of September 1943*, Cambridge, Cambridge University Press, 2000.

Andrew, Christopher, *Secret Service: The making of the British intelligence community*, London, Heinemann, 1985.

Atkinson, Rick, *The Day of Battle: The war in Sicily and Italy, 1943–1944*, London, Little, Brown, 2007.

Battaglia, Roberto, *Storia della Resistenza italiana*, Turin, Einaudi, 1964.

Beevor, J. G., *SOE: Recollections and reflections, 1940–45*, London, Bodley Head, 1981.

Benello, Franco, *Ricordo del 1944–45: Ultimo anno di guerra*, privately printed, 1995.

Binney, Marcus, *The Women Who Lived for Danger: The women agents of SOE in the Second World War*, London, Hodder & Stoughton, 2002.

Blumenson, Martin, *Salerno to Cassino*, United States Army in World War II: The Mediterranean Theater of Operations, 3, Office of the Chief of Military History, US Army, Washington, DC, 1969.

Bosworth, R. J. B., *Mussolini*, London, Arnold, 2002.

*British Security Coordination: The secret history of British intelligence in the Americas, 1940–45*, introduction by Nigel West, London, St Ermin's, 1998.

Carver, Michael, Baron, *The Imperial War Museum Book of the War in Italy, 1943–1945*, London, Sidgwick & Jackson in association with the Imperial War Museum, 2001.

Castellano, General Giuseppe, *Come firmai l'armistizio di Cassibile*, Verona, Mondadori, 1945.

Churchill, Winston S., *The Second World War*, vol. 5: *Closing the Ring*, New York, Bantam Books, 1962.

Churchill, Winston S., *The Second World War*, vol. 6: *Triumph and Tragedy*, New York, Bantam Books, 1962.

Clark, Martin, *Mussolini*, London, Pearson, 2005.

Cooke, Peter (ed.), *The Italian Resistance: An anthology*, Manchester, Manchester University Press, 1997.

Cooper, Adolphus Richard, *The Adventures of a Secret Agent*. London, Frederick Muller, 1957.

Cooper, Adolphus Richard, *Born to Fight*, Edinburgh, Blackwood, 1969.

Corvo, Max, *The O.S.S. in Italy, 1942–1945: A personal memoir*, New York, Praeger, 1990.

Croce, Benedetto, *Croce, the King and the Allies: Extracts from a diary by Benedetto Croce, July 1943–June 1944*, translated by Sylvia Sprigge, London, Allen & Unwin, 1950.

Croft, Andrew, *A Talent for Adventure*, Hanley Swan, Worcs, S.P.A., 1991.

Davidson, Basil, *Special Operations Europe: Scenes from the anti-Nazi war*, London, Gollancz, 1980.

Deakin, F. W., *The Brutal Friendship: Mussolini, Hitler and the fall of Italian Fascism*, London, Weidenfeld & Nicolson, 1962.

Deane-Drummond, Anthony, *Return Ticket*, London, Collins, 1953.

Delzell, Charles F., *Mussolini's Enemies: The Italian anti-Fascist resistance*, Princeton, Princeton University Press, 1961.

Dodds-Parker, Douglas, *Setting Europe Ablaze: Some account of ungentlemanly warfare*, Windlesham, Surrey, Springwood, 1983.

Downes, Donald, *The Scarlet Thread*, London, Derek Verschoyle, 1953.

Dulles, Allen Welsh, *From Hitler's Doorstep: The wartime intelligence reports of Allen Dulles, 1942–1943*. University Park, PA, Pennsylvania State University Press, 1996.

Earle, John, *The Price of Patriotism: SOE and MI6 in the Italian-Slovene borderlands during World War II*, Lewes, Sussex, Book Guild, 2005.

Ehrman, J., *Grand Strategy*, vol. 5: *August 1943–September 1944*, London, HMSO, 1956.

Elliott-Bateman, Michael (ed.), *The Fourth Dimension of Warfare*, vol. 1: *Intelligence/Subversion/Resistance*, Manchester, Manchester University Press, 1970.

Ellwood, David, *Italy, 1943–1945*, Leicester, Leicester University Press, 1985.

Farran, Roy, *Operation Tombola*, London, Collins, 1960.

Federazione Italiana Associazioni Partigiane (FIAP)/Special Forces Club, *No. 1 Special Force and the Italian Resistance: Proceedings of the conference held at Bologna, 28–30 April 1987, under the auspices of the University of Bologna*, vols 1 and 2, Bologna, Cooperativa Libraria Universitaria Editrice Bologna, 1990.

Foot, M. R. D., *SOE in France*, London, HMSO, 1966.

Foot, M. R. D., *SOE in the Low Countries*, London, St Ermin's, 2001.

Foot, M. R. D., and J. M. Langley, *MI9: Escape and evasion, 1939–1945*, London, BCA, 1979.

Franks, Norman L. R., *Double Mission: RAF fighter ace and SOE agent, Manfred Czernin, DSO, MC, DFC*, London, William Kimber, 1976.

Funk, Arthur Layton, *Hidden Ally: The French resistance, special operations, and the landings in southern France, 1944*, New York, Greenwood Press, 1992.

Gallegos, Adrian, *And Who Are You?*, London, Adelphi, 1992.

Gobetti, Eric (ed.), *1943–1945: La lunga liberazione*, Turin, Franco Angeli, 2007.

Graham, Dominick, and Shelford Bidwell, *Tug of War: The battle for Italy, 1943–1945*, London, Hodder & Stoughton, 1986.

Green, Andrew, *Writing the Great War: Sir James Edmonds and the official histories, 1915–1948*, London, Frank Cass, 2003.

Grose, Peter, *Gentleman Spy: The life of Allen Dulles*, London, Andre Deutsch, 1995.

Harris, C. R. S., *Allied Military Administration of Italy, 1943–1945*, London, HMSO, 1957.

Hastings, Stephen, *The Drums of Memory: An autobiography*, London, Leo Cooper, 1994.

Holland, James, *Italy's Sorrow: A year of war, 1944–45*, London, Harper Press, 2008.

Hood, Stuart, *Pebbles From My Skull*, London, Hutchinson, 1964.

Horne, Alistair, *Macmillan, 1894–1956*, London, Macmillan, 1988.

Howard, Michael, *Grand Strategy*, vol. 4: *August 1942–September 1943*, London, HMSO, 1972.

Howarth, Patrick, *Undercover: The men and women of the Special Operations Executive*, London, Routledge & Kegan Paul, 1980.

Jackson, W. G. F., *The Battle for Italy*, London, Batsford, 1967.

Jackson, W. G. F., *The Mediterranean and Middle East*, vol. 6: *Victory in the Mediterranean*, pt 2: *June to October 1944*, History of the Second World War, United Kingdom Military Series, London, HMSO, 1987.

Jackson, W. G. F., *The Mediterranean and Middle East*, vol. 6: *Victory in the Mediterranean*, pt 3: *November 1944 to May 1945*, History of the Second World War, United Kingdom Military Series, London, HMSO, 1988.

Jakub, Jay, *Spies and Saboteurs: Anglo-American collaboration and rivalry in human intelligence collection and special operations, 1940–45*, with a foreword by Sir Douglas Dodds-Parker, London, Macmillan, 1999.

Kesselring, Albert, *The Memoirs of Field-Marshal Kesselring*, London, William Kimber, 1953.

Koestler, Arthur, *Scum of the Earth*, London, Collins, 1955.

Lamb, Richard, *The Ghosts of Peace, 1935–1945*, London, Michael Russell, 1987.

Lamb, Richard, *War in Italy 1943–1945: A brutal story*, London, John Murray, 1993.

Lees, Michael, *Special Operations Executed in Serbia and Italy*, London, William Kimber, 1986.

Lett, Gordon, *Rossano*, London, Hodder & Stoughton, 1955.

Lewis, Laurence, *Echoes of Resistance: British involvement with the Italian partisans*, Tunbridge Wells, Costello, 1985.

Lewis, Norman, *Naples '44: An intelligence officer in the Italian labyrinth*, London, Eland, 1983.

Lussu, Joyce, *Freedom Has No Frontier*, London, Michael Joseph, 1969.

Luzi, Alfredo (ed.), *Max Salvadori: L'uomo, il cittadino*, Fermo, Andrea Livi, 1996.

MacDonald, Callum, *The Killing of SS Obergruppenführer Reinhard Heydrich*, New York, Collier, 1990.

Macintosh, Charles, *From Cloak to Dagger: An SOE agent in Italy, 1943–1945*, London, William Kimber, 1982.

Mackenzie, W. J. M., *The Secret History of SOE: The Special Operations Executive, 1940–1945*, London, St Ermin's, 2000.

Macmillan, Harold, *The Blast of War, 1939–1945*, London, Macmillan, 1967.

Macmillan, Harold, *War Diaries: Politics and war in the Mediterranean; January 1943–May 1945*, London, Macmillan, 1984.

Madge, Tim, *The Last Hero: Bill Tilman; A biography of the explorer*, London, Hodder & Stoughton, 1995.

Mauri, Enrico Martini, *Partigiani penne nere*, Milan, Mondadori, 1968.

Ministero Della Difesa, Stato Maggiore Dell'Esercito, Ufficio Storico, *L'Azione dello Stato Maggiore Generale per lo sviluppo del movimento di liberazione*, Rome, 1975.

Molony, Brigadier C. J. C. [et al.], *The Mediterranean and Middle East*, vols 5 and 6, History of the Second World War, United Kingdom Military Series, London, HMSO, 1973–1984.

Morgan, Philip, *The Fall of Mussolini*, Oxford, Oxford University Press, 2007.

Munthe, Malcolm, *Sweet is War*, London, Duckworth, 1954.

Murphy, Christopher J., *Security and Special Operations: SOE and MI5 during the Second World War*, Basingstoke, Palgrave Macmillan, 2006.

Newby, Eric, *Love and War in the Apennines*, Newton Abbot, Readers' Union, 1972.

Newby, Wanda, *Peace and War: Growing up in Fascist Italy*, London, Collins, 1991.

Nicolson, Gerald W. L., *The Canadians in Italy, 1943–1945*, Ottawa, Queen's Printer, 1956.

Nicolson, Nigel, *Alex: The life of Field Marshal Earl Alexander of Tunis*, London, Weidenfeld & Nicolson, 1973.

*Operation Foxley: The British plan to kill Hitler*, introduction by Mark Seaman, London, Public Record Office, 1998.

O'Reilly, Charles T., *Forgotten Battles: Italy's war of liberation, 1943–1945*, Oxford, Lexington Books, 2001.

Pawley, Margaret, *In Obedience to Instructions: FANY with the SOE in the Mediterranean*, Barnsley, Leo Cooper, 1999.

Peniakoff, Vladimir ('Popski'), *Private Army*, London, Jonathan Cape, 1950.

Pickering, William, with Alan Hart, *The Bandits of Cisterna*, London, Leo Cooper, 1991.

Pizzoni, Alfredo, *Alla guida del CLNAI*, Bologna, Il Mulino, 1995.

Pond, Hugh, *Salerno*, London, William Kimber, 1961.

Read, Anthony, and David Fisher, *Colonel Z: The life and times of a master of spies*, London, Hodder & Stoughton, 1984.

Reid, P. R., *Winged Diplomat*, London, Chatto & Windus, 1962.

Richards, Brooks, *Secret Flotillas: The Clandestine sea lines to France and French North Africa, 1940–1944*, London, HMSO, 1996; also expanded second edition: London, Whitehall Publishing in association with Frank Cass, 2004.

Robertson, K. G. (ed.), *War, Resistance and Intelligence: Essays in honour of M. R. D. Foot*, Barnsley, Leo Cooper, 1999.

Salvadori, Massimo, *The Labour and the Wounds: A personal chronicle of one man's fight for freedom*, London, Pall Mall Press, 1958.

Seaman, Mark (ed.), *Special Operations Executive: A new instrument of war*, London, Routledge, 2006.

Secchia, Pietro, and Filippo Frassati, *La Resistenza e gli alleati*, Milan, Feltrinelli, 1962.

Simpson-Jones, Peter, as told to Philip Brutton, *Nine Lives, or The Felix Factor*, London, Elliot & Thompson, 2005.

Smith, R. Harris, *OSS: The secret history of America's first Central Intelligence Agency*, Berkeley, University of California Press, 1972.

Sogno, Edgardo, *Guerra senza bandiera*, Bologna, Il Mulino, 1995.

*The Special Operations Executive: Sound archive oral history recordings*, compiled and edited by Kate Johnson, London, Imperial War Museum, 1998.

Stafford, David, *Britain and European Resistance, 1940–1945: A survey of the Special Operations Executive, with documents*, London, Macmillan, 1980.

Stafford, David, *Camp X: Canada's school for secret agents, 1941–45*, Toronto, Lester & Orpen Dennys, 1986.

Stafford, David, *Secret Agent: The true story of the Special Operations Executive*, London, BBC, 2000.

Strawson, John, *The Italian Campaign*, London, Secker & Warburg, 1987.

Stucchi, Giovanni Battista, *Tornim a baita: Dalla campagna di Russia alla Repubblica dell'Ossola*, Milan, Vangelista, 1983.

Tilman, H. W., *When Men and Mountains Meet*, Cambridge, Cambridge University Press, 1946.

Tompkins, Peter, *A Spy in Rome*, London, Weidenfeld & Nicolson, 1962.

Tudor, Malcolm Edward, *Escape from Italy, 1943–45*, Newtown, Powys, Emilia, 2003.

Tudor, Malcolm Edward, *Special Force: SOE and the Italian resistance, 1943–1945*, Newtown, Powys, Emilia, 2004

Urban, Joan Barth, *Moscow and the Italian Communist Party: From Togliatti to Berlinguer*, Ithaca, Cornell University Press, 1986.

Valiani, Leo, *Tutte le strade conducono a Roma*, Bologna, Il Mulino, 1983.

Warren, Major Harris G., *Special Operations: AAF aid to European resistance movements, 1943–1945*, [AAF Historical Office 1947] Manhattan, Kansas, Sunflower University Press, 1947.

Whinney, Patrick, *Corsican Command*, Wellingborough, Stephens, 1989.

Wilkinson, Peter, *Foreign Fields: The story of an SOE operative*, London, I. B. Tauris, 1997.

Wilkinson, Peter, and Joan Bright Astley, *Gubbins and SOE*, London, Leo Cooper, 1993.

Windsor, John, *The Mouth of the Wolf*, Sidney, British Columbia, Gray's Publishing, 1967.

Woods, Christopher, 'A Tale of Two Armistices', in K. G. Robertson (ed.), *War, Resistance and Intelligence: Essays in honour of M. R. D. Foot*, Barnsley, Leo Cooper, 1999.

Woods, Christopher, 'SOE in Italy', in Mark Seaman (ed.), *Special Operations Executive: A new instrument of war*, London, Routledge, 2006.

Woodward, Sir Llewellyn, *British Foreign Policy in the Second World War*, vol. 2, London, HMSO, 1971.

Wylie, Neville, *Britain, Switzerland, and the Second World War*, Oxford, Oxford University Press, 2003.

Wylie, Neville (ed.), *European Neutrals and Non-belligerents during the Second World War*, Cambridge, Cambridge University Press, 2002.

# Index